Physiological Correlates of Human Behaviour

Vol. I: Basic Issues

Physiological Correlates of Human Behaviour
Vol. I: Basic Issues

Edited by

Anthony Gale

Department of Psychology
University of Southampton
Southampton

John A. Edwards

Department of Psychology
University of Reading
Reading

1983

ACADEMIC PRESS

A Subsidiary of Harcourt Brace Jovanovich, Publishers

London   New York

Paris   San Diego   San Francisco

São Paulo   Sydney   Tokyo   Toronto

ACADEMIC PRESS INC. (LONDON) LTD.
24/28 Oval Road
London NW1

United States Edition published by
ACADEMIC PRESS INC.
111 Fifth Avenue
New York, New York 10003

British Library Cataloguing in Publication Data

Physiological correlates of human behaviour.
Vol. 1
1. Psychology, Physiological
I. Gale, A.   II. Edwards, J. A.
612'.8   QP360

ISBN 0-12-273901-9
LCCCN 82-73802

Typeset by Oxford Verbatim Ltd.
and printed in Great Britain by
St. Edmundsbury Press, Bury St. Edmunds, Suffolk

List of Contributors

P. A. *Ackles*, Department of Psychology, University of Illinois, Urbana Champaign, Illinois 61820.

J. G. *Beaumont*, Department of Psychology, University of Leicester University Road, Leicester, LE1 7RH.

J. *Boddy*, Department of Psychology, The University, Manchester, MI3 9PL.

S. *Cox*, Department of Psychology, University of Nottingham, University Park, Nottingham, NG7 2RD.

T. *Cox*, Department of Psychology, University of Nottingham, University Park, Nottingham, NG7 2RD.

J. B. *Davidoff*, University College, Singleton Park, Swansea, SA2 8PP.

J. A. *Edwards*, Department of Psychology, University of Reading, Earley Gate, Whiteknights, Reading, RG6 2AL

B. A. *Farrell*, "Leyswood", Cotswold Road, Cumnor Hill, Oxford.

A. *Gale*, Department of Psychology, University of Southampton, Highfield, Southampton, SO9 5NH.

J. G. *Lindsley*, Massachusetts School of Professional Psychology, 785 Centre Street, Newton, Massachusetts, O2158.

D. T. *Lykken*, Minnesota Twin Study, Psychiatry Research Unit, 682 Diehl Hall, University of Minnesota, Minneapolis, Minnesota 55455.

B. C. J. *Moore*, Department of Experimental Psychology, Psychological Laboratory, Downing Street, Cambridge.

S. W. *Porges*, Department of Psychology, University of Illinois, Urbana Champaign, Illinois, 61820.

G. G. *Ratcliff*, Harmarville Rehabilitation Center, Inc., P.O. Box 11460, Guys Run Road, Pittsburgh PA. 15238.

M. *Thirlaway*, Department of Psychology, University of Nottingham, University Park, Nottingham, NG7 2RD.

S. R. *Truax*, Department of Psychology, University of Illinois, Urbana Champaign, Illinois 61820.

C. *Van Toller*, Department of Psychology, University of Warwick, Coventry, CV4 7AL.

D. M. *Warburton*, Department of Psychology, University of Reading, Whiteknights, Earley Gate, Reading, RG6 2AL.

K. *Wesnes*, Department of Psychology, University of Reading, Whiteknights, Earley Gate, Reading, RG6 2AL.

M. *Zuckerman*, Department of Psychology, University of Delaware, Newark, Delaware 19711.

Preface

All students of psychology are required to follow courses in physiological psychology, the biological bases of behaviour, or neuropsychology. Those who have an inadequate background training in biology experience some difficulty in coming to grips with terminology and are confused by anatomy and biochemistry. Others are also disenchanted by the fact that physiological psychology seems to focus largely upon animal behaviour, while many students are more concerned with the understanding of human behaviour. At some universities, human physiological psychology is studied, but typically as an advanced option or even only at postgraduate level. The study of physiological correlates of human behaviour over the last twenty years or so, has gone under the name of *psychophysiology*. It is a sad reflection of the state of psychological sciences that physiological psychologists and psychophysiologists rarely talk to each other. They attend different conferences and publish in different scientific journals. Few of the many excellent and comprehensive textbooks in physiological psychology cover more than the odd topic or two which has an immediate bearing upon those psychological processes studied by the experimental psychologist; and neuropsychology is only just beginning to establish links with experimental psychology. The present three volumes attempt to bridge some of the gaps and draw together disciplines which, in our view, should be working in collaboration. Thus we offer a unique combination of topics for the reader.

Physiological Correlates of Human Behaviour comes in three volumes because the sheer range of enquiry which now constitutes biological psychology inhibits a combination of all major topics under one set of covers. Even so, many topics which receive generous treatment in introductory textbooks, have been excluded. If space had allowed, we would have included chapters devoted to evolution, behavioural genetics, language, social psychophysiology, and sociobiology. We have tried, in selecting our contributions, to identify essentials, while filling major gaps in the available literature.

Moreover, this is not a series of textbooks, for range of treatment would of necessity have encouraged superficial coverage. Rather, we have commissioned internationally established authorities to prepare accessible, straightforward and yet critical accounts of the present state of the art. The aim has been to deal with a set of well defined research areas in depth, so that the reader can capture the full flavour and excitement of contemporary research.

Thus we hope that lecturers and postgraduate students, as well as undergraduates, will find this volume offers not only an introduction to biological research into human behaviour, but a spur and stimulus to further reading and research endeavour. Each of our authors has recommended additional readings, apart from the references provided within the text.

The term *correlates* which appears in our title, requires delicate and sensitive "unpacking". The business of relating subjective experience, behaviour and physiology is probably one of the most complex enterprises which human scientists will ever have to face. Some of our authors are bolder than others in staking their claims; this reflects the enthusiasm and zeal with which they tackle Nature. Sometimes it is necessary, like a thoroughbred racehorse, to wear blinkers and romp ahead. Others prefer a more painstaking and cautious approach to the finishing post. We hope that the different personalities and cognitive styles of our authors shine through. Indeed it is in the nature of science that the optimal approach to complex problems is to mix the broad brush with attention to fine detail. Virtually all our authors have written basic textbooks themselves or have made fundamental contributions to their disciplines. We owe them a profound debt of gratitude for staying so close to the briefs we gave them. By approaching leading authorities in their fields, we know we have obtained for the reader's benefit not only a freshness and liveliness of approach but a far more authoritative and up-to-date account than we could have achieved on our own. We hope the reader will agree that they have managed to express very sophisticated problems in straightforward language yet without sacrificing complexity.

The three books in this series will be appropriate for courses in experimental psychology, individual differences, and psychopathology, as well as mainstream physiological psychology. Students of medicine and psychiatry will find that Volume III (*Individual Differences and Psychopathology*) in particular is highly relevant to their psychological studies.

We have already expressed our thanks to our authors. We must acknowledge the understanding of David Henderson of the Teaching Media Department at the University of Southampton, who in redrawing all our graphs and figures has exercised a satisfying combination of aesthetic virtue and technical skill; thanks are also due to Peter Jack, who was responsible for some of the detailed anatomical drawings. Liz Gale provided constant support to one of us and Marg Kuiack assisted and coaxed us through the final stages of preparation of the manuscript; to them also go special thanks.

June, 1983   Anthony Gale
University of Southampton   John Edwards

Contents

Contents

Contents of Other Volumes

1 Introduction

A. Gale
and J. Edwards

Our authors have been commissioned to write three types of contribution for this volume. There are basic accounts of anatomy, physiology, and biochemistry (Boddy and Van Toller), reviews of substantive bodies of psychological and neuropsychological research (Lindsley, Warburton, Davidoff and Ratcliff, Moore, Beaumont, Cox *et al.*, Warburton and Wesnes, and Zuckerman), and essays on problems of research design and the interpretation of complex data (Farrell, Porges *et al.*, and Lykken).

As the title for the Series implies, *Physiological Correlates of Human Behaviour* is essentially concerned with biological accounts of *human* behaviour and experience. Volumes II and III are concerned with *Attention and Performance* and *Individual Differences and Psychopathology* respectively. However, human studies cannot be understood without a thorough understanding of the fundamental principles which govern the operation of the nervous system. Ethical and sheer practical difficulties impose limits upon human research, and so much of our basic knowledge concerning biological correlates must be derived from infra-human species. While much of the emphasis in this book is therefore upon animal research, a constant attempt is made to cross-refer back to the human case. Thus for example, the chapters on vision and hearing focus on direct analogies between findings derived from human and animal studies and are not designed to give the comprehensive coverage normally found in textbooks of physiological psychology. Such an approach reveals both the power of cross-species comparison and the limitations imposed by extrapolation from animal data.

The shift from animal to human research itself raises a number of difficulties. To the complexity of physiology is added first the rich variability of human behaviour, and secondly our unique capacity to communicate by language and to reflect upon our own experience. Farrell in Chapter 2 and

PHYSIOLOGICAL CORRELATES OF HUMAN
BEHAVIOUR   ISBN 0-12-273901-9

Porges *et al.* in Chapter 11 consider the logical limits of the term *correlation* and the problems of interpretation which arise when we try to integrate data from the three domains of description, namely physiology, behaviour and subjective report of experience.

In setting out the contents of this volume, we have followed both the logical order inherent in the chapters and the traditional layout for textbooks in physiological psychology, moving from basic sensory processes through to more complex and integrated processes. However we place Farrell's chapter, which is unique to collections of this sort, very much at the beginning because the problems he raises are common to all three volumes in the Series. The reader is recommended to read his essay very carefully before sampling other parts of the book.

In each of the three volumes we list a number of key themes which recur throughout and we list below those themes which appear in all the contributions to this volume. The reader will find that he returns constantly to the problems below, because they represent the major challenges to our understanding of the relationship between our nervous systems and our behaviour.

I. Some Key and Recurrent Themes in this Book

A. *Common Principles of Operation in the Nervous System*

Human and infra-human species share an environment with certain common and invariant features. It is not altogether surprising therefore that evidence of continuity exists within nervous systems across species. These continuities are represented in electrophysiological and biochemical systems. Such systems have "wired-in" and plastic features. Inasmuch as systems are "wired-in" they can be seen to have functional characteristics in common. Reproduction, defence and the means of sustaining life are clear candidates. It seems that approach and avoidance and reward and punishment systems are essential and these must be associated with means of registering and storing information about the environment. Such systems must be flexible and must have means of recuperation following extremes of use; they have evolved within a particular ecology, and under some circumstances pressures upon them may be so great that a stress reaction occurs. The statements in this paragraph may seem very straightforward, but they have strong implications for a biological approach to human behaviour. They also set the scene for the majority of chapters in all three volumes of *Physiological Correlates of Human Behaviour*.

B. *Functional Integration*

It might be tempting, given the notion of invariant features within and across species, to identify particular behaviour functions with particular anatomical structures. However a key principle of operation is functional integration. This means that a particular functional unit is involved in several functional systems, each of which has both individual and general functional properties. The electrophysiological and biochemical pathways which have been discovered are not only extensive in themselves, but have extensive connections throughout the nervous system. Thus a simple-minded notion of localization of function is impossible and a distinction needs to be drawn between *necessary* and *sufficient* conditions for a function. Thus a lesion could lead to observed disruption of a behavioural function; but the part or parts damaged within the brain can only logically be seen as necessary to the execution of the function i.e. as one of the functional units or paths between units. Only systematic control lesions in other areas can lead to the conclusion that they also are *not* involved in the function. This means that potentially many brain areas could be implicated.

C. *The Complexity of Neurophysiological Enquiry*

Data from a variety of sources may be seen to converge upon a particular set of unifying constructs. Thus, for example, data from psychophysics, animal preparations, histology, experimental psychology and clinical neurophysiology may be integrated to devise *general* principles of perceptual processing. However one of the difficulties which our authors point to is the use of ill-defined and almost vernacular terms to draw links across these different sources of data. To say that a monkey "sees" a banana and that during the time when it is displaying interest in the banana certain brain areas are observed to be active, is not to say that the monkey experiences what a human subject experiences when "seeing" a banana. While the word "see" has common elements in both contexts, the two sets of attributes in the monkey and human case are not isomorphic or interchangeable. The difficulty of translating concepts from one descriptive domain to another is not insuperable, since we are already accustomed to exchanging explanatory concepts between for example the electrophysiological and biochemical domains; but in the case of human experience and subjective report of experience, we appear to have difficulty. The reader should follow the careful distinctions drawn by Farrell between the various logical uses of the term *correlation*.

D. *Logical Difficulties of Dissociation*

Different psychological functions, observed as different behaviours, may be represented in the nervous system by one or many neurophysiological systems. The reverse is the case also; one neurophysiological system may be associated with one or many psychological functions. We are not observing a simple structure in which various operations proceed in parallel. Thus it is extremely difficult to draw conclusions from individual experiments derived from limited experimental procedures. Similarly, it is misleading to limit one's enquiry to one level of description. Moreover, the relation between different levels of explanation may be a hierarchical one. For example, description at the level of heart rate changes presupposes certain mechanisms, both mechanical and biochemical, which control the heart's operation. To ignore these, or to assume their *modus operandi*, may lead to the devising of misleading experiments and inappropriate explanations.

E. *Individuation*

While there are general laws, each individual organism represents a unique case. Individual differences in nervous system dispositions interact with environmental features to produce a unique patterning of experience. In the human case, the individual may be seen to reflect upon his experience and alter not only its representation in memory, but his own future behaviour. This modulation of information transfer provides yet another source of complexity for neurophysiological explanation. Patterns of rearing, past learning, social and epidemiological variables and life events all influence the ways in which the nervous system responds to a physically defined stimulus. This implies that a stimulus cannot just be devised at the experimenter's convenience; the salience or meaning of a stimulus cannot be defined in purely physical terms for its meaning lies within the interaction between the organism and the stimulus. There is a growing awareness in experimental psychology that to neglect individual differences, is to throw out part of the baby with the bathwater of the error term.

II. Conclusion

The themes we have discussed briefly above are not only evident in this volume but in Volumes II and III. The identification of common problems across such a broad range of subject areas reveals the potential for integration among those disciplines concerned with the biological correlates of behaviour. The reader might find it helpful to adopt the following classification of problems: (i) the identification of *ideas, constructs* or *variables* which explain phenomena; (ii) clarification of the *logical relationships* which hold among constructs; (iii) the devising of *empirical or operational definitions* of the constructs, which allow for the testing of *specific hypotheses*; (iv) devising *methodological solutions* and *experimental procedures* which yield data which have a direct bearing upon the hypotheses; (v) *interpreting and explaining* the data both in terms of their *internal logical coherence*, their *relationship with other data* sets, and their *implications* for the theoretical constructs which inspired the initial questions asked.

Some of our authors are obliged to focus on some of these aspects at the expense of others. In part, this reflects the history of the particular area of the discipline in which they are engaged. The reader, however, is in the privileged position of being able to stand back and impose a comprehensive and rigorous framework upon all the contributions to this book.

2 The Correlation between Body, Behaviour and Mind

B. A. Farrell

I

At the present time physiological psychologists and related workers appear to be very much influenced by an important regulative presumption or principle. This can be stated in different, but equally acceptable, ways. These psychologists presume that the whole wide and varied range of (i) behaviour, human and infra-human, as well as (ii) the mental functioning of organisms are "dependent" on their bodily structures and functioning – more especially those of the nervous system. Accordingly, their interest as psychologists is to try to discover how this dependency works so as to give rise to the activity of human and infra-human organisms. Psychologists use a number of words and expressions to pin point this interest. Thus, they speak of studying "the localization of function", the "centre" for this or that activity, "the neural basis" of it, "the mechanism" that mediates this or that behaviour, and so on. If we want to use just one word here, we could say that they are interested in finding out how the constituents of the two domains – body, on the one hand, and behaviour-cum-mind, on the other – "correlate" with each other. It is generally agreed that some of the words and expressions they use to describe their interest are less helpful than others. And it is quite evident that all of them are in need of clarification. Hence, it is advisable to examine some of these words and expressions, in order to see just what psychologists are doing when they investigate this field.

I shall pick on a small, but central, segment of this very large subject in the hope that, by so doing, I may be able to throw some light on the enterprise as a whole.

II

Let us begin with some easy first steps. As we all know, for an organism to adapt with success it is necessary for its nervous system to be able to take

PHYSIOLOGICAL CORRELATES OF HUMAN BEHAVIOUR
ISBN 0-12-273901-9

account of the world outside itself, of "noxious" disturbances to the body, and of the internal states of the rest of the body, so as to maintain the equilibria on which the body depends. The organism achieves this sensitivity by means of the machinery of different types of receptors – with related internal apparatus – which handle the inputs of energy concerned. Similarly on the side of reactivity. To be able to make an avoidance response (for example), the organism has to possess the necessary effectors.

When we investigate the machinery of (say) the visual receptors and system, we do so partly in order to discover what constituents of the system, with their functioning, are necessary for the normal visual sensitivity and behaviour of the organism. Suppose we find that when a primate is deprived of its striate area – with subsequent degeneration of the lateral geniculate – the animal becomes and remains incapable of discriminating shape via feature sensitivity. This gives us good grounds for saying that the striate cortex is necessary for the animal to discriminate shape via its sensitivity to features. Of course we may be wrong here. It *may* turn out that some other part of the visual system can take over this role of the striate area. In this case we only have good grounds for making some alternative claim – perhaps that the presence of the striate area is one of a disjunctive set $(x_1$ or x_2 or ... or $x_n)$ of necessary conditions for shape discrimination via feature detection (see p. 12).

In this part of the enterprise, therefore, we are hunting for conditions in the body on which adaptive behaviour depends. The hope is to find dependency conditions that are necessary; and the closer we are to the periphery of input and output, the more reasonable does this hope seem to be. Furthermore, if we discover that X is a non-disjunctively necessary condition for Y, then it follows that if Y happens X must have happened also. Hence, we can say that the occurrence of Y is correlated in this way with the occurrence of X – where X is a necessary dependency condition for Y. Such a discovery would typically represent the beginning of further enquiry.

Now, when a rat (for example) adapts successfully to an object in its visual field, the animal has standardly to discriminate and react appropriately to one or more of certain properties of the object – in particular, its shape, size, movement(s) and colour. These properties are noted by the animal initially via its sensitivity to different properties of the light; the animal's retina picks these out, and passes them on. At this point we resort to two widely used metaphors. We say that, when the light energy impinges on the visual receptors, it is (i) "coded" or "encoded", and (ii) the "information" it contains is transmitted. These metaphors use the intentional concepts of coding and information; and these have to be elucidated away into extensional concepts and discourse, before we can incorporate what these metaphors help us to say into the extensional discourse of science (Wilkes,

1978). Fortunately, this elucidation does not seem to be too difficult, and merely requires industry.

As we are all aware, our knowledge of how the nervous system encodes and transmits information has been greatly extended by some epoch-making work in recent decades. We now know a great deal about what happens at the synapse, about the chemistry of neuronal transmission, about single neurone specificity, and so on. It would seem that this impressive accumulation of knowledge provides us with some of the conditions necessary for the organism to react to features of the input, and so to produce an adaptive response. Thus, if the input is light, the nervous system reacts to its intensity by a change in the frequency of neural discharge. When a monkey reacts differentially to the presentation of a monkey's hand, some of the necessary conditions for this reaction are to be found in the activity of specific neurones in the inferotemporal cortex. Similarly, when a new-born infant gives evidence of form discrimination, we have some reason to believe that it possesses certain mechanisms, probably cortical, the presence and activation of which are necessary for this discrimination.

It is obvious, then, that in these sections of the field, we are concerned with the ways in which parts, states and events, in the body are necessary for behaviours. We have been dealing, therefore, with the familiar relation of necessary antecedent and consequent – where the former helps to bring about or produce the latter. We can say that, in this sort of work, we are doing correlational studies, in the hope of being able to uncover causal connections between antecedents and behavioural consequents.

But this is the easy part of our enquiry; the next stage is more difficult.

III

Consider again the encoding and transmission of information. When the visual system reacts to the intensity of light by variations in the frequency of discharge, we are dealing with the familiar relation of causal antecedent and consequent. However, when the neural impulses exhibit a certain frequency, it is clearly *not* the case that these events in the nerve fibres cause or produce a coding or encoding. They *are* the encoding of stimulus intensity. Likewise, the travelling spike potentials do not cause or produce the transmission of information. They *are* this transmission. What sort of "are" and relation are we dealing with here?

It seems correct to say, as a first move, that this is the "are" of identity. It is not the case that we are correlating two sets of events – those that make up the encoding plus the transmitting of information, *and* the neural events in the visual system. We are obviously dealing with one and the same set of events; and we are simply describing them in different ways.

But this is not the whole story. It is clear that we introduced and explained the words "encoding" and "information transmission" in standard ways; and that these ways enable us, in principle, to derive an important consequence. From statements describing what happened in certain nerve fibres during a certain interval, we can derive the consequence that these nerve fibres encoded this or that feature of the visual input, and transmitted the connected information during this interval. So we are dealing with two different discourses (or languages) and descriptions. The one is a neuro-electro-cum-chemical language with descriptions of these same types, which set out events going on in the nervous system during the interval or time involved (e.g. the events of impulse frequency). Let us call this (for short) the NP discourse. The other discourse is a psychological one (the P discourse, for short) with descriptions of this same type; and these pick out and emphasize the role played by the same set of events, which we are dealing with, in the ongoing adaptive activity of the organism. These events encode what the light input tells the organism about its intensity; and they pass on this information.

All this is far from being as wordy and trivial as it may sound. For, with the single example of light intensity behind us, we can go on to specify – in a *very* approximate way – a general relation of fundamental importance to the whole enterprise of correlational studies. In the example of light intensity, it is clear (i) that what we are referring to in the P discourse is contemporaneous with what we are referring to in the NP discourse. (ii) Our present knowledge is such as to justify the statement that it is necessary, for the P discourse here to be true, that the discourse of NP be true also. (iii) As we have noted, the P discourse here can be derived from the NP. Hence, we can use the latter to explain the former. Now, where these three propositions (i), (ii) and (iii) are true about the discourse of NP and P in any instance, we can say that the items, as described in the NP discourse, subserve or mediate, the same items as described in the P discourse. It is natural here to speak loosely and to say that, when we investigate some set of items using both of these descriptions, we are studying how certain bodily parts, states and events subserve, or mediate, certain psychological states, events and activity, and that the latter are identical with the former. It is natural also to say that we are now studying correlations between bodily states, events, etc., and psychological states, etc. This use of the word "correlation" is plainly quite different from the one we have introduced above (p. 9), and it is quite fundamental to the whole enterprise (see Clark, 1980).

IV

The animal and the human infant does not only rely on inbuilt machinery and processes to adapt appropriately; it also has the ability to learn, and so to remember past interactions with the world. If we are to follow our controlling regulative presumption or principle, we have to postulate that the nervous system of the infant has the ability, not only to transmit information, but also "to store" it, "to compare" a new packet of information with what is in store, and then, in the light of this comparison, to transmit "instructions" to the effector system. We all know that a great amount of impressive preliminary work has been done into the ways the nervous system enables the organism to do all this. But we also know that as yet we have not arrived at a firm consensus about these ways. Indeed, it could be said that we know very little indeed about "the neural basis of learning and memory".

Suppose, for the purpose of elucidation, we adopt, as the most promising exploratory hypothesis, the view that the neural basis of learning is to be found in certain changes that occur at the synapses in neural circuits. In following up this hypothesis, we would obviously look into some complex and subtle causal chains. We would look into how the transmitted impulses arriving at the presynaptic terminal produce changes in (say) the membrane, how this affects the transmitter substances, which in turn affect the membrane of the post-synaptic neurone, and how these synaptic changes in the particular neural circuits concerned interlock to produce the new response. Hence, when we search for the neural basis of learning on this hypothesis, *part of* what we are looking for are the minute particular entities, with their properties, which are necessary to account for the causal chains and dependencies, on which learned responses in general depend. The same will be true, no doubt, of any other hypothesis we adopt about the neural basis of learning.

However, when we go hunting for the basis of learning, we are also interested in something else about the whole varied panorama of learning phenomena. Thus, when we ask about (for example) the basis of imprinting, of the important temporal relations between the UCS and CS in classical conditioning, or of the well established phenomenon of PREE in operant conditioning, we are also concerned to find out what it is in the nervous system *in virtue of which* the person or animal is able to respond in these ways. It is clear that, in so far as we are concerned to find this out, we are *not* looking for causal dependencies. We are looking for states, events, etc. which will give us subserving dependencies. What we are searching for is a reasonably supported discourse of NP which will stand to the discourse of psychology in the general relation of subserving that we sketched above. With such an NP discourse on hand, we could then specify and describe what it is in the nervous system that enables an organism to exhibit imprinting; to react to the UCS and CS as it does; and to exhibit PREE. We could then explain these powers, and related behaviour in a powerful way, which we cannot do at the present time.

It is evident then that psycho-physiologists and others are liable to have a *dual* interest when they pursue their correlational work. They are likely to be interested in the causal connections between states, events, etc. at the particular level of minuteness at which they are working. However, they are also likely to be concerned with explaining items referred to and described in the P discourse, by means of items referred to and described in the discourse of NP. If they are concerned to do this, then it means that they are interested in exploring the subserving relation, and in discovering the connections between levels that this relation involves. When psychophysiologists, and others, pursue this interest, they run into a formidable and well known obstacle that we have met before.

When we considered encoding and the transmission of information above, we made a supposition which seems to be reasonable at the present time. We supposed that *only if* certain events occurred in the nervous system (namely, changes in the frequency of discharge and the passage of impulses along the nerve fibre) would the encoding of light intensity occur, and the information about intensity be transmitted. That is, for the latter to occur, it is necessary that the former should also occur. Given that this is so, we can then describe the subserving relation as we did above (pp. 9–10). This relation enables us to derive statements about encoding and transmission in the P discourse from statements about neural, and related, events in the discourse of NP. But we all know about facts such as the recovery of function and the multiplicity of neural machinery; and these go to make the nervous system a very flexible one. It is this flexibility which makes it difficult to claim that *one*, and *only* one, set of states, events, and so on, in the system is necessary for a particular psychological power – even if the latter be something fundamental to survival such as the ability to drink, feed or to acquire new motor habits. In all these contexts, therefore, it is doubtful whether we can maintain proposition (ii) in our elucidation above of the subserving relation.

The consequence of this is that we cannot explain an animal's ability to learn new motor responses (for example) by reference to statements, in the discourse of NP, about only one distinguishable group of structures, states, events, and so on. Hence, we cannot use the strong relation of subserving we introduced above (pp. 9–10). We have to weaken it. We have to say that what physiological psychologists, and others, are also interested in is the relation between the statements describing any particular psychological power, and the statements about the disjunctive set $(x_1 \text{ or } x_2 \ldots x_n)$ of neuro-physiological states, events, and so on, any *one* member of which is necessary for the possession and exercise of a particular power. In so far as the nervous system has the flexibility mentioned in the last paragraph, we shall have for the present to use and explore this weaker relation of subserving. The flexibility of the nervous system is indeed a great empirical obstacle to progress. But it is not a logical obstacle that makes the enterprise an impossible one. And the weaker relation of subserving is good enough to enable psychophysiologists, and others, to get on with their work.

V

But this whole enquiry has further complications which we have skidded over so far.

When we say that a child has learned to recognize its mother's face, we are no longer only talking about the transmission of information. We are also saying, in effect, that the child has the ability to process the information in ways sufficient to enable it to recognize the mother's face.

Observe that the word "recognize" comes from ordinary discourse. It does not follow (let us always remember) that such words are valid pointers to the truth. But if we are going to start our scientific work with them (and this is what usually happens in science), then we have to look at them carefully to prevent them misleading us. Thus, if we do not look carefully at the word "recognize", we may be misled into supposing that when we use it we are referring to some mysterious, ineffable, inner event in a mental theatre. For it is clear that it refers to an achievement, which does not occupy time, which it seems difficult to bring into time at all, and which therefore is very mysterious indeed. If we are to deal adequately with *these* features of the use of the word, we can only do so by constructing a psychological model which will analyse and incorporate them – along with the other known features of this type of functioning. With such a model in our possession, we will obviously be less tempted to think of recognition as some ineffable inner event (Ryle, 1949; Geach; Farrell, 1972; 1972/3).

What is more, it is only when we have articulated a fairly good model of recognition, and related activity, that we will have a fairly clear idea of what it is that an NP account is required to explain, and therefore what the neuro-physiological states, etc., are supposed to subserve. However, in spite of all the excellent psychological work that has been done on recognition, it is doubtful whether we do possess good models of recognition – ones which are sufficient to explain the phenomena referred to by this word, and its cognates, in their ordinary use. In the absense of such a model it is evident that to speak *simpliciter* of, for example, "the neural basis of learning" is liable to give us an over optimistic and misleading picture of the work accomplished in this field. It seems quite clear that there is still a very large gap indeed between what we know of the psychology of learning, and what we know about the neuro-physiology involved. Hence the work that has been done on "plastic mechanisms at the synapse", for instance, is even more preliminary and exploratory than we are apt to suppose.

This brings us to the heart of the problem of studies in the "correlation" between body and mind.

When the infant Jane gives the mother evidence that it recognizes her, ordinary discourse will lead us to say, *inter alia*, that "Jane saw her". But we also hesitate about saying this. Why? Consider the witness in a court of law, who gives evidence about a car accident, and says that he saw the car quite plainly. This statement entails that "he was aware of the car", and that "he was conscious of it". If we have good and sufficient reason to believe that the witness is telling the truth, then we have equal reason to believe that these entailed statements are also true. So we now have evidence not only that the witness discriminated the input by identifying the object in the low-level way that even a cow seems able to do; we also have evidence that the witness discriminated the input by recognizing the object as a car. But to say this is to say, in effect (and to speak briefly and roughly), that the nervous system of the witness processed the input by "interpreting", or "categorizing" it in a certain way. It was in a position to do this because, presumably, the witness had previously mastered the concept of a car, and so acquired the power to use it. On the occasion of the accident, the nervous system of the witness exercised this power in its processing – it functioned in a way which gives us reason to assert that the witness applied the concept of car, and thereby enabled him to say, truly, in court that he saw the car. It is necessary, therefore, that input be "categorized" in the way just sketched to enable the witness to make his statement in court, and to provide the evidence that he was aware of the car (see Bruner, 1971).

But when we say of the infant Jane that she saw the mother, we do not have the evidence to believe that the infant had mastered the relevant concepts at this stage of its development. Hence we have no evidence that it processed the input in ways which are necessary for it to do before it can give us evidence that, for example, it was aware of the mother. Hence, we have good reason to hesitate about saying *simpliciter* that it saw the mother.

The same seems to apply to all modalities, not just vision, and to the whole of our conscious experience. Psychologists take account of this crucial and pervasive feature of our functioning in their emphasis on the role of symbolism, interpretation and internal representations in their work on agnosic states, and so forth. But they do not seem to appreciate as clearly as they might just how this feature bears on our correlational enterprise.

Well, how does it bear on the search for the neuro-physiological states, events, and so on, which subserve and so correlate with our conscious functioning?

From what we have said above (p. 13), it is clear that a necessary early step towards progress will be to construct a helpful, psychological model of conscious functioning. Such a model would have to account, at least, for the exercise of concepts on input, and for the acquisition of related perceptual beliefs about the world, as well as of our other propositional attitudes. All this plunges us into an enormously involved area, bristling with difficulties. It seems generally agreed that the discourse of NP has already been good enough, in different places, to help in developing P discourse and models. On the other hand, it seems clear that we are nowhere near developing adequate psychological models of conscious functioning at the present time. Hence we cannot yet model this functioning in ways which are particularly useful for the development of NP discourse. This negative fact helps to explain why psychologists in general are still so influenced by the pre-scientific Cartesian picture of the mind. This, in turn, helps to explain why they are apt to suppose that, when I see, feel, and so on, some ineffable mental event takes place, and that my stream of consciousness is made up of such events on the inner stage of my mind. Adequate psychological models of conscious functioning would help psychologists to shed this traditional Cartesian picture; and to talk instead about mental functioning in ways that are congruent with the development and outlook of their own science at the present time.

VI

The fact that we simply do not possess adequate models of conscious functioning brings out that some talk by psychologists on this subject is premature and confusing. For example, when we consider the secondary components of evoked potentials (EP), we may be tempted to identify them with conscious perception (see Boddy, 1978). But this would be wholly premature. They may just be some necessary antecedents of this perception. When we bear in mind how involved the achievement of conscious perception really is, it is obvious that we are only safe at present in claiming, at most, that the secondary components of EP are manifestations of *part of* the complex of neural states, and similar events, that subserve the psychological phenomena of conscious perception. Moreover, it does not make sense to speak to these potentials as being identical with the witness seeing the car. Even if we could show that the potentials occurred over the same interval of time as the psychological events leading up to the achievement by the witness of seeing the car, the latter is not a straightforward process in time, as we have noted. On top of all this, if we say that it is the secondary components which are identical with conscious perception, where and how do the particular entities that make up the nervous system come in? Clearly, the identity we are in search of is between (i) the states, events, etc. described in an adequate psychological model of perception in P discourse, and (ii) the entities, events, etc. described in the discourse of NP, which explains the psychological model. The items described in the discourse of NP would then subserve those described in the P discourse. In this way, and as we have seen above, they could be said to be the same identical items differently described at different levels for dissimilar purposes. It is therefore plainly unhelpful and confusing to speak *simpliciter* of the secondary components of EP being identical with conscious perception.

All this makes it clear that there is still an enormous gap between these two types of discourse, P and NP, in this part of the field. We have a very long way to go before we can speak in non-inflationary and unconfusing ways about the neural basis of consciousness.

VII

At some stage, however, psychologists are liable to feel uneasy about their efforts to close the gap between the two discourses, P and NP.

For one thing, they may feel that, in so far as they do close the gap, to that extent does the discourse of P become logically expendable. It may seem to be eliminable in favour of the discourse of NP. Is this uneasiness justified?

The short answer to this complicated question is: No. Consider an example that is close at hand. We know that the nervous impulse travels at different speeds along fibres of different diameters. This phenomenon is explained by reference to events such as depolarization, and differences in electrical resistance. Here then we have two discourses, the one concerned with the rate of impulse transmission along nerve fibres, the other concerned with electrical and chemical phenomena. The latter explains the phenomena referred to by the former; and the items described in the one subserve those described in the other. Yet it is quite clear that the latter discourse – about depolarization and the rest – has not eliminated the former in practice. Nor is it ever likely to do so, because they have different roles to play and logical jobs to do. Likewise, and even more conspicuously, the discourses of P and NP about conscious functioning are at different levels of description and explanation. It is manifest that they have, and will continue to have, very different roles to play and jobs to do (see Clark, 1980).

Psychologists are also liable to be uneasy for quite a different reason about the prospects of closing the gap between the discourses of P and NP. They may be inclined to say that, no matter how adequate our psychological models are of (say) ordinary human perception or of our stream of consciousness, these will never be able to include the *quality* of our perception, or of our conscious life in general. For, though they may be able to include the fact that the witness recognized the object as a green car, they will not be able to include the experience of "green" that he had at the time. The qualia of perception, and of experience in general, will be omitted. Hence, the NP discourse cannot possibly ever explain these phenomena, and no events subserving them can ever possibly be found.

This argument raises difficult issues that are of great interest to philosophers, and which we cannot pursue adequately here. However, it is worth noting that it has been argued that whereas P discourse cannot be eliminated (as we have just seen), discourse about qualia can be. For when we strip off, and put into our psychological model, all the categorizing that the witness exercised here, we also strip off all the empirical properties of the object. Nothing is left in the object to which the word "qualia" can be used to refer. But, be this as it may, the important fact for psychologists to notice is that the whole argument is irrelevant for their purposes. Even if qualia are in some way genuine entities, but ones which they cannot in principle include in their psychological models, then they can safely ignore them, and just get on with their own business (Farrell, 1962; Wittgenstein, 1953).

Attempts to close the gap between P and NP discourse run into other difficulties, which philosophers have emphasized in recent years. In particular we may be faced by the problem of incorporating belief, and other propositonal attitudes, into the discourse of NP, and thereby into the language of science. But psychologists, physiological psychologists, and other workers in this field, do not seem to have been bothered much, if at all, by these difficulties. For they have not put practical obstacles in the way of their work. Accordingly, it seems safe and wise to recommend psychologists, and their partners, to ignore these difficulties for the present, and just get on with the enterprise of extending the discourses of P and NP, and of bringing them closer together.

VIII

We have noted that the word "correlation" can be used in this field to refer to two quite different relations. (i) Where item A (e.g. some set of events) is a necessary condition for item B, then the occurrence of B will be correlated with that of A. (ii) Where the psychological discourse of P is related in certain ways (which we have sketched above) to that of NP, then we can say that the subserving states, events, and so on, described by NP are correlated with the states, etc. described by P. We noted, also, that the relation of subserving has two forms – the strong and the weak; and so the word "correlation" applies to two sets of events, etc., which stand to each other in either one of these two sub-relations.

But the workers in this field are concerned with other relations, in which the items concerned can also be said to be correlated. Suppose, for example, it is claimed that physiological measures of skin conductance and of the threshold of flicker and click fusion go along with schizophrenic impairment, especially social withdrawal. This is a claim which by itself just states a concomitance of fact, and we can correctly describe it as a correlational claim. It leads naturally to a further claim: the properties of the nervous system, which are manifested in the physiological measures mentioned, are conditions that predispose a person to schizophrenic impairment. One could also describe this as a correlational claim – one connecting predisposing conditions and consequences. Clearly, the field taken as a whole is very diversified; and different sorts of physiological enquiries may be concerned to reveal different sorts of relations and correlations between body, behaviour and mental functioning.

It is all too evident, therefore, that in this field the word "correlation" serves as a blanket term to cover a variety of relations. To use one word to cover all of them is liable to mislead us into thinking that there is only one relation here that we are concerned to investigate. Above all, the word is also liable to mislead us into retaining a traditional Cartesian picture of mental functioning, in which bodily items stand somehow in a one to one relation with mental items, such as qualia, that appear in the inner theatre of one's mind. As we have noted, this traditional picture is not congruent with the drift of psychological enquiry. It is obstructive and should be dropped.

Acknowledgements

I am greatly indebted to Professor L. Weiskrantz, F.R.S. for his kind help in preparing this paper. But he is not responsible for the views and errors it contains.

Further Reading

Nagel, E. (1961). "The Structure of Science". Routledge and Kegan Paul, London.
This is a classical account of the logical problems involved in relating different "levels" of explanation.
Armstrong, D. M. (1968). "A Materialist Theory of the Mind". Routledge and Kegan Paul, London.
This is an extended exposition and defence of the "Identity" theory of the mind and brain.
Putnam, H. (1975). "Mind Language and Reality" Vol. 2, Chs 14–22. Cambridge University Press, Cambridge.
A collection of papers in which the author examines a number of contemporary issues in the philosophy of mind, which bear on the problems raised by this volume.
Dennett, D. (1978). "Brainstorms". Bradford Books.
A collection of lively papers, in which the author presents a "functionalist" account of the mind.

References

Boddy, J. (1978). "Brain Systems and Psychological Concepts", Chs 11–12. Wiley and Sons, Chichester and New York.

Bruner, J. S. (1971). "Beyond the Information Given", Ch. 1. Norton, New York.

Clark, A. (1980). "Psychological Models and Neural Mechanisms". Clarendon Press, Oxford.

Farrell, B. A. (1950). Experience. *In* "The Philosophy of Mind" (V. Chappell, ed.), (1962). Prentice-Hall, Englewood Cliffs, New Jersey.

Farrell, B. A. (1972). Thoughts and Time. *Phil. Q.* **22**, 140–8.

Farrell, B. A. (1972/3) Temporal Precedence. *Proc. Aristotelian Soc.* **73**, 193–216.

Geach, P. (no date) "Mental Acts". Routledge and Kegan Paul, London.

Ryle, G. (1949). "The Concept of Mind", esp. Ch. 5. Hutchinsons, London.

Wilkes, K. (1978). "Physicalism". Routledge and Kegan Paul, London.

Wittgenstein, L. (1953). "Philosophical Investigations" e.g. paras 138–197. Blackwell, Oxford.

3 The Nervous System: Structure and Fundamental Processes

J. Boddy

Abstract The computer metaphor of information transmission and storage may be borrowed to help characterize the ways in which the nervous system works. The neurone and the ways in which it is involved in the storage and transmission of information is the basic building block of the nervous system, and without it there would be no consciousness or thought. Basic anatomical structures are described and illustrated, from the more primitive parts of the brain to those which have evolved to sustain the highest functions of human intelligence and behaviour. When viewed as a system or set of interrelated systems, it is clear that no individual function can be identified with particular anatomical regions or structures. The brain demonstrates the most elaborate example of a complex and integrated system.

I. Introduction

In order to be able to understand the physiological mechanisms of behaviour, it is necessary to acquire basic information about the overall layout of the nervous system, its mode of operation and organizational principles. The student must possess cognitive maps and conceptual frameworks that will make subsequent information on specific topics intelligible.

The nervous system is an information system for the body that accomplishes communication, information processing and initiation and control of action. In the construction of electronic computers man has mimicked the functions of his nervous system in many respects. Computers receive, code, identify, compute, restructure, manipulate and store information and give various forms of output, as nervous systems do. Computer analogies are thus useful to gaining a conceptual grasp of nervous system functions, although it should always be remembered that the details of the underlying mechanisms differ in fundamental ways.

PHYSIOLOGICAL CORRELATES OF HUMAN
BEHAVIOUR   ISBN 0-12-273901-9

The unique central processor of the human (and all mammallian) nervous systems is the brain, encased within the skull. Information from the sense organs is transmitted to the brain by the sensory nerves, either directly or via the spinal cord which travels in the vertebral column. Whilst some simple reflex responses are mediated by the spinal cord, the brain plays the major role in "reading" incoming information, assessing its significance and organizing responses. Information, particularly about the causal (or probabilistic) relation between the individual's responses and painful or rewarding events, are stored within the brain for future reference. The brain is unique in that it generates consciousness of both current events and past events and, in humans at least, consciousness of self. Consciousness is a property that is very difficult to attribute to a computer. The brain organizes responses and effects their execution by issuing signals to the muscles, via motor nerve pathways that descend through the spinal cord and exit through the nerve root at the relevant level for the muscle to be contracted.

II. The Basis of Neural Information Transmission

A. *The Neurone*

It is best to start our examination of the nervous system by observing the structure and properties of its basic functional unit – the neurone. The neurone is a variant of the organic cell that is the building block of all living organisms. Its elongated processes and property of irritability specialize it for information transmission. The neurone is able to transmit information coded into electrical and chemical events, and it is towards an understanding of these fundamental processes, which underlie all mental life and behaviour, that we will aim in the following section.

The central feature of the neurone (see Figs 1 and 2) is the cell body or soma (also perikaryon), ranging from 45 to 100 μm in diameter, at the centre of which is the nucleus. The nucleus contains the genetic material, which carries the instructions controlling the production of proteins and enzymes fundamental to the cell's structure and internal processes. From the cell body branching processes emerge called dendrites which give a tree-like appearance. They are around 5 μm in diameter and are collectors of information from other neurones (see Fig. 3). A more elongated cable-like process, called the axon (diameters ranging from 1 μm to 1 mm), is the transmission line along which information is passed out from the cell body to the terminals at its far end. These terminals pass on the information to other neurones or muscles. Sometimes the axon is encased in an electrically insulating sheath of myelin, formed by the wrapping around of a species of cells called neuroglia,

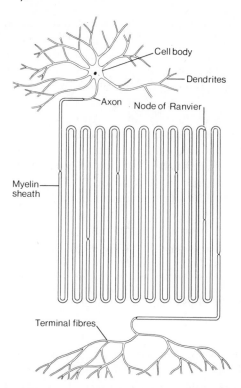

Fig. 1 *Diagrammatic representation of a Neurone; a cell specialized for the transmission of information. Branching processes called* dendrites *form a tree-like network around the cell body. They are collectors of information from other neurones, which might be numbered in the thousands. Information is transmitted down the* axon *in the form of an electrical impulse. In this figure an axon 1 cm long, and magnified around 250 times, is shown folded so that all the features of the neurone can be drawn to scale. In large creatures axons can be measured in metres. This axon is insulated by a* myelin sheath *with periodic gaps called* nodes of Ranvier. *Towards its end the axon may branch to form many terminal fibres that may synapse with one or many other neurones.*

which is punctuated at intervals of around 1 mm by gaps called the nodes of Ranvier. The axon may divide into several branches towards its termination, in order to pass on information to several different postsynaptic cells. The axon terminals each have a swelling called the synaptic knob which sits in close apposition, although not actually touching, to another neurone (at its cell body a dendrite or sometimes its axon) making a junction called the synapse. If the synapse is axo-dendritic then the synapse is formed by juxtaposition of the synaptic knob with a protuberance called a dendritic spine (see Figs. 4a and 4b).

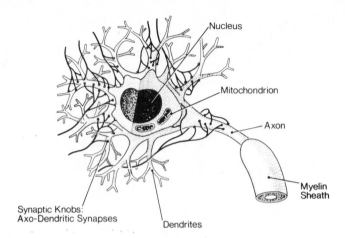

Fig. 2 *Cell body of a neurone. The cell body contains the complex metabolic machinery of the cell. The inner nucleus contains the genetic material that is responsible, through its control of protein production, for the structural and functional characteristics of the cell. Many synaptic knobs at the axon terminals of other cells form synapses on the dendites, cell body and even the axon of the cell shown.*

The human nervous system contains enormous numbers of neurones, it being estimated that the brain alone contains up to 14 billion. In the peripheral nervous system, serving the sense organs and the effectors, neurones have very long myelinated axons (measuring in metres in large animals), which travel in large bundles of white appearance (due to the myelin) referred to as nerves or nerve tracts. In the information processing areas of the brain the neurones have short unmyelinated axons (down to micrometres in length) and concentrations of cell bodies give such areas a grey appearance. Neurones do vary somewhat in their form, but they have sufficient in common for us to consider the functional properties of a composite neurone.

The constituents of the neurone are contained within a membrane. Within the neurone electron microscopy reveals a number of minute structures, including mitochondria, endoplasmic reticulum, neurofilaments, microtubules and synaptic vesicles, that are important for the metabolic activities within the cell and all exist in a fluid medium. The cell membrane, consisting of two layers of lipid (fat) molecules with embedded protein molecules, is about 5 μm thick and separates the internal fluid or axoplasm from the extracellular fluid in which all neurones must be bathed. The membrane maintains its integrity as a boundary between these fluid media despite the fact that the membrane exhibits some of the properties of a fluid itself. It is the dynamic properties of

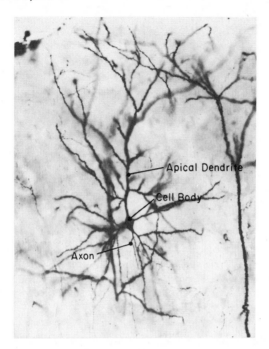

Fig. 3 *Light micrograph showing the main structural features (cell body, dendrites and axon) of a cortical pyramidal neurone. The myriad microscopic protuberances on the dendrites are called dendritic spines and are the location of synapses. The axon of this cell is both slender and short compared with the dendrites and is identifiable by the absence of dendritic spines. The LM is from the visual cortex of a rat.*

this membrane that permit the neurone to transmit information, coded into electrical impulses. It is in the patterns of such impulses that the physical basis of human consciousness and thought lies.

B. *Axonal Transmission*

We will first consider the properties of the axonal membrane which allow it to transmit electrical impulses of a more or less constant size and form, from cell body to axon terminal. In an inactive neurone the membrane is semi-permeable, like a sieve, and only allows certain substances to pass through the pores in its structure by a process of osmosis. The extracellular fluid is an electrolytic solution, in which salt has dissociated to yield positively charged sodium ions (Na^+) and negatively charged chloride ions (Cl^-). These ions exist in concentrations that are about ten times higher outside than inside the

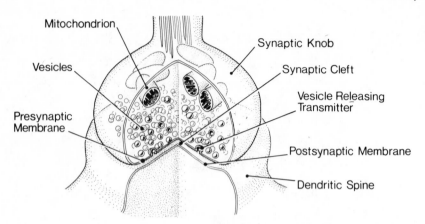

Fig. 4a *A single synapse. The synaptic knob that forms the axon terminal of the pre-synaptic neurone is separated from the post-synaptic membrane by a synaptic cleft around 200 nm wide. The post-synaptic membrane forms the upper surface of a protuberance from the dendrite called a* dendritic spine. *Spherical sacs called* synaptic vesicles *contain transmitter substance which is released to cross the synaptic cleft when an impulse arrives at the pre-synaptic terminal.*

cell. As the cell membrane is almost totally impermeable to them they cannot diffuse inside the cell to equilize the concentration on both sides of the membrane. Within the cell the axoplasm contains positively charged potassium ions (K^+) in a concentration ten times higher than that outside of the cell, together with negatively charged protein ions. As the existence of positively and negatively charged ions inside of the cell has arisen from the dissociation (splitting) of molecules which are electrically neutral, they must cancel each other out. Thus there would be a net charge of zero if the membrane prevented movement of any of these ions to the outside of the cell. In fact the membrane is selectively permeable to potassium and potassium only. The consequence of this is that potassium ions move (by diffusion under osmotic pressure) along their concentration gradient to the outside of the cell. The selective migration of the potassium ions to the outside of the cell creates a growing excess of negative ions inside of the cell and positive ions outside of it. This imbalance generates an increasing electrical force that opposes diffusion out of the potassium ions. Eventually the opposing osmotic and electrical forces reach an equilibrium (i.e. become equal and opposite) and the trans-membrane ion flow ceases. The ion imbalance at this equilibrium point leaves the interior of the cell negative with respect to the exterior. This equilibrium potential for potassium can be calculated from the Nernst equation (see Kuffler and Nicholls, 1976, Chapter 5) when the interior and exterior concentrations of the diffusible ion are known. The theoretical value of 75 mV

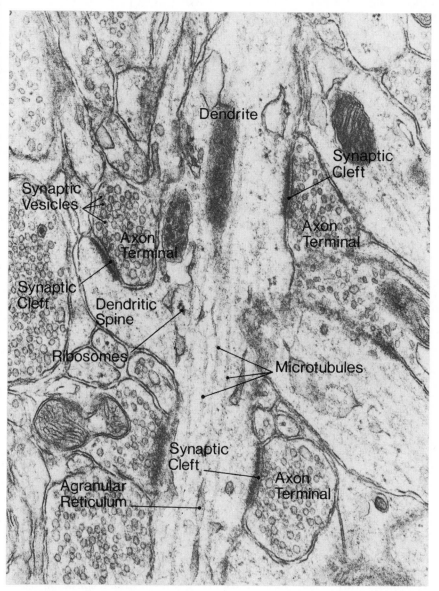

Fig. 4b *Electronmicrogaph of Axodendritic Synapses.* Three axon terminals are shown, two making direct contact with the shaft of the dendrite and one making contact with a dendritic spine. The synaptic vesicles can be clearly seen. The EM is taken from the thalamus of a rat.

differs slightly from the empirically determined value of 70 mV (interior negative), the difference being attributable to a slight inward leakage of positive sodium ions tending to reduce the negativity of the interior relative to the exterior.

We see then that in the inactive neurone there is a resting potential of 70 mV across the membrane (see Fig. 5). The basis of information transmission in the neurone is a brief electrical impulse, called the action potential, nerve impulse or neurone spike, that travels down the axon. The action potential is a transient change in the membrane potential, that occurs when the membrane abruptly becomes permeable to sodium ions and probably decreases its permeability to potassium ions. Control of the membrane potential is taken over by the sodium ions as they flood in along their concentration gradient (leaving the negative chloride ions outside), seeking their

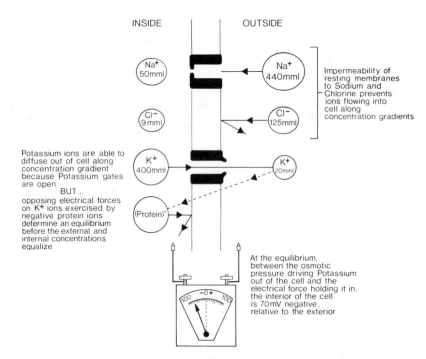

Fig. 5 *The ionic basis of the nerve cell resting membrane potential. The ionic concentrations (in millimols = mml) on the inside and the outside of the membrane are shown. Only potassium ions can freely pass through the membrane along their concentration gradient, but this movement is opposed by the electrical attraction of interior negative ions. When the electrical force exactly matches the opposing osmotic pressure the cell interior is at 70 mV negative relative to the exterior.*

equilibrium potential according to the Nernst equation. This is found when the interior of the neurone reaches 55 mV positive with respect to the exterior, at the peak of the action potential (see Fig. 6). The process giving rise to the action potential is referred to as depolarization. After about 1 ms, the sodium channels are closed by the membrane potential and control is returned to the potassium ions which now flow out through more slowly opening channels until the potassium equilibrium potential (the resting potential of the cell) is restored.

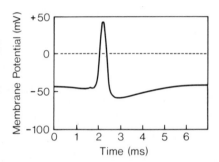

Fig. 6 *The neural action potential (nerve impulse or neural spike discharge). It is shown here as it would appear on an oscilloscope screen. The graph plots the membrane potential, recorded from electrodes inside and outside of the cell, changing over time. The action potential appears, after 2 ms, as an abrupt reversal of the membrane potential lasting just under a millisecond. It is followed by an overshoot of the resting potential before a gradual return to its normal value. Slight discrepancies between the values of membrane potential shown in the diagram and those cited in the text reflect slight differences between species and preparations. The axon potential depicted is that originally recorded from the giant axon of the squid by Hodgkin and Huxley (1939).*

It is clear that with repeated generation of action potentials more and more sodium will move into the cell and potassium out, even though only minute quantities move on any one occasion. This ion exchange caused by action potentials is countered by a metabolic pump, energized by adenosine triphosphate (ATP), that exchanges sodium ions inside the neurone for potassium ions outside and thus maintains the correct concentration gradients between the two sides of the membrane (See Figs 6 and 7). The sodium–potassium coupled pump also counters leakage of sodium ions across the membrane in the resting neurone. (see Kuffler and Nicholls, 1976, Chapter 12).

In recent years it has been established that sodium and potassium have separate channels in the cell membrane (Hille, 1976). For instance it has been found that the puffer fish poison tetrodotoxin (TTX) selectively prevents

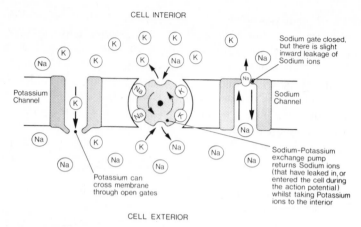

Fig. 7 *Sodium–potassium exchange pump. In the resting neurone a metabolic pump in the membrane exchanges sodium ions that have entered the cell for potassium ions that have left it, in order to maintain the resting membrane potential.*

opening of the sodium channels, while tetraethylammonium allows inward flow of sodium but prevents any subsequent outward flow of potassium. The sodium and potassium channels appear to be gated by charged protein molecules that open or close the channels by changing their shape in response to changes in the membrane potential (Hille, 1978). This is an important principle to appreciate as it is the basis for the triggering of the action potential and for its propagation along the axon.

The axon potential originates at the axon hillock of the cell where graded potential changes, whose origin will be discussed later, produce electrical currents that make the initial segment of the axon more positive than normal. This shift in potential starts to open the sodium gates. If the inflow of sodium sufficiently exceeds the outflow of potassium then the gate opening process feeds upon itself (by positive feedback between the membrane potential and the gate opening mechanism) and sodium explosively enters the neurone. The sodium gates, originally opened by a conformational change in the gating molecule, are closed by a second conformational change produced at longer latency, by the same potential responsible for gate opening (Hille, 1978).

The initiation of the action potential at the axon hillock produces currents that spread down the axon. By changing the transmembrane voltage these currents initiate opening of the sodium gates further down the axon that leads to the appearance of the axon potentials at these more distal locations. The axon potential thus proceeds down the axon by constantly regenerating from the electrical effects it projects ahead of itself (see Fig. 8). At any one point the action potential is terminated by closure of the sodium and opening of the potassium gates. The sodium gates, where the gating molecules assume a special closure conformation (see Stevens, 1979; Hille, 1978), remain refractory to reopening for a period so that the action potential cannot regenerate itself in the rear by currents that project equally as far in that direction. Indeed the post-action potential inactivation of the sodium channels is responsible for a refractory period during which re-stimulation of a neurone fails to generate a new action potential.

The action potential makes a smooth progression down unmyelinated axons that has been compared to the passage of a flame down a fuse. However it progresses down myelinated axons by jumping from node to node in a manner referred to as saltatory conduction. The action potential jumps because no ions (thus no current) can flow through the insulating myelin and the currents set up by the action potential are forced to flow to the next node down the line where they produce depolarization and thus an action potential. Because the insulating sheath causes the current to spread down the inside of the axon more readily, conduction is faster along myelinated axons. This is why the long conducting axons, such as those innervating the peripheral musculature are seen to be myelinated. Long conducting axons

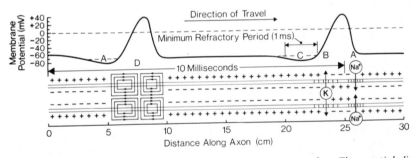

Fig. 8 *The generation and propagation of the nerve impulse. The spatial distribution of the nerve impulses (action potentials) are shown as they move down an axon. At the leading edge (A) of an impulse an influx of sodium ions reverses the membrane potential (depolarization). Behind this zone (at B) an efflux of potassium ions starts to restore the resting potential. There is a refractory zone (at C) where the membrane potential has overshot its normal resting level. The impulse moves down the axon like a wave down a water channel, because depolarization at any one point generates currents (D) that flow forward to open sodium channels ahead of the impulse. The impulse cannot move backwards because of the temporary "locking" of the sodium gates following passage of an impulse. Smooth progression of an impulse only occurs down unmyelinated axons. On myelinated axons the impulse jumps from nodes to node in a mode of progession known as saltatory conduction.*

and/or axons mediating rapid reflexes are also usually found to have larger diameters than others, because speed of conduction is also increased as axonal diameter is enlarged.

C. *The Synapse*

Having gained some understanding of the generation and conduction of the action potential down axons, we must now turn to look at events at the synapse, the junction between neurones, that lead to the arrival of an action potential at the presynaptic terminal initiating an action potential in the postsynaptic neurone. Understanding of the synaptic mechanisms is critical to understanding virtually any aspect of nervous system function as the synapse is the basis of the nervous system's integrative and logical properties, the probable location of information storage and the site of action of many chemical agents affecting nervous system function and thus both experience and behaviour.

Until the 1930s it was generally thought that each neurone in a chain influenced the next by direct physical contact. The theory that each neurone is separated from the next was first argued by the brilliant Spanish anatomist Ramon y Cajal (1934) and later verified by electronmicroscopy. The synaptic knobs of axon terminals are apposed to postsynaptic membranes at distances of between 20 and 50 nm, either at depressions on top of the synaptic spines of the dendrites (see Fig. 4) or at depressions directly on the cell body. Although it has recently been observed that at the molecular level there are structures that span the synaptic cleft (gap) these do not appear to be of major significance in the transmission of information.

At the synapse the transmission of information shifts from electrical (or electrochemical) to chemical. The synaptic knobs contain small spherical sacs, called synaptic vesicles, that are filled with packets of a transmitter chemical such as acetylcholine or noradrenaline. The vesicles appear to be formed by the "pinching" off of a segment of the membrane of the synaptic knob away from the junctional region; they then migrate to the junctional region. The arrival of an action potential at the synaptic knobs causes depolarization to occur that involves influx not only of sodium but also of calcium ions. The calcium ions are essential for the next stage, which is the release of the packets of transmitter from the vesicles when they fuse with the presynaptic membrane to which they are attached. The fusing of the vesicle to the membrane thus replaces the membrane pinched off earlier to form the vesicle. The release of transmitter from the presynaptic terminal has a delay of about 0·5 ms that slows transmission time in multisynaptic pathways. (for a more detailed account of the synaptic vesicle and transmitter release see Kuffler and Nicholls, 1976, Chapter 10)

It has been estimated that there are about 10 000 molecules of transmitter chemical in a single vesicle package and that about 1000 of these take around 100 μs to cross the synaptic cleft and attach to special receptors on the postsynaptic membrane (see Stevens, 1979). The receptors are protein molecules in the membrane and when the transmitter molecules bind to them they open channels in the membrane that increase its permeability to both sodium and potassium, with a slight advantage to sodium (see Fig. 9). The new equilibrium potential when both sodium and potassium can move across the membrane is around zero and this shift from the resting potential is called an excitatory postsynaptic potential (EPSP). EPSPs actually vary in their size according to how many channels are opened.

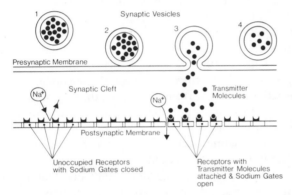

Fig. 9 *Chemical transmission at the synapse. Vesicles filled with transmitter chemical move up to the membrane. The influx of sodium and calcium when an impulse reaches the terminal causes vesicles to fuse with the presynaptic membranes and discharge their contents. Transmitter molecules diffuse across the synaptic cleft and individually attach to receptor molecules in the post-synaptic membrane, causing the sodium channels to open. Vesicles are reclaimed from the pre-synaptic membrane and re-filled with transmitter substance.*

The chemically mediated opening of the membrane channels is brief (about 1 ms) and the transmitter molecule quickly disengages and drifts back into the synaptic space. A transmitter molecule has the potential of repeatedly attaching to different receptor sites and thus prolonging its postsynaptic depolarizing effects until it drifts out of the synaptic cleft. Normally this is prevented by an enzyme (such as acetylcholine esterase) that degrades the transmitter and thus inactivates it. Also some transmitter molecules are removed from the synaptic space by reuptake by the presynaptic terminal. It is necessary to inactivate transmitter molecules after an EPSP as otherwise they would prolong postsynaptic depolarization and prevent the recovery of the resting potential, required before a further impulse can be initiated. It is observed that drugs that mimic transmitters and are excitatory in lower doses, block neural activity when administered in high doses because their persistence at the synapse causes permanent depolarization (known as a depolarization block).

It should be noted that many of the drugs acting on the nervous system act on the synaptic mechanisms of chemical transmission. For example, amphetamines mimic the effects of the catecholamine transmitters (such as noradrenaline) at their receptors, monoamine oxidase inhibitors (antidepressants) destroy the enzymes responsible for degradation of catecholamines and thus potentiate their effect, and α-bungarotoxin (a snake venom) is one of many drugs that block transmission by occupying receptor sites.

Radioactively labelled α-bungarotoxin has been used to map the distribution of receptors to which it binds on postsynaptic neurones. It has been shown that, whilst receptors are normally densely concentrated in the synaptic junctional zones, a few exist at extra-junctional sites (Kuffler and Nicholls, 1976, Chapter 10). Furthermore there is some evidence for mobility of the receptors involving them moving into junctional zones when the synapses are active and away from them when they are inactive. The protein receptor molecules can move through the membrane by diffusion as it has some fluid-like properties. It has been suggested that the enhancement or diminution of postsynaptic membrane sensitivity by junctional accumulation or dispersal of receptors is the mechanism involved in the storage of information by the nervous system (Cronly-Dillon, 1980, personal communication).

We must return to the electrical effects of synaptic activation and note that the excitatory postsynaptic potentials, generated when the receptors open the sodium and potassium channels, do not actively propagate themselves away from the junctional region. This is because the membrane of the soma, unlike the axonal membrane, is not normally electrically excitable. Instead the EPSP spreads decrementally, which is to say with decreasing amplitude the farther away from the junctional region. However as many synaptic knobs converge on any one neurone, EPSPs from adjacent synapses will overlap and summate when simultaneous excitation occurs or when one EPSP follows another before it fades away. If sufficient spatial and temporal summation occurs over an entire neurone, then the depolarization produced at the axon hillock will be enough to cross the threshold for generation and propagation of an action potential.

There is a further important element in the additive process determining whether or not an action potential will be propagated and that is the inhibitory synapse. Some axon terminals release an inhibitory transmitter, of which the only known example is γ-aminobutyric acid, that binds to its own special receptor sites and, by opening channels that admit chloride into the neurone, causes hyperpolarization. In other words the interior of the neurone becomes even more negative than its usual resting value of −70mV, to −90 mV in fact. This potential change, which is referred to as an inhibitory postsynaptic potential (IPSP), makes it more difficult for excitatory influences to depolarize the cell to its firing threshold. Thus at any point in time it is the sum of the excitatory and inhibitory influences that decide whether or not a neurone will pass on information. We might also observe that a phenomenon of presynaptic inhibition has been reported (e.g. see Eccles, 1964), where an inhibitory terminal synapses (axon-to-axon) at a presynaptic excitatory terminal (see Fig. 10). There it has the capacity to reduce excitatory effects by reducing the output of transmitter chemical.

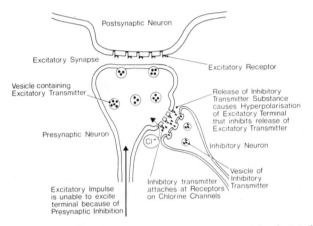

Fig. 10. *Presynaptic inhibition. Inhibitory neurones may make their influence felt at the presynaptic terminal rather than at the postsynaptic membrane.*

The concept of inhibition in neural function is an important one to understand, as many of the brain mechanisms mediating psychological processes involve the interaction of excitatory and inhibitory influences. For example inhibitory influences would appear to terminate eating behaviour in satiety. Within the nervous system many terminals may synapse on a single neurone and those terminals may come from many converging neurones. When we remember that it is the summation of many excitatory and inhibitory influences that determine whether or not a neurone will fire, we can begin to appreciate the enormous range of logical possibilities implicit in the junctional arrangements of neurones. At a relatively simple level, the extraction of visual features by single neurones in the visual cortex (see Chapter 8 by Davidoff and Ratcliff) is likely to be due to the converging interaction of excitatory influences in the visual system.

The brain has many subsystems, serving different behavioural functions, which are not clearly differentiated by anatomical boundaries. One of the

ways in which separation is achieved is by operating with different transmitter chemicals which definitely include acetylcholine, noradrenaline and
adrenaline and almost certainly include dopamine and serotonin. The only
clearly identified inhibitory substance is γ-aminobutyric acid (GABA).
Chemically specific systems, concerned with such functions as sleeping,
eating, reward and punishment, may course through several anatomical
structures, often originating in the brain stem and projecting to widespread
subcortical and cortical locations. These systems are discussed by Van Toller
(see Chapter 5) and Lindsley (see Chapter 6).

III. The Organization and Structure of the Nervous System

The major subdivisions of the nervous system (NS) are the **peripheral nervous
system (PNS)**, consisting of all the sensory and motor nerve tracts outside of
the brain and spinal cord, and the **central nervous system (CNS)**, consisting of
the brain and spinal cord. The brain is sometimes referred to as the **higher
nervous system (HNS)**. The peripheral NS is subdivided into the **somatic NS**,
which controls the skeletal muscles used to execute voluntary acts, and the
autonomic NS, which controls the smooth muscles of internal organs (heart,
lungs etc.) whose responses are involuntary.

The nerve tracts which supply the skeletal muscles and somatosensory
receptor organs are distributed by the 31 segmental levels of the spinal cord,
which is encased and protected by the 33 bony vertebrae. The spinal cord is a
direct evolutionary descendant of the notochord, the primitive head to tail
neural tube that heralded the beginning of the vertebrate line, in primitive
chordate worms. The sensory and motor nerves at any segmental level merge
into an unsegregated tract. Just before entering the spinal cord, the sensory
and motor nerves serving one side of the body separate, the former to enter
the spinal cord at the dorsal (towards the back) nerve root, the latter to enter
at the ventral (towards the belly) nerve root (see Fig. 11). At each segmental
level there is a pair of nerve roots for each side of the body. In cross-section the
spinal cord shows a distinctive "butterfly shaped" central gray area, consisting of nerve cells, which process and switch information at the segmental
level. External to the central gray is white matter, in which one can discern the
segregated fibre tracts or funiculi in which the ascending and descending
axons travel.

A. *The Brain Stem*

At the rostral (head, top) end of the spinal cord, the **decussation of the
pyramids** (right to left and left to right cross-over of the pyramidally cross-

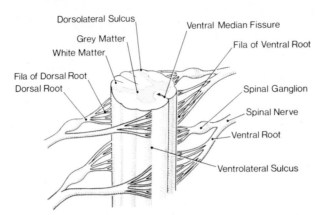

Dorsolateral Sulcus
Grey Matter
White Matter
Fila of Dorsal Root
Dorsal Root
Ventral Median Fissure
Fila of Ventral Root
Spinal Ganglion
Spinal Nerve
Ventral Root
Ventrolateral Sulcus

Fig. 11 *View of a part of the spinal cord showing disposition of spinal nerve roots entering at different segmental levels and sectioned to show the cross-sectional plan.*

sectioned descending motor tracts) marks the transition to **brainstem** (see Fig. 12). This is the lowest part of the brain, both in the sense that it was the earliest to evolve and that it controls some of the most basic functions, such as respiration and reflex aspects of chewing and swallowing. The most caudal (towards the bottom, towards the tail) structure of the brainstem is the **medulla oblongata** (or just medulla) or **myellencephalon**. On the ventral surface of its upper part is a large rounded prominence called the **pons**. This is largely a fibre tract connecting the two deeply fissured hemispheres of the **cerebellum**, a large dorsally situated structure whose primary functions seem to be in the precise timing and co-ordination of muscular movements on the basis of continuous feedback of position information from the sense organs in the muscles. At the level of the cerebellum the central canal, which runs the length of the spinal cord, opens up to form the **4th ventricle**.

The level of the pons and cerebellum is sometimes referred to as the **metencephalon**. Above it is the most rostral brainstem structure, the **midbrain** or **mesencephalon**. On the dorsal surface of the midbrain, sometimes referred to as the **tectum**, are two lower (left and right) and two upper protruberances called the **inferior** and **superior colliculi**. The inferior colliculus is a relay in the auditory system and the superior colliculus an ancient part of the visual system. Rostral to the colliculi and at the termination of the groove that separates them is the **pineal body**, an enigmatic structure that is sensitive to light and appears to influence gonadal function. Ventral to the tectum the brainstem enlarges to form the two massive **cerebral peduncles** (literally "feet" of the cerebral hemispheres) in which the dorsal portion, carrying ascending sensory pathways, is referred to as the

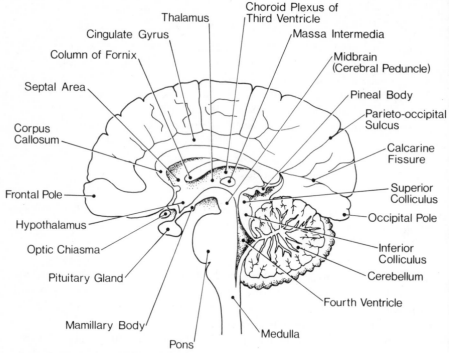

Fig. 12 *Medial sagittal section of the brain. The principle structures of the brainstem and diencephalon can be seen as well as some cortical structures.*

tegmentum and the ventral portion, carrying the descending motor fibres, is referred to as the **basis pedunculi**.

There are two other important features of the brainstem that we should note. The first is the entry of 10 of the 12 cranial nerves, largely serving sensory and motor functions for the head, at different levels of the brainstem. The second is a network of neurones that ascends through the central core of the brainstem, and has extensive connections to cerebral structures above it, called the **brainstem reticular formation** (**BSRF**). It is a structure without clear boundaries as its neural processes intermingle with adjacent sensory and motor tracts. The BSRF is a legacy of the brain of the earliest vertebrate worms. It is a key structure as it appears to have primary responsibility for maintaining the waking state and is an indispensible substrate for consciousness. The BSRF is often referred to by its more functional name, the **reticular activating system** (**RAS**). This brief description of the brainstem omits mention of many component structures and of the structural and functional differentiation within the BSRF. Interested readers should consult more detailed sources such as Moyer (1980) or Gardner (1975).

B. The Diencephalon

Located rostral to the brainstem is the **cerebrum** or brain proper (see Fig. 12). At the base of the cerebrum, rostral and anterior to the midbrain, and continuous with it, are the phylogenetically old structures of the **diencephalon** the **hypothalamus** and **thalamus**. The successive layers of neural structures which encase the diencephalon on all sides except for its basal surface, generally represent the additions of successive phases of evolution of the brain. The outer mantle of the brain, the **cerebral cortex**, by far the most highly developed in man, is the most recent evolutionary addition to the brain and the source of behavioural flexibility, elaborated perceptual abilities and intellect.

C. The Hypothalamus

At the very base of the brain, just anterior (in front of) to the cerebral peduncles, is the **hypothalamus** (see Figs 13 and 14). The medial surface (towards the middle of the brain) in the upper part forms the wall of the **3rd ventricle**. Although small in relation to other structures in the brain, the hypothalamus appears to be of vital importance in both voluntary and autonomic aspects of the behaviours most directly affecting survival; regulation of food and water intake, temperature regulation, reproductive behaviour and emotional arousal. Many small nuclei can be differentiated in the hypothalamus (see Figs 13 and 14), although their boundaries are not sharply drawn. Also the extent to which these subdivisions are a key to localization of function is contentious. The nuclei are named according to their position. The most anterior nuclei are the **lateral** (side) and **medial pre-optic nuclei** and the **supra-optic nucleus**, named according to their relation to the **optic chiasma** (the cross-over of the optic nerve just below the hypothalamus) and particularly associated with sexual behaviour. Next is the **anterior nucleus**. This is followed by the **dorsomedial** and **ventromedial nuclei**, respectively associated with aggressive behaviour and feeding behaviour. At the rear is the **posterior nucleus** which is above the **mammillary body**, a rounded projection from the basal diencephalon. Flanking the medial hypothalamic nuclei is the **lateral hypothalamic area**, also associated with feeding behaviour. There are extensive afferent and efferent connections of the hypothalamus with both lower and higher brain structures. The **medial forebrain bundle**, which appears to be important in the pleasure linked reinforcement of behaviour, originates in the **septum** (Figs 13 and 14) and connects with the pre-optic and ventromedial nuclei as it courses through the hypothalamus down to the midbrain tegmentum.

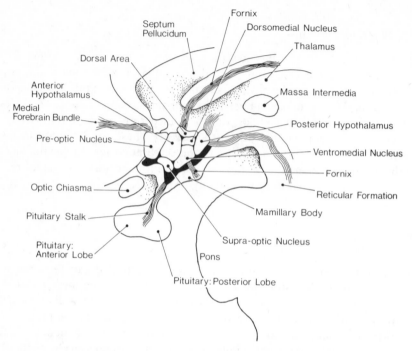

Fig. 13 The sub-divisions and adjacent structures of the hypothalamus.

Vital efferent connections of the hypothalamus are made, via the **infundibulum** or neural stalk, with the posterior **pituitary gland** (or **hypophysis**), where many hormones affecting bodily functions are secreted (Fig. 13).

D. *Thalamus*

The sensory fibres of the brainstem tegmentum project rostrally to the large ovoid mass of the **thalamus** (Figs 13, 14, 15), the largest diencephalic structure. Its medial surface faces the third ventricle. The two thalami are connected by a band of fibres called the **massa intermedia**. The thalamus is a complex structure which is best known for having major relay nuclei (where trans-synaptic transmission occurs) for all of the sensory systems and accomplishing preliminary information processing. The sensory nuclei include the **lateral geniculate nucleus** of the visual system and the **medial geniculate nucleus** of the auditory (acoustic) system. Each gives rise to fibres which travel to the specific cortical projection area for its modality. In contrast, the **intralaminar** and **reticular nuclei** receive input from the brainstem reticular

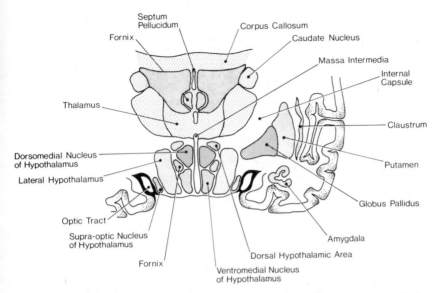

Fig. 14 *A cross-sectional view of the diencephalon. The structures of the diencephalon and the basal ganglia (corpus striatum) can be seen. Limbic system structures which are shown are the fornix, septum pellucidum and amygdala.*

formation, whose rostral projections they are sometimes considered to be, and are the origin of fibres which project diffusely to widespread cortical areas. This **diffuse thalamic projection system** (DTPS), as it is sometimes called has been identified as the possible substrate for selective attention and the generation of conscious awareness. The extensive cortical and subcortical connections of the thalamus suggest a much wider functional involvement than is currently attributed to it.

E. *The Basal Ganglia* (or *corpus striatum*)

The thalamus is surrounded by a quite large and complex arrangement of structures collectively referred to as the **basal ganglia** (Figs 14 and 15). Laterally they are separated from the thalamus by the "V" shaped band of motor fibres, projecting to the cerebral peduncle, called the **internal capsule**. The poorly understood functions of the basal ganglia seem to include control of aspects of motor activity, including posture, balance and locomotion. Principal structures flanking the thalamus are the inner **globus pallidus** and outer **putamen**, collectivelly called the **lenticular nucleus**. The **caudate nucleus** is at its most massive anterior to the thalamus and has a long tail arching over the top of the thalamus and wrapping around to project anteriorly to its termination near the **amygdala** in the temporal lobe.

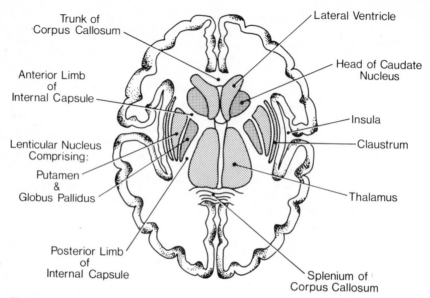

Trunk of
Corpus Callosum

Anterior Limb
of
Internal Capsule

Lenticular Nucleus
Comprising:

Putamen
&
Globus Pallidus

Posterior Limb
of
Internal Capsule

Lateral Ventricle

Head of Caudate
Nucleus

Insula

Claustrum

Thalamus

Splenium of
Corpus Callosum

Fig. 15 A horizontal section of the brain showing all the major structures of the basal ganglia (corpus striatum).

F. *The Rhinencephalon and Limbic System*

The term rhinencephalon (see Figs 11, 14 and 16) literally translates from the Greek as "smell brain", which it once was. However in more recently evolved species it appears to have other important functions in emotion and memory. The **olfactory bulb** and tract must obviously be included, and the immediately adjacent **orbito-frontal cortex** (piriform lobe) is considered to be a rhinencephalic structure. The largest component is the **hippocampus**, an elongated structure in the temporal lobe whose dorsal surface forms the floor of the **inferior horn** of the **lateral ventricle**. At its posterior extremity the hippocampus curves up and gives rise to a massive band of fibres called the **fornix**. The fornix arches over the thalamus and descends to terminate in the mammillary body of the hypothalamus. Also included in the rhinencephalon is the **septum pellucidum**, a thin sheet of neural tissue suspended between the corpus callosum and the fornix below it. The **corpus callosum** is the massive band of communicating fibres between the two hemispheres.

The rhinencephalon is part of a wider system called the **limbic system**. It additionally includes the **cingulate gyrus**, a fold of cortex lying across the corpus callosum, and the **amygdala** a mass of gray matter in the dorsomedial region of the tip of the temporal lobe, in contact with the tail of the caudate

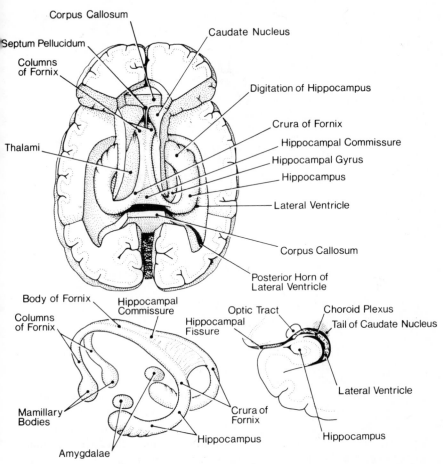

Fig. 16 *This stepped horizontal section of the brain permits a good 3-dimensional visualization of some of the major structures of the limbic system: the hippocampus and fornix. Notice the location of the hippocampi on the floors of the lateral ventricles and, in the bottom diagram, notice the position of the amygdala in relation to the hippocampus.*

nucleus. The limbic system is especially associated with the production of emotional behaviour and has intimate connections with the hypothalamus, which is sometimes included as a limbic system structure.

G. *Cerebral Hemispheres and Cerebral Cortex*

The two distinctive halves of the brain above the diencephalon are known as the cerebral hemispheres (see Fig. 17). They are joined, below the anterior–

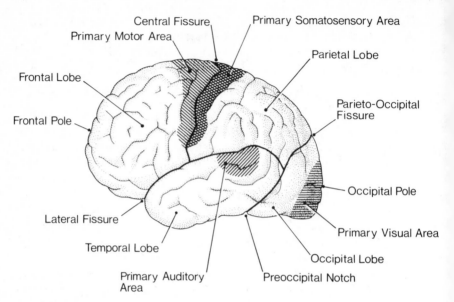

Fig. 17 *A lateral view of the brain showing the boundaries of the four lobes of the cerebral cortex, the primary sensory areas and the primary motor area.*

posterior **longitudinal fissure** by the **corpus callosum** that permits exchange of information between them.

The visible outer mantle of gray matter (with its concentrations of cell bodies) is known as the **cerebral cortex**. Its surface appearance of a complex series of deep fissures and convolutions, known as **sulci** and **gyri,** permit the attainment of a very large surface area within a small enclosure. This greatly increases the number of cells that can be accommodated. In the human cortex, which is the most convoluted (with the exception of dolphins), we find by far the greatest number of neurones of any species, and the highest intelligence.

1. Microscopic anatomy of the cortex

Knowledge of the microscopic anatomy of the cortex is becoming more important for the understanding of certain brain functions (see Gardner, 1975, Chapter 17 for full account). Visual inspection has identified 6 diffe-rent layers of neocortex, on the basis of sizes and shapes of cells. The triangular shaped **pyramidal cells** of layers 3 and 5 are the most prominent cell types. They are the origin of output signals, and are distinguished by the possession of large and conspicuous **apical dendrites**, which rise vertically to the cortical surface and are thought to be critically involved in the generation of gross cortical electrical activity.

Recently a more functional approach to the cellular architecture of the cerebral cortex has led to the recognition that it is vertically organised into columns, each with its own specific input, and with chiefly inhibitory influences between columns (e.g. Chapter 8 on vision).

2. Gross anatomy of cerebral cortex (see Fig. 17)

On the lateral aspect of the brain the **central fissure (fissure of Rolando)** divides the **frontal lobe** from the **parietal lobe**. The **lateral fissure (fissure of Sylvius)**, running more-or-less horizontally at the bottom of the central fissure, divides off the distinctive finger of the **temporal lobe** from the frontal and parietal lobes above it. The **occipital lobe** at the posterior extremity of the brain is demarcated on the lateral aspect, by an imaginary line joining the end of the **parieto-occipital fissure** to the **pre-occipital notch**. The most important cortical gyri are indicated on Fig. 17 and the reader should note the logic of the nomenclature. Function is most clearly localized at the cerebral cortex on the sensory projection areas. For instance the **occipital pole** is the visual area, a segment of the **superior temporal gyrus** is the auditory area and the **post-central gyrus** is the somatosensory area. Electrical stimulation of these areas in a conscious human patient induces diffuse sensations in the modality concerned. The precentral gyrus is the origin of voluntary motor commands. Electrical stimulation produces contraction of muscle groups as a function of area stimulated. On both the sensory cortex and motor cortex there is systematic mapping of either the peripheral receptors (or receptor area on the retina) or effectors (muscle groups) reflecting their spatial arrangement on the body. The mapping is distorted by the fact that the size of the cortical area allocated to a receptor zone or body part is a function of its importance to the organism.

Areas of the cortex which are not clearly sensory or motor are certainly concerned with interpretation of information received through the senses, intellectual function and probably memory. Areas specifically concerned with language have been identified from the examination of brain damaged patients and these are discussed elsewhere in this volume.

IV. Anatomy and Functional Systems

It should be understood that it is rarely possible to straightforwardly identify any functional system of the brain with one of the specific, visibly distinct structures of classical neuro-anatomy. A particular system may course through several structures and a single structure may contain segments of several systems. Classical neuro-anatomy, which pre-dates most current knowledge of brain function, provides an outline map within which the details of functional systems can be traced and interrelated.

For much fuller information on the structures of the nervous system of interest to physiological psychologists, the reader should consult Moyer's (1980) neuro-anatomical text.

Further Reading

Eccles, J. C. (1964). "The Physiology of Synapses". Springer-Verlag, Berlin.
Definitive publication (at time of publication) by the foremost pioneer in the field of research.
Eccles, J. C. (1973). "Understanding the Brain". McGraw-Hill, New York.
More general book on the brain, primarily concerned with neurophysiology, by the pioneer of research on synaptic function,
Hille, B. (1976). Ionic basis of resting and action potentials. *In* "The Nervous System: Vol. 1, Cellular Biology of Neurons, Pt. 1." (E. Kandel, ed.), pp. 99–136. American Physiological Society, Bethesda, Maryland.
Up-to-date account of fundamental neural processes.
Kuffler, S. W. and Nicholls, J. G. (1976). "From Neurone to Brain: A cellular approach to the function of the nervous system". Sinauer, Sunderland, Massachussetts.
Excellent book from which intelligent novices with some scientific background can gain a good understanding of the fundamental processes of the nervous system. There are excellent diagrams and illustrations and interesting and very useful accounts of the classical experiments which laid the foundations of modern neurophysiology.
Moyer, K. (1980). "Neuroanatomy". Harper and Row, New York.
Clear, well labelled and aesthetically pleasing drawings of the nervous system which are a great help to learning its anatomy. A number of diagrams are specifically orientated to understanding the physiology of behaviour.
Stevens, C. F. (1979). The neurone. An article in "The Brain", a Scientific American Book. W. H. Freeman, Oxford. Originally published in *Scient. Am.* **241**(3), pp. 48–59.
Readily intelligible, excellently illustrated and up-to-date brief account of neural function.

References

Cooke, I. and Lipkin, M. (eds), (1972). "Cellular Neurophysiology". Holt, New York.
Eccles, J. C. (1964). "The Physiology of Synapses". Springer-Verlag, Berlin.
Gardner, E. (1975). "Fundamentals of Neurology" 7th edn. W. B. Saunders, Philadelphia.
Hille, B. (1976). Ionic basis of resting and action potentials. *In* "The Nervous System: Vol. 1, Cellular Biology of Neurons, Pt. 1" (E. Kandel, ed.), pp. 99–136. American Physiological Society, Bethesda, Maryland.
Hille, B. (1978). Gating in sodium channels of nerve. *A. Rev. Physiol.* **38**, 139–152.
Hodgkin, A. L. and Huxley, A. F. (1939). *Nature* **144**, 710.

Katz, B. (1978). The release of the neuromuscular transmitter and the present state of the vesicular hypothesis. *In* "Studies in Neurophysiology". (R. Porter, ed.), pp. 1–21. Cambridge University Press, Cambridge.

Kuffler, S. W. and Nicholls, J. G. (1976). "From Neuron to Brain: A cellular approach to the function of the nervous system". Sinauer, Sunderland, Massachussetts.

Moyer, K. (1980). "Neuroanatomy". Harper and Row, New York.

Ramon y Cajal, S. (1934). "Les preuves objectives de l'unite anatomique des cellules nerveuses". Trob. Lab. Inest. Biol. Univ. Madrid.

Stevens, C. F. (1979). The Neuron. *Scient. Am.* **241**(3), 48–59. Also published in "The Brain". W. H. Freeman, Oxford.

4 Information Processing and Functional Systems in the Brain

J. Boddy

Abstract Chapter 3 set out the key features of the anatomy and structure of the nervous system. In this Chapter we turn to an examination of how information is processed and how systems are organized to produce psychological functioning. The simple principle of a binary (on–off) state for the neurone is seen to be inadequate for even quite primitive aspects of sensory coding. Place coding is an essential principle which helps us in the understanding of the capacity of the nervous system to recognize complex patterns of stimulation. The synapses represent the brain's logic system, and inputs and outputs are controlled by inhibitory and excitatory processes. Inhibition and excitation may be seen to operate at a functional level within larger systems and may subserve aspects of reward and punishment, thereby controlling the basic mechanisms of adaptation. Continuous feedback is a basic principle of all control systems and it is clear that the brain is able to monitor the consequences of actions upon the world, and also to regulate the absorbtion and release of energy. Information relating to adaptation is stored by subtle changes in the strength and patterning of the multiple connections between neurones. It is explained that cell assemblies in the brain and their interconnections do not respond in a passive or consistent fashion as is the case with man-made electronic systems; rather the multiple pathways respond in a probabilistic mode. When we move to a consideration of larger functional systems we see that the old-fashioned notion of localization of function can no longer be supported, for the neural substrates of any particular function are distributed through several structures; the same pathways may participate in a variety of functional systems. Some systems like the visual system show clear evidence of hierarchical organization and a great deal is known about the neurophysiological mechanisms which underlie vision. Evoked potentials provide a window to the sequences involved in information processing, from the appraisal of physical characteristics of the stimulus, to the appreciation of its meaning within the flux of neural events. The capacity to maintain alertness and to respond selectively to stimuli is mediated by a particularly diffuse functional system. It stretches from the core of the brain stem outwards to all cortical structures, and works in conjunction with the diffuse thalamic projection system, which is thought by some authorities to be the source of conscious awareness. Finally brain structures involved with the regulation of vegetative function and survival are described, together with the chemical substances known to operate in pathways as elaborate and extended as any revealed by electrophysiological studies. However much we know about individual anatomical structures, functional

PHYSIOLOGICAL CORRELATES OF HUMAN
BEHAVIOUR   ISBN 0-12-273901-9

systems and pathways, we must never forget that all parts of the nervous system are constantly active, and that communication and mutual influence between systems is always present. Thus all parts of the nervous system are mutually interdependent.

I. Coding and Integration in the Nervous System

A. *Pulse Coding*

Living organisms such as ourselves have the capacity to detect and assign meaning to stimulus patterns in our environment and to respond to them according to our needs. We have seen (Chapter 3) how the neurones, the units of the nervous system which are the basis of this capacity, actively propagate an electrochemical impulse. We now need to understand how the external world is represented in patterns of neural impulses. We need to know how the nervous system codes information.

At first sight coding in the nervous system is very simple. A neurone offers only two possibilities: that it transmits an impulse or that it does not. All nerve impulses are essentially the same, varying little in the potential change involved. They appear to be the basis of a binary code (which counts from a base of two) like that commonly used in computers. However, when we come to examine the details we find that rather different principles are involved.

The simplest stimulus dimension that has to be coded is that of intensity. How bright is a light? How loud is a sound? Even here complexity starts to creep in as two principles appear. Intensity is partly coded by the frequency with which the neurones transmit impulses and partly by the number of neurones activated within a nerve tract. The latter principle is made possible by the fact that some neurones have higher activation thresholds than others.

B. *Place Coding*

The frequency of impulses travelling down a neural axon might inform the brain how intense a stimulus is, but it does not tell it what type of stimulus is being detected. This brings us to the most important coding principle operating in the nervous system – place coding. Environmental stimuli are, in effect, sources of energy that impinge upon sense receptors tuned to receive different classes and bands of energy. Our receptors are well known; eyes, ears, nose, tongue, labyrinth (for spatial orientation), tactile and kinaesthetic (muscle sense). The different sensations which we become aware of arise because the nerve tracts from the receptors travel to specific destinations in the brain. An impulse in an optic tract axon is essentially similar to one in the auditory pathway, but gives rise to a visual sensation because it activates neurones in the visual cortex, at the occipital pole of the brain (see Fig. 1). If a neurone in

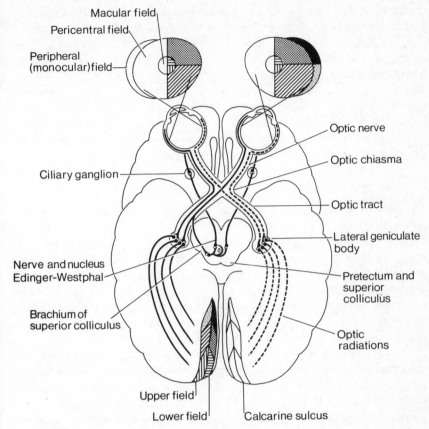

Macular field

Pericentral field

Peripheral (monocular) field

Optic nerve

Optic chiasma

Ciliary ganglion

Optic tract

Lateral geniculate body

Nerve and nucleus Edinger-Westphal

Pretectum and superior colliculus

Brachium of superior colliculus

Optic radiations

Upper field

Lower field   Calcarine sulcus

Fig. 1 *The visual system: the eye, the optic nerve and its route to the visual projection area of the occipital lobe. The shaded sectors indicate how the retina is topographically mapped on the visual projection area.*

the visual system could be disconnected and re-connected to the auditory projection area on the superior temporal gyrus then it would give rise to auditory and not visual sensations.

Knowing the principle of place coding one is able to start accounting for the capacity of the nervous system to recognize complex patterns. The most obvious extension of the principle is the visual system. The retina of the eye is a spatially extended surface upon which a spatially patterned external stimulus is projected. As the neural connections from the retina achieve topographical mapping of the retina at the cortex, place coding can account for the representation of spatial information in the brain (see Fig. 1). However, this is only the beginning, as the coding of environmental information is much more than just a process of passive representation. It involves analysis and accentuation of the most important identifying features of a pattern.

The principle of place coding is used to represent information other than simple spatial relationships. For instance in the visual system information about the presence of different wavelengths of light (different colours) and about the presence of specific features, such as a light–dark boundary with a specific orientation, is coded by the activation of cells at specific cortical locations, that are activated only by specific features. In the auditory system where all patterns are temporal rather than spatial, different frequencies of sound, or tones, are coded by separate nerve pathways.

C. Synaptic Integration

The nervous system has very complex capabilities for analysing input signals and issuing output to the effector organs. The key to the understanding of these capabilities lies in understanding the functions of the synapse. The synapses are the source of the brain's logic. Within the brain up to 4000 presynaptic neurones may converge on one postsynaptic neurone, and, conversely, one presynaptic neurone may give rise to processes synapsing on many postsynaptic neurones. Also the synapse multiplies the possibilities of action in the nervous system as there are inhibitory as well as excitatory influences on the readiness of the postsynaptic neurone to fire.

We have already seen in the previous chapter how a process of spatial and temporal summation of excitatory and inhibitory synaptic potentials decides whether or not a neurone will fire. The presynaptic influences on a cell determine the status of a "logical gate" (see Fig. 2). A cell might give an output in response to several different combinations of synaptic input, which are equivalent in the sense that they all generate sufficient excitatory potentials to reach the cell's activation threshold. This important function as an "OR" gate gives the cell the ability to abstract equivalence. For instance there are cells in the visual cortex that respond specifically to bars of light projected onto the retina at a specific orientation, irrespective of retinal location. This presupposes that the orientation specific cell is triggered by any of several inputs representing equivalent bars of light at different retinal locations. Lower down in the system there are cells that respond to bars of light at specific retinal locations because of the additive influence of input from each of the line of retinal points stimulated by the bars (see Fig. 3).

D. Excitation and Inhibition

The capacity of one neurone to inhibit another is a very important property of the nervous system. In the sensory systems lateral inhibition (see Chapter 8 on vision) is used to accentuate important attributes of a stimulus pattern.

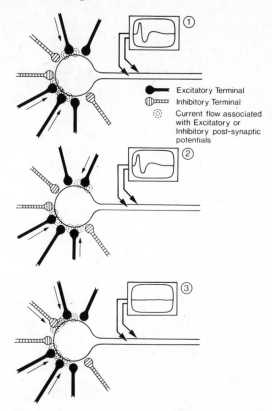

Fig. 2 *The principles of neural logic: the hypothetical case of a postsynaptic neurone with multiple presynaptic terminals, both excitatory and inhibitory, is shown. (1) AND gate mode of operation in which it has required simultaneous activation of three presynaptic terminals to generate a postsynaptic impulse. (2) OR gate operation illustrated by the generation of a postsynaptic impulse by an alternative group of three excitatory synapses. (3) The blocking of a postsynaptic impulse when adequate presynaptic excitatory influences are countered by the influence of an inhibitory presynaptic terminal. From these hypothetical illustrative cases a large number of schemes for opening and closing of neural gates can be visualized.*

Survival behaviours may be controlled by the balance between excitatory and inhibitory influences. The regulation of eating behaviour is an example of this. Internal nutrient deficits and external olfactory, gustatory and visual stimuli generate excitatory inputs to the hunger mechanism, which leads to food seeking behaviour and eating if they predominate. Aversive gustatory and olfactory stimuli, the cumulative effects of oropharyngeal stimuli (from mouth and pharynx) from eating and the detection of rising or high levels of

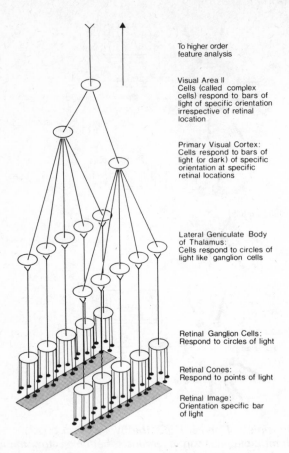

To higher order
feature analysis

Visual Area II
Cells (called complex
cells) respond to bars of
light of specific orientation
irrespective of retinal
location

Primary Visual Cortex:
Cells respond to bars of
light (or dark) of specific
orientation at specific
retinal locations

Lateral Geniculate Body
of Thalamus:
Cells respond to circles of
light like ganglion cells

Retinal Ganglion Cells:
Respond to circles of light

Retinal Cones:
Respond to points of light

Retinal Image:
Orientation specific bar
of light

Fig. 3 *Schematic diagram showing patterns of convergence in the visual system which would allow single cortical cells to be activated by bars of light of specific orientation, irrespective of retinal location. This is an example of a hierarchical system, in this case to accomplish feature analysis.*

utilisable fuels in the body all generate inhibitory influences tending to suppress the feeding mechanism if it is active (see Fig. 4 and Boddy, 1978, Chapter 4). Oomura *et al.* (1967) recorded the activity of single neurones in the hypothalamic centres associated with feeding and satiety respectively, and found evidence that each centre had the capacity to inhibit neural activity in the other.

Gray (1971) has presented evidence for the existence of anatomically separated excitatory and inhibitory systems of fundamental importance in the regulation of our behaviour. The systems become conditioned to environmental stimuli on the basis of rewards and punishments. An inhibit-

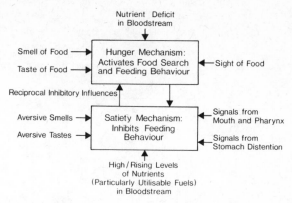

Fig. 4 *Simplified schematic diagram showing how feeding behaviour is regulated by reciprocal inhibitory influences which a hunger mechanism and a satiety mechanism exercise on each other. All inputs into each mechanism are excitatory, but the influence of each mechanism on the other is inhibitory.*

ory mechanism in the hippocampus and medial septal nucleus suppresses behaviour which has previously been punished or which has repeatedly failed to elicit a reward from a formerly rewarding source. An excitatory system including the septal area, lateral hypothalamus and medial forebrain bundle activates behaviour which has previously been rewarded or has secured successful escape from a punishment. Gray has attempted to account for personality differences on the extraversion–introversion dimension, in terms of differences in sensitivity of the mechanisms mediating reward based excitation of behaviour and punishment based inhibition of behaviour.

Inhibition is of particular importance at all levels in the motor systems, permitting precise and co-ordinated execution of muscle movements. For example, the cerebellum, which imparts smoothness and accuracy to limb movements on the basis of comparing copies of command information from the cerebral cortex, with feedback information from the movement, exercises a purely inhibitory influence to modulate signals in descending motor pathways (see Fig. 5).

E. *Feedback*

A principle that is used pervasively in neural subsystems is that of feedback control. Every subsystem is organised so that the results of any unfolding action initiated, whether external or internal, are continuously fed back, either to the command centre or to a comparator which has received a copy of the original command. Feedback is the first principle of control engineering. It permits continuous error correction during ongoing movements that

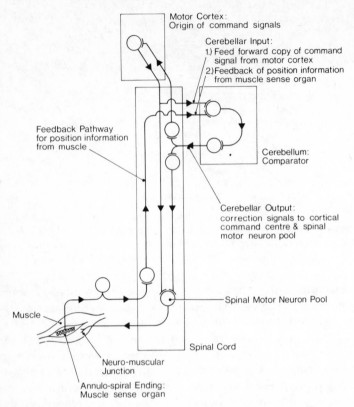

Fig. 5 *Simplified schematic diagram to illustrate how the cerebellum achieves the feedback control of movement.*

ensures accuracy and also enables a moving target to be tracked. The simplest example of feedback in the nervous system is "recurrent collateral inhibition", which occurs in the motor neurone pools at each segmental level of the spinal cord (see Fig. 6). Each motor neurone receives command signals from higher levels in the nervous system and transmits them to the muscles via the central motor nerve roots. The axons have collateral branches that emerge before they leave the cord and synapse with inhibitory neurones (called Renshaw cells). These inhibitory neurones complete a simple circuit by synapsing with the original motor neurone, as well as with other neurones of the spinal motor neurone pool. Thus, whenever a motor neurone is activated it initiates inhibitory influences that are fed back to it. This is clearly negative feedback in the sense that it tends to reduce the level of activity in the original command neurones. Its function appears to be to prevent a "runaway"

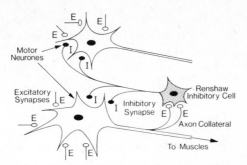

Fig. 6 *The principle of negative feedback illustrated by the circuit for recurrent collateral inhibition. The inhibitory Renshaw cell opposes excitatory influences on the cell which originally excited it.*

response in spinal motor neurones that will result in an uncontrolled muscular contraction.

We saw a more elaborate example of feedback control in the reference to cerebellar function at the end of the last section. The cerebellum appears to receive a copy of command signals issued to the musculature by the motor cortex (see Thach, 1968). Feedback information from the proprioceptive sense organs in the moving muscles and from other sense organs is compared with the copy of the command signal in the cerebellum and a continuous series of corrections is made to ensure a smooth and accurate movement (see Fig. 5). In persons suffering from cerebellar damage an attempt to perform a simple action, like touching the end of the nose with a finger, is marked by an escalating series of wavering movements that appear to arise because of loss of ability to make small corrections to an ongoing movement.

The system for regulating food intake may be considered as another example of feedback control. If the vetromedial hypothalamic nucleus is lesioned (destroyed) an animal will over-eat and become very obese. This appears to occur because the ventromedial hypothalamus mediates negative feedback from oropharyngeal (mouth and pharynx) sensation and the post-ingestional effects of food that normally leads to termination of eating behaviour and its suppression until nutrient levels are low again. In the absence of this negative feedback eating behaviour is controlled largely by the positive feedback from food, namely smell and taste. Thus as long as "good smelling", "good tasting" food is present, eating continues unabated with no regard to the factors that normally signal satiety.

Sometimes feedback comes along routes outside of the nervous system. For example the hypothalamus controls the release of follicle stimulating hormone, and later luteinizing hormone, from the pituitary gland during the female sex cycle. It is the feedback of oestrogen and progesterone, released into the bloodstream from the ovary, that influences the hypothalamus to switch from follicle stimulating hormone to luteinizing hormone production during the ripening of an ovum.

F. Plasticity

The knowledge that the neurone is a transmission line for information coded into electrical impulses suggests analogues between the nervous system and man-made electrical circuits. It can easily appear that the key to the understanding of brain function is simply to work out the diagram of a fixed circuit. However, one of the most important properties of the nervous system is its plasticity, the modifiability of its patterns of internal connections, that is the basis of its capacity to change its response to a given stimulus. This is the basis of learning and memory, for which the capacity increases the more highly evolved the brain is. At a neural level the storage of information would appear to involve subtle changes in the pattern and strength of connections between neurones. As an organism is continuously receiving and/or processing information, even possibly while asleep, we must suppose that there are continuous changes in the circuitry of its nervous system. Speculation about the nature of the plastic changes underlying memory and learning focus on the synapse. The activation of functionally dormant synapses or change in sensitivity at operative synapses are obvious ways in which the logic of a neural network could be changed as a basis for information storage. The physiological basis of memory and learning is elaborated upon in Chapter 7 of this volume.

G. The Statistical Nature of Neural Activity

It is important to appreciate the fundamental ways in which neural circuits differ from manmade electronic circuits, in which signals are carried by a single passive wire. Communication between any two locations in the nervous system is carried by multiple pathways in each of which the carrier is an active element. Thousands of neurones serve where a single wire would carry the message in a manmade system.

Furthermore, an individual neurone is not bound to respond identically to repetitions of a particular input signal, particularly when one comes to look at neurones in the brain that are involved in information processing. An individual neurone might show spontaneous spike activity when there is no stimulus at all. Alternatively, activity might be absent or attenuated when a stimulus does occur. This variability in responsiveness presumably reflects modulation of the cell's excitability by intrinsic or external factors. It would seem to be inconsistent with reliable transmission of information. We must consider the activity of the ensemble of cells accessed by a stimulus to understand how that stimulus is uniquely represented in the brain. It is in the overall pattern of excitation of an ensemble of cells that the identity of a repeated stimulus is retained. Individual cells may drop into or out of the pool of responding cells without affecting the overall pattern of response. The time at which a member cell of an ensemble will fire after a repeated identical input varies from occasion to occasion, but over many repetitions shows a frequency distribution whose shape is identical to the waveshape of the overall response of the ensemble. The specific probabilities of cells responding at different points in time after a specific input ensures that the ensemble will yield an identical response to an identical input due to a process of spatial averaging. This theme is elaborated upon by Thatcher and John (1977).

H. *Neural Systems: Localized, Specific and Diffuse*

The brain is usually discussed in terms of the functional systems into which it can be subdivided. System functions might come under such headings as vision, audition, perception, regulation of food intake or sexual behaviour. It is easiest to suppose that the different functional systems will be localized in clearly identifiable structures. Historically a great deal of investigation of the brain has been concerned with the localization of function in specific structures. Prime examples of systems with specific anatomical localization are the sensory systems. For example, input to the visual system (see Fig. 1) occurs at the light sensitive surface of the retina of the eye. It travels along the clearly defined optic tract to the partial left–right cross-over at the optic chiasma, and from there to the first sensory relay at the lateral geniculate body of the thalamus. Beyond the thalamus the pathway fans out to gain access to the primary visual cortex at the occipital pole of the brain. There the retina is topographically mapped. The visual cortex is essential for vision and the loss of any part results in the loss of part of the visual field. However, information must go beyond the primary visual cortex if pattern perception or anything other than diffuse visual sensation is to be experienced. The final stage of the route to conscious perception becomes much more difficult to trace in the dense neural networks of the cerebral hemispheres.

In recent times it has become apparent that the notion of clearcut localization of function is inadequate. The neural substrate serving a specific function may be distributed through several structures and a specific structure may carry circuits serving several different functions. Neural pathways concerned with different functions, such as eating and drinking, may be interleaved. The notion of "diffuse localisation" has been evoked to characterize a neural substrate which is specific at the neurone level, but which is interleaved with other systems and widely distributed throughout the brain. A flexible approach to the question of localization of function needs to be maintained. This theme is developed later in the chapter.

I. *Hierarchical systems*

Some brain systems show signs of being hierarchically organized. This is particularly apparent in the visual system where the hierarchical organization appears to be essential to pattern recognition. Adjacent to the primary visual cortex, which receives input from the lateral geniculate nucleus of the thalamus, are secondary and tertiary visual areas to which visual input goes in turn. The classical work of Hubel and Wiesel (1962) has shown that, as one progresses from the primary to tertiary visual area, individual cells respond specifically to progressively more complex shapes projected upon the retina. The visual areas appear to form a hierarchical system in which the lowest levels of the hierarchy analyse the simplest elements into which visual pattern can be dissected and higher levels analyse progressively more complex shapes projected upon the retina. The visual areas appear to form a hierarchical system in which the lowest levels of the hierarchy analyse the simplest elements into which visual pattern can be dissected and higher levels analyse progressively more complex features formed from the simplest elements. For instance cells at the lowest level of the hierarchy will respond to light–dark boundaries of a specific orientation at a specific retinal location. At a higher level they will respond to orientation irrespective of retinal location and higher still they might respond to the intersection of two boundaries at different orientations. Such a hierarchical feature analysis system clearly forms an important part of the neurophysiological mechanisms of perception (see Fig. 3).

J. *Brain Potentials and Neural Information Processing*

Because the activity of single neurones in the brain bears only a statistical relationship to a particular input signal, we have seen that the massed activity of populations of neurones must be studied as well as unit activity, to understand how information is represented in the brain. There is the advantage in the study of the massed activity of brain cells that it can be carried out without the necessity of destructive invasion of brain tissue, which can compromise the interpretation of the results, apart from anything else. The development of techniques for the non-invasive recording of massed neural electrical activity from the brain has meant that investigators have been able to use normal humans in experiments on information processing by the brain.

The electrical activity of the human brain was first recorded externally by

Hans Berger, an Austrian psychiatrist, in the 1920s. He named the weak pulses that he picked up from electrodes on the scalp the electro-enkephalogram (English form electroencephalogram), a name that has stuck, although often shortened to EEG. The validity of Berger's work was unfortunately not recognised until the late 1930s, but after this the recording of the EEG in clinical neurology and experimental research became increasingly common.

The weak oscillations of the EEG signal are picked up between two small silver electrodes. They may be stuck on over two active brain sites (bipolar recordings) or over an active and an indifferent (inactive) area (monopolar recording). At the EEG machine the signal is amplified by a factor of 100 000 or more and the amplified signal used to drive pen galvanometers that write out a graph of the fluctuations in voltage over time on a sheet of paper moving at a constant speed. These days it is common for the amplified EEG signal to be fed directly into a digital computer for further analysis.

Paradoxically the raw EEG signal is stronger the less an individual is doing. In the resting individual a rhythmic pattern of high voltage waves with a frequency of around 10 Hz is seen. It appears to arise because cells that are not involved in information processing have resting rhythms that are drawn into synchrony with each other. The frequency and voltage characteristics of the raw or background EEG normally index an individual's state on an arousal continuum that determines the speed and efficiency with which information is processed.

The brain activity elicited by transient stimuli requiring processing is usually rather difficult to discern against the background activity in the raw record. Stimulus related activity can only be clearly revealed by averaging the EEG samples immediately following a number of stimulus occurrences. The resulting waveform is referred to as an evoked potential (see Fig. 7). It is a phenomenon that has been widely recorded in investigations of how external information is represented in ensembles of neurones in the brain (see Thatcher and John 1977 for review).

The spike discharge of neurones lasts for only 1 ms while the waves of an evoked potential last for tens or even hundreds of msecs. The most obvious interpretation is that the evoked potential represents an "envelope" of spike discharges of cortical neurones. Careful recording from microelectrodes in or adjacent to single cells has shown that this is not so and that the voltages recorded from the scalp are primarily slow oscillations of membrane potential (EPSPs and IPSPs) summed across many synchronized cells. As slow membrane potentials have not been directly implicated in information processing this observation seems to devalue the EP as a window on aggregated neural activity during information processing. However, Fox and O'Brien (1965) have shown that the frequency distribution of impulses evoked in a

62

J. Boddy

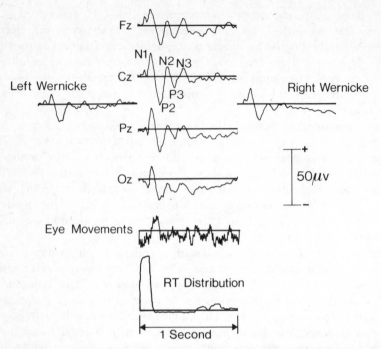

Fig. 7 Averaged evoked potential, to a series of briefly presented words, recorded at different locations on the scalp. It has been suggested that the series of negative (N) and positive (P) waves reflect the successive stages in the processing of information.

single neurone in the period immediately following many repetitions of a flash of light, closely resembles the waveshape of the slow membrane potential recorded in the same epoch (see Fig. 8). This observation indicates that the evoked potential waveshape at least indirectly reflects the fluctuating levels of impulse activity in the period following a stimulus. Although this doctrine has been widely accepted, Donald (1979) has recently pointed out that in only a small proportion of the units activated does the pattern of impulse activity conform to the evoked potential waveshape. This observation emphasizes the need for caution in interpretation of the informational significance of the evoked potential.

The evoked potential following a stimulus in any sensory modality is composed of a series of waves that persist for half a second or more (Fig. 7). It has been suggested that the successive waves in the evoked potential reflect the waves of neural activity underlying the successive stages in the processing of information (see Boddy, 1978, Chapters 11 and 12). The earliest waves (or

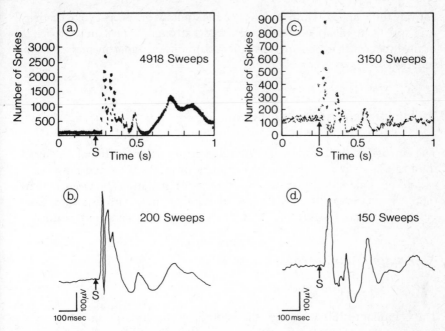

Fig. 8 *Graphs showing the similarity between evoked potential waveshapes (b and d) and the spike discharge frequency distributions (a and c) of single cells in the visual cortex plotted over the same time period following a repeated flash stimulus, Fox and O'Brien (1965).*

components) of the EP (100 ms latency) are most prominent over the cortical projection area for the sense involved and seem to reflect the activation of cells that analyse the stimulus into its component features (Campbell and Maffei, 1970; Regan, 1972). Intermediate (approximately 100–200 ms latency) and long latency components are recorded over wide areas of the scalp and are relatively small over the sensory projection area. They appear to be associated with high level pre-conscious stimulus analysis and attainment of meaning, processes underlying selective attention and conscious perception (Boddy, 1981). The wide distribution of the later EP components suggests that there is a loss of anatomical specificity when signals travel beyond the sensory projection area into the subsystems concerned with complex pattern recognition and conscious perception. It appears that after preliminary analysis, signals travel downwards from the cortex to the non-specific areas of the thalamus, which in turn excites large areas of the cortex via diffuse projection pathways (e.g. see Goff, 1969) to generate the later EP components. Whilst the system responsible for simple sensation is highly specific and localized, the perceptual mechanism it interfaces with is almost entirely unlocalized. The fact that a simple stimulus produces evoked activity that spreads to all areas of the cortex argues strongly against an approach to brain function that presupposes strict anatomical compartmentalization of function.

II. Functional Systems in the Brain

The aim of this section is to define and classify the major functional systems of the brain and to convey an understanding of their nature and purpose. It should be understood that there are a series of gradations between systems that are anatomically specific and those that are anatomically diffuse. Furthermore it is possible for a system to be partly specific and partly diffuse.

A. *Anatomically Specific Systems*

1. *Sensory systems*

These fundamental systems of the body have the very specific purpose of transmitting information from the sense receptors to the brain for interpretation. This specificity of purpose is reflected in the readily identifiable pathways, relay nuclei in the brainstem and/or thalamus and the well defined localization of sensory projection areas of the cortex. At the cortex itself there is gross topographic mapping of the receptor surface, whether it be retina (see Fig. 1) or skin surface. At a microscopic level the analysis of stimulus qualities, such as visual features or musical notes, is accomplished by distinct columns of cells, localized within the sensory cortex and identifiable by their common response characteristics. However we have seen that for interpretation the feature analysed sensory information seems to be handed on to a more diffuse system. We must note in passing that some analysis of sensory input is accomplished at the receptor organ and at sensory relays, particularly in the thalamus. For instance, recording of the activity of single neurones in the thalamic relay of the visual system has shown that they are influenced in a complex fashion by receptive fields on the retina that cover many receptors. Whereas in parts of the receptive field, normally a disc or annulus will respond to stimulus onset, other zones will respond to stimulus offset (Hubel and Wiesel, 1961). The pre-cortical relays appear to accomplish the preliminary phases of the process of feature analysis which we have seen is completed at the cortex. Recent research on vision is reviewed by Davidoff and Ratcliff in Chapter 8.

2. *Motor systems*

(Refer to Chapter 3 for anatomical details). There are also fundamental systems that initiate and control movement and locomotion. The subtlety of our motor activities, particularly exercise of manual skills, is reflected in the complexity of a multi-level system, whose details are far from understood. The highest level and executive centre for the motor systems is in the pre-frontal gyrus of the cerebral cortex. Electrical stimulation of points on this motor cortex in an intact animal or human produce contractions of specific muscle groups. This technique has been used for mapping of the motor cortex, where the principle of allocating the largest cortical zones to the most important muscle groups is observed. It is interesting to note that in conscious human patients muscle movements elicited by motor cortex stimulation are experienced as forced upon the individual and beyond the control of the will. Thus the motor cortex is not the ultimate origin of impulses for acts that are experienced as consciously willed.

Within the motor cortex the large pyramidal cells (Betz cells) give rise to the efferent fibres of the pyramidal motor system that course down through the internal capsule, through the ventral region of the cerebral peduncle into the spinal cord. At the segmental levels in the spinal cord the descending fibres synapse on the motor neurone pools of the spinal gray, from which motor fibres are distributed to the muscles.

Whereas the motor cortex issues global commands for action, the details of execution of action, the carrying out of over-learnt skills and locomotion and the regulation of postural adjustments appear to be mediated by an extensive extra-pyramidal motor system. This includes the basal ganglia and the cerebellum. It has proved difficult to attribute precise functions to the structures of the basal ganglia. There is some evidence that in lower animals innate action patterns are produced by these structures (Tower, 1936). In humans, lesions of the different extra-pyramidal structures lead to a variety of motor disorders including the postural rigidity and tremor of Parkinson's disease (globus pallidus and putamen), the involuntary rapid jerky movements of Huntington's chorea (striatum generally), the slow repetitious writhing movements of athetosis (putamen) and the violent flailing movements of hemiballismus (subthalamic nucleus). These syndromes seem to implicate the extra-pyramidal system in co-ordinating rhythmicity and postural adjustments.

The other vital structure of the extra-pyramidal motor system is the cerebellum, the role of which in imparting smoothness and precision to movements we have already considered in the sub-section on feedback (see also Fig. 5). The fact that patients with cerebellar damage show decomposition of movement and report loss of ability to delegate details of movement control to the subconscious is consistent with the cerebellum being a vital control centre for manipulative skills. The fact that overlearnt skilled movements, such as playing the piano, can be carried out even after section (cutting) of the pyramidal tract (Ruch, 1960) suggests that the cerebellum may store the command sequences for such skills.

3. Lateralized functions

In recent years data from patients with brain damage has created a lot of interest in the idea that different aspects of cognitive functioning are lateralized in one or the other of the cerebral hemispheres. Language function has been particularly associated with the left hemisphere because of the specific language deficits associated with damage to different areas. The right hemisphere has been particularly associated with spatial abilities and perception of rhythm. The association of circumscribed cortical areas with subcategories of language function, such as understanding speech, articulation of speech, understanding written language and writing, is in surprising contrast to the apparent diffuseness of the systems for general perceptual interpretation and for other functions.

B. Anatomically Diffuse Systems

1. Arousal system

The pre-eminent example of a diffuse system is the reticular arousal system (anatomical details outlined in Chapter 3; see also Fig. 9). This system originates in the central core of the brainstem as a diffuse multi-synaptic ascending network of cells. Individual cells in the reticular system may receive input from all the sensory modalities and the forebrain. Their multiple branching axons may project rostrally to diencephalic and neocortical structures and caudally to the central gray of the spinal cord. All cortical structures are accessed by the diffuse rostral (upwards) projections of the reticular activating system (RAS).

During a creature's normal waking hours, the RAS exerts a continuous "tonic" influence that sustains the capacity of the cortex and other cerebral structures to process input to the level of awareness. In early "classical" studies of the RAS, the permanent somnolence that followed section of the RAS at the base of the cerebrum indicated that the RAS was indispensible to wakefulness. In a relaxed, inattentive animal a warning signal or novel stimulus in any sensory modality will trigger the RAS, via its collateral afferent connections, to transmit arousing signals to the entire cerebral cortex. There is both neurophysiological and behavioural evidence that the

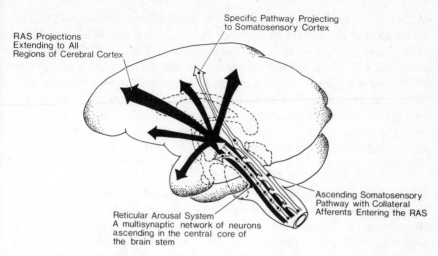

Specific Pathway Projecting
to Somatosensory Cortex

RAS Projections
Extending to All
Regions of Cerebral Cortex

Ascending Somatosensory
Pathway with Collateral
Afferents Entering the RAS

Reticular Arousal System
A multisynaptic network of neurons
ascending in the central core of
the brain stem

Fig. 9 *Schematic diagram of the reticular arousal system and its diffuse connections to the cerebral cortex.*

RAS increases the efficiency with which the cortex processes incoming information and organizes responses (e.g. Fuster, 1958). There is histological evidence that at the cortex the terminals of the rostrally projecting RAS fibres synapse in low densities over widely diffused dendritic locations of the cortical afferent cells. Via this pattern of connection the RAS fibres appear to modulate the excitatory state of cortical cells rather than triggering spike activity. Thus they determine the probability that spike activity will be elicited by the specific afferents, with their synapses narrowly distributed at the somatic ends of the dendrites (Thatcher and John, 1977, pp. 109–110).

2. Selective attention and consciousness

In addition to a system that regulates generalized arousal there is a mechanism for selective attention. Its focus has been tentatively located in the non-specific thalamic nuclei (Lindsley, 1960). The mechanisms of selective attention have been extensively investigated using evoked potential (EP) recording. The earliest components of the EP (<100 ms), of greatest amplitude over the sensory projection areas, and apparently originating from specific pathway activation, are not modulated by pharmacological (drugs) or behavioural manipulations of attention. They have therefore been identified with pre-attentive, pre-conscious processing. In contrast the intermediate and late components of EPs increase or decrease in amplitude as a function of whether the evoking stimulus is attended to or not. These later components appear to reflect the activation of the cortex by the non-specific thalamic system, subsequent to activation of the diffuse thalamic projection system (DTPS) by specific cortical areas. This and other evidence has led to the suggestion that the DTPS is at once the mechanism for attention focusing and the generator of conscious awareness (Goff, 1969). Penfield (1969) has described a "centrencephalic integrating system" which receives input from the cortex and appears to be responsible for generating the stream of consciousness. It is interesting to note that, although the elaborated perceptual intellectual and memory abilities of humans are attributed to the highly enlarged cortex, the vital substrate of consciousness is identified in phylogenetically ancient structures of the brain stem and diencephalon.

3. Systems for survival

It is not surprising that we find the mechanisms of basic survival focused in brain structures that appeared early in evolution, the hypothalamus and limbic system (for anatomical details see Chapter 3). Some studies have produced evidence of fairly precise localization of function, such as the identification of the lateral hypothalamus as an eating centre because lesion of this area leads to refusal to eat (see Boddy, 1978, Chapter 4). However, the fact that most survival behaviours can be influenced by stimulation of widespread points in the hypothalamus and limbic system suggests that the controlling neural systems ramify throughout the area, even if there is a primary focus at a specific location. The range of survival behaviours includes regulation of food and water intake, reproductive behaviour, thermo-regulation and fearful and aggressive behaviour. In some cases the multiple structures implicated in a class of behaviour seem likely to represent the different levels of an hierarchical system. For example there is evidence that the fragments of emotional responses that can be elicited by stimulation of areas of the midbrain are integrated into successively larger units of behaviour by the hypothalamus and amygdala (De Molina and Hunsperger, 1962). Other researchers (e.g. Fisher, 1964) have conceived of drive systems in terms of neural circuits coursing through several hypothalamic and limbic system structures parallel to each other. It has been suggested that the circuits for different drives are differentiated by the nature of the transmitter substance released at synapses. For example noradrenaline has been identified as the transmitter in the circuit for feeding behaviour, while acetylcholine has been identified as the transmitter in the drinking circuit. A description of mechanisms underlying habitual substance use is given by Warburton and Wesnes in Chapter 14.

C. Chemically Specific Systems

We have just seen that anatomically diffuse systems for hunger and thirst might be characterized in terms of the specificity of their synaptic transmitter substance. In recent years there has been more emphasis on identifying chemically specific systems than anatomically specific ones, partly because of the development of tracing techniques in which the use of specific reagents cause particular transmitters to fluoresce (Falk *et al.* 1962).

Major systems that have been described include a serotoninergic system that induces sleep, a cholinergic system concerned with attention and arousal, a dopaminergic system concerned with motor activity and a noradrenergic system mediating the reinforcing effects of behaviour. The ascending serotoninergic, cholinergic and noradrenergic systems all have their origins in different brainstem zones and project to widely diffused diencephalic and neocortical locations.

The reader should note that the number of functional systems in the brain far outnumbers the known neurochemicals so that no functional system is uniquely labelled by its transmitter chemical. Indeed the same neuro-chemicals have been implicated in systems with seemingly contradictory functions. For instance noradrenaline has been identified as the transmitter for both a behaviour activating system (Wise and Stein, 1969) and for a behaviour inhibiting system (Gray, 1978).

A noradrenergic system of particular interest is the behavioural reinforce-ment system anatomically focused in the septal area, medial forebrain bundle and lateral hypothalamus, which mediates the repetition of reinforced behaviours (reward or successful escape from punishment) and apprears to give rise to the subjective feelings of pleasure. Depletion of noradrenaline in this system has been identified as a correlate of depression, in which pleasure cannot be experienced. Depression can be lifted by the administration of drugs that increase the amount of adrenaline functionally available at central synapses. The importance of this system and a reciprocally related system, tentatively cholinergic, that inhibits punished or non-rewarded behaviour is discussed in more detail in Gray's chapter (3) in volume 3. Useful introduc-tions for the reader interested in chemically specific systems in the brain are given by Warburton (1975) and Brown and Cooper (1979).

III. The Autonomic Nervous System (see Fig. 10)

The autonomic nervous system is of vital importance and is distinct from other systems under discussion because of its primary concern with involuntary bodily functions. It should be noted, however, that the doctrine that the autonomic nervous system (ANS) is entirely independent of volun-tary control has been challenged in recent years.

Although the sensory nerves from the organs innervated may be included in

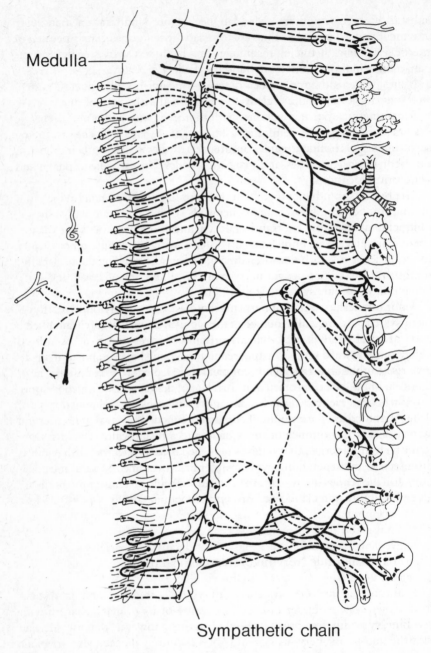

Medulla

Sympathetic chain

Fig. 10 *The autonomic nervous system. Solid lines represent preganglionic fibres, dashed lines postganglionic fibres.*

the ANS, the term usually refers to a system of motor pathways which exit, via cranial nerves and spinal nerves, to innervate glands, smooth muscles in the viscera (heart, lungs, stomach, intestines, kidney) and walls of blood vessels and the reproductive organs. Every organ is innervated by both the parasympathetic and sympathetic branch of the ANS in a reciprocal relation-ship. The parasympathetic NS tends to reduce function (e.g. lower heart rate), and is generally concerned with preservation, accumulation and storage of energies in the body. The sympathetic NS on the other hand tends to increase function, as a concomitant to mobilization of the body's energy resources to deal with emergencies. It is responsible for all the visible and invisible manifestations of emotion, which include the changes routinely measured by psychophysiologists, including changes in skin resistance, heart rate, blood volume, etc.

The parasympathetic and sympathetic branches of the ANS have rather different organization. Both systems synapse on nerve ganglia external to the CNS proper, before innervating target organs. Pre-ganglionic para-sympathetic fibres exit from cranial nerves (III, VII, IX, X) and from the sacral segment of the spinal cord. They follow typically long unbranching pathways to ganglia adjacent to organs innervated. Post-ganglionic fibres are thus short and the terminals are cholinergic (release acetylcholine). Clear separation of neural pathways allows individual activation of organs.

The pre-ganglionic fibres of the sympathetic NS emerge from ventral spinal nerve roots of the thoracic and upper lumbar regions of the spinal cord. They synapse with short, multi-branching axons on a chain of ganglia, which form a sympathetic nerve trunk just outside and lateral to the spinal cord, extend-ing from the base of the skull to the lower end of the spine. The diffuse connections of the sympathetic nerve trunk preclude individual activation of organs so that all those innervated tend to be activated together. In addition to the viscera, post-ganglionic sympathetic fibres innervate the adrenal gland, peripheral blood vessels, sweat glands and erector pilorum muscles in the skin (that make body hairs stand on end) and their terminals are noradrenergic (release noradrenaline). Thus by triggering the release of noradrenaline from the adrenal gland the sympathetic nervous system potentiates its effects on the body. This brief section neglects many details and paradoxes of ANS function and the reader requiring further information should consult Van Toller (1979), and his chapter (5) in this volume.

IV. The Nervous System and other Body Information Systems

The nervous system interfaces with the blood stream, which is another information carrying vehicle in the body. The blood stream carries important information about the internal environment; whether nutrients fluids and body temperature are within their homeostatic limits. It was thought that the hypothalamus was effectively a sense organ for the internal environment, able to monitor all the important constituents of the blood its volume (for fluid balance) and temperature. However it now appears that there are other monitoring sites within the body, such as the kidney and the liver, from which information is transmitted to the brain via either neural or hormonal routes.

A. Endocrine System

The bloodstream is most important as a carrier for the hormones. These chemical messengers are released into the bloodstream from their site of manufacture in the endocrine glands and are carried by it to the target organs which they influence. The pivotal endocrine gland is the pituitary, suspended on a neural stalk beneath the hypothalamus, which exercises a controlling influence on it. The anterior lobe secretes many hormones; adreno-corticotrophic hormone (ACTH), follicle stimulating hormone (FSH), and thyrotrophic hormone (thyroxin) influence the growth and secretory activities of the subordinate glands, the adrenals, gonads and thyroid respectively. Somatotrophic hormone (STH) stimulates bodily growth and repair and prolactin stimulates the production of milk. The posterior lobe of the pituitary secretes anti-diuretic hormone (ADH) that reduces excretion of water when fluid balance is in deficit, and oxytocin that produces contractions of the smooth muscles of the uterus during labour.

Amongst the subordinate endocrine glands the adrenal medulla (inner segment) secretes adrenaline and noradrenaline when activated by the sympathetic nervous system during emotional arousal. This promotes the release of glucose (metabolic fuel) from store, increases the heart rate and produces dilation of the blood vessels that supply the brain and muscles. All these changes give support to vigorous muscle activity, which might be required in an emergency. Noradrenaline is also a neurotransmitter the presence of which prolongs the activating effects of the sympathetic nervous system. The adrenal cortex produces hydrocorticosteroid hormones that also promote the release of glucose from fat stores in the body during periods of urgent need. The gonads produce hormones that stimulate the sex drive and organize other aspects of the reproductive process. The reproductive functions are particularly noteworthy for their close integration between neural and hormonal mechanisms. For instance the hormones secreted by the gonads strongly influence the mechanism for sexual drive and coital activity. Before leaving this topic we should also recall that most hormones have multiple functions. Adrenaline, for example, promotes the conversion of glycogen to glucose, stimulates vasodilation and increases the coagulative properties of the blood.

For further information on the endocrine system Ebling and Highnam (1969) is a useful introduction. Chapter 13 of this volume by Cox *et al.* shows how the endocrine system is implicated in stress.

V. A Systems Approach to the Nervous System

There is a danger that our familiarity with contemporary man-made electrical and mechanical systems will predispose us to think about brain mechanisms in a "compartmentalized" manner which is quite inappropriate. The brain does not consist of a series of separate boxes which are switched "on" or "off" in specific situations (e.g. hunger) and perform their functions in isolation. The brain must be viewed as a dynamic organization of interacting subsystems. Barry Commoner's (1972) first law of ecology that "everything is connected to everything else" is entirely applicable to the brain. The observation that an external stimulus produces neural perturbations that invade all brain structures (John, 1972) exemplifies the connectedness of the brain's subsystems. The principle is further illustrated by the observation that the arousal of one motive state, by natural or even artificial means (e.g. brain stimulation), increases the likelihood that behaviour associated with other motive states can be elicited by appropriate stimuli. For instance aggressive behaviour is more easily elicited in a hungry animal or human than a satiated one. The hypothalamic circuits mediating drive states are closely interwoven so that it is hardly surprising that the activation of one circuit will lower the threshold of adjacent circuits by electrical and possibly chemical excitatory processes.

No subsystem of the brain is ever completely inactive, even in deep sleep. The diverse inputs to the brain modulate activity in the subsystems rather than switching them "on" and "off". The pattern of modulation varies as a function of the nature of the input and the status of the subsystem. The status of the subsystem is a function of the interrelated factors of their biochemical status, the organism's motive state and prior history. A sensory input will be responded to in terms of its emotional connotations, its relevance to current needs and its relevance to past events. We might note, for instance, that although the subsystems for motivation and emotion are focused in the hypothalamus and limbic system, disconnection of the frontal lobes from subcortical regions results in profound motivational and emotional changes. Even in discussion of experimental damage to hypothalamic structures there have been arguments over the question of whether changes in eating behaviour arise because of direct disruption of the mechanisms for hunger or changes in a creature's emotional response to food. We should note that the reticular activating system in particular continually exercises a capacity to modulate all of the subsystems of the brain through its widely ramifying projections.

VI. The Neural Representation of External Reality and Subjective States

A multitude of observations make it clear that the brain interprets the external and internal environments, and organizes objectively observable responses to them which promote an organism's survival. Less directly, we infer from observable responses and particularly from verbal behaviour that the brain is the source of conscious experience and the seat of the mind. Indeed it is important to understand that our consciousness of our world, its sights, sounds and smells, is entirely determined by the structure and properties of our sensory systems and brain. For instance the property of colour is intrinsic to our brain's interpretation of the electromagnetic radiation, at specific wavelengths that is reflected by surfaces that are seen as being coloured, and not to the surfaces themselves. Our sensory organs enable us to detect certain classes of energy, within certain frequency spectra, which give us information relevant to our survival. There are forms of energy, such as X-rays, which we are not equipped to detect and which we are therefore unaware of without the aid of special instruments. Our sensory and interpretive systems (within the brain) give us awareness of a world of solid objects separated by spaces. This contrasts sharply with the underlying nature of the world inferred by physicists and chemists. The solid objects of our brain's world are conceived of as arrangements of particles separated by spaces and the "spaces" of our world are described in terms of their gaseous content.

Sensation and conscious awareness can only occur when the impulses from the sense receptors reach the brain. For instance destruction of the visual projection area leads to partial or total loss of vision, depending on the extent of the damage. A vestigial capacity to detect light and dark may be mediated by archaic visual centres in the thalami and colliculi (see Davidoff and Ratcliff, Chapter 8).

The boundary which nerve impulses must cross before they give rise to consciousness is very difficult to define. We have already seen that conscious awareness is dependent on the excitation of diffuse activation systems, as well as specific sensory projection areas. The contents of conscious awareness at any one moment are probably determined by the blended activity of multiple systems, which variously determine such qualities as vividness, elaboration of detail, degree of focus, attribution of meaning and emotional colouration.

There is much evidence that our percepts are the result of a process of synthesis from sensory and stored data, rather than a passive projection of sensory data (Neisser, 1967). This and other evidence tends to exclude the sensory projection areas from direct involvement in conscious awareness and associates conscious awareness with non-specific systems in central structures of the brain such as the thalamus.

Whereas the mechanisms of perceptual synthesis usually produce a reasonably faithful representation of external reality, there are circumstances, particularly dreaming and hallucinations, in which the stream of consciousness appears to be synthesized entirely from stored information (in effect memories) and is thus totally subjective. Penfield (1952) appears to have triggered the synthesis of a stream of consciousness, which replayed past events in a patient's life, when he electrically stimulated the brains of conscious patients during operations for epilepsy. He called the experiences "recollective hallucinations".

The inevitable corollary to the fact that the neural systems of the brain generate consciousness is that the qualities of consciousness are a function of the physical integrity and biochemical status of the brain. Physical damage to the brain results in loss, distortion or degradation of consciousness, depending on the locus of the damage. Changes in consciousness may include loss of parts of a sensory field, loss of the ability to focus attention, loss of the ability to resolve detail, loss of ability to extract meaning and loss of, or abnormal, emotional responses.

The citizens of the industrialized world are no strangers to the chemical (pharmacological) manipulation of consciousness. They regularly use drugs to get to sleep, reduce anxiety or elevate mood. Some people use drugs that distort and make conscious experience more vivid. All these facts reinforce the view that the qualities of conscious experience are determined by multifarious influences on a hypercomplex physical system.

Further Reading

Boddy, J. (1978). "Brain Systems and Psychological Concepts". Wiley and Sons, Chichester.
Part 4 on "Information Systems" covers the coding and processing of information in the brain.
"The Brain" (1980), a Scientific American Book. W. H. Freeman, Oxford. A clear, up-to-date and lavishly illustrated collection of readings. It includes a chapter on information processing in the visual system by Hubel and Weisel, recently awarded a Nobel prize for their epoch-making work.
Brown, K. and Cooper S. J. (1978). "Chemical Influences on Behaviour". Academic Press, London and New York.
Up-to-date readings on chemically specific neural subsystems mediating behaviour.

Ebling, F. J. G. and Highnam, K. C. (1969). "Chemical Communication". Edward
Arnold, London.
An introduction to the endocrine system.
Kuffler, S. W. and Nicholls, J. G. (1976). "From Neuron to Brain: A Cellular
Approach to the Function of the Nervous System". Sinauer, Sunderland,
Massachussetts.
Part 1 on the "Neural Organization for Perception" is a dissertation on fundamental
aspects of information processing in the brain.
Thatcher, R. W. and John, E. R. (1977). "Functional Neuroscience: Vol. 1, Founda-
tions of Cognitive Processes". Lawrence Erlbaum, Hillsdale, New Jersey.
Looks at the neural basis of cognitive processes and is particularly concerned with
developing the arguments concerning the statistical nature of neural activity in
information processing.
Warburton, D. M. (1975). "Brain, Behaviour and Drugs". Wiley and Sons,
Chichester.
Useful introduction to chemically specific subsystems in the brain.
Van Toller, C. (1979). "The Nervous Body: An Introduction to the Autonomic
Nervous System". Wiley and Sons, Chichester.
A good introduction to the autonomic nervous system and its relevance to behaviour.

References

Boddy, J. (1978). "Brain Systems and Psychological Concepts". Wiley and Sons,
Chichester.
Boddy, J. (1981). Brain potentials, perceptual mechanisms and semantic categorisa-
tion. *Biol. Psychol.* **12**, 43–61.
Brown, K. and Cooper, S. J. (1979) "Chemical Influences on Behaviour." Academic
Press, London and New York.
Campbell, F. W. and Maffei, L. (1970). Electrophysiological evidence for the existence
of orientation and size detectors in the human visual system. *J. Physiol., Lond.* **207**,
635–652.
Commoner, B. (1972). "The Closing Circle". Jonathan Cape, London.
De Molina, A. F. and Hunsperger, R. W. (1962). Organisation of the subcortical
system governing defence and flight reactions in the cat. *J. Physiol., Lond.* **160**,
200–213. Reprinted in D. G. Stein and J. J. Rosen, eds (1974). "Motivation and
Emotion". pp. 123–136. Macmillan, New York.
Donald, M. (1979). Limits on current theories of transient evoked potentials. *In*
"Cognitive Components in Cerebral Event-Related Potentials and Selective
Attention: Progress in Clinical Neurophysiology, Vol. 6" (J. E. Desmedt, ed.),
pp. 187–199. Karger, Basel.
Ebling, F. J. G. and Highnam, K. C. (1969). "Chemical Communication". Edward
Arnold, London.
Falk, B., Hillarp, M., Thieme, G., and Torp, A. (1962). Fluorescence of
catecholamines and related compounds condensed with formaldehyde. *J.
Histochem. Cytochem.* **10**, 348–364.
Fisher, A. E. (1964). Chemical Stimulation of the Brain. *Scient. Am.* **210**(6), 60–68.
Fox, S. S. and O'Brien, J. H. (1965). Duplication of evoked potential waveform by
curve of probability of firing of single cell. *Science* **147**, 888–890.

Fuster, J. M. (1958). Effects of stimulation of brain stem on tachistoscopic perception. *Science* **127**, 150.

Goff, W. R. (1969). Evoked potential correlates of perceptual organisation in man. *In* "Attention in Neurophysiology" (C. R. Evans and T. B. Mulholland, eds) pp. 169–193. Butterworths, London.

Gray, J. (1971). "The Psychology of Fear and Stress'. Wiedenfield and Nicolson, London.

Gray, J. (1978). The Neuropsychology of Anxiety. *Br. J. Psychol.* **69**, 417–434.

Hubel, D. H. and Wiesel, T. N. (1961). Integrative action in the cat's lateral geniculate body. *J. Physiol., Lond.* **155**, 385–398.

Hubel, D. H. and Wiesel, T. N. (1962). Receptive fields, binocular interaction and functional architecture in the cat's visual cortex. *J. Physiol., Lond.* **160**, 106–154.

John, E. R. (1972). Switchboard versus statistical theories of learning and memory. *Science* **177**, 850–864.

Lindsley, D. B. (1960). Attention, Consciousness, Sleep and Wakefulness. *In* "Handbook of Physiology: Section I, Neurophysiology, Vol. III" (J. Field, H. W. Magoun and V. E. Hall, eds.), pp. 1553–1593. American Physiological Society, Washington D.C.

Neisser, U. (1967). "Cognitive Psychology". Appleton-Century-Crofts, New York.

Oomura, Y., Ooyama, H., Yamamato, T. and Naka, F. (1967). Reciprocal relationship of the lateral and ventromedial hypothalamus in the regulation of food intake. *Physiol. and Behaviour*, **2**, 97–105.

Penfield, W. (1952). Memory Mechanisms. *Arch. Neurol. Psychiat.* **67**, 178–198.

Penfield, W. (1969). Consciousness, Memory and Man's Conditioned Reflexes. *In* "On the Biology of Memory" (K. H. Pribram, ed.). Harcourt, Brace and World Inc., New York.

Regan, D. (1972). "Evoked Potentials in Psychology, Sensory Physiology and Clinical Medicine". Chapman and Hall, London.

Ruch, T. C. (1960). The cerebral cortex: Its structure and motor functions. *In* "Medical Physiology and Biophysics" (T. C. Ruch and J. F. Fulton, eds), pp. 249–276. Saunders, Philadelphia.

Thach, W. T. (1968). Discharge of Purkinje and cerebellar nuclear neurons during rapidly alternating arm movements in the monkey. *J. Neurophysiol.* **31** 785–797.

Thatcher, R. W. and John, E. R. (1977). "Functional Neuroscience: Vol. 1, Foundations of Cognitive Processes". Lawrence Erlbaum, Hillsdale, New Jersey.

Tower, S. S. (1936). Extra-pyramidal action from the cat's cerebral cortex: motor and inhibitory. *Brain* **59**, 408–444.

Warburton, D. M. (1975). "Brain, Behaviour and Drugs". Wiley and Sons, London.

Van Toller, C. (1979). "The Nervous Body: An introduction to the autonomic nervous system and behaviour". Wiley and Sons, Chichester.

Wise, C. D. and Stein, L. (1969). Facilitation of brain stimulation by central administration of norepinephrine. *Science* **163**, 229–301.

5 Biochemistry of the Nervous System

C. Van Toller

Abstract A general introduction to cellular components leads to consideration of the fundamental units of proteins, carbohydrates, and lipids. Discussion then turns to the essential role of the organic catalysts called enzymes. These serve to build up and break down the fundamental units of the three classes of compounds, which in their larger forms are called macromolecules. Control of the basic metabolic processes within a cell are controlled by the genetic information that is contained by the nucleic acids within the cell nuclei.

The action and types of transmitter substances are then discussed. These range from acetylcholine through to the catecholamines, the amino acids and the recently discovered role of polypeptides as neurotransmitters.

The chapter then considers the ways in which psychologists interested in biochemical functions have attempted to use them in their models to explain learning and behaviour. In this section we consider nucleic acids and macromolecular theories of learning and, finally, correlations of the catecholamines with behaviour.

I. Introduction

The greatest difficulty encountered by a person writing a chapter about the chemistry of the body in a psychophysiological text, lies in the fact that traditionally it has not been an area of central concern to psychophysiologists. They have concentrated on the more easily and readily quantifiable electrical signals that can be picked up from various parts of the body. Yet the very signals that they have recorded are to a large extent the product of the underlying biochemical reactions of the body. This is not an attempt to argue for a reductionist position, but merely to point out that for too long psychologists have mumbled about the whole being greater than the sum of the parts, when what they should have been saying was, the whole is equal to the sum of the parts plus their interactions. Just as the artist studies anatomy to help him to draw his models more accurately, so many of the phenomena

PHYSIOLOGICAL CORRELATES OF HUMAN
BEHAVIOUR   ISBN 0-12-273901-9

that puzzle us now, may become clearer when our conceptions include knowledge of the basic chemical processes. For too long our textbooks have told us that the information transmission in the nerve cell is by electro-chemical means and have then gone on to tell us about the electrical properties, whilst largely ignoring the chemical ones.

To the unaided eye the brain is composed of white and grey matter with obvious connections between different areas. With the use of a microscope it becomes apparent that the tissues are composed of billions of cells with numerous interconnections. Within and between these cells complex bio-chemical processes occur. At each of these levels we can produce and test hypotheses. The secret lies in conceptions that include the interactions both within and between the levels. As Christie and Woodman (1980) have pointed out, many of the simpler biochemical assays can be purchased in kit form and they require little expertise to use them. Their use to support more conventional measures may considerably extend our knowledge and under-standing. In this way, we shall come to understand biochemical contributions to the total behavioural processes.

The second major problem in attempting to write such a chapter concerns the vast amount of information that needs to be included. I have of necessity been general in approach, attempting to give preliminary understanding and perhaps waken interest in a fascinating area. I have also tried to show how psychologists have attempted to use knowledge about the biochemical processes in their theoretical and experimental attempts to understand behaviour.

One of the fundamental facts of biochemistry is, however profligate mother nature may have been in terms of species, the basic cellular reactions are very similar throughout the animal kingdom. These facts are remarkable if you stop to consider how long it is since yeast and muscle cells parted company, but they still use the same metabolic steps to convert glucose to energy. Despite many changes and countless mutations the cell has clung to its old chemical habits. However, there are still certain essential differences. A drinking companion has long bemoaned the fact that, whereas the yeast cell's final product is alcohol, his own muscle cells can only produce lactic acid.

The human body can be thought of as an energy producing system, which enables it to carry out the various transductions that are required for the behavioural processes. The temperature of a human body fluctuates around 37°C, so its energy cannot be obtained in the manner of a steam engine, against a heart gradient, but must be obtained from the various chemical reactions that are carried out at the constant temperature, acidity/alkalinity and pressures found within the human body. Apart from these constants, there are certain dietary essentials that must be ingested along with the normal food intake. Generally a normal diet includes sufficient amounts of these, but for more specific details the reader is referred to Vander *et al.* (1980).

II. The Chemistry of the Cell

Although physicists are concerned with the smaller elements of the atom such as protons and electrons, the atom is usually the smallest particle that concerns biochemists, with their main interest centred upon the molecules that are formed when the atoms of two or more elements combine. A good example of this process is where an atom of sodium and an atom of chlorine combine to form a molecule of sodium chloride or common salt.

The main organic compounds within the cells of our bodies are proteins, carbohydrates, lipids and nucleic acids. All of these classes of organic compounds are complex and may be formed of many thousands of molecules, but thankfully all are based upon relatively simple units that are repeated in various combinations. Organic substances composed of numerous molecules are called macromolecules. A schematic diagram of a cell is shown in Fig. 1, with the main structures and their functions noted. A nerve cell would look similar but have an axon, which might be myelinated or unmyelinated,

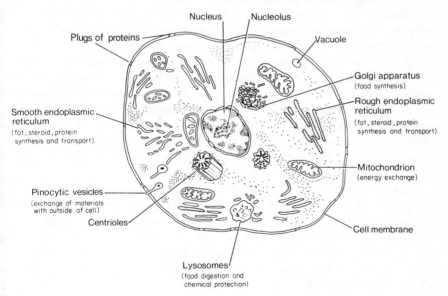

Fig. 1 *Schematic drawing of a cell showing its important components and their functions.*

leading away from the cell body down towards the synapse, through which communication is made with other cells (see Chapter 3, Fig. 1).

A. *Proteins*

The basic elements that form proteins are typically carbon, hydrogen, oxygen and nitrogen, and sometimes phosphorus and sulphur. These basic elements are bonded together to form the amino acids which themselves form the basic units of complex protein chains. The amino acids are

Glycine	Alanine	Tryptophan	Tyrosine
Methionine	Phenylalanine	Cysteine	Lysine
Serine	Threonine	Glutamic acid	Isoleucine
Glutamine	Aspartic acid	Leucine	Asparagnine
Histidine	Valine	Proline	Arginine

Proteins are the most abundant class of organic substance found in the cellular proto- or cytoplasm. The main classes are nucleoproteins, phosphoproteins, glycoproteins and lipoproteins. Proteins also form the important organic catalysts called enzymes. Amino acids are organic acids with a carboxyl (COOH) group and an amino (NH_2) group attached to either side of a carbon atom. The carbon atom also has a side chain designated as R, and it is in their R chains that each of the twenty amino acids differ. Separate amino acids bond together by a chemical condensation reaction between the COOH and the NH_2 groups which result in a molecule of water (H_2O) being produced. The reverse process is called hydrolysis. The individual bonds between the amino acids are called peptide bonds and the lengths of amino acids that result are called polypeptide chains. The variation between different types of polypeptide chains can be enormous but they are constant for any single type of polypeptide chain. Protein molecules often consist of more than one polypeptide chain held together by numerous weak bonds, such as hydrogen bonds. There are also some covalent interpolypeptide bonds, such as sulphur links which are called disulphide bonds.

Depending on its basic shape a protein may be fibrous or globular. Fibrous proteins are relatively insoluble in water and have the property of elasticity; examples are the collagen in cartilage and the horny keratin in hair and nails. Globular proteins are soluble in water and can be crystallized; examples are the albumin or the white of an egg, haemoglobin in the blood, and a number of hormones. Globular proteins form the catalytic enzymes which are so essential for the metabolic processes of the cell.

Proteins must not be thought of as being laid out simply as two-dimensional chains. They are often coiled and folded into complex three-dimensional structures. Thus protein macromolecules are folded into complex spatial patterns, and the particular configuration that any type of protein assumes will be crucial in determining its distinctive biological properties. For example trypsin, which is an enzymatic protein with a molecular weight of 34 000, has only one active site along its length.

In addition to these complexities there is the problem of isomers, which occur when two proteins have exactly the same chemical composition but differ in shape and structure. Three basic types of isomerism exist, these are: structural isomers, geometric isomers and optical isomers. Structural isomers are proteins with different structures; geometric isomers have different spatial arrangements in certain parts of the molecule; and optical isomers occur when two proteins are the mirror image of each other. Isomers of compounds may exhibit very different properties. Indeed, for any particular reaction, one form may be very active while the other form is quite inactive. Even without considering the complex interactions with the other organic substances we have still to discuss, it is easy to see that the combinations and permutations can mount up to large numbers very quickly. It must also be recognized that not all amino acids are used in protein synthesis. Taurine, which is said to be the most abundant amino acid in the body, is a good example. In common with some other amino acids, taurine is thought to act as an inhibitory neurotransmitter substance.

B. *Carbohydrates*

The basic elements of carbohydrates are carbon, hydrogen and oxygen. The smallest components of carbohydrates consist of monosaccharides which are linked together into polysaccharides by glycosides. Carbohydrates are sugars and starches and they range from the simple sugars that provide energy for metabolic processes within the cell to more complex sugars such as cellulose and chitin which have important functions in providing cellular support. For example, chitin is found in the exoskeletons of the invertebrate animals such as insects and crayfish. Carbohydrates can also be found as bodily lubricants at joint surfaces. Carbohydrates fall into the following classes, simple sugars, polysaccharides, starches, glycogen, cellulose. Carbohydrates as simple sugars are essential to cellular respiration and they provide energy for the transfer of cellular materials and the metabolic processes within the cell. The oxidation of glucose provides most of the energy for the cell. One of the major functions of cells is to store energy in the form of starch, to provide energy for future requirements. For example, it is important that muscle cells have large reservoirs of energy to allow for periods of intense and rapid muscular activity. Starches form the basis of the energy store and are unable to pass out of the cell once formed. Like the lipids or fats that we will consider next, the body can store considerable amounts of carbohydrates. Simple sugars or monosaccharides are built up into larger polysaccharides by the chemical process, mentioned in the protein section, called condensation. The reverse process of breaking down the polysaccharides is called hydrolysis. In general polysaccharides lack the three-dimensional complexities of the proteins, but the fact that they are branched adds its own problems for attempts to understand them. In addition they have the complication of numerous isometric forms, with the same basic six carbon chains. The brain is virtually completely dependent on glucose for its energy.

C. Lipids

The elements that form lipids are principally carbon, hydrogen and oxygen, but lipids may also contain other elements such as phosphorus and nitrogen. Lipids are composed of two types of compounds; an alcohol group called a glycerol and certain organic acids called fatty acids. Fatty acids are chains of from sixteen to eighteen carbon atoms. Palmitic, stearic and oleic account for 90% of the fatty acids in the brain. Fatty acids are spoken of as saturated and unsaturated, the distinction being that unsaturated fatty acids contain less than the maximum number of hydrogen atoms because certain of the carbon atoms that form the backbone of the fatty acid have double bonds. An oil differs from a fat only in that it has a lower melting point; in general the more double bonds the lower the melting point. Fatty acids formed with the alkali metals sodium and potassium are more or less soluble in water; the other fatty acids are completely insoluble in water. These properties are called hydrophilia and hydrophobia respectively, and are vital in terms of the formation of cell membranes. The macromolecules of lipids are called triglycerides.

Fats are probably the best known group of lipids. They have a characteristic greasy feel and are soluble in ether. Apart from their role in providing protection for the delicate internal organs of the body and providing insulation against heat loss, fats are the most concentrated form of energy stored by the body. Weight for weight fats give twice as much energy as the carbohydrates. This largely comes about because, compared to carbohydrates, fats are more fully reducible compounds.

A number of vital vitamins and hormones called steroids are often classified as lipids, because their solubility characteristics are similar to those of the fats, waxes, oils and the phospholipids of the brain. Steroids are complex molecules composed from a basic pattern of four interlocking carbon atoms.

Since the last century it has been known that a number of hereditary diseases causing mental illness arise from defects in lipid metabolism, but few, if any, of the psychological texts contain reference to the importance of the lipids. This is strange because many of the standard physiological psychology texts are built around the concept of the nerve cell and most of the nerve cells in the body have their neurones surrounded by a fatty sheath of myelin called the sheath of Schwann. The myelin has an important role in aiding the electric impulse along the neurone. In fact, half of the dry weight of the brain is composed of phospholipids, so clearly any adequate understanding of the function of the brain requires an understanding of lipid metabolism.

D. *Enzymes*

In the earlier sections where proteins, carbohydrates and lipids were discussed, it was pointed out that for all of these organic substances there was a basic unit that was used to build up the complex macromolecules. It is the building up and breaking down of macromolecules that is the concern of enzymes, and within an individual cell there may be 3000 different types of enzymes. All enzymes are proteins, although it is important to point out that the converse of this statement is not true. Enzymes are biological catalysts which mediate chemical reactions that would take weeks or months to complete without their help. For example, one molecule of a certain enzyme can catalyse the transformation of 500 000 molecules of the substance with which it is reacting every minute. Like inorganic catalysts, organic catalysts are unchanged at the end of the reaction but organic catalysts have specific and precise functions. Platinum is an inorganic catalyst which acts in a variety of reactions, but an enzyme will have a very limited and precise action. In the protein section, mention was made of the enzyme trypsin which despite a molecular weight of 34 000 has one single active site on its surface.

In general, enzymes are globular proteins which are soluble in water and contain active sites located on the complex geometry of their surfaces. Certain enzymes are aided in their reactions by co-enzymes which are simple organic or inorganic compounds. The role of a co-enzyme is to facilitate attachment of the enzyme to the reactive site on the substrate. Many vitamins function as co-enzymes and that is why they are so important, despite the small amounts required.

The general action of an enzyme is indicated by the suffix "ase" and the name of the class of compound it reacts with. For example, enzymes that split proteins are called proteases and those that split carbohydrates are called carbohydrases.

The action of a number of poisons and antibiotic drugs is via their ability to block enzymatic activity and thereby prevent the normal metabolic processes from proceeding. Within individual cells there is a need to have the right enzymes available at the right time. Remember that enzymes will need to distinguish the very small changes that are sometimes found between isomers of macromolecules. Within cells the metabolic processes proceed according to precise and planned pathways, and within these processes enzymes carry out their specific roles. For example, conversion of glucose to carbon dioxide takes about thirty different steps and at certain points small amounts of energy are made available to the cell. The action of any one enzyme will be to break the chain at certain points along its length when it encounters certain amino acid links. Enzymes do this with great precision and it is this very precision that enables poisons and antibiotics to interfere with either the shape of the enzyme or the reactive site on the substrate. The activity of enzymes within cells is controlled by the nuclear activity within the cell and also hormones which attach to the outside surface of the cell and cause changes in levels of metabolic activity.

E. Nucleic acids

Within a cell the metabolic activity proceeds under the direction of the genetic information, stored in the nucleus of the cell in the form of nucleic acids. In general nucleic acids are robust and as we shall see they are arranged in such a way as to minimize biological degradation, for it is clearly very important that genetic information passed on is faithfully reproduced. This is true for both control of the intracellular metabolic activity and any daughter cell should cellular division take place. There are two types of nucleic acid: deoxyribonucleic acid (DNA) and ribonucleic acid (RNA). DNA is found mainly within the nucleus as genes on chromatin threads, and RNA is found within the nucleolus and on the ribosomes that are located throughout the cell.

Nucleic acids are formed from the elements; carbon, hydrogen, oxygen, nitrogen and phosphorus. These elements form into three types of basic molecule: pentose sugars, which in the case of DNA is a deoxyribose sugar and in the case of RNA is a ribose sugar; phosphoric acid; and nitrogen bases. Four types of nitrogen base are found in DNA; two are purines (adenine and guanine) and two are pyrimidines (cytosine and thymine). The nitrogen bases for RNA are the same except that the pyrimidine base thymine is replaced by uracil.

The basic unit of a nucleic acid is termed a nucleotide and consists of a sugar, a phosphorus group and one of the nitrogen bases. DNA is found as two chains of nucleotides wrapped around each other as a double helix or spiral. The chains consist of alternating sugar and phosphorus groups with cross links between the chains consisting of a pyramidine and a purine base pair. The cross links are located on the sugar groups of the chains. The smallest unit of genetic information consists of three adjacent nucleotides called a codon. A codon specifies a single amino acid. Each cell in the body contains a complete set of the 46 chromosomes that comprise the hereditary code for humans, although any one cell will use only a small amount of the total genetic information. When a cell divides, DNA undergoes replication and any daughter cell will contain an identical set of DNA.

In general terms the function of RNA is to transcribe the genetic information from DNA and to carry it out into the cell, to sites where the actual process of synthesis is to take place. There are a number of different types of RNA of which messenger RNA (mRNA) and transfer (tRNA) are the most important. mRNA leaves the nucleus through nuclear membrane pores and travels along structured pathways to the ribosomes. tRNA is crucial for its role in assembling amino acids in the specific order required. The intermediate compounds formed from the nucleic acids often act as co-enzymes for the metabolic processes of the cell.

It has been noticed that certain primitive cells can survive for appreciable periods in the absence of the nucleus, which indicates that the metabolic processes do not need the constant intervention of the nucleic acids. On the other hand the importance of the nucleus is indicated by the action of phages or viruses, which penetrate the cell and enter the nucleus where they use their own DNA to instruct the cell to produce the metabolic processes that the virus requires. The cell continues this process until it swells up to a huge size and bursts, thereby releasing particles of virus which will diffuse out. Some will by chance attach themselves to other cells and repeat the process.

The action of viruses suggests the possibility of alteration in the metabolic processes of cells, and a question may be raised as to whether or not such changes may come about as a result of learning. As we shall see in a later section, most attempts to understand changes in a cell as a result of learning have centred around the nucleic acids.

III. The Cell Membrane

Earlier concepts of the cell membrane being plastic to allow for cellular growth have been replaced by concepts of it being a liquid, indeed some authorities conceive of the cell membrane as a collection of ordered phospholipids on the surface of the cell. Whatever the final story, the membrane is a very active and critical part of cellular activity whereby chemical substances are actively transported into the cell. The cell membrane consists of a double layer of phospholipids with a distinct space between them. The phospholipids have hydrophilic heads and hydrophobic tails. At certain points the phospholipids are penetrated throughout their width by plugs of protein. At other points depressions are found, called pinocytic vesicles, that are open to the outer surfaces of the wall. Particles that collect in the vesicles are taken into the cell by a process of pinching-off. The fluid mosaic model of the cell membrane suggests that the membrane is not confined to the cell wall but continues into the interior of the cell, presumably to aid the processes of transporting materials into the cell. Recalling that half the dry weight of the brain consists of the phospholipids, we can begin to have some conception of the activity that is continuously being carried out by the cellular membranes of the brain and to this we must add the activity of other cells that are laid down in blocks of tissue throughout our bodies.

It should by now be apparent that the cell is a place of high activity and continuous movement. For example, the nerve cell needs energy not only for the metabolic activity and the production and movement of the transmitter substance but also actively to pump ions into and out of the axon during the transmission of the action potential (see Chapter 4). In certain nerves this can be a continuous process occurring all day and every day for a lifetime. The commonest intermediary for storing energy in cells is adenosine diphosphate (ADP), which takes up energy from the glucose cycle using phosphate and converting the adenosine diphosphate into adenosine triphosphate (ATP) in a reversible reaction. $ATP \rightleftharpoons ADP + P$. The energy rich ATP is able to release its energy when required leaving the ADP to enter into another turn of the energy cycle. Mitochondria are the main source of ATP and the removal of the ATP from them will cause other ATP to flow to the depleted spot.

IV. Neurotransmitters

The main emphasis in this section is on nerve cells or neurones, but it must be recognised that there are many different types of cells within the brain (for example glial and astrocyte cells), which play important supporting roles for the normal functioning of nerve cells. In fact although the brain contains many millions of nerve cells, at the molecular level you could cross vast Saharas of space without locating an actual nerve cell.

Nerve cells are the means by which the brain communicates directly with other brain areas and peripheral parts of the body. Although there are many different types of nerve cell, they all have in common: dendritic processes, which serve to collect and collate information from adjacent nerve cells; a cell body, which contains the nucleus and the axon hillock; and the axon, which relays the electrical impulse down to the synaptic junctions.

A nerve cell axon may be less than a few millimetres in length or it may be, in the case of a large animal, several metres in length. It follows from this point that the nuclear instructions about the metabolic processes of any particular cell may be a considerable distance from the end of the axon. An axon is not like an inert length of electrical wire from time to time passing an electric current, but an area where considerable biochemical activity takes place even when nervous impulses are not passing along its length. Time-lapse photography of a living axon reveals a peristaltic-like movement (Ochs, 1965). Presumably these movements represent bursts of metabolic activity; however, it has been calculated that the slowest known rate of nervous conduction is five times faster than the transport of metabolic waves down an axon. This may lead us imprudently to conclude that biochemical processes cannot play a primary role in terms of information processing in the nerve cell. But if we conceive of biochemical processes as chains of "firemans' buckets", we can see that a chemical exchange can be instantaneous. Wassermann (1978) has argued persuasively that we have over-emphasized the electrical properties of nerve cells and that a truer understanding of their functions will come only when we have a more complete understanding of their biochemical properties. Ochs (1972) has also discussed the fast transport of materials in nerve fibres.

The chemical substance that any particular nerve cell uses at its synaptic areas is synthesized within the neurone and stored at the synaptic junctions in vesicles. Upon the arrival of an electrical impulse at a synapse a quantity of the chemical is released and crosses the synaptic cleft to activate a receptor site on an adjacent nerve cell. Almost at the moment of release the transmitter chemical is either broken down into an inactive form or taken back into the releasing nerve cell to be used again. For the transmitter substance acetylcholine, it has been calculated that between 1000 and 10 000 molecules are contained in each quantum and each quantum represents the simultaneous release of several vesicles. Elmquist and Quastel (1965) have said that in some nerve cells there may be about 1000 quanta available for immediate release and about 500 000 quanta ready for use. In total these would be sufficient for about 10 000 impulses even if further synthesis was prevented. There appear to be about three basic types of synapse (Shepherd, 1979), with the walls of the axon at the synapse being spanned by sub-units of six proteins within the bipolar lipid walls. All transmitter chemicals are either low molecular weight water soluble amines, or amino acids and related substances. It is not possible to identify any specific transmitter with a general action. A transmitter may have an excitatory action at one point and an inhibitory action at another point. A neurotransmitter is usually considered to have a short action time course. Those with a long time course are usually referred to as neuromodulators. As we shall see in a later section, the main emphasis for the investigation of transmitter substances has arisen from interest in psychopharmacological drugs. However, we should recall the statement made by Katz (1966), who pointed out that the more one learned about an individual nerve cell the less likely one felt to make generalizations concerning nerve cells.

A. Criteria

There are certain criteria which are used to identify a transmitter substance. These have been listed by Kruk and Pycock (1979) and can be summarized as follows:

(i) the chemical must be found within the nerve cell, and the enzyme and substrates required for its synthesis must be present in the nerve cell;
(ii) enzymes which inactivate the transmitter must be present at the synapse;
(iii) the application of a synthetic neurotransmitter chemical at the post synaptic receptor site should mimic the effects of the normal transmitter chemical;
(iv) during normal stimulation the transmitter chemical must be present in the synaptic cleft;
(v) electrical stimulation of the nerve cell must result in the normal calcium dependent release of the chemical.

For a few of the well established neurotransmitters it is possible to demonstrate that in the peripheral parts of the body these criteria are satisfied. Within the deeper areas of the brain this is clearly not so simple and it is assumed that the same basic processes occur. Currently there is an ever increasing list of chemicals that appear to satisfy some if not all of the criteria listed above and these are usually spoken of as putative neurotransmitters or occasionally as neuromodulators.

B. Neurotransmitter Substances

Recent discoveries about transmitter substances and the ever increasing number of biochemical substances that seem to qualify as neurotransmitters or at least as neuroregulators are serving to confuse what was originally a very simple concept of having two or three transmitter substances for the whole of the nervous system.

Acetylcholine (ACh) was the first neurotransmitter substance to be identified nearly one hundred years after the idea of chemical transmission in the nervous system had been proposed by Du bois Reymond. The original findings were made by research workers examining the structure and function of the autonomic nervous system. For a fuller account the reader is advised to read Van Toller (1979) and Day (1979). Acetylcholine is found in the brain and at the neuromuscular junctions, as well as in the preganglionic nerves of the sympathetic nervous system and the nerves of the parasympathetic nervous system. It is synthesized from acetyl co-enzyme A and choline and inactivated after release from the nerve cell by the enzyme acetylcholinesterase (AChE). Drugs that affect ACh include physostigmine, which by inhibiting AChE allows ACh to build up in the extracellular space. A small proportion of ACh is taken back into the releasing nerve cell. There are two types of cholinergic receptors labelled muscarinic and nicotinic, after the drugs that were initially found to stimulate them selectively. Nicotinic receptors have the faster reaction times and are found at the neuromuscular junctions. Certain drugs act selectively at the different receptors; for example atropine acts as a false transmitter at muscarinic receptors, but not at nicotinic receptors.

The next most important class of neurotransmitter substances are called the catecholamines and they include noradrenaline and dopamine. Catechol-amines are derived from the amino acid phenylalanine in the following metabolic chain: phenylalanine → tyrosine → dopa → dopamine → noradrenaline → adrenaline. Because the metabolic process terminates with adrenaline, which is an important hormone related to the autonomic nervous system, noradrenaline and dopamine were initially felt to be unimportant and merely precursors of the final product adrenaline. However, this was shown to be incorrect and they are now known to be important neurotransmitters in their own right. Recent discoveries about the catecholamines owe much to the discovery of fluorescence techniques which allow very low levels of the catecholamines to be detected in the nervous system. Using histochemical fluorescence techniques it is now possible to visualize noradrenergic and dopaminergic pathways in the brain (Livett, 1973; Anlezark *et al.*, 1973).

Noradrenaline is found in the postganglionic nerves of the autonomic nervous system and the limbic system, which is an important area of the brain acting as the central coordinator for the multitudinous activities of the nervous network throughout the brain. After noradrenaline has been released into the synaptic cleft most of it is retaken into the releasing nerve cell to be used again, but two enzymes catechol-O-methyltransferase and monoamine oxidase serve to inactivate and break down noradrenaline. The former enzyme has an extracellular action while the latter has an intracellular action. The drug amphetamine prolongs the action of noradrenaline by limiting the rate it can be taken back into the cell and cocaine acts to reduce the effectiveness of the released noradrenaline by blocking the noradrenergic receptors.

Dopamine is a transmitter with more restricted distribution in the brain and although dopaminergic pathways have been traced from the brain stem up to the cerebral cortex, the major concentrations appear in the basal ganglia. The basal ganglia are clusters of nerve cell bodies that are found just below the cerebral cortex and are essential for somatic movement. A disease, mainly of old age, called Parkinsonism is marked by low levels or the absence of dopamine in the basal ganglia and is treated by administering large dosages of L-dopa, a precursor of dopamine that can traverse the blood-brain barrier and enter the vascular circulation of the brain.

Serotonin is an indoleamine that is formed from the amino acid tryptophan and has been implicated in the sleep-waking cycle (see Chapter 6). The hallucinogenic drug lysergic acid diethylamide (LSD-25) is thought to act on serotoninergic receptors but its actual action is not understood. Initially the hallucinogenic properties of LSD-25 were thought to mimic those found in schizophrenia and this led to a suggestion that serotonin malfunction caused schizophrenia. A short review of the biochemical theories of schizophrenia can be found in Lipinski and Matthysse (1977). In general, serotonin appears to function more like a local neuroendocrine or neuromodulator than a neurotransmitter. This is also true of melatonin, which is synthesized in the pineal gland and appears to have an important role in the biorhythms of the body. Melatonin levels of the pineal gland show increasing levels at night and decreasing levels by day (Van Toller, 1979).

There are five recognized amino acids that have neurotransmitter or neuro-modulator roles in the nervous system and a number of these revolve around glutamic acid. Glutamic acid is metabolized in the mitochrondia of cells and it appears to act as a stimulator for nerves in the spinal cord. With the addition of ammonia to glutamic acid, glutamine is formed; by decarboxylation gamma-aminobutyric acid (GABA) can be formed; by removing a carbon atom, aspartic acid can be formed. Thus around glutamic acid and its metabolities we find a complex of transmitter substances. GABA is interesting because it is known to be an inhibitory neurotransmitter substance. The importance of inhibitory transmitter substances becomes obvious if we consider that when a fast reaction is required it is better to have the nerve cell inhibited rather than to have to initiate a reaction from a dormant nerve cell. Cystathionine, a complex sulphur containing amino acid, also appears to act as an inhibitory neurotransmitter substance.

In recent years there has been increasing evidence that certain polypeptide chains may act as neurotransmitters or neuroregulators (Kruk and Pycock, 1979; Polak and Bloom, 1979; Zetler, 1978). Although the presence of peptides that are found in both the gut regions and the brain have been known since the 1930s, it has only been with the introduction of immunocyto-chemistry that the exact locations and nature of these peptides has been revealed. At present about eight are known but it is important to point out that the actual question as to whether or not they are truly transmitter substances has still to be finally settled. One area of research that revealed the importance of peptides acting within the nervous system concerned investigations into morphine and the search for synthetic compounds with similar powerful analgesic functions. Part of this research concentrated on morphine receptor sites and one of the questions asked was what were the endogenous biochemicals that acted on these receptors. The answer was that there appeared to be substances that came to be called endorphine (from ENDO-genous moRPHINE). Endorphine and another related peptide called enkephalin are fragments of a polypeptide chain consisting of 91 amino acids called β-lipotropin. Endorphine and enkephalin are found in high concentrations in the hypothalamus, the amygdala and other important areas of the limbic system of the brain related to pleasure and pain. The action of the neuroactive peptides is thought to be inhibitory and they serve to regulate nerve cells in a way that is not clearly understood at the present time. A synthetic peptide, Org 2766, that is an analogue of the pituitary peptide ACTH $_{4-9}$, has recently been proposed as a peptide related to the ageing process (Pigache, 1982; Rigter, 1982).

V. Hormones

An adequate consideration of hormones would form a separate chapter but some consideration should be given to hormones if only for their important role in determining levels of biochemical activity within individual cells (Lee and Laycock, 1978).

Hormones act as chemical messengers affecting the rates and directions of ongoing cellular activity. They serve to supplement and extend the activities of the nervous tissues. Hormones are chemicals secreted by the endocrine glands and transported in the blood stream to specific sites of action on cell walls where they regulate the internal reactions. Unlike vitamins and enzymes, hormones are not a source of energy. The older view of hormones, being released and having general reactions at sites a considerable distance from the releasing endocrine gland, has been modified. Local hormones with discrete actions are known to exist in the gut region of the body and are also thought to exist within the brain (Polak and Bloom, 1979). As we have already mentioned, peptides and other neural modulators appear to have a hormone-like role.

In common with biochemical causation, hormones raise the "chicken and egg" problem as to whether they initiate reactions or are merely the result of reactions. Leshner (1978) reviewed the literature relating to hormones and behaviour and concluded that, when the animal is exposed to an appropriate stimulus, a hormone will affect whether or not a behavioural reaction will occur and with what intensity. His point is that hormones do not cause or stimulate behaviour *per se* but they markedly affect the intensity of behavioural reactions.

The menstrual cycle, with its fluctuating hormone levels and correlated changes of moods and behaviour, is an area that has been reviewed by Bell *et al.* (1975). Many more recent articles can be found in the journal "Psychophysiology". It is now thought that the overall control of the hormones in the body lies with the complex circuitry of the limbic system, rather than with the important pituitary and its associated hypothalamic connections. In the light of what was said in an earlier section about certain of the neurotransmitter substances acting as inhibitors, it is interesting to consider what inhibits the sex hormones until puberty is reached. The basic hormones are available in the body but do not produce reactions until certain critical stages of development are reached.

Clearly, former distinctions between the long term action of the hormones and the short term actions of transmitter substances have been blurred and the discovery of neurally active peptides seems to indicate local and perhaps precise neurohormones. The half life of enkephalin *in vivo* is said to be in the order of 4–5 seconds. Pearse (1978) has coined the phrase "diffused neuroendocrine" to help explain some of the complexities.

VI. Synaptic Facilitation

The idea that learning involves modifications to nerve cells is quite old. However, it received a considerable impetus when Hebb (1949) proposed that the specific physiological mechanism for short term memory was local reverberatory synaptic circuits and that long term memory involved synaptic facilitation, which with common use lead to the build up of brain connections. Rosenzweig *et al.* (1960) set up a research programme that involved measuring brain levels of acetylcholinesterase. They were using the hypothesis that rats reared in an enriched environment would show increased levels, reflecting increased activity of the cholinergic nerve cells. Kretch (1968) has summarized this and later work which overall failed to confirm the original ideas, although a strain of rats bred for their maze brightness ability did have ACh/AChE ratios that were in line with the original idea. An excellent discussion of the cholinergic nerve cell has been written by Warburton (1975), who considers the cholinergic system from the physiological, pharmacological and behavioural aspects. Gardner-Medwin (1969) has proposed a more recent theoretical model relating to synaptic activity and learning but overall these ideas have not led to a very fruitful area of behavioural research.

VII. Macromolecules and Learning

Katz and Halstead (1955) proposed a specific biochemical model of learning, arguing that learning caused the random configuration of certain polypeptide chains to change to specific orientations. The converse of learning, extinction, involved the gradual denaturation of the learning-induced configuration. Protein macromolecules are large enough and have a sufficiently complex surface area and structure to make this idea possible. However, before their idea could have any impact, Watson and Crick (Watson, 1968) proposed their DNA model and attention turned towards discovering the roles of DNA and RNA in the learning processes.

The many experiments that were carried out on this problem can be categorized as follows: (i) blocking RNA and protein synthesis and observing the effects on learning processes; (ii) measuring levels of proteins and certain amino acids during and after learning; (iii) adding RNA and amino acids to the diets of animals and observing the effects on the learning processes; (iv) conditioning an animal and extracting RNA from its brain and using this to inject into a recipient animal to see if the latter was aided in learning the original task.

The last category was by far the most controversial and it was claimed (Babich *et al.*, 1965) that cross species facilitation of learning has been achieved between rats and hamsters. Apart from problems in extracting the RNA there were often problems related to behavioural tasks used. For example, most of the learning tasks used involved activity and if one of the main effects of adding RNA to an animal's diet is to cause a general increase in activity then any learning involving activity would be helped. In this sense injected RNA might be having a general pharmacological role. Also, injected RNA can be broken down in the body to its component parts and these will be utilized by the body. So, any non-specific RNA given to control animals might also serve to aid them. Finally, Byrne (1966) and twenty-one other workers in the area published a letter in the journal *Science* pointing out that they had all experienced negative findings, when attempting to show the transfer of learning via the extraction of RNA from a donor animal and its introduction into a naive recipient.

Theoretical models explaining the action of RNA on learning varied, from Hyden and Egyhazi (1963) who suggested that RNA from the glial cells transferred into nerve cells and altered the metabolic rate, to Landauer (1964) who argued that changes in the metabolic activity or protein configuration modulated the actual action potential within the nerve cell. As Glassman and Wilson (1970) pointed out, even if it can be shown in a learning situation that alterations in RNA or protein levels have taken place we would still need to determine the more difficult question of whether or not learning *per se* or emotional, motivational, visual, auditory, olfactory, sensorimotor or a host of non-specific effects had produced the changes.

After virtually eliminating the causal role in learning of nucleotides and proteins, attention switched to more restricted but still worthwhile aims. In particular attention centred on the peptides which had been largely neglected since the Watson and Crick model. Ungar (1972 and 1973) demonstrated

that a specific peptide called scotophobin could be extracted from a trained
animal and injected into a naive donor animal where it produced a similar
fear of light. The importance of peptides also came to light from another
source, in which the effects of the adrenocorticotrophic hormone (ACTH) on
a learning task was shown. This study was carried out by Bohus and De Wied
(1966). They found that, if they injected the first ten amino acids of ACTH
but replaced the seventh amino acid phenylalanine by its mirror image
isomer, they were able to speed up extinction of an avoidance task. The exact
meaning and relationships of these findings are not clear, but biochemical
processes clearly play a role in the learning processes. At a future date it is to
be hoped that these relationships may be unravelled. Certainly the recent
interest in peptides as neurotransmitters or neuroregulators serves to make
the problem more intriguing, but the crucial point about whether or not the
brain does contain compounds coded for specific learning has still to be
settled (Org 2766 and aging has already been mentioned; Pigache, 1982).

Starting from the ideas of Jouvet (1972), who argued that serotonin nerve
cell pathways in the brain are important for slow wave sleep activity and the
noradrenaline nerve cell pathways are important for active states, Ellison
(1979) has examined the role of these biochemicals in terms of evolutionary
characteristics. He points out that serotonin brain levels are high in situations
where an animal feels safe and secure. Noradrenaline brain levels are high in
situations of excitement and arousal. Both of these conditions are necessary
for an animal to function adequately and they represent alternating states of
anabolic and catabolic activity. Animals need to venture out to find food and
to explore, but at the same time they need to conserve energy by resting. The
latter state is done either in a safe physical niche or by hiding in a school of fish
or a flock of birds.

VIII. Catecholamines and Behaviour

Many attempts have been made to use adrenaline and noradrenaline as an
index of brain function. A more complete account of the role and functions of
the catecholamines is given in Van Toller (1979).

One of the main interests in examining the effects of the catecholamines is
that they may help us distinguish between learning and performance. The
reason for this lies in their separate actions. Adrenaline has the wider action
of the two. It is mainly released from the adrenal medulla and has a general
hormone action affecting the body's cells. Little, if any, adrenaline is found in
the central nervous system. Noradrenaline is found in small amounts in the
adrenal medulla, but the main concentrations are found in noradrenergic
postganglionic fibres of the sympathetic nervous system and the noradrenergic

nerve fibres in the brain. An important function of the sympathetic nervous system is control of the vascular system and it has a vital role in distributing blood to areas of the body which need it. For example, the need for muscular movement results in the sympathetic nervous system moving the blood into the muscular tissues. This movement arises from the vasoconstriction and vasodilation of the blood vessels. The need for the movement of blood arises from the fact that the vascular system is larger than the vascular volume. Thus, noradrenaline could be held to be an index of the muscular energy being expended at any time. Adrenaline has a wider, more general priming effect on lots of different tissues and could be said to measure cellular tonus.

Goodall (1962) assayed urinary samples taken from subjects exposed to gravitational stress in a large centrifuge. He found that adrenaline levels appeared to be related to the amount of anxiety evoked by the situation. Noradrenaline appeared to be related to the physiological stress induced by being whirled around in the centrifuge. Goodall found that adrenaline levels decreased gradually over days as a subject's anxiety level adapted to the psychological stress involved in the centrifugation process. The physiological stress induced by the centrifugation process remained constant over days, and this was reflected by noradrenaline levels not showing the adaptations found for adrenaline. Subjects showing high anxiety levels in the situation did not show progressive decrements in their excreted adrenaline levels.

Frankenhaeuser (1971) has summarized a series of studies measuring the excretion rate of catecholamines. Within certain limits, it was found that plotting level of adrenaline against performance, gave a dose response curve showing small increases in efficiency. Catecholamine levels during moderate activity rose to twice normal resting levels, while moderate stress produced increases of up to three to five times normal resting levels. Mental activity produced increases in adrenaline but not noradrenaline. Physical work produced increases in both catecholamines.

In another series of studies dividing subjects into low and high adrenaline output groups, it was shown that catecholamine output matched behavioural efficiency. Using the Stroop colour–word test that requires close concentration, it was found that a group of subjects having high adrenaline output performed consistently better than a group showing low adrenaline output. Similarly in a choice reaction time experiment, subjects showing high adrenaline output recorded faster reaction times compared to subjects with low adrenaline output. Assays made of the excreted adrenaline levels in habitual "morning" and "evening" workers showed that the peaks of the subject's adrenaline output matched periods of optimal performance. Thus it would appear that catecholamine output matches performance efficiency and level of alertness. This finding was extended by an experiment in which it was found that night-time resting levels of adrenaline showed a significant positive correlation with the intellectual level of young children, as measured by conventional intelligence tests.

These studies carried out in Stockholm implicate adrenaline as an important hormone for coping with a variety of social and psychological stressors, and also show that adrenaline excretion is related to cognitive and behavioural performance. However, large individual differences in catechol-amine output exist which may, in part, relate to previous conditioning and learning.

A clinical condition called pheochromocytoma, where excessive amounts of the catecholamines are excreted, has enabled various metabolites or break-down products of the catecholamines to be determined. Gitlow et al. (1971) reported that 20–35% of the 3-methoxy-4-hydroxyphenylglycol (MHPG) metabolite excreted in the urine of humans arose from cerebral catecholamine metabolism. Following these discoveries, a number of studies have been reported in which the metabolite was assayed in patients suffering from manic depression (Maas et al., 1971; Bond et al., 1972; Fawcett et al., 1972; Maas et al., 1972; Jones et al., 1973). These authors showed that levels of MHPG secreted rose during the manic phases of the manic–depressive cycle and fell during the depressive phases of the cycle. The suggestion made by these authors was that the changing levels reflected the level of brain activity. However, it could be claimed that the levels of MHPG reflected alterations of muscular activity during the different phases of the cycle rather than brain activity. Goode et al. (1973) tested this idea by using subjects over a period of several days, comparing a rest period with a 2-hour period of isometric and isotonic exercises. These authors found no increases in MHPG levels following the exercise periods and concluded that their results sup-ported the suggestion that the results obtained from manic–depressive patients were not likely to be due to differences in muscular activity. In addition, Maas et al. (1971) have argued that the changes in MHPG levels were not a byproduct of concurrent biochemical changes taking place in the brain.

The studies reported above indicate a relationship between noradrenaline metabolism in the brain and cognition. Rubin et al. (1970) reported a study that investigated urinary MHPG levels in naval pilots and their navigators during three training exercises, related to landing aircraft on the flight deck of a warship. The phases were: (i) simulated flight deck landings at the shore base; (ii) day-time landings on a carrier ship; (iii) night-time flight deck landings on the carrier ship. Night-time landings on a moving carrier are said to be the most difficult and complicated task demanded of the naval pilots. They call for a number of complex perceptual-motor skills and precise spatial orientation. The levels of MHPG found in the urine of the pilots and navi-gators were shown to be commensurate with the difficulty of the landings. In all cases the pilots were said to show higher levels than their navigators. Clearly in such a dangerous situation there is a strong stress component, for the dangers are very apparent and real. In considering this point Rubin and his collaborators point out that, in an earlier study which examined the levels of cortisol in the blood, it was the pilots who showed increases on flying days and not the navigators. The authors finally concluded that the MHPG changes appeared to be related to the intensity of concentration, attention and alertness required to perform the task, and furthermore these factors did not diminish with experience.

Frankenhaeuser *et al.* (1976) have reported a study in which 4-hydroxy-3-methoxyphenylethylene glycol (MOPEG) excretion levels were analysed in male and female students. Both groups performed equally well in an examination; however, self-report questionnaires revealed that males felt confident and successful whereas the females reported discomfort and lack of confidence. Urinary excretion of cortisol, adrenaline, noradrenaline and MOPEG were found to increase in both sexes. In the male group the levels of adrenaline and MOPEG increased significantly.

The discovery of the metabolite MHPG appears to point the way for future research, and further detailed examination of the relationships between cognition and biochemical metabolism is required. Although a number of differences between the various studies exist there is a promise that in the future catecholamine assays will enable us to have an index of central nervous system activity.

IX. Conclusions

The brain contains at least three massive and diffuse chemical pathways and the behavioural significance of these is now being revealed.

Reviewing the literature reveals a slow growth of interest in the relationship between biochemistry and behaviour which has in the more recent past been extended to include environmental factors and cognitive stress (Frankenhaeuser and Gardell, 1976).

One area of great potential concerns the interactions between the electrical and the biochemical activity of the brain. Adams (1976) has reported on the use of electrochemical techniques of voltammetry and chronamperometry, which allow for instantaneous determinations about the release of transmitter substance within the brain. The development of this type of technique will allow us to build more precise pictures of the chemical pathways in the brain and this knowledge will serve to complement our existing understanding of electrical pathways in the brain. Another technique with potential is the use of immunological methods as a means of producing precise lesions in nervous tissue (Van Toller and Tarpy, 1972). Psychophysiologists have ignored electrical (d.c.) currents in their studies (Becker *et al.*, 1962), presumably because they have a very slow time course. Longitudinal studies would be required for an adequate understanding of their function. However, d.c. electrical activity may serve to influence biochemical reactions, particularly in the mood and emotion states. Biochemical mechanisms may also play important roles in the biological rhythms which are now becoming recognized as critical to human performance (see Vol. II, Chapter 4).

Margolis (1975) has suggested that specific proteins act as markers for smells and, although at this time the evidence is far from complete, we can expect this type of biochemical research to provide us with valuable information about the sensory systems. Finally, we may expect that some of the findings now being made in the areas of genetic engineering will find application in the brain biosciences. For example, Parkinsonism is a disease caused by the lack of adequate levels of the transmitter substance dopamine in the dopaminergic nerves of the basal ganglia. The present means of treatment is to administer low dosages of a dopamine precursor called L-dopa which produces a number of side effects. In the future it may prove possible to induce the relevant nerve cells to produce their own dopamine by affecting cell nuclei, which in turn will affect the metabolic processes in the cell body.

Further Reading

Rose, S. and Sanderson, C. (1979). "The Chemistry of Life" 2nd edn. Penguin, Harmondsworth.
A popular and good introduction which is used as a course text by the Open University.
Kramer, L. M. J. and Scott, J. K. (1979). "The Cell Concept". Macmillan, London.
A sound introduction to most aspects of cellular activity written from a biological view point.
Keeton, W. T. (1980). "Biological Science" 3rd edn. Norton, New York.
A very good American glossy textbook with plenty of informative illustrations and photographs. Unfortunately relatively expensive.
Vander, A. J., Sherman, J. H. and Luciano, D. S. (1980). "Human Physiology: The Mechanisms of Bodily Function". McGraw-Hill, New York.
A clear lucid account of human physiology. Again, unfortunately relatively expensive.
Lee, J. and Laycock, J. (1978). "Essential Endocrinology". Oxford University Press, Oxford.
Written primarily for medical students but it is a sound and relatively cheap book.
Brown, T. S. and Wallace, P. M. (1980). "Physiological Psychology". Academic Press, London and New York.
Written in the standard format for a physiological psychology textbook but more up to date than most of the current books in this area and it has a good glossary.
Van Toller, C. (1979). "The Nervous Body: An Introduction to the Autonomic Nervous System and Behaviour". Wiley and Sons, Chichester.
Relates behaviour to autonomic function.

Warburton, D. M. (1975). "Brain, Behaviour and Drugs". Wiley and Sons, Chichester.
Contains a very good account of research relating to the cholinergic systems of the brain.
Leshner, A. I. (1978). "An Introduction to Behavioural Endocrinology". Oxford University Press, Oxford.
Covers the behavioural aspects of hormones in a lucid manner.
Watts, G. O. (1975). "Dynamic Neuroscience: Its Application to Brain Disorders". Harper and Row, New York.
A complex but well integrated account of brain chemistry in abnormal states.

Edward Arnold Publishers (London) publish some cheap and well written booklets in a series called Cell Biology and Biochemistry. A number would be excellent readings as an introduction to biochemistry and cell biology. The journal Scientific American often contains relevant articles written by leading experts in the field. In particular, the September 1979 issue contains ten papers on various aspects of brain function.

References

Adams, R. (1976). Probing brain chemistry with electroanalytic techniques. *Analyt. Chem.* **48**, 1128–1138.
Anlezark, G. M., Crow, T. J. and Greenway, A. P. (1973). Impaired learning and decreased cortical norepinephrine after bilateral locus coerulus lesions. *Science* **181**, 682–684.
Babich, F. R., Jacobson, A. L. and Rubash, S. (1965). Cross species transfer of learning: effect of RNA from hamsters on rat behaviour. *Proc. Nat. Acad. Sci.* **54**, 1299–1309.
Becker, R. O., Bachman, C. H. and Friedman, H. (1962). The direct current control system, a link between environment and organism. *N.Y. St. J. Med.* **15**, 1169–1176.
Bell, B., Christie, M. J. and Venables, P. H. (1975). Psychophysiology of the menstrual cycle. *In* "Research in Psychophysiology" (P. H. Venables and M. J. Christie, eds). Wiley and Sons, Chichester.
Bohus, B. and De Wied, D. (1966). Inhibitory and facilitatory effect of two related peptides on extinction of avoidance behaviour. *Science* **153**, 318–320.
Bond, P. A., Jenner, F. A. and Simpson, G. A. (1972). Daily variations of the urine content of 3-methoxy-4-hydroxyphenylglycol in two manic-depressive patients. *Psychol. Med.* **2**, 81–85.
Byrne, W. L. *et al.* (1966). Memory Transfer. *Science* **153**, 658.
Christie, M. and Woodman, D. D. (1980). Biochemical Methods. *In* "Techniques in Psychophysiology" (I. Martin and P. H. Venables, eds). Wiley and Sons, Chichester.
Day, M. D. (1979). "Autonomic Pharmacology". Churchill Livingstone, Edinburgh.
Ellison, G. D. (1979). Chemical Systems of the brain and evolution. *In* "Brain, Behaviour and Evolution" (D. A. Oakley and H. C. Potkin, eds). Methuen, London.
Elmquist, D. and Quastel, D. J. M. (1965). Presynaptic action of hemicholinium at the neuromuscular junction. *J. Physiol., Lond.* **177**, 463–482.
Fawcett, J., Maas, J. W. and Dekirmenjian, H. (1972). Depression and MHPG excretion. *Archs Gen. Psychiat.* **26**, 246–251.
Frankenhaeuser, M. (1971). Behaviour and circulating catecholamines. *Brain Res.* **31**, 241–262.

Frankenhaeuser, M. and Gardell, B. (1976). Underload and overload in working life: outline of a multidisciplinary approach. *J. Human Stress* **2**, 35–46.

Frankenhauser, M., von Wright, M. R., Collins, A., von Wright, J., Sedvall, G. and Swann, C.-G. (1976). "Sex differences in psychoneuro-endocrine reactions to examination stress" Report No. 489. Department of Psychology, University of Stockholm.

Gardner-Medwin, A. R. (1969). Modifiable synapses necessary for learning. *Nature* **223**, 916–918.

Gitlow, S. E., Mendlowitz, M., Bertoni, L. M., Wilk, S. and Wilk, E. K. (1971). Human norepinephrine metabolism. Its evaluation by administration of tritiated norepinephrine. *J. Clin. Invest.* **50**, 859–865.

Glassman, E. and Wilson, J. E. (1970). The incorporation of uridine into brain RNA during short experiences. *Brain Res.* **21**, 157–168.

Goodall, Mc. C. (1962). Sympathoadrenal response to gravitational stress. *J. Clin. Invest.* **41**, 197–202.

Goode, D. J., Dekirmenjian, H., Meltzer, H. Y. and Maas, J. W., (1973). Relation of exercise to MHPG excretion in normal subjects. *Archs Gen. Psychiat.* **29**, 391–396.

Hebb, D. O. (1949). "Organization of Behaviour". Wiley and Sons, Chichester.

Hydén, H. and Egyhazi, E. (1963). Glial RNA changes during a learning experiment in rats. *Proc. Nat. Acad. Sci. U.S.A.* **49**, 618–624.

Jones, F. D., Maas, J. W., Dekirmenjian, H. and Fawcett, J. (1973). Urinary catecholamine metabolites during behavioural changes in a patient with manic depressive cycles. *Science* **179**, 300–302.

Jouvet, M. (1972). The role of monoamines and acetylcholine-containing neurons in the regulation of the sleep-waking cycle. *Ergebn. Physiol.* **64**, 166–307.

Katz, B. (1966). "Nerve, Muscle and Synapse". McGraw-Hill, Maidenhead.

Katz, J. J. and Halstead, W. C. (1955). Protein organization and mental function. *Comp. Psychol. Monogr.* **2C**, 1–39.

Kretch, D. (1968). Brain Chemistry and anatomy: implications for behaviour therapy. *In* "Mind as Tissue" (C. Rupp, ed.). Harper and Row, New York.

Kruk, Z. L. and Pycock, C. J. (1979). "Neurotransmitters and Drugs". Croom Helm, London.

Landauer, T. K. (1964). Two hypotheses concerning the biochemical basis of memory. *Psychol. Rev.* **71**, 167–169.

Lee, J. and Laycock, J. (1978). "Essential Endocrinology". Oxford University Press, Oxford.

Leshner, A. I. (1978). "An Introduction to Behavioural Endocrinology." Oxford University Press, Oxford.

Lipinski, J. and Matthysse, S. (1977). Biological theories of schizophrenia. *In* "Biological bases of Psychiatric Disorders" (A. Frazer and A. Winokur, eds). Spectrum, New York.

Livett, B. G. (1973). Histochemical visualization of adrenergic neurones. *Br. Med. Bull.* **29**, 93–99.

Maas, J. W. Dekirmenjian, H. and Fawcett, J. (1971). Catecholamine metabolism in depression and stress. *Nature* **230**, 330–331.

Maas, J. W., Fawcett, J. A. and Dekirmenjian, H. (1972). Catecholamine metabolism, depressive illness, and drug response. *Archs Gen. Psychiat.* **26**, 252–262.

Margolis, F. L. (1975). Biochemical markers of the primary olfactory pathway: a model neural system. *In* "Advances in Neurochemistry" Vol. 1. (B. W. Agranoff and M. H. Aprison, eds). Plenum Press, New York.

Ochs, S. (1965). "Elements of Neurophysiology". Wiley and Sons, Chichester.

Ochs, S. (1972). Fast transport of materials in mammalian nerve fibres. *Science* 176, 252–259.

Pearse, A. G. E. (1978). Diffuse neuroendocrine system: peptides common to brain and intestine and their relationship to the APVD concepts. *In* "Centrally Acting Peptides" (J. Hughes, ed.), pp. 49–57. Macmillan, London.

Pigache, R. M. (1982). A peptide for the aged? Basic and clinical studies. *In* "Psychopharmacology of Old Age" (D. Wheatley, ed.), pp. 67–96. Oxford University Press, Oxford.

Polak, J. M. and Bloom, S. R. (1979). The neuroendocrine design of the gut. *Clinics Endocr. Metab.* 8, 313–330.

Rigter, H. (1982). A peptide for the aged? Animal studies. *In* "Psychopharmacology of Old Age" (D. Wheatley, ed.), pp. 97–112. Oxford University Press, Oxford.

Rosenzweig, M. R., Kretch, D. and Bennett, E. L. (1960). A search for relations between brain chemistry and behaviour. *Psychol. Bull.* 57, 476–492.

Rubin, R. T., Miller, R. G., Clark, B. R., Poland, R. E. and Ranson, J. C. (1970). The stress of aircraft carrier landing II. 3-methoxy-4-hydroxyphenylglycol excretion in naval aviators. *Psychosomatic Med.* 32, 589–597.

Shepherd, G. M. (1979). "The Synaptic Organization of the Brain" 2nd edn. Oxford University Press, Oxford.

Ungar, G. (1972). Seminar on the requirements for resting hypotheses about molecular coding of experience: transfer studies. *Psychopharmacol. Bull.* 8, 5–13.

Ungar, G. (1973). Scotophobin bioassay. *Psychopharmacol. Bull.* 9, 21–31.

Vander, A. J., Sherman, J. H. and Luciano, D. S. (1980). "Human Physiology: The Mechanisms of Body Function" 3rd edn. McGraw-Hill, Maidenhead.

Van Toller, C. (1979). "The Nervous Body: An Introduction to the Autonomic Nervous System and Behaviour". Wiley and Sons, Chichester.

Van Toller, C. and Tarpy, R. M. (1972). Hypothermia and behaviour of immuno-sympathectomized mice. *In* "Nerve Growth Factor and its Antiserum" (E. Zaimis, ed.). Athlone Press, London.

Warburton, D. M. (1975). "Brain, Behaviour and Drugs". Wiley and Sons, Chichester.

Wasserman, G. D. (1978). "Neurobiological theory of psychological phenomena". Macmillan Press, London.

Watson, J. D. (1968). "The Double Helix: a Personal Account of the discovery of the Structure of D.N.A.". Weidenfeld and Nicolson, London.

Zetler, G. (1978). Active peptides in the nervous tissue. *In* "Advances in Biochemical Pharmacology" Vol. 18. (E. Costa and M. Trabucchi, eds). Raven Press, New York.

6 Sleep Patterns and Functions

J. G. Lindsley

Abstract We sleep approximately one third of our lives. Most of us think of this as a time when psychological function is held in abeyance: twenty years of suspended psychological activity for sixty years of life! In this chapter, we first correct this idea, with data from animal and human studies, then begin to explore the intricacies of what does occur during sleep. We then ask, how is the brain organized to produce these events, and what vital function is reflected in the events of sleep we are able to observe? Finally, we arrive at some tentative conclusions; then look to the future and the terrain of inquiry still to be traversed.

I. Introduction

Historically, sleep was a phenomenon that fell between the interests of psychologists and biologists, and not squarely into either camp. As an apparently reflexive behaviour involved in the recuperation of the body at the end of the day, it had little to interest the psychologist. Apparently less dynamic than the more complicated survival functions such as feeding behaviour, it seemed not to have caught the interest of biologists.

The phenomenon of sleep, however, is of great value to physiological psychology, because the study of sleep will help us to comprehend how psychological function arises from the workings of the brain. Methodologically, sleep is particularly amenable to the search for relationships between physiological and behavioural levels of analysis, because it is a relatively unambiguous behaviour that appears in fairly similar form in lower mammals and humans. This permits the use of animal models. Substantively, sleep is linked with phenomena well beyond the reflexive level: (i) we dream during sleep, suggesting that sleep bears some relationship to thoughts and feelings; (ii) the structure of sleep is vulnerable to disruption by emotional distress and clearly is not just reflex behaviour, but rather is a behaviour subject to higher order control; (iii) some of the chemical pathways involved in the production of sleep are also deeply implicated in the development of

PHYSIOLOGICAL CORRELATES OF HUMAN
BEHAVIOUR   ISBN 0-12-273901-9

affective disorders such as depression and anxiety, and thought disorders such as schizophrenia; and (iv) not only is sleep a behaviour which seems to absorb the shock of one's ups and downs, but it appears to be a period of time during which events happen that affect the way a person uses her or his daily experience.

It is quite likely that a great deal will be learned about how psychological function arises from the unique organization of the brain when we understand, at a physiological level, the relationships among thought disorders, affective disorders, and sleep. Simply understanding the physiological substrates of sleep will cast much light on the understanding of waking life.

The original lack of interest in sleep by psychologists was understandable. Through to the middle of this century sleep was considered to be simply the absence of waking, and was thought to be brought about passively. It was generally accepted that one remained awake only as long as there were sufficient stimulation to maintain arousal. As stimulation decreased – usually as the sun went down – waking was thought to recede, with one passively slipping into the nothingness of sleep; that is, into a state of no psychological function.

Times changed. Ideas were modified. In 1949, Moruzzi and Magoun identified the reticular formation as the part of the brain central to waking vigilance (Moruzzi and Magoun, 1949). Stimulation of the system produced cortical desynchronization. Behaviourally, it aroused the sleeping cat from its slumber, and in the waking animal produced more acute perceptual discriminations and faster reaction times. The first physiological foothold into an understanding of waking vigilance, and therefore perhaps of consciousness, was established. With this finding, it was possible to test the hypothesis that sleep is the result of cessation of sensory input. The reticular formation (discussed in detail in a later section of this chapter) receives collateral input from virtually every system of the body. Denervation of the sensory apparatus, therefore, should bring about behavioural and electrophysiological sleep. Not so, it turned out. As long as the reticular formation was intact, a normal cycling of the cortex between the electrophysiological signs of wakefulness and those of sleep was observed.

Later experiments by Hess (e.g. Hess, 1954) also in the cat demonstrated that stimulation of certain hypothalamic and pontine structures would produce behavioural and electrophysiological sleep. Jouvet, in turn, found that he could prevent sleep by lesioning specific brainstem structures (Jouvet, 1969).

The work of Moruzzi and Magoun and of Jouvet will be discussed in detail, when we turn to a discussion of the biological substrates of sleep. The importance of the Moruzzi and Magoun, Hess and Jouvet work was that, when taken together, it probably set aside forever the notion that sleep is simply the absence of wakefulness: sleep can be produced by activating brain structures with electrical stimulation, and can be eliminated by removing certain brain structures. That is, sleep is itself an active phenomenon, which requires the integrity and active participation of certain brain structures.

After the establishment of sleep as an actively produced event, the study of sleep became more interesting. However, before deeper questions could meaningfully be posed, the study of sleep had first to enter into a descriptive phase. If sleep were an active process, there clearly was a great deal to be learned about which parts of the body participated in the activity.

II. What are the Characteristics of Sleep? A First Step in Understanding it

Even if we accept that sleep is actively induced, it is difficult to overcome the belief that sleep is a time when nothing much is going on. The aspects of sleep of which the layman is most aware are that it involves an absence of intentional transaction with the environment; usually an absence of any kind of complex behaviour; usually an absence of normal waking function such as urination; and an absence or near absence of muscle tone. One's eyes are closed so no light comes in, and one's ears are deaf to the auditory world. However, the descriptive research was to reveal that beneath the quietness and darkness of sleep there is a great complex of events occurring.

During sleep, transformations occur in virtually all systems of the body, including but not restricted to the central nervous system. So intricate and so organized are the events which occur that one begins to set aside simple notions of the function of sleep, and to wonder about the complicated inner events which create such outer complexities.

A. *Electroencephalographic Characterization of Sleep*

The earliest characterization of the events of sleep was largely in terms of electroencephalographic (EEG) activity. We owe our understanding of what is to follow to the technique of electroencephalography made possible by Berger's work in 1929; to the electroencephalographic characterization of sleep by Aserinsky and Kleitman in 1953; and to the work of Dement and Kleitman in 1957. Some of the first data demonstrating that sleep was not a monotonous simple state were from scalp EEG recordings of sleeping people. Aserinsky, Kleitman, Dement and others noted systematic transitions of the EEG from one rhythm to another, and saw that these changes through the night were patterned.

Kleitman found that a person begins the night with an easily disrupted sleep, during which waking alpha rhythm disappears and reappears a few times, and then is gradually lost. During this phase the EEG assumes a low voltage desynchronized character, including at times a regular 4–6 Hz pattern. As the first stage of sleep of the night, this sequence of events was named **stage 1**. After a few minutes a pattern appears characterized chiefly by frequent 12–14 Hz spindle-shaped tracings, known as sleep spindles; and to a greater or lesser degree, depending upon the individual, high voltage spikes known as K-complexes. This phase was called **stage 2**. Soon, the spindles and K-complexes disappear and the phenomena of stage 2 are gradually replaced by delta waves to give **stage 3**. Finally, during the period named **stage 4**, delta waves come to occupy the major part of the record. The sleeper then proceeds back through the stages, from 4 to 3 to 2 and, then apparently, back to stage 1. This second and subsequent "stage 1" of the night is somewhat reminiscent of the first, but more reminiscent of alert waking. Yet, while during waking and during the first stage 1 of the night the sleeper can be easily aroused, during this "stage 1" the sleeper is particularly unarousable, and the eyes dart from side to side. To this odd stage Kleitman gave the name emergent stage 1 (E-1).

Kleitman's observation came to have more meaning when it was recognized that this last emergent stage 1 is a phase of sleep so different from the other four stages that it is not really a part of the stage 1 to 4 progression at all. Rather, it is as unique a state as waking arousal. With this realization, the EEG structure of sleep was cast in sharper relief. Sleep consisted not of five continuous *stages*, but was organized around two discrete *states*.

The first four stages of sleep can now be understood as belonging to a single state, referred to as **S-sleep**. It takes its name from the *s*low waves of stages 3 and 4. The state which previously had been called emergent stage 1 is now called **D-sleep** (as well as REM sleep and paradoxical sleep, for reasons which will become apparent). D-sleep takes its name from the *d*esynchronized rhythm which dominates the EEG record. The view that D-sleep is a different state from S-sleep is reinforced by the fact that similar periods, differing markedly from the remainder of sleep, are found in mammals, to some extent in the sleep of birds, but not at all in fish, amphibians or reptiles. It would appear that D-sleep can be differentiated from S, and is evolutionarily a new development. Lest the reader be thoroughly confused at this point, we have summarized the names of each phase of sleep in Table I.

Recognition that the two states are the major subdivisions of sleep permits us to formulate better the pattern of EEG changes across the night. In the normal individual without a sleep disorder, the two states of sleep alternate with each other through the sleeping period, for a total of about four or five cycles. Each complete S-to-D cycle lasts about 90–110 minutes. The relationship between S and D is dynamic, not simply a monotonous alternation. Early

EEG and Eye-Movement Records

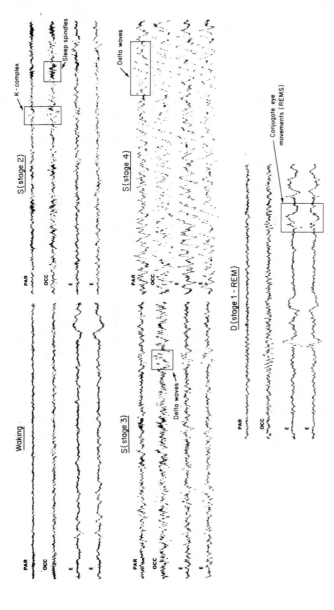

Fig. 1 *Representative EEG and eye movement records in the human of waking; stages 2, 3 and 4 of S-sleep; and of D-sleep. Notice the spindles and K-complexes of stage 2; the delta waves apparent to some extent in stage 3 and dominating the record in stage 4. Notice also the conjugate eye movements (REMs) of D-sleep. PAR = parietal cortex recordings; OCC = occipital cortex recordings; E = eye leads.*

Table I Summary of alternative terminologies for various epochs of sleep

Basic state	Name	Relationship to S or D sleep	Derivation of name
S	non-REM or NREM	synonymous with S-sleep	takes its name from the absence of REMs (rapid eye movements) during this state
	SWS	Slow wave sleep. Refers to stages 3 and 4 of S-sleep	takes its name from the presence of slow, delta waves which appear in the EEG record during these stages of S-sleep
D	REM sleep	synonymous with D-sleep	takes its name from the presence of REMs (rapid eye movements) during this state
	FWS	fast wave sleep; synonymous with D-sleep	takes its name from the low voltage fast activity which appears in the EEG record during this state.
	paradoxical sleep	synonymous with D-sleep	takes its name from the apparent paradox of a very high arousal threshold in the presence of the kind of EEG record associated with alert waking
	emergent stage 1	synonymous with D-sleep, and largely of historical interest	historically, the appearance of D-sleep immediately following Stage 2 of S appeared to be the re-emergence of Stage 1 EEG activity

in the night, S-periods are relatively long, D-periods quite short. As the night proceeds the proportions shift, with S-periods becoming progressively shorter and the associated D-periods longer. By the end of the night, D will have accounted for 20% of the record in the normal adult.

The progression of events within the state of S is also dynamic. During the first S-period, stage 1 is followed by stages 2, 3 and 4 in rapid succession; then 3 and 2 occur once again before the first D-period is ushered in. As the night goes on, the sleeper dips progressively less deeply into S before transition to D until, by the early morning hours, stages 3 and 4 have virtually disappeared, and D effectively is alternating with stage 2.

Figure 2 depicts the oscillation between S and D, and the changes in the electrophysiological organization within S as the night proceeds. What is most striking is the remarkable consistency of these dynamic patterns from night to night and individual to individual. The consistency would imply a central mechanism with tight control over the production of the different states. The transformations seem almost to be the footsteps of sleep's inner workings as they move toward completion of some kind of goal.

B. *Other Physiological Correlates to the States and Stages of Sleep*

We now have presented in intricate detail much of what is known of the EEG signs of sleep. Effectively, what we have described are the movements of a

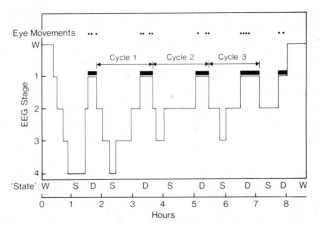

Fig. 2 *Organization of the states and stages of sleep of a normal young adult, derived by averaging many all-night recordings. The bars above "stage 1" in cycles 1, 2 and 3 represent D-periods, and show graphically the similarity of the stage 1 and the D EEG pattern. Above the bars are dots, representing the rapid eye movements which occur also during D-sleep. Reprinted from Hartmann (1973) with permission from the author. W = waking; S = synchronized sleep; D = desynchronized or dreaming sleep.*

very complex dance, performed each night with surprising regularity. But these are only the outward manifestations of yet more complex inner events. To make sense of these outward signs, we must now view them in the context of other physiological events with which they are intimately associated. Although historically the several phases of sleep were defined by electrophysiological events and eye movements, we know now that each is formed by a highly organized cluster of autonomic, skeletomuscular, endocrine and, perhaps, cognitive events as well.

Table II summarizes the entire pattern of events specific to each state and stage. In the column labelled "endocrine events", we have chosen to include only that event with which we will deal exclusively in the text.

1. S-sleep

Generally speaking S-sleep can best be characterized as calm and stable. Sympathetic autonomic signs gradually decrease, reaching their lowest level during stage 4. Heart rate and respiratory rate gradually slow; body temperature and blood pressure are gradually lowered. Electromyographic (EMG) activity is also low; the skeletal muscles are hypotonic in stage 4. One of the more salient endocrine events to occur during stages 3 and 4 is the release of a hormone called human growth hormone (HGH), which is discussed later. HGH is also secreted during the day, but in response to specific events rather than in a cyclic fashion. With respect to perceptual events, the sleeper becomes progressively less responsive to the environment. By stage 4, the sleeper is very difficult to arouse, perhaps as resistant to arousal as he will be at any other time during sleep. When aroused, the person is disoriented, and rarely reports dreamlike mentation, although the individual may recall some thought-like cognitive content. And, as above, an EEG rhythm far slower than the waking rhythm is gradually established.

Taking into account the entire pattern of events depicted for S-sleep in Table II, the impression is that stages 1 and 2 are organized around the initial inhibition of waking function, while the second half of the stage – stages 3 and 4 – are organized around a function yet unknown, but lying at the heart of sleep. The attenuation of a person's cognitive, perceptual and behavioural transaction with the world, and of the systems necessary to support it, appears to be a pre-requisite to the rest of sleep (pun intended!). Of all the events of S-sleep, HGH release and perhaps the synchronous activity of SWS appear to be the most intimately related to the essential function of sleep.

2. D-sleep

With the introduction of D-sleep, the outward dance assumes a less placid tone. During D, as with S, there is a tonic background of lowered sympathetic activity. However, superimposed upon this are phasic disruptions such as

Table II The outward physiological manifestations of sleep, arranged by state, and by stages within the state of S-sleep

State	Stage	Scalp EEG events	Autonomic events	Skeletomotor events	Cognitive events	Endocrine event	Arousal threshold
S	1	low voltage desynchronized; some 4–6 Hz activity	heart rate and respiratory rate slowed; blood pressure and temperature lowered	restlessness at times; muscle tone beginning to fall	drifting thoughts		low
	2	12–14 Hz spindles; K-complexes	autonomic signs continue in same direction	restful; muscle tone continues to fall			somewhat higher
	3	at least 20% of record shows delta waves	autonomic signs continue in same direction	perhaps whole body movements; muscle tone continues to fall	if sleeper wakened, will report thoughts, not dreams; will be disoriented		somewhat higher
	4	at least 50% of record shows delta waves	autonomic signs slow and stable	large anti-gravity muscles hypotonic; peaceful and restful	same as above	human growth hormone secreted	quite high
D		low voltage, desynchronized; sawtooth waves	autonomic signs show phasic irregularities; penile and clitoral tumescence	virtual atonia of anti-gravity muscles tonically; phasic rapid eye movements (REMs); phasic muscle activity	if sleeper awakened, 60–90% of time dreams reported; will quickly reorient		quite high

cardiac acceleration, bursts of rapid breathing, penile and perhaps clitoral erections, and so forth. Skeletomuscular activity is similarly affected. The tonic background is virtually one of complete atonia (in contrast to the hypotonia of S). Even ungulates (single-hooved animals such as the horse) which manage to stand during S-sleep must recline during D because of the atonia. Superimposed upon the tonic muscle atonia are many phasic events, including body jerks and lateral darting of the eyes – rapid eye movements or REMs. These REMs have provided one of the synonyms for D-sleep, REM sleep; S-sleep at times is therefore called non-REM or NREM sleep. In the endocrine system, few significant changes have been noted. Some data suggest, however, that events at the molecular level slowly unfold during D-sleep, increasing in magnitude with each subsequent D-period. This is enlarged upon later.

An important departure from S in the cognitive or perceptual realm is that the person awakened from a D-period will be quite oriented, and report rich cognitive, perceptual and affective material. The person has been dreaming. Dreams occur predominantly if not exclusively during D. The presence of dreaming which occurs almost exclusively during this state may provide a clue to the function of sleep. Certainly dreaming was virtually the only aspect of sleep which caught the imagination of psychologists for many decades. We now can look at the dream within a larger context.

Finally, the arousal threshold for D is relatively high, almost as high as during the deepest portions of S-sleep. In other mammals, such as the cat and rat, Jouvet has found the arousal threshold to be distinctively higher during D than during S. The discrepancy between EEG phenomena, reminiscent of alert awakening, and the behavioural phenomena of D, were so striking that Jouvet was led to refer to this state of sleep as **paradoxical** sleep.

C. In Summary

S-sleep and D-sleep, the basic units of sleep, differ from each other along a number of specific dimensions; but a given state shows some rather surprisingly constant features within an individual from night to night, within a species, and even across mammalian species. Each state is characterized, not only by a unique set of electrophysiological phenomena, but also by a unique pattern of autonomic, skeletomuscular, endocrine and perceptual/cognitive events. The non-random organization of events across systems during each state of sleep, and the orderly but gradually shifting relationship between the two states, may provide clues to the function of sleep.

III. Biological Substrates of Sleep

With the peripheral physiological correlates to the overall behaviour we call sleep now unfolded, we move you forward from a descriptive era into an explanatory one. It is time to probe one step further beneath the surface to discover the systems of the brain involved in producing the peripheral events. We present the search for the biological substrates chronologically so that the reader can observe the process of discovery – and of "mis-discovery".

A. *The Work of the Mid-twentieth Century*

Between the end of the 1940s and the middle of the 1960s, much effort was directed toward uncovering the biological substrates of the electrophysiological signs of wakefulness. As discussed briefly earlier in this chapter, the landmark work of Moruzzi and Magoun in 1949 had re-energized research efforts by those who had for so long sought the neurophysiological basis of conscious life. Concerns about the biological substrates of sleep were left as mere fallout from the major enterprise.

What we are about to present is complex. Therefore, before we begin to fill in the details, we will mark out the general outline (Fig. 3a). In the mid-twentieth century the picture of sleep which emerged consisted of three components: (i) a component responsible for cortical desynchronization – presumably the electrophysiological correlate of waking vigilance; (ii) a second component responsible for cortical synchronization (or at least cortical recruiting responses, an EEG rhythm resembling the spindles of stage 2 sleep); and (iii) holding the two systems in dynamic balance was a third component which acted by holding the desynchronizing system at bay, thereby releasing the synchronizing system to exert its influence and sleep to ensue. In this conceptualization, release of the synchronizing system and behavioural sleep were considered as synonymous. This tripartite skeleton of the detailed discussion to follow is depicted in a highly schematic form in Fig. 3a. As we develop the details in the text, we shall correspondingly develop the details in successive panels of Fig. 3.

The area of the brain to which the function of cortical desynchronization was ascribed is a mass of tissue, reticulated or net-like in appearance, which surrounds the central canal of the brainstem along its entire length. As alluded to earlier, the landmark finding of Moruzzi and Magoun (1949) was that electrical stimulation of this reticulated mass, dubbed then and known today as the reticular formation (RF), resulted in cortical desynchronization. It was already known at that time that spontaneous alertness to the environment was associated with a desynchronized cortex. RF stimulation therefore

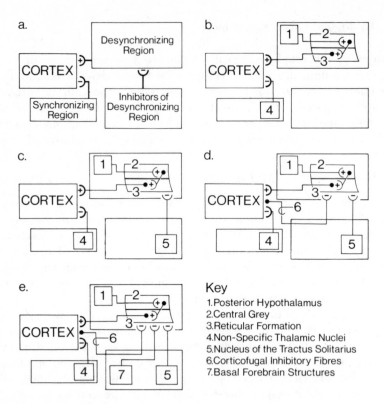

Fig. 3 *Highly schematic diagram of the organization of the sleep–wake system as it was understood through the mid-1960s. (a) General overview of the assumed major functional units of the system; (b) non-specific thalamic nuclei identified as the neural substrate of the synchronizing region; posterior hypothalamus-central grey-reticular formation complex identified as the neural substrate of the desynchronizing region; (c) – (e) the Nucleus of the Tractus Solitarius, corticofugal inhibitory fibres, and basal forebrain structures added successively; each believed to form a portion of the neural substrate of the functional unit of the system which inhibits the desynchronizing region, releasing the synchronizing region from inhibition.*

yielded a cortical rhythm known to be a correlate of environmental responsivity. Thus, the findings of Moruzzi and Magoun appeared at last to have actually uncovered the brain structure responsible for waking vigilance. However, it has never been clear which portion of the anatomically defined reticular formation, and/or which fibre tracts originating there, actually reach the cortex to influence it in so profound a way. Despite the electrophysiologically supported association between the reticular formation and waking arousal, anatomical support, which requires the finding of direct connections between that anatomically defined system and the cortex, could not be found. Subsequent investigators have therefore come to refer to the "reticular activating system" or RAS, rather than the reticular formation itself in its entirety, as the substrate of waking arousal. That is, they refer to a system of fibres and nuclei associated in some important way with the reticular formation.

While the reticular formation, or at least a hypothetical construct called the reticular activating system which is somehow related to it, seemed therefore critical to cortical desynchronization, it rapidly became evident that waking vigilance required the integrity not only of the RAS, but of something else in addition. It was already known that the RAS receives input from, and is activated by, the several sensory systems. But in addition a clue was taken from Von Economo, who had long ago recognized that encephalitis lethargica (sleeping sickness) was associated with damage to a part of the brain just rostral to the brainstem wherein the RF resides. The part of the brain under consideration is called the posterior hypothalamus. In 1965, Demetrescu *et al.* demonstrated in experimental animals that lesions restricted to the posterior hypothalamus produced tonic (i.e. constant) somnolence (or at least lack of waking vigilance). Only when a sensory stimulus was presented to animals with such damage was it possible to record desynchronization from the cortex. Even under those circumstances, cortical desynchronization was stimulus bound; that is, it began and ended with the sensory stimulation. But when we are awake, we are awake and responsive continuously. The RAS therefore, though obviously important to waking desynchronization, is not sufficient for it to occur. These data required that we differentiate between tonic and phasic (i.e. sporadic, time limited, discrete) arousal, conceptually and anatomically. It is now well established that in order for there to be sustained, tonic arousal, the RAS requires continuous input from the posterior hypothalamus. Figure 3b and subsequent panels of Fig. 3 depict schematically the entire route that appears to be involved between the activity of the posterior hypothalamus and desynchronization of the cortex. To get a sense of the anatomical picture in a less schematic form, envision the brain stem as the stem of a mushroom through the centre of which runs a central canal for carrying cerebrospinal fluid (CSF). Immediately surrounding the central canal, as would a concentric cylinder, is a thin layer of cells which cumulatively are called the central grey. Within the ventral portion of a cylinder effectively surrounding the central grey is the reticulated mass of the reticular formation. And the posterior hypothalamus: envision it as an accumulation of cell bodies sitting atop the brain stem. Putting it all together as we now understand it, the posterior hypothalamus communicates with the RAS via the cells of the central grey. The RAS drives cortical desynchronization, the central grey drives the RAS and the posterior hypothalamus drives the central grey. But what drives the posterior hypothalamus? The possibilities and theories are many, but the ultimate driving force giving rise to the phenomena of the waking brain remains unidentified.

We turn our attention now to cortical synchrony. If one region of the brain subserves cortical desynchrony, surely there must be a second separate area subserving synchrony? Weinberger *et al.* (1965) reported that low frequency stimulation of the non-specific thalamic nuclei created cortical synchrony, or at least the development of a cortical recruiting response, i.e. an increasingly larger number of cortical neurones being drawn into recurrent bursts of fairly rapid highly synchronous EEG activity, much like the spindles of stage 2. These thalamic nuclei are called non-specific nuclei because their activity is not specific to a particular sensory modality or motor event. A series of lesion studies demonstrated that fibres responsible for synchronizing the cortex ascended from these nuclei to influence the cortex directly. At the same time, high frequency stimulation of these same nuclei turned out to have a desynchronizing influence. However, this latter effect appeared to be mediated by another set of fibres, which were descending and exerted their influence via the RAS, secondarily activating it. The antagonistic systems therefore identified were the RAS, subserving desynchronization, and the non-specific thalamic nuclei – so-called pacemakers after the pacemakers in the heart – subserving synchronization.

With a synchronizing system and a desynchronizing system identified, the question then became: what mediated the supremacy of the one over the other at a given point in time? This translated into the question: what systems were responsible for inhibiting the RAS so that the thalamic nuclei could exert their effect? Implicit in the second question was the idea that the influence of the RAS would hold sway unless acted upon by another force. Interestingly this general principle seems to hold throughout the nervous system: structures involved in activating a function seem to dominate until actively inhibited.

Other discoveries in the early 1960s involved identification of areas in the lower brain stem which, when stimulated, inhibited the RAS and released the thalamic synchronizing system from inhibition. In Fig. 3c, we therefore add this piece. Prominent among these findings was the identification of the nucleus of the tractus solitarius in the lower brainstem as an important RAS inhibitor (Bonvallet and Allen, 1963). Seeming perhaps solitary to the anatomists who named it, it is a long narrow band of cell bodies lying parallel with and in close proximity to the caudal–dorsal axis of the lower portion of the reticular formation. We hasten to point out, as we begin to present many different anatomical sites, that knowing more of the anatomy involved in turn provides a better understanding of the topic under consideration. Of functional interest in this case is that the N. tractus solitarius receives its input from the vagus nerve. The vagus nerve carries information about blood pressure, gut distention, and other autonomic phenomena. Effectively, the greater the amount of pressure in the blood vessels, the gut, or the lung, the more likely the reticular activating system is to be inhibited, and cortical synchronization to be recorded. Perhaps this organization accounts in part for the sleepiness we all experience at the end of a large, belly-filling meal, or the relaxation we feel when we take a deep breath and distend the lungs.

In Fig. 3d a second posited source of RAS inhibition has been added. The notion in the early 1960s was of two possible roles of the cortex in bringing about its own inhibition. Demetrescu *et al.* (1965) advanced the idea that there existed an intermediary intracortical inhibitory network of neurones which would be activated by ascending diffuse influences. Bonvallet and Allen (1963), in a similar vein, advanced the notion that there existed cortico-fugal fibres also with the capacity to attenuate the activity of the RAS, and therefore with the capacity indirectly to attenuate cortical desynchrony. This notion arose from the earlier belief documented by French (1960) that there existed in the cortex "suppressor strips" from which arose corticofugal fibres of the sort described above. In both these cases the idea was that cortical activation tends to be maintained within adaptive limits, i.e. homeostatically controlled, by the process of negative feedback; if the cortex receives too much input from the RAS it can attenuate its own responsivity through a number of mechanisms. We summarize this proposed form of RAS inhibition in Fig. 3d with a single corticofugal pathway.

Finally, Clemente and Sterman (1963) and others identified yet another system which could inhibit the central core of the activating system and presumably release the synchronizing system from inhibition (Fig. 3e). This was the basal forebrain area, and included structures we now identify as the N. accumbens, the preoptic nucleus of the hypothalamus, the medial portion of the olfactory tubercle, and the amygdala. Stimulation of these structures induced, in animals, not simply an attenuation of waking EEG desynchronization but rather a very natural looking sleep. The sleep included most of the behavioural changes usually and naturally associated with readiness to sleep. Interestingly, Nauta and Domesick (1982) have demonstrated anatomically that there are tight reciprocal connections between the limbic system – with which the basal forebrain is intimately associated – and the potential for constant conversation among these systems and the RAS.

Let us consider some possible implications of this last set of connections. As we understand it, the limbic system plays a central role in emotion. Identification of the "basal forebrain–RAS connection" may help account for the everyday observation that some kinds of emotional experience are associated with increased sleep, and others with decreased sleep and even insomnia.

Perhaps the basal forebrain synchronizing area permits the production of sleep in response to some emotional states. And perhaps inhibition of these basal forebrain areas "cuts off" at least one avenue of RAS inhibition in response to other kinds of emotional situations, thus permitting wakefulness during the sleep period.

These were most of the pieces of the puzzle available in the first half of the sixties. Some ideas, such as the notion of corticofugal inhibitory fibres and intracortical inhibition, were simply never supported at all. However, most of the initial observations were verified; only the interpretation of those data has changed – the story is turning out to be considerably more complex than the final picture presented schematically in its full form in Fig. 3e. To summarize, the picture includes a central desynchronizing system, consisting of the posterior hypothalamus–central grey–RAS complex; a central thalamic synchronizing system; and a number of pathways which feed into the RAS with the capacity to inhibit it.

B. Evidence of the Mid-sixties

From this point on, advances in knowledge about sleep and arousal were rapid, particularly concerning the former. The earlier work was focused more upon the production and inhibition of arousal than directly on the production of sleep, with the Clemente and Sterman work probably being the most important exception.

Jouvet (1969) for example focused quite specifically upon sleep, and not simply on the inhibition of waking. He added two more anatomical elements to be considered in the larger picture of control systems responsible for the state of vigilance. These were (i) the raphe nuclei of the brain stem, which he believed to be directly involved in the production of sleep; and (ii) shifting attention from the RAS to some small oddly bluish nuclei each called the locus coeruleus (as in cerilean blue), he suggested another system which could account for cortical desynchronization: the cortical desynchronization of sleep. Jouvet also introduced a possible scheme for understanding the transition from wakefulness to S-sleep, and from S-sleep to D-sleep, which involved these two areas of the brain. It was also he who coined the now-popular term, discussed in the early portion of this chapter, "paradoxical sleep". Recall the apparent paradox that cortical desynchronization, previously believed to be associated uniquely with waking arousal and alertness, can co-exist with the behavioural state of very deep sleep.

The raphe (meaning crossed) nuclei lie along the entire lower and mid-brainstem, on the floor of the central canal. Removal of 90% of the area in cats resulted in permanent elimination of S-sleep and, because S-sleep seems a necessary prerequisite to D, elimination also of D-sleep. Coincident with the elimination of sleep, he found that these lesions virtually depleted the forebrain of a neurotransmitter called serotonin (or 5-hydroxytryptamine). Jouvet hypothesized that activation of these ascending raphe fibres, communicating with the cortex via the neurotransmitter serotonin, lay at the heart of the production of slow wave sleep. At last the cortical synchronization of waking was separated from the cortical synchronization of sleep.

Two important additional observations supported the synchronization component of Jouvet's hypothesis.

(i) Injections of a drug called parachlorophenylalanine (PCPA) in intact cats blocked the production of serotonin by interrupting the metabolic pathway which produces it (see Fig. 4). The injection *also* produced behavioural waking for as long as the compound was active in the system. To prove that this was not just a non-specific toxic effect of PCPA, 5-hydroxytryptophan was injected into PCPA treated cats. Serotonin is produced from the dietary amino acid precursor called tryptophan. The first step in the metabolic pathway is the conversion of tryptophan into a compound called 5-hydroxytryptophan. The PCPA prevented this step. Injection of 5-hydroxytryptophan therefore picked up the metabolic pathway on the other side of the block. It also permitted sleep to occur in these cats once more. Corroborating these results in humans, there are some indications (e.g. Hartmann, 1977) that orally ingested tryptophan produces sleep in at least some individuals. This is a particularly useful finding for insomniacs who prefer not to use central nervous system depressants as sleep aids. As above, tryptophan is the dietary precursor of serotonin. It has the advantage of being orally ingestable, and being able to cross the blood brain barrier so that serotonin can be produced from it once it has been ingested.

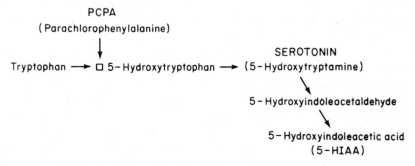

Fig. 4 *Anabolic (synthetic) and catabolic (breakdown) pathway for serotonin. The enzymes necessary to catalyse the successive transformations from tryptophan to serotonin, and from serotonin to 5-HIAA, are not shown. Parachlorophenylalanine (PCPA) is shown to be a blocker of the tryptophan to 5-hydroxytryptophan conversion. See text for more complete description.*

(ii) Histofluorescent techniques, which permit some neurotransmitters actually to be visualized under a special kind of microscope, have demonstrated that the raphe nucleus comprises the cells of origin of virtually the entire ascending serotonin system (Dahlstrom and Fuxe, 1964). Of particular importance was the ability to demonstrate that these fibres do indeed reach the cortex. It was an enormous realization to recognize that nuclei in the brainstem as small and almost as inconspicuous as the raphe nuclei could have the apparent ability to influence the activity of the entire neocortex in a manner as global and pervasive as what happens during sleep.

The work on the desynchronizing RAS and the synchronizing thalamic nuclei was perhaps a blind alley in uncovering the biological substrates of sleep. Realizing this, let us continue to shift our focus more squarely onto the electrophysiological signs of sleep. We continue with Jouvet's formulation of how desynchronization during D-sleep is generated.

Jouvet found that lesions of the locus coeruleus – nuclei also lying just outside the classically defined reticular formation – disturbed what he called paradoxical sleep, but *did not* disturb what he called slow wave sleep (SWS). In fact, not only did these lesions prevent the occurrence of paradoxical sleep's cortical desynchronization, but he also observed them to release from inhibition the muscular atonia of D-sleep as well as to cause the PGO spikes usually seen during D-sleep to begin occurring during S-sleep.

The histofluorescence technique revealed that fibres arising from the locus coeruleus terminated massively on the neocortex, as well as on other cortical and subcortical structures; and that the neurotransmitter secreted by the axons was noradrenaline (Dahlstrom and Fuxe, 1964). Indeed, it was discovered that virtually all the noradrenaline secreted by the brain arose from the cells of this exceedingly small pair of nuclei, and was released by the proliferation of axons arising from it. Once again, a small part of the brain capable of the kind of profound and global effect on the cortex that one would have to account for in a discussion of sleep had been identified.

Finally, Jouvet posed the question: what underlies the orderly alternation of S-sleep with D-sleep (or SWS with paradoxical sleep). He postulated that, as SWS progressed, there would be a natural build-up of a compound called 5-HIAA, the catabolic by-product of the serotonin progressively released throughout S-sleep. This 5-HIAA might eventually reach a critical level and somehow trigger the activity of the locus coeruleus. Based upon other experiments too detailed for the scope of this chapter, he actually postulated that 5-HIAA in association with acetylcholine released from elsewhere would trigger the activity of the locus coeruleus and D-sleep.

By the end of the 1960s therefore there were many more pieces of the puzzle. From the waking point of view, the RAS was believed to be central in waking arousal, and the thalamic nuclei were believed to be important in waking cortical synchrony. On the sleeping end, there are the raphe nuclei which appear to be the core system involved in cortical synchrony during sleep, and the basal forebrain/limbic system which can trigger the activity of the raphe system, perhaps in response to an emotional need for sleep. With more pieces being added to the puzzle, the semblance of a hierarchical system controlling sleep begins to emerge. The raphe–locus coeruleus system perhaps represents the basic sleep system, and higher structures which converge on these may represent the capacity for sleep to be produced on the basis of important contingencies. Just as one general principle of brain activity is that structures remain active unless acted upon by an inhibitory force, hierarchical control over basic biological functions, such as eating and sleeping, represents another general principle. We eat because of a nutritional need of the body; but we also become hungry and eat *in anticipation* of needing food – higher needs influencing lower ones. Similarly, we presumably always sleep in response to information about the presence of a biological sleep need (whatever that is!), but tend also to sleep when the world is too much with us; that is, *in anticipation* of needing sleep.

Let us diverge a moment now from our story to consider a piece we slipped, probably unnoticed, into the puzzle box collection. Because of its implications for modern-day thinking about brain function, it is important the piece be noted explicitly.

Through the mid-sixties, the thinking focused almost exclusively upon anatomical circuitry as revealed by histological techniques such as lesion-degeneration techniques. For convenience, we shall call these "anatomical techniques". In this context, the concern was with identifying the several structures and their interconnections which were important to the sleep–wakefulness and synchrony–desynchrony continua. The work of Jouvet (among others) in its concern with neurotransmitters, shifted the focus onto pathways in the brain as revealed by neurochemical histological methods; that is, onto chemical pathways in the brain. Chemical pathways are indeed anatomically identifiable fibre tracts; but, in addition, they have particular neurotransmitters at their synapses in common. A large fibre tract identifiable by "anatomical" techniques can, upon close inspection, be seen to be made up of a number of discrete chemical pathways. The medial forebrain bundle for instance, which is an "anatomically" identifiable fibre tract, is made up of the serotonergic chemical pathway originating in the raphe nuclei, as well as of separate noradrenaline and dopamine chemical pathways. New histological techniques, like the histofluorescence technique described above, showed the chemical pathway to be the critical unit of analysis, rather than the larger "anatomically" defined pathway of which it might be a part. That is, the several chemical pathways within a larger anatomically defined pathway may together converge upon a single target structure in the brain.

However, to understand how that target structure is affected by activity in the anatomically defined tract, one must know which of the chemical pathways within the tract is activated. It is the neurotransmitter released onto the target structure which ultimately determines how the target structure will be affected at a particular moment in time. In this regard, activity within the serotonergic raphe efferents, not generally within the medial forebrain bundle, seemed critical for the development of slow wave sleep.

Jouvet's work marked the beginnings of the new era of neurochemistry – an era which has been flourishing ever since. This past decade has seen the discovery of around 200 peptides and polypeptides in the brain. These are biochemicals built up of the basic amino acids from which the classical neurotransmitters are derived; biochemicals some small portion of which have already been implicated as functional neurotransmitters. The full implications of this important new dimension are just beginning to be appreciated. Although intimately involved with sleep, especially as it relates to psychiatric disorders, further discussion of neurochemicals is well beyond the scope of the immediate chapter. The reader interested in pursuing the topic is encouraged to consult Chapter 5 by Van Toller and the works cited in the general reference section at the end of this chapter. But let us now return to the Jouvet story and the emerging picture of the biological substrates of sleep.

Despite the compelling nature of the evolving picture, there are some difficulties with Jouvet's formulation. With respect to the raphe-serotonin portion of the hypothesized organization: (i) Although destruction of the raphe nuclei creates permanent arousal in cats, electrical stimulation of the raphe nuclei also interrupts ongoing sleep and produces behavioural arousal. Though there are a number of ways in which these conflicting data can be reconciled, the necessary research combining both procedures is not available; (ii) Although the histofluorescence technique revealed serotonergic raphe fibres terminating at the neocortex, the density of such terminals was quite small. It was difficult to believe that this apparently scant innervation could account for the major EEG changes seen during sleep; and (iii) as above, raphe fibres travel to the cortex via the medial forebrain bundle in association with noradrenergic fibres originating from the locus coeruleus, and with dopaminergic fibres. Section of either the raphe nucleus or of the fibres arising from the raphe, which travel in the medial forebrain bundle, depletes the forebrain of serotonin. As stated above, the section of the raphe nuclei also creates persistent arousal, whereas section of the medial forebrain bundle does not. Interruption of the route from the raphe nuclei to the cortex *fails* to disrupt sleep. This would appear to disqualify the ascending raphe fibres as the instigators of sleeping synchrony.

With respect to the locus coeruleus portion of the hypothesized organization, the ascending noradrenaline fibres from the locus coeruleus to the cortex have now been implicated in *waking* arousal. Indeed, it is no longer clear if it is the RAS, or if it is the ascending noradrenaline fibres from the locus coeruleus which underlies waking arousal (see Warburton on mechanisms underlying learning; Chapter 7). While a direct connection between the fibres of the reticular formation and the neocortex has never been observed, histofluorescence techniques have clearly indicated anatomical connections between the noradrenergic locus coeruleus fibres and the neocortex. The evidence for these noradrenergic fibres subserving waking desynchronization is compelling. Amphetamine ("speed") has the effect of increasing the amount of noradrenaline at the synapses in the brain and also has the effect of producing profound wakefulness and cortical desynchronization.

It is possible that the noradrenaline fibres of the locus coeruleus subserve only the cortical signs of D-sleep. These are quite similar to the cortical EEG signs of waking arousal. That would in part be consistent with Jouvet's hypothesis. Were that the case, one would then have to seek other systems – systems yet to be identified – which would subserve the remaining signs of D-sleep, and influence the *type* of information which is processed during that state. Again, answers are far from clear.

By the end of the 1960s, we were left with a picture assembled from many more puzzle pieces than were available earlier in the decade; but the picture was a lot less clear. It became apparent that there must be many other pieces of the puzzle yet to be discovered, before a coherent picture could be confidently created once again.

C. *The Current State of the Art*

In some respects, all we have to go on in our continuing search for the biological substrates of sleep are (i) the model available to us from other systems which control biological functions; (ii) the observable phenomena of sleep; and (iii) the clear sense that *something* about the raphe system and *something* about the locus coeruleus system are central to sleep. It would be unwise to try to present the reader with a picture assembled out of the known pieces of information. We would, in effect, be attempting to make a complete picture without even knowing if we had all the pieces of the jigsaw puzzle (i.e. all relevant data); and without having the to-be-completed picture on top of the puzzle box to guide us (i.e. without knowing what the function of sleep is).

We therefore begin this section by expanding on the information already known: we will begin by discussing the new findings about the raphe system.

1. *The raphe system: a finger in every pot*

If there is indeed a central system with major control over production of sleep, is it the raphe system? New facts about the raphe system have come to light in the late 1970s and early 1980s which deal with some of the problems described above. They strongly support the theory that the raphe system plays a central role in the initiation and perhaps maintenance of sleep.

Using a new histological technique more sensitive than histofluorescence, there have been discovered massive inputs to the cortex from the raphe nuclei. The new technique is called radioimmunochemistry and essentially, involves the injection of radioactively labelled antibody, to an enzyme associated with the metabolism of the neurotransmitter in question – in this case serotonin. Stained tissue is then evaluated for the presence of the antibody-antigen complex, which shows up as areas of radioactivity. The input to the cortex from the raphe nuclei has been found by this method to be so massive that it is now believed that serotonergic raphe fibres actually contact every single cell of every layer of the neocortex (Lidov et al., 1980). This finding lends far more credence to the hypothesis that the small raphe nuclei have the kind of pervasive global organized influence on the neocortex that would be necessary to initiate and maintain sleep. These findings resolve one of the problems presented earlier.

The second important problem was that section of the medial forebrain bundle, while causing depletion of forebrain serotonin, did not interfere with sleep. Were the medial forebrain bundle the only connection between the raphe nuclei and the cortex, it would be difficult to continue to believe that sleep production is dependent upon the raphe system. However, these same immunohistochemical studies (Lidov et al., 1980) have identified a second route between the raphe nuclei and the neocortex. It is highly possible that the role of the raphe system in sleep depends upon this second, newly discovered pathway. This remains to be evaluated.

Other structures receiving the rapidly diverging input from the raphe nuclei include limbic structures, such as the cingulate cortex, the hippocampus, the septum and the hypothalamus. These limbic structures appear to have some involvement with emotion, but also involvement with memory functions. The raphe also distributes to extra-pyramidal structures such as the substantia nigra and the striatum (caudate nucleus and globus pallidus). These structures are believed to have some involvement in motivated locomotion. There is also output from the raphe nuclei to portions of the thalamus.

Thus, serotonergic fibres arising from a relatively circumscribed area of the brainstem appear to have a widespread influence on large parts of the brain. The influence seems generally to be an inhibitory one. But how many of these projections somehow permit the raphe to fulfill its putative sleep-inducing role; and how many of these serve quite a different purpose? In the future these new findings may provide the key to understanding why sleep dysfunctions, such as hypersomnia or insomnia, frequently occur with affective or thought disorders. Like sleep these disorders have a global impact on a person, affecting cognition, "affective state" and even locomotion; and it is also believed that at least some of these disorders, such as depression, involve a dysfunction of the serotonin system.

2. *The suprachiasmatic nucleus: one of the pots*

Perched atop the optic chiasm, at the lower border of the hypothalamus, is a small nucleus in rather a propitious position. It receives input from the retina, and maintains a substantial bi-directional anatomical relationship with the serotonergic raphe cells. A lesion to this nucleus in rats selectively disrupts the diurnal cycles of two hormones, ACTH and melatonin (Moore and Eichler, 1972), and slow wave sleep (Yamaoka, 1978). The ACTH cycle and the melatonin cycles are usually entrained to the light–dark cycle; that is peaks and troughs of ACTH and melatonin secretion are closely related to the rise and fall of the sun. Presumably, the retinal input to the suprachiasmatic nucleus would permit this nucleus to entrain body rhythms to the light–dark cycle. Reciprocal connections between the raphe and the suprachiasmatic nucleus would permit synchronization between the light–dark cycle and the sleep–wake cycle.

3. *The locus coeruleus: any more evidence about its association with D-sleep?*

While it still seems likely that there is a relationship between the raphe nuclei and S-sleep, the evidence for the contribution of noradrenergic locus co-eruleus fibres to D-sleep is becoming less convincing. Single unit recordings from the locus coeruleus indicate a *decrease* in the rate of firing with the onset of D-sleep. In fact it has even been suggested that output from the locus coeruleus inhibits D-sleep, and that the decrease in activity of these cells permits D-sleep to develop. Nor have lesion studies upheld the role of the locus coeruleus in D-sleep.

It has been learned (Morgane, 1972) that fibres from the ventromedial portion of the locus coeruleus synapse upon the raphe, implying perhaps some role for the locus coeruleus in sleep (perhaps inhibiting the activity of the raphe nuclei to permit, rather than cause, the beginning of D-sleep). Fibres from the dorsolateral portion of the locus coeruleus ascend in the medial forebrain bundle to the cerebral cortex and other telencephalic sites; to the colliculi and geniculates, indicating some kind of relationship perhaps with visual and auditory sensory systems; and to the cerebellar cortex (Morgane, 1972). Interestingly one of the nuclei of the cerebellum, the fastigial nucleus, appears to play a role in sleep induction.

Overall, however, very little is understood about the direct role which the locus coeruleus might play in the production of sleep.

4. The FTG system: an alternative to the locus coeruleus?

Lying just lateral to the locus coeruleus are a group of giant cells, cumulatively called the magnocellular region of the reticular formation, or the gigantocellular tegmental fields (FTG system). Lesions to this area selectively eliminate D-sleep, decrease PGO spikes to 15% of their normal frequency, and eliminate the muscle atonia which would have been associated with D-sleep. The same lesion induces adipsia (elimination of drinking behaviour), aphagia (elimination of feeding behaviour), impaired motor function, elimination of lateral eye movements, and impairment of urinary retention. The lesions also reduce stage 2 of sleep to 60% of normal (Jones, 1979). Another interesting observation is that D-sleep and stage 2 sleep are selectively increased in length in a group of persons, studied by Hartmann, who customarily require 10 or more hours of sleep at night. This is discussed in more detail in the final section of this chapter.

There exist distinct ascending and descending paths interconnecting giant reticular cells and the locus coeruleus. It is possible that Jouvet's lesions inadvertently damaged the underlying FTG cells. It is also possible, as is suggested by Hobson *et al.* (1975), that the interaction between the FTG system and the locus coeruleus is responsible for sleep.

From a functional point of view, it is worthy of note that a single lesion to the FTG system can at once influence many of the systems that play a role in sleep, especially systems which control lateral eye movements (which normally occur as REMs during D-sleep) and urinary retention (an event which in general also occurs during sleep).

5. A few more tidbits

There are many other bits and pieces to the sleep story, two of which we will present below.

(i) Lesions to the septal region in the rat result in increased D-time while not affecting S-sleep at all (Yamaoka, 1978). The septum appears to be the pacemaker for the hippocampus, a structure which receives input from noradrenergic locus coeruleus fibres as well as from serotonergic raphe fibres, and which seems to have an inhibitory influence on the reticular formation. Lesions to the medial basal hypothalamus disturb the entire rhythm of sleep. And lesions to the suprachiasmatic nucleus seem preferentially to disturb the slow wave sleep cycle. Thus it would appear that these limbic and hypothalamic structures also participate in the organization of sleep.

(ii) Sleep spindles are one of the prominent events of stage 2 sleep. They are recorded in the somatosensory cortex, and are eliminated by lesions which leave SWS intact. This would imply that portions of the brain which produce the EEG rhythm, characteristic of stages 3 and 4 of sleep, are separable from the portion of the brain which produce this phasic phenomenon of stage 2. The lesions which selectively eliminate sleep spindles are in two nuclear groups of the thalamus: the ventrobasal complex and the ventrolateral complex (Steriade *et al.,* 1971). These areas are involved with sensation from the body.

6. *What's it all about?*

How do we begin to assemble all these pieces? The answer is: with great difficulty. Perhaps a quotation from Peter Morgane is appropriate here: "The behavioural and EEG phenomena comprising the sleep states must involve neural integration at many levels in the brain stem" (Morgane, 1972); to which we might add, "and additionally in the diencephalon, limbic system and striatum." Not surprisingly for a phenomenon which affects virtually all systems of the organism for lengthy periods of time, large portions of the brain are implicated in the control of sleep. In the absence of knowing the function of sleep, we are lacking an organizing focus around which to arrange all the data which have been collected. So we conclude this section of the chapter with a model – taken from other functional systems – which might help the enterprising reader to assimilate all the information about biological substrates:

(i) One set of lower motor neurones controls the chewing motions of the mouth; another the secretion of gastric acid; and yet another the peristaltic activity of the gastrointestinal tract. In like manner, we would assume that, for each separate activity which occurs during sleep, there must inevitably be a set of neurones with immediate control over it.

(ii) What is interesting about feeding behaviour is the *coordination* of many different systems around the central goal of eating and providing nutrition to the body when the body needs it. Similarly, sleep is a sequence of phases consisting of a patterning of systems. In feeding, hypothalamic nuclei such as the ventromedial and lateral nuclei appear to organize much of the patterning around feeding behaviour. Thus we would expect to find a similar system in the brain responsible for the implementation of sleep, which would have the capacity to produce a similar coordination across systems during sleep.

(iii) Movements toward initiating feeding appear to be dependent upon the absence of output from a so-called satiation or anti-hunger system. In seeking biological substrates for sleep, the tendency has been to seek structures or systems which actively antagonize waking – the so-called "anti-waking" centres or systems; and, quite separately, to seek structures or systems which actively promote sleeping. It remains unclear whether separate anti-waking and "pro-sleep" centres, or systems, exist or if both functions might pertain to the same system.

(iv) Although there does not seem to be a homologue in the feeding system, it is important to point out here that we need not only to understand the neural mechanisms which cause sleep to be initiated, but we must also understand the mechanisms responsible for movement back and forth between S and D within sleep, and among stages 1 and 4 within S-sleep. Such a system would have to account for the basal entrainment of the sleep–wake cycle to the light–dark cycle as well, an issue considered in detail in the new field of chronobiology.

(v) Finally, we need to consider decision making in the brain. In response to what eventualities is sleep initiated and terminated? What kind of information must the sleep-controlling regions of the brain receive in order that their activity be affected? If sleep is like other consummatory behaviours, such as feeding, we would expect first of all for there to be feedback systems from target organs to maintain homeostatic levels of "sleep" as a function of whatever sleep is providing; as a function of the here-and-now needs of the body. With respect to feeding, according to the glucostatic hypothesis, there exists an optimal level of blood glucose. Information about blood glucose is fed to the ventromedial hypothalamus. Low levels, which should be associated with a nutrition need-state of the body, are associated with a failure to activate the ventromedial hypothalamus. In turn, the ventromedial hypothalamus is prevented from inhibiting the activity of the lateral hypothalamus. The lateral hypothalamus, released from inhibition, then appears to be active in the initiation of feeding. We still do not know the whole story with respect to the feeding system. But at present, we know even less of the story vis-à-vis the sleep system. Again, we are not quite sure what kind of information we are speaking of when we refer to information about a sleep need. Nonetheless, were we to discover the function of sleep, i.e. what is accomplished by sleeping, we might imagine such a closed-loop negative feedback system organized at the level of the hypothalamus to be operative, maintaining a homeostatic level of whatever it is that sleep accomplishes.

(vi) Along the same lines, the body does not always regulate functions in response to the here-and-now needs of the body. People can have the experience of hunger even when their here-and-now nutritional state does not seem to justify the feeling. Similarly, people become extremely sleepy even when, one might assume, the here-and-now situation did not seem to justify it. Clearly, sleep is not always entrained to the day–night cycle. Despite the uncanny regularity of the structure of sleep from person to person and across species, deviations can and do occur. The delicate balance between wakefulness and sleep can be shifted in favour of vigilance in response to an anticipated need to be aware of the environment. Some insomnia – difficulty initiating or maintaining sleep – occurs in the presence of anxiety. Anxiety can be well understood as the need to remain vigilant in the presence of an anticipated threat at the temporary expense of sleep.

Clearly all of this would suggest that there must exist higher order systems which, on the basis of anticipated need, or some other kind of not-strictly-physiological need, can influence and override the systems which would tend to regulate sleep according to a diurnal rhythm. The limbic system, and the limbic forebrain (also called the basal forebrain area) would seem to be prominent candidates. Both systems process "psychological" information, and both have direct access to the raphe system as well as to the brainstem systems concerned with behavioural arousal.

IV. The Function of Sleep

It should be abundantly clear to the reader by now that – while a great deal is known about the outward manifestations of sleep, and that while a fair amount is known about the neuroanatomy and neurochemistry responsible for these outward signs – we are very much in a quandry about what function is served by the events of sleep described in such detail.

We are reasonably certain that there is a biological need for sleep, but in truth we have no proof even of that. Virtually all methods which attempt to prove that sleep is necessary in order that life continue have flaws. For example, in animal research it has been the custom to prevent sleep by forcing the animal to walk a treadmill by shocking it if it stops; or requiring that it swim continuously. Yet it is unclear whether the death which ultimately results arises from the absence of sleep, or from the presence of the chronic stressors.

Despite the common-sense notion that sleep is necessary for bodily re-cuperation, we are even less sure of what the function of sleep might be. Methodologically, deriving the function of sleep is even more complex than deriving proof that sleep must occur for life to continue. A major problem is that the hallmark of sleep is the occurrence of survival-related events *within* the individual. Thus, to know truly the significance of the outward manifestations of sleep, we must therefore look within. Ironically, the problem of identifying the function of sleep is made particularly difficult *because* the critical events occur inside. Much in contrast to inquiry into the function of various waking events, there is little in the way of overt behaviour or verbal report to provide direction.

One approach used by sleep research is to evaluate the waking behaviour of sleep-deprived individuals. By observing the kinds of waking phenomena which are disrupted in the absence of part or all of sleep, one can then logically infer what function might have been served had that portion of sleep been permitted to occur. Although apparently sound, the strategy has clear limitations. Should the investigator care to know specifically the effects of SWS deprivation, for instance, it will be found that SWS deprivation also interferes with D. Similarly, because events at night are cyclic, selective deprivation of D is bound to disturb whatever goes on during S. Just as with the strategy of brain lesions, wherein a lesion disrupts not only the structure at which it was aimed but also the entire system of which the structure is a part, it is extremely difficult to disrupt one part of sleep without disrupting another. Should the investigator care to look at the effects of total sleep deprivation, data are still difficult to interpret. The effects of generalized stress resulting from the deprivation are difficult to separate from the more specific effects of sleep deprivation.

A strategy convergent with the sleep deprivation approach is to reason inductively from the outer manifestations of sleep to what the critical inner events must be. The resultant hypotheses can then be evaluated with the help of techniques such as sleep deprivation in humans and animals; and selective brain lesion in the case of animal research.

A. S-sleep: What's it all about?

1. K-complexes: a stage 2 event

During stage 2, one of the characteristic occurrences is the appearance of K-complexes. These appear with varying frequency from individual to individual, and in some individuals not at all. They are understood to be evoked potentials, occurring either in response to specific exteroceptive stimulation or spontaneously. The "spontaneous" K-complexes are believed to be responses to covert internal stimuli.

K-complexes are in some respects different from evoked potentials. The latter habituate rapidly to a monotonously repeated stimulus, while K-complexes do not (Church et al., 1978). The significance of this difference is unknown. Although the K-complex would therefore appear to be the outer manifestation of cortical responsiveness to sensory stimulation, it is unclear whether the K-complex reflects that the responsible stimulus has alerted the sleeping brain, or that the stimulus has been refused entry to higher level processing.

Data which support the view that the person may have been alerted at the time that the K-complex appears include the observations that K-complexes precede most body movements during stage 2 (although they are not invariably followed by body movements) (Sassin and Johnson, 1968); that the K-complex occurs in association with sympathetically mediated autonomic signs, such as an increased number of spontaneous skin potentials and decreased electrodermal resistance (Johnson and Karpan, 1968); and they occur during stage 2, one of the lightest states of sleep.

Observations more consistent with the possibility that K-complexes are in response to stimuli that failed to reach higher levels of processing include the fact that the individual generally does *not* awaken; and that the changes in heart rate associated with the K-complex – a biphasic cardiac acceleration–cardiac deceleration pattern – are opposite in direction to what one would expect from the waking individual alerted by a stimulus. Cardiac deceleration followed by cardiac acceleration is the pattern observed in the waking individual orienting to a novel stimulus (Graham and Clifton, 1966).

Future research must decide if the K-complex reflects gating out of sensory input, or if it is the outer manifestation of sensory information being permitted in. Whichever the case, however, the existence of the K-complex during stage 2 makes clear that sensory input is available to the cortex, and therefore has the potential of being processed further. Stage 2 would appear to be a recurrent choice point in sleep. Alternating with D-sleep even after the remainder of S has dropped out, stage 2 presents the sleeper with the opportunity to withdraw from sleep in response to potentially important stimuli, but to be protected against the intrusion of stimuli which are not particularly important.

The threshold below which stimuli are treated as unimportant and above which they are treated as important, is probably quite individual. In this regard in one form of insomnia, called "difficulty in maintaining sleep", sleep is fragmented. The person falls asleep, but then awakens at intervals through the night. The need for high level vigilance possibly interferes with the need to sleep. The events of stage 2 would appear to be biased toward permitting virtually any stimulus available to the system to be processed fully; and away from extruding stimulus input from awareness.

It will be interesting to determine if the differences in the number of K-complexes across individuals differentiate between sound sleepers and those with this form of sleep disruption. A positive result would yield information about the kind of central process reflected by the K-complex, and perhaps about the mechanisms involved in protecting sleep from the intrusion of external stimulation.

2. *Delta waves and human growth hormone: stages 3 and 4 of S-sleep*

For what ultimate purpose is sleep being protected? While an understanding of the events of stage 2 may reveal a great deal about the gating of sensory information, the stage 2 phenomena seem not to have yielded information about the ultimate purpose of sleep itself. More seems to have been learned from the events of stages 3 and 4 in this regard.

One of the more singular events which occurs during stages 3 and 4 is the secretion of human growth hormone (HGH). HGH is released by the anterior pituitary gland into the blood stream in response to growth hormone releasing factor (GRF) from the ventromedial hypothalamus (VMH) (the VMH is a nucleus believed to be important for the termination of feeding behaviour). The ventromedial hypothalamus is stimulated to produce the releasing factor in response to alpha adrenergic agonists, such as noradrenaline and dopamine in the human; and inhibited from doing so by beta adrenergic agonists. As we have seen the major sources of noradrenaline in the brain are the neurones of the locus coeruleus. As described earlier, we are now beginning to believe that an area of the brain adjacent to the locus coeruleus, called the FTG system, is most central to some D phenomena (Hobson et al., 1974). The fact that noradrenaline potentiates the production of HGH, and that HGH production occurs during SWS, would suggest that the locus coeruleus becomes active either at the end of a D-period in preparation for the next S-period; or that it is actively releasing noradrenaline during SWS.

The effect of HGH is to promote protein synthesis via gene activation (Ganong, 1975). Its actions are mediated by compounds called somatomedins, believed to be produced as a result of HGH action in the liver. The hormone is called growth hormone because, by facilitating protein synthesis, it promotes growth and tissue repair.

The release of HGH is inhibited during D-periods, and decreases with deprivation of stages 3 and 4 (Sassin et al., 1969). Thus, HGH secretion clearly seems to be a SWS phenomenon. HGH secretion as a prominent SWS event is consistent with the commonsense hypothesis that sleep is a time of bodily recuperation. Additional hard data to support the hypothesis, however, are equivocal.

The amount of SWS, and therefore possibly the rate of HGH secretion, are slightly but significantly greater for athletes than for non-athletes (Baekland and Lasky, 1966). These data would support the bodily recuperation hypothesis. Yet, a study carried out on Navy corpsmen found no difference in rate of HGH secretion after days of no exercise, of light exercise, or of moderate exercise (Zir et al., 1971). If HGH secretion is related to exercise at all, it is apparently reflected over time, not on a day-to-day basis. Other studies, such as that of Horne (1978), have produced similar negative results.

Independent of a potential role of S-sleep in general growth and repair of body tissue, the secretion of HGH is consistent with a second possible role of sleep. HGH, which facilitates the production of protein, can potentially have an effect on the nervous system. The enzymes involved in the elaboration of neurotransmitters (as well as other enzymes), and most probably also the post-synaptic receptors of neurones, are elaborated from a protein substrate.

Following total sleep deprivation, a number of changes occur which would be consistent with an actual structural alteration of neural tissue in at least some parts of the brain (Horne, 1978). There are psychological changes, which include irritability, a decreasing ability to be vigilant during monotonous tasks such as signal detection, and occasionally depression. Visual anomalies occur, such as difficulties with visual accommodation and binocular convergence (Sassin, 1970) ("I'm so tired that I can't see straight!"); and distortions of visual perception, including hallucinations in some people. It is difficult to know if the latter is more properly understood as a psychological change or as a primary change in the visual system, or an interaction between the two. Since visual hallucinations are not constant features of total sleep deprivation, it is possible that they arise from a combination of psychological predisposition and alterations in visual perception. Finally, there is a distortion of the waking EEG, with the alpha waves less prominent than usual (Naitoh et al., 1969). It is therefore at least possible that one role of SWS is the maintenance of critical parts of the nervous system.

Another piece of data from total sleep deprivation studies is significant. Early during recovery from this kind of deprivation, the person spends an extended amount of time in stage 4 – a so-called stage 4 rebound. Further into the recovery period, there is a similar expansion of D-time, or REM, known in the literature as a REM rebound. Hence, during both recovery from total sleep deprivation and during normal sleep, SWS always precedes D. One gets the impression that "SWS prior to D" in both these situations is a necessary relationship, in fact suggestive of the possibility that certain events of SWS are causally linked to the phenomena of D.

B. *D-sleep: does it subsume the ultimate function of sleep?*

Most of the theories about the function of sleep have focused on the function of D. We present below a sample of two such hypotheses. Both are consistent with the idea that the HGH secretion of SWS results in the production of protein which becomes important during the D-periods.

One of the provocative observations about the relationship of HGH secretion to D-sleep is that HGH production is increased following deprivation of D. Normally, HGH production is inhibited during D. The impression is that an event normally occurring during D-periods actively inhibits the release of HGH. With D absent, HGH secretion is disinhibited. Beta adrenergic agonists, such as adrenaline (and noradrenaline to a lesser extent) are known to inhibit HGH production. Noradrenaline is a powerful alpha adrenergic agonist, but is believed also to have weak beta adrenergic properties. We do not yet know how to integrate this information into the above discussion.

Repair and maintenance of the noradrenergic systems form the basis of a hypothesis developed by Hartmann, about the function of D-sleep (Hartmann, 1973). In one series of studies he looked at naturally long and naturally short sleepers (Hartmann et al., 1972). He found that the most important difference in the sleep of the two groups was that the long sleepers spent far more time in D and stage 2 than did the short sleepers. He discovered that these long sleepers differed from the short sleepers in personality also. The long sleepers tended to be worried people, people for whom the world was not a straightforward place. They were people who had the need, to use his term, constantly to "reprogramme" themselves. In contrast, short sleepers with lesser D-times tended to have vocations which were largely physical, and found the world far more of a straightforward place. Hartmann reasoned that the increased reprogramming that the long sleepers seemed to do, and the increased D-time, might be related.

Hartmann hypothesized that D-time is a time during which the neural circuits involved in relating to the world are repaired and reprogrammed. We add the possibility that D-time may be a time when the enzymes necessary to produce neurotransmitters are replenished. Hartmann pointed specifically to the repair of noradrenaline pathways as the work of D-sleep. The central idea of his hypothesis is that during waking noradrenaline pathways are particularly responsive to stressful situations, and that they would therefore be called upon in proportion to the amount of psychological stress and need for reprogramming encountered by the individual during the day. The function of D-sleep, and perhaps of the entire night of sleep, is understood to have been accomplished when these pathways are "ready for another day". Amphetamines act to increase the amount of noradrenaline at the synapse, and also to produce wakefulness. By certain standards, the person awakens "too soon". According to the "noradrenaline system maintenance hypothesis," the noradrenaline artificially induced by amphetamine simply has short circuited the sleep process by supplying inappropriate feedback.

A second hypothesis about the function of D-sleep would also include the production of protein (e.g. Tilley and Empson, 1978). In its general form, the hypothesis suggests that D-sleep has a central role in the consolidation of memory. The secretion of HGH-protein is relevant here, because it has come to be believed that long term memory at a molecular level involves the elaboration of new protein, mediated by heightened RNA activity. The type of protein involvement is unknown, but may have to do with the elaboration of enzymes important to an increase or decrease in the production of neurotransmitters in selected pathways of the brain; or it may have to do with changes in the structure of post-synaptic receptors at specified synapses.

More data are needed before definitive answers can be presented. What is salient here is that memory consolidation appears somehow to involve the elaboration of protein, and that HGH promotes protein production.

Consistent with this hypothesis is the observation that most people have the impression that information incompletely processed before bedtime seems to have completed its processing by the time the person has awakened in the morning. Thoughts half recalled before bedtime are often fully available upon awakening. The phrase, "If you're having trouble making a decision, sleep on it," also refers to this point.

Dreams are often made up of familiar elements arranged in odd, at times bizarre, configurations. Freud hypothesized that dreams were an individual's subconscious effort to work out emotional problems, to satisfy needs and generally to deal with affective data. The familiar elements of the manifest dream – the story part rather than the latent true meaning of the dream – might have been incorporated from the events of the day, but the incorporation did not represent a particularly important part of the dream process. In contrast, according to a memory consolidation hypothesis, dreams are simply the by-products of the consolidation of newly acquired information into pre-existing schemata.

If memory consolidation is the central role of D-sleep, the elaboration of HGH just prior to each of the early D-periods in a night can be understood as essential to the process.

These two hypotheses, of S-sleep being the time when noradrenaline systems are repaired and reprogrammed and D-sleep being the time when memory consolidation occurs, are not mutually exclusive. In some respects, Hartmann's hypothesis would appear to subsume the memory consolidation hypothesis, focusing largely upon the assimilation of information specific to stressful events. In many respects, the hypotheses are quite different. The central points which the student might take with her or him is that most discussions about the function of sleep eventually come to focus upon the D-state; and that the secretion of HGH during SWS is probably central to the function of sleep.

V. Directions for the Future

We have left the reader with more questions than answers. We have presented two main hypotheses about the function of sleep. However, although both proposed functions are important, neither seems so critical that its elimination through sleep deprivation would directly compromise life. There is clearly a great deal left to discover.

The most solid findings have been at the most superficial level of analysis:

138

the outward manifestations of sleep. But, as we come to have a better idea about the function of sleep, we will come to have better ideas about the kinds of psychophysiological changes we need to uncover. We are now becoming fairly confident that the important events of sleep occur at the molecular level, and that the events at more superficial levels are reflections of the molecular events. Soon, we expect to add to the description of sleep information on systematic changes in classical neurotransmitters, and/or polypeptide neuro-modulators.

Even without a coherent picture that would point the search along a particular path, we have many leads to follow. Human growth hormone release is potentiated by dopamine as well as noradrenaline. Very little attention has been paid to the role of dopamine systems in sleep, yet the acute phase of schizophrenia is associated with acute sleep disturbance, and the blockade of dopamine synapses is the physiological change most closely associated with significant clinical change following pharmacotherapy. These observations would suggest the need to evaluate the role of dopamine systems in sleep.

An entire new class of polypeptides which function as neurotransmitters has been identified. We have barely begun to look at these in the context of sleep. Large peptides which appear, respectively, to produce S-sleep and D-sleep have now been identified. This work needs to be pursued.

We also do not know whether one or several functions occur under the darkness of sleep: are we seeking a single main function of sleep, or several independent ones? Nor do we know whether S and D play separate or complementary roles. If the roles are complementary, we must look ulti-mately for the function of sleep as a whole, rather than for the function of each state of sleep separately.

There are many subsidiary questions, including why psychological dis-orders and disorders of sleep are so closely associated. Probing into the neural and endocrine mechanisms that underly the events of sleep continues to be an actively pursued enterprise. While a great deal is known, there is a great deal yet to be learned.

The creative use of *all* the information known about sleep will someday help us to uncover its function. Even beyond that, by having understood completely the events of sleep, we will be one step closer to understanding how the functions of mind arise from the unique neural organization and chemistry of the brain. By having understood *what kind* of question to pose in our inquiry into sleep, we will at one and the same time have begun to know what kind of question will be most fruitful in opening the doors of the brain to reveal the secrets of the mind.

Persevere, and in the end one finds what one seeks.

Further Reading

General

Chase, M. H. (ed.) (1972). "Perspectives in the brain sciences, Vol. I: The Sleeping Brain". Brain Information Services, Brain Research Institute, University of California, Los Angeles.
Kleitman, N. (1963). "Sleep and Wakefulness" 2nd edn. University of Chicago Press, Chicago.
Koella, W. P. (1967). "Sleep: Its nature and physiological organization". C. C. Thomas. Springfield, Illinois.

K-complexes

Johnson, L. C. and Karpan, W. Z. (1968). Autonomic correlates of the spontaneous K-complex. *Psychophysiol.* **4**, 444–452.
Sassin, J. F. and Johnson, L. C. (1968). Body motility during sleep and its relation to K-complexes. *Exp. Neurol.* **22**, 133–144.

Growth Hormone

Ganong, W. F. (1975). "Review of Medical Physiology" 8th edn. Lange Medical Publications, Los Altos, California.
Sassin, J. F., Parker, D. C., Johnson, L. C., Rossman, L. G., Mace, J. W. and Gotlin, R. W. (1969). Effects of slow wave sleep deprivation on human growth hormone release in sleep: preliminary study. *Life Sciences* **8**, 1, 1299–1307.

Total Sleep Deprivation

Horne, J. A. (1978). A review of the biological effects of total sleep deprivation in man. *Biol. Psychol.* **7**, 55–102.

Neurochemistry and Psychological Function

Barchas, J. D., Berger, P. A., Ciaranello, R. D. and Elliott, G. R. (eds) (1977). "Psychopharmacology: From Theory to Practice", Oxford University Press, New York.
Cooper, J. R., Bloom, F. E. and Roth, R. H. (1978). "The Biochemical Basis of Neuropharmacology". Oxford University Press, New York.

Functions of Sleep

Hartmann, E. (1973). "The Functions of Sleep". Yale University Press, New Haven and London.
Tilley, A. J. and Empson J. A. C. (1978). REM sleep and memory consolidation. *Biol. Psychol.* **6**, 293–300.

References

Aserinsky, E. and Kleitman, N. (1953). Regularly occurring periods of eye motility and concomitant phenomena during sleep. *Science* **118**, 273–274.

Baekland, F. and Lasky, R. (1966). *Percept. Mot. Skills* 23, 1203.

Berger, H. (1929). Uber das Elektroenkephalogramm des Menschen. *Arch. Psychiat. Nervkrankh.* 87, 527.

Bonvallet, M. and Allen, M. B. (1963). Prolonged spontaneous and evoked reticular activation following discrete bulbar lesions. *Electroenceph. Clin. Neurophysiol.* 15, 969–988.

Church, M. W., Johnson, L. C. and Seales, D. M. (1978). Evoked K-complexes and cardiovascular responses to spindle-synchronous and spindle-asynchronous stimulus clicks during NREM sleep. *Electroenceph. Clin. Neurophysiol.* 45, 443–453.

Clemente, C. D. and Sterman, M. B. (1963). Cortical synchronization and sleep patterns in acute restrained and chronic behaving cats induced by basal forebrain stimulation. *Electroenceph. Clin. Neurophysiol.* 24, 172–187.

Dahlstrom, A. N. and Fuxe, K. (1964). Evidence for the existence of monoamine-containing neurons in the central nervous system, I. Demonstration of monoamines in the cell bodies of brain stem neurons. *Acta Physiol. Scand.* 62, Suppl. 232, 1–55.

Dement, W. and Kleitman, N. (1957). Cyclic variations in EEG during sleep and their relation to eye movements, body motility, and dreaming. *Electroenceph. Clin. Neurophysiol.* 9, 673–690.

Demetrescu, M., Demetrescu, M. and Iosif, G. (1965). The tonic control of cortical responsiveness by inhibitory and facilitatory diffuse influences. *Electroenceph. Clin. Neurophysiol.* 18, 1–24.

French, J. D. (1960). The reticular formation. *In* "Handbook of Physiology II" 1281–1306.

Ganong, W. F. (1975). "Review of Medical Physiology" 8th edn. Lange Medical Publications, Los Altos, California.

Graham, F. K. and Clifton, R. K. (1966). Heart rate change as a component of the orienting response. *Psychol. Bull.* 65, 305–320.

Hartmann, E. (1973). "The Functions of Sleep". Yale University Press, New Haven and London.

Hartmann, E. (1977). L-tryptophan: a rational hypnotic with clinical potential. *Am. J. Psychiat.* 134, 366–370.

Hartmann, E., Baekland, F., Zwilling, G. (1972). Psychological differences between long and short sleepers. *Arch. Gen. Psychiat.* 26, 463–468.

Hess, W. R. (1954). "Diencephalon: autonomic and extrapyramidal functions". Grune and Stratton, New York.

Hobson, J. A., McCarley, R. W., Freedman, P. and Pivik, R. T. (1974). Time course of discharge rate changes by cat pontine brain stem neurons during sleep cycle. *J. Neurophysiol.* 37, 1297–1309.

Hobson, J. A., McCarley, R. W. and Wyzinski, P. W. (1975). Sleep cycle oscillation: reciprocal discharge by two brainstem neuronal groups. *Science* 189, 55–58.

Horne, J. A. (1978). A review of the biological effects of total sleep deprivation in man. *Biol. Psychol.* 7, 55–102.

Johnson, L. C. and Karpan, W. Z. (1968). Autonomic correlates of the spontaneous K-complex. *Psychophysiology* 4, 444–452.

Jones, B. E. (1979). Elimination of paradoxical sleep by lesions of the pontine giganto-cellular tegmental field in the cat. *Neurosci. Letts.* 13, 285–293.

Jouvet, M. (1969). Biogenic amines and the states of sleep. *Science* 163, 32–41.

Lidov, H. G. W., Grzanna, R. and Molliver, M. E. (1980). The serotonin innervation of the cerebral cortex in the rat – an immunohistochemical analysis. *Neuroscience* 5, 207–227.

Moore, R. Y. and Eichler, V. B. (1972). Loss of a circadian corticosterone rhythm following suprachiasmatic lesions in the rat. *Brain Res.* **42**, 201–206.

Morgane, P. (1972). The Neural Circuitry of Sleep. *In* "The Sleeping Brain" (M. H. Chase, ed.) pp. 91–100. Brain Information Services, Brain Research Institute, University of California, Los Angeles.

Moruzzi, G. and Magoun, H. (1949). Brain stem reticular formation and activation of the EEG. *Electroenceph. Clin. Neurophysiol.* **1**, 455–473.

Naitoh, P., Kales, A., Kollar, E. J., Smith, J. C. and Jacobson, A. (1969). Electroencephalographic activity after prolonged sleep loss. *Electroenceph. Clin. Neurophysiol.* **27**, 2–11.

Nauta, W. J. H. and Domesick, V. B. (1982) Neural Associations of the Limbic System. *In* "Neural Substrates of Behaviour" (A. Beckman, ed.), 175–206. Spectrum, New York and London.

Rechtschaffen, A. and Kales, A. (eds). (1968). The manual of standardized terminology, techniques and scoring system for sleep stages of human subjects. National Institutes of Health Publications No 204.

Sassin, J. F. (1970). Neurological findings following short term sleep deprivation. *Archs Neurol.* **22**, 54–56.

Sassin, J. F. and Johnson, L. C. (1968). Body motility during sleep and its relation to the K-complex. *Expl Neurol.* **22**, 133–144.

Sassin, J. F., Parker, D. C., Johnson, L. C., Rossman, L. G., Mace, J. W. and Gotlin, R. W. (1969). Effects of slow wave sleep deprivation on human growth hormone release in sleep: preliminary study. *Life Sciences* **8**: I, 1295–1307.

Steriade, M., Apostol, V., Oakson, G. (1971). Control of unitary activities in cerebellothalamic pathway during wakefulness and synchronized sleep. *J. Neurophysiol.* **34**, 211–217.

Tilley, A. J. and Empson, J. A. C. (1978). REM sleep and memory consolidation. *Biol. Psychol.* **6**, 293–300.

Weinberger, N. M., Velasco, M. and Lindsley, D. B. (1965). Effects of lesions upon thalamically induced electrocortical desynchronization and recruiting. *Electroenceph. Clin. Neurophysiol.* **18**, 369–377.

Yamaoka, S. (1978). Participation of limbic-hypothalamic structures in circadian rhythm of slow wave sleep and paradoxical sleep in the rat. *Brain Res.* **151**, 255–268.

Zir, L. M., Smith, R. A. and Parker, D. C. (1971). Human growth hormone release in sleep: effect of daytime exercise. *J. Clin. Endocr. Metab.* **32**, 662–665.

7 Towards a Neurochemical Theory of Learning and Memory

D. M. Warburton

Abstract This chapter is a selective review of the evidence on the neurochemical systems which are correlated with the psychological processes that are involved in learning and memory. The evidence reviewed is the result of extensive biochemical, psychopharmacological and neurophysiological research undertaken over the last twenty years. Thus the discussion concentrates on the neural mechanisms mediating reinforcement, consolidation and transient and permanent memory, and the data from the diverse fields of research is integrated within this framework.

I. Introduction

This chapter is about the neural mechanisms that seem to be involved in the processes of learning and memory. It deals with the way in which information from the outside world is selected and stored and then made available to the organism to be expressed in behaviour. The focus of this approach is on neurochemical substrates for the behavioural systems, that have been postulated by learning theorists.

Thus the chapter has a behavioural framework although the explanatory concepts are neurochemical. It is an assumption of this approach that the same neurochemical systems are basic to the learning of human beings as to other animals. In order to minimize the probability of error in extrapolation, the majority of studies that are discussed are based on mammals.

II. Stability and Plasticity in the Brain

A person can be considered as a three stage information processing system. There is an input stage, a decision stage and an output stage. The boundaries of the input and output stages are the environment and represent the points of

PHYSIOLOGICAL CORRELATES OF HUMAN
BEHAVIOUR   ISBN 0-12-273901-9

interaction between the organism and his world. For mammals the decision stage is usually in the brain, which has evolved as an organ for processing information. The billions of neurones in the brain are not randomly connected but are organized as neural networks (Warburton, 1975). The inputs to these networks come from extero-receptors and intero-receptors distributed throughout the body. Extero-receptors, such as the rods and cones of the eye, transduce information from the external environment while intero-receptors, such as the glucoreceptors of the hypothalamus, transduce information from the internal environment. Transduction involves the conversion of energy from the environment into a pattern of electrochemical changes which are transmitted along neurones. This coded input is integrated with information which is already in the network, to determine the behavioural output.

Points of integration are at the convergence of neurones on to a single receiving neurone, which may receive inputs from a large number of neurones. The amount of excitation or inhibition that an input neurone contributes will depend on a number of factors, including the amount of transmitter released, the size of the synapse and the number of synapses on the end of the neurone. As a result an input neurone with many large synapses that produce a large quantity of transmitter will have a much greater influence on behaviour than a neurone with a few small synapses that only release a small amount of transmitter when activated.

The genes determine the major interconnections within a neural network, and the properties of most neurones are established at birth or soon after. Chemical stimulation studies in animals and histochemical staining studies of animal and human brains have shown that there are sequences of neurones which have the same transmitter substance, similar enzymes and are functionally interrelated (Warburton, 1975). Once these neural networks are established embryonically, they normally remain unchanged throughout the life of the person. For example, a homeostatic system must maintain stability within certain limits and so a given input will invariably result in the same output. The capacity of the person to survive depends on the existence of an invariable quantitative relation between input and output and so it relies directly upon the unchanging function of neurones in the network.

However, there must be other neurones in the human nervous system that have plasticity, so that they can change in response to inputs. As a result the plastic neurone's output is not constant but changes as a result of the person's experience. If there were no plastic neurones, the input would merely activate networks where the output depends on inherited neural interconnections, and behaviour would be invariable. The presence of plastic neurones ensures that the output will depend on both the inherited connections and the acquired connections, so that the output will be a resultant of the present information from the receptors and stored information about past inputs.

The problem that will be tackled in this chapter is how information can be stored to change the input–output properties of the system.

Most researchers in this field would agree with the assumption of Hebb (1949), that some growth or metabolic change takes place at the synapse to change the efficiency of synaptic transmission. For example, growth of the synaptic terminals (including terminal sprouting) would alter the size of the postsynaptic potential, since larger synapses will secrete a larger quantity of transmitter even though the amount secreted per unit area remains the same. Alternatively, the area of the neurone terminals may remain the same but the number of vesicles released by a given change in deplorization may increase or decrease. A third kind of synaptic modification would involve no change in the amount of transmitter released but would involve an increase or decrease in the sensitivity of the postsynaptic membrane. All of these changes would involve a modification in the normal synthesis of the proteins required for the neural structures and transmitter production.

The change in protein synthesis required for growth could be initiated in seconds although the actual change in the neurone would take much longer. This would fit in with the evidence that certain types of simple learning may proceed very rapidly and even on one trial some neurones may have only two states, an "unlearned" state and a "learned" state. Parsimoniously it could be suggested that all plastic neurones have this property and that incremental learning involves the accumulation of a large number of changed neurones which change state in an "all-or-none" fashion. This conceptualization would fit the all-or-none (Markovian) interpretations of human learning that have been made by many theorists (see Restle and Greeno, 1970).

In summary, people are born with a set of neural networks, which enable them to integrate excitatory and inhibitory information from the internal and external environments and respond accordingly. The function of some of these networks is unvarying and a given input will elicit the same output each time. In addition, there are plastic neurones whose input to the neural networks can be modified, and so responding will be based on both past and present information. The modifications in the functioning of the synapses are due to new growth or altered metabolic processes. In this way behaviour is changed by the environmental stimulus input.

III. Reinforcement

One important class of input is information about the consequences of actions and behaviour changes as a result of these outcome stimuli. In classical learning theories outcome stimuli were called reinforcing stimuli and it was believed that the probability of responses was modified by these stimuli (see Mackintosh, 1974). This idea was originally proposed by Thorndike (1903), who believed that there were inherited connections between stimuli and responses and some of these could be modified to establish new connections. These new connections were "stamped in" automatically as a result of the occurrence of a "confirming reaction" in the brain (Thorndike, 1933) that was produced by outcome stimuli. As a result the outcome stimuli came to be called reinforcers because they strengthened connections. Thorndike's idea of connections went far beyond stimulus–response bonds and included associations between any stimuli which occurred internally or externally (Thorndike, 1903).

A major controversy in learning theory has been the nature of the reinforcing stimuli. One approach has been to argue that stimuli can be divided absolutely into events which are reinforcing and those which are not (Skinner, 1938) and to argue that there is some common underlying factor that defines a reinforcing stimulus. Hull (1952) proposed that all reinforcing stimuli are drive reducing in some sense; for example food is a reinforcer because it reduces hunger in the deprived animal. However, experiments with reinforcing stimuli such as saccharin and light onset, that were not drive reducing, contradicted this theory (see Kimble, 1961).

A second approach is to argue that there is no such thing as a dichotomy of stimuli between two classes but rather there is a continuum, with some stimuli more reinforcing in relation to others (Bevan and Adamson, 1963). According to this theory, stimuli that have occurred over the recent trials in a situation are averaged, to determine an internal norm or referent. A new stimulus is evaluated relative to this norm and will be a positive reinforcer if it is above the norm. Reinforcement magnitude will be measured relative to the internal standard and not in absolute terms. This magnitude will determine the amount of change in arousal which will alter future performance in some way.

As response-produced stimuli are merely defined by their effectiveness in changing arousal level, a number of the controversies in learning theory are unimportant; it does not matter for the theory whether the reinforcing stimuli are pleasurable or aversive and whether they are drive reducing or not; drive reduction is only important if it changes arousal appropriately. Latent learning results are handled quite easily because it is the arousal changes that are important, and not whether the experimenter presented specific response-contingent stimuli. Finally, there will be no difference in principle between primary and secondary reinforcers.

Let us consider the possible neural mechanisms for reinforcement and changes in arousal.

A. *Reinforcing Stimulation in the Brain*

One of the most important findings for the neural theory of reinforcement mechanisms was the discovery that animals would respond in order to receive electrical stimulation of certain parts of the brain (Olds and Milner, 1954). Before considering the anatomy of self-stimulation, we will consider the relation of this stimulation to the effects of natural reinforcing stimuli. Major pieces of evidence on this issue have been collected by Rolls and his colleagues (1975). As we have described in Chapter 14, Rolls recorded from single cells in the lateral hypothalamus during self-stimulation. Cells, which responded after a short latency to electrical reinforcing stimulation, were tested further with the natural reinforcing stimulation of food and water. Some neurones fired when water was put in the mouth of the thirsty animal, but not when isotonic saline or glucose were introduced, nor when the tongue was cooled with air. Some neurones were activated when the hungry monkey tasted food and even when it saw food, but not when it saw an inedible object (see Rolls, 1975). Thus, hypothalamic cells were activated selectively by natural reinforcers and by stimuli associated with these reinforcers (e.g. the sight or smell of food), in other words secondary reinforcing stimuli, but only if the animal was deprived. Reinforcing brain stimulation mimicked the effect of the natural stimuli on these cells, and suggests that the brain pathways that mediate self-stimulation may mediate the reinforcing effects of natural stimuli. It is particularly significant that the secondary reinforcing stimuli also activated the same neuronal pathways.

The precise neural pathways which mediate reinforcement have proved difficult to disentangle. The problem has been complicated by evidence that self-stimulation behaviour is not a consequence of a reinforcement system alone. The studies of Deutsch (Deutsch and Deutsch, 1973) and of Gallistel (1973) indicated that the medial forebrain bundle contained a drive pathway as well as a reinforcement pathway. However, the sets of neurones which pass through this region have different origins in the hindbrain and project to different places in the forebrain. Experiments by Routtenberg (Huang and Routtenberg, 1971) and Crow (1972a) found high rates of self-stimulation responding were obtained when electrodes were placed close to the dopamine neurones in the hind-brain, even when the stimuli were not contingent upon responses. This latter observation suggests that the dopamine pathways are associated with non-specific drive rather than a response-contingent reinforcement system.

The studies of Huang and Routtenberg (1971) also implicated the brachium conjunctivum in self-stimulation. These fibres have their origins in the dorsal nuclei around the locus coeruleus, and Crow (1972b) obtained self-stimulation responding from electrode sites close to the locus coeruleus. Histochemical staining (Ungerstedt, 1971) has demonstrated that there is a dorsal noradrenaline pathway, which has its cell bodies in the locus coeruleus and passes along the brachium conjunctivum and ascends together with the dopamine fibres in the medial forebrain bundle. The dorsal noradrenaline pathway innervates practically all areas of the brain, but especially the cerebral cortex, cerebellar cortex and the hippocampus. If lesions are made in the brachium conjunctivum at sites that support self-stimulation, fluorescence histochemistry showed that there was an accumulation of noradrenaline in the dorsal pathway from the locus coeruleus (Clavier and Routtenberg, 1974). These results suggest that the reinforcement component of self-stimulation acts via the dorsal noradrenaline pathway to the hippocampus, neocortex and cerebellum.

B. The Mechanisms of Reinforcement

The next problem is to consider how this pathway is involved in changing associations. Crow (1972b; 1973) points out that there is an association, between the dorsal noradrenaline pathways from the locus coeruleus and the central connections of gustation, which may mediate the reinforcing effects of gustatory stimulation and is believed to be reinforcing. As an independent part of the hypothesis, Crow suggested that it is the projection of the dorsal noradrenaline fibres to the neocortex which initiates the plastic changes involved in learning. This suggestion was similar to one made by Kety (1972), who postulated that the cortical release of noradrenaline might provide sufficient additional excitation to refire sensory cells that had recently been fired by an input of information. At the sensory cortex many cells are active during processing of a sensory input and all these will be affected by the reinforcement mechanism. With a number of repetitions of this process the random activity in the synapses would be averaged out and the essential adaptive connections would be formed.

Clues about the action of the reinforcement system on brain activity have to be derived from cortical recording. Certain stimuli produce a steady potential shift at the cortex, reward contingent positive variation (RCPV) (Rowland et al., 1967), which can be elicited by a novel neutral stimulus, such as a light flash. However, there is a rapid decrement in the potential when the stimulus is repeated, except when a reinforcing stimulus has been given. A food-deprived cat showed a large response when lapping food and this declined as the animal satiated. Anaesthetization of the cat's mouth showed that it is the gustatory input which is crucial for the shift for this consummatory response. The steady potential was not specific to food intake reinforcement, but could be obtained by perineal stimulation in the oestrous cat and rat and by positively reinforcing electrical stimulation of the lateral hypothalamus. It was not specific to positive reinforcing stimuli and was elicited by aversive electrical shock to the skin and aversive hypothalamic stimulation. If a neutral stimulus was paired with a positive or negative reinforcing stimulus then the previously neutral stimulus elicited the steady potential shift, which showed that a secondary reinforcing stimulus had the same effect, provided the animal was deprived.

As well as the steady potential shift there is high voltage slow activity at the cortex, which appears after the onset of the steady potential and is called post-reinforcement synchronization (PRS). Clemente, Sterman and Wyrwicka (1964) found that PRS depended on the quality of the food reward and that it could be produced by a previously neutral stimulus which had been paired with a reinforcing stimulus. Marczynski (1969; 1971) studied both RCPV and PRS and found that both potential changes depended on the quality of the reinforcing stimulus, so that substitution of water for milk abolished them. He also found that the sensory evoked potentials were larger during the post-reinforcement period in comparison with the evoked potentials to the same stimuli after non-reinforcement.

From these findings we can construct a picture of the effects of reinforcing stimuli on cortical information processing. The stimulus activates the reinforcement pathway, which inhibits electrocortical arousal at the cortex for a brief time. According to a current theory of attention (Warburton, 1978; 1979), cortical desynchronization enables selection of stimuli in the environment by masking the smaller evoked potentials with desynchronized activity. However, when the reinforcement pathway inhibits the desynchronization all evoked potentials at the cortex are enhanced. The magnitude of the evoked potential initiates the change in the characteristics of the cortical cells which we will call consolidation. After a single presentation of a reinforcing stimulus the evoked potentials of many stimuli would be enhanced; but with successive presentations the activity from randomly occurring stimuli would be averaged out. As a result only the patterns of activity which occurred constantly in contiguity with stimuli which inhibited electrocortical activity would be consolidated.

IV. Consolidation for Permanent Storage

Consolidation refers to the changes in the nature of the memory trace which make it relatively insensitive to external interference. The evidence for a period of memory fixation is strong; it is commonly observed clinically that after a blow on the head cases of retrograde amnesia can occur (Russell and Newcombe, 1966). Most laboratory studies of retrograde amnesia in animals have used electroconvulsive shock. All studies which have investigated the training–shock interval have found a gradient of susceptibility, but the steepness seems to depend on shock intensity, complexity of the task, strain, sex and even time of test. Other treatments which have retroactive effects are hypothermia (lowering of temperature) and hypoxia (lack of oxygen) (McGaugh, 1966).

Other experiments, with anaesthetics like ether and pentobarbital, show that memory consolidation can be disrupted by drugs during the first hour after acquisition (McGaugh and Petrinovich, 1965). A parallel set of drug studies has examined the effects of stimulants on acquisition. The most complete investigations have been on strychnine, by McGaugh and his co-workers. For example, McGaugh and Krivanek (1970) examined the effects of dose and time of injection on a black–white discrimination acquisition in mice. It was clear from the results that most doses of strychnine, injected immediately after three trials in the maze, facilitated consolidation. Consolidation was measured by the number of errors to a criterion during training on the following day. For each dose, errors to a criterion increased with increases in the training–injection intervals up to one hour. This suggested that the mechanisms affected by the strychnine could only be activated to modify consolidation in the first hour after acquisition, with the greatest effect at five minutes. Studies with other drugs have supported a time dependent effect, although the gradient varies with the drug used to measure it (McGaugh and Dawson, 1971).

In an attempt to locate the anatomical pathways involved in consolidation, Alpern (1968) injected strychnine into the mesencephalic reticular formations of rats just dorsal to the ventral tegmental region and obtained clear facilitation of learning. Facilitation of memory storage has also been obtained by post trial electrical and chemical stimulation of the mesencephalic reticular formation close to the ventral tegmental region (Alpern, 1968; Denti et al., 1970).

Recordings of electrocortical activity have been made after electrical stimulation of these regions, after strychnine and after electroconvulsive shock. It was found that the amount of post-training synchronization was correlated with subsequent retention scores, and that the electroconvulsive shock appeared to lower the probability of synchronized activity during the 30 minute period after training (Landfield et al., 1972). This would link these studies with the reinforcement experiments, since both seem to involve synchronized activity in the cortex. Thus, amnesic treatment may work by blocking cortical synchronization, while facilitating drugs may work by inducing or prolonging post-reinforcement synchronization, and so increase the probablity of initiating the chemical processes involved in the permanent storage of information.

V. Long Term Storage

In the late 1940s studies on the genetic coding of information were begun. The molecular biologists pointed out the analogy between memory as individual specific storage of information and heredity as species specific storage of information and wondered if memory molecules were synthesised in the central nervous system as the result of learning. Inherited information is encoded in the sequences of nucleotide bases in deoxyribonucleic acid (DNA). These molecules are very stable and resistant to changes in their physical and chemical environments and each molecule reproduces itself during cell division. The control of cell function by DNA is accomplished by the production of proteins, including enzymes. Synthesis of proteins is mediated by a second type of nucleic acid, ribonucleic acid, which is a copy of some of the information that is coded by the DNA molecule and specifies the unique combination of amino acids required for synthesising any one protein.

There are two possible ways by which information could be stored in the nervous system by changes in protein synthesis: (i) *instruction*, in which qualitative changes would occur in the nucleotide sequences of the DNA, or more likely the RNA, to produce a new protein; or (ii) *selection*, whereby specific portions of the DNA molecules would be activated to increase selected types of proteins (Schmitt, 1962). One strong argument against the instruction theory is that changes in the genetically determined RNA would disrupt normal cellular metabolism, and that the novel protein synthesized would elicit a foreign protein reaction (Briggs and Kitto, 1962). In addition, this sort of theory does not explain how neural activity could induce a molecular rearrangement which is thereafter immune to further electric changes (Morrell, 1964).

One version of the selection theory is the gene expression theory (Flexner *et al.*, 1967). It proposes that protein molecules are the final storage molecules and that the essential biochemical change in memory storage is not modification of DNA and RNA, but increased production of already available species of RNA from DNA by a change in the pattern of gene expression produced by neural activity during training. The additional RNA will then specify more protein and the newly synthesized proteins will modify the characteristic of synapses to facilitate future neural transmission. In addition, the proteins or their products act as inducers of their own specific RNA, maintaining the concentration of the inducer proteins above the critical level for further gene induction, which enables the change in neural function to persist. Evidence for protein storage of memory has come from studies which have measured specific changes in protein synthesis mechanisms after training, and studies which have manipulated protein synthesis with drug and tested memory.

Some of the first biochemical studies on the macromolecular hypothesis were carried out in the Soviet Union in the mid-1950s. These were followed by the major studies of Hydén in Sweden on the changes in RNA in single neurones after a learning experience. These early studies did not have adequate controls for non-specific stimulation, but in later studies evidence was found of changes in the relative quantities of the types of RNA in the cortex of trained rats (Hydén and Lange, 1965). Soon after training there appears to be increased activity of RNA polymerase in cell nuclei (Rose and Haywood, 1977), indicating the start of RNA synthesis; and work with radioactive amino acids has demonstrated greater incorporation of these amino acids into RNA in trained animals (Glassman, 1969; Rose and Haywood, 1977). It would be expected from the hypothesis that enhanced RNA production would lead to increased protein synthesis, and there is certainly evidence of more incorporation of amino acids into protein in trained animals (Gaito *et al.*, 1969; Hershkowitz *et al.*, 1975· Rose and Haywood, 1977). Analyses of brain protein have even demonstrated increased production of a protein known as S-100 (Hydén and Lange, 1970) which may be related to synaptic structure. Altogether there is encouraging evidence which is consistent with the activation of protein synthesis by learning.

Unfortunately, these studies are only correlational and do not necessarily demonstrate a causal link between the changes in RNA and protein synthesis, and memory. Physiological stimulation of any body tissue results in increased synthesis of these macromolecules and trained animals must inevitably receive more information input than the controls. Nevertheless, the changes that have been observed are consistent with a selectional theory, even if they do not establish it unequivocally. More convincing evidence has come from studies which have made protein synthesis the independent variable and memory the dependent variable.

Many tests of the hypothesis have been carried out using drugs which inhibit cerebral RNA and protein synthesis at various stages of the transcription from DNA, such as acetoxycycloheximide, actinomycin, anisomycin, 8-azaguanine, and puromycin. It has proved important to use a wide variety of drugs because of the side effects of the drug which make interpretation of the results of a single study equivocal. When the drug is injected before training, acquisition proceeds normally in the animals, even though there is over 90% inhibition of protein synthesis, but when tested six hours or more later there was evidence of memory impairment (Barondes and Cohen, 1967; 1968a and 1968b). However, tests in the period immediately after acquisition (up to three hours) have shown that the information is still retained at this time (Barondes and Cohen, 1967; Squire and Barondes, 1972). Post-trial injections of a protein synthesis inhibitor are also effective in impairing memory (Flexner and Flexner, 1966; Barondes and Cohen, 1968a), but the effectiveness of post trial injections wanes over time (Barondes and Cohen, 1968b), as in the consolidation studies. These studies and others like them suggest that amnesia is produced when protein synthesis is inhibited shortly before and shortly after acquisition, but that the registration of information is unaffected. The amnesia that was produced by a protein synthesis inhibitor could be prevented by an injection of amphetamine three hours after training at a time when protein synthesis was recovering (Barondes and Cohen, 1968b), which suggests that amphetamine reinstated the processes for the long term storage of information. This reinstatement of memory could be abolished by a further dose of the protein synthesis inhibitor. One interpretation of the reinstatement phenomenon is that the amphetamine activated the noradrenaline reinforcement pathway and initiated the consolidation process again.

In summary, there seem to be at least two forms of information storage. One form of storage is initiated by the input of information and persists for at least three hours. It is a labile change and can be enhanced and weakened by treatments which act on the pathways that control electrocortical arousal, but it is insensitive to the inhibition of protein synthesis. The second form of storage is also initiated at the same time as the labile storage, or shortly thereafter and gradually becomes more and more resistant to any form of disruption over a period of hours. If it is disrupted before the decay of the labile form of storage, the process of permanent storage can be reinstated, which implies that the two forms of storage are not independent. Disruption by protein synthesis inhibitors suggests strongly that this second type of storage involves a permanent quantitative change in protein production.

These changes would be localized in the plastic neurones active during the acquisition session. Changes in protein could be in the nature of increases in transmitter synthesizing enzymes, which would increase the presynaptic stores of transmitter making more available for release at each synapse and so increasing the probability of the postsynaptic neurone reaching threshold. Alternative sorts of neural change might be the development of new synaptic connections, in the form of more presynaptic terminals or more postsynaptic receptors. The outcome of any of these changes would be functionally equivalent to increased transmitter synthesis in terms of enhanced transmission in brain pathways.

VI. Conclusions

In this selective account I have presented the neural substrates for the psychological processes that are believed to be involved in learning and memory. The storage of information begins with some event which produces a transient change in electrocortical arousal. The neural system which produces this change is probably the ascending noradrenaline pathway which runs from the locus coeruleus to the cortex. In some way this system interacts with the sensory input to initiate information storage. At first two forms of storage are initiated – a transient change in synaptic transmission and an activation of the mechanisms of protein synthesis. The transient changes decline but the altered protein synthesis results in permanent alterations in synaptic activity, so that the synapse functions more effectively in future. Information is not stored at a single synaptic locus in the brain but in the changed firing probabilities of a set of neurones located in many parts of the brain.

Although this account represents a synthesis of the major neurochemical mechanisms that are thought to be involved in learning and memory, the reader must be cautioned about the strength of the conclusions. Both the pharmacological and biochemical approaches have inherent difficulties which critical researchers recognize.

The methodological problem of the pharmacological studies lies in the incompleteness of our knowledge about drug action. It may be known that a drug changed the brain levels of a neurochemical, and that there were concomitant changes in performance. However, we cannot unequivocally conclude that the changes in behaviour were related to changes in the neuro-chemical unless it can be established that *all* other possible neurochemical effects are non-existant or irrelevant for the behavioural change. Total exclu-sion is impossible, but the evidence becomes stronger when a set of studies use drugs of markedly differing structures and widely differing biochemical modes of action but with one action in common. No learning and memory study has achieved this aim. Indeed, there are no drugs which are known to enhance protein synthesis, so the only evidence comes from the few drugs which disrupt synthesis.

The flaw in the biochemical approach is that the studies are only correla-tional and there is a logical fallacy in arguing from correlation to causality. It has been demonstrated that there are systematic changes in neurochemicals when a response has been acquired, but we cannot be sure of the exact interrelationship between the two sets of events. It is conceivable that the neurochemical changes may not be correlates of learning, but of one of the other behavioural events which must also occur during acquisition of behaviour, such as sensory input, attentional changes, stress, decision making or response programming. The same criticism that was levelled at the pharmacological studies can also be made about the biochemical research, because unless we can show that other neurochemical changes are irrelevant or do not occur, we cannot conclude with certainty that our measured neurochemical change causes the behavioural change. It may be that the actual changes which code memory are too small and too widely distributed throughout the brain neurones to be detected, and that all we will ever measure will be the more dramatic neurochemical events which initiate information storage. The answers to all these uncertainties will only come from future methodologically sophisticated research.

Further Reading

Many of the references for this chapter have been deliberately selected from secondary sources to enable the reader to follow up areas in detail. However, since completion of the chapter an important conference book has become available:
Brazier, M. A. B. (Ed.) (1979). "Brain Mechanisms in Memory and Learning: from single neuron to man". Raven Press, New York.
This book discusses in detail various hypotheses about cellular changes during learning. Important supplements to the material in this chapter are to be found in the chapters by J. L. McGaugh, R. Mark and N. P. Bechtereva.

References

Alpern, H. P. (1968). "Facilitation of Learning by Implantation of Strychnine Sulphate in the Central Nervous System". Unpublished doctoral dissertation, University of California, Irvine.
Barondes, S. H. and Cohen, H. D. (1967). Delayed and sustained effect of acetoxycycloheximide on memory in mice. *Proc. Nat. Acad. Sci. USA* **58**, 157–164.
Barondes, S. H. and Cohen, H. W. (1968a). Memory impairment after subcutaneous injection of acetoxycycloheximide. *Science* **160**, 556–557.
Barondes, S. H. and Cohen, H. W. (1968b). Arousal and the conversion of 'short-term' to 'long-term' memory. *Proc. Nat. Acad. Sci.* **61**, 923–929.
Bevan, W. (1963). The pooling mechanism and phenomena of reinforcement. *In* "Motivation and Social Interaction: Cognitive determinants". (O. J. Harvey, ed.), pp. 18–44, 453–472. Ronald, New York.
Bevan, W., and Adamson, R. (1963). Internal Referents and the Concept of Reinforcement. *In* "Decisions, Values, and Groups" (N. F. Washburne, ed.), Vol. 2., pp. 453–472. Pergamon, New York.
Bloch, V. and Deweer, B. (1968). Role accelerateur de la phase de consolidation d'un apprentissage en un seul essai. *C. R. Acad. Sci.* **266**, 384–387.
Bloch, V., Denti, A., and Schmaltz, G. (1966). Effects de la stimulation reticulaire sur la phase de consolidation de la trace amnésique. *J. Physiol. Paris* **18**, 469–470.
Briggs, M. H. and Kitto, G. B. (1962). The molecular basis of memory and learning. *Psychol. Rev.* **69**, 537–541.
Clavier, R. M. and Routtenberg, A. (1974). Ascending monoamine-containing fiber pathways related to intracranial self-stimulation: histochemical fluorescence study. *Brain Res.* **72**, 25–70
Clemente, D. C., Sterman, M. B., and Wyrwicka, W. (1964). Post-reinforcement EEG synchronization during alimentary behaviour. *Electroenceph. Clin. Neurophysiol.* **16**, 355–365.

Crow, T. J. (1972a). A map of the rat mesencephalon for electrical self-stimulation. Brain Res. **36**, 265—73.

Crow, T. J. (1972b). Catecholamine-containing neurones and electrical self-stimulation: 1. a review of some data. Psychol. Med. **2**, 414—421.

Crow, T. J. (1973). Catecholamine-containing neurones and electrical self-stimulation. 2. A theoretical interpretation and some psychiatric implications. Psychol. Med. **3**, 66—73.

Denti, A., McGaugh, J. L., Landfield, P. W. and Shinkman, P. (1970). Facilitation of learning with posttrial stimulation of the reticular formation. Physiol. Behaviour **5**, 659—662.

Deutsch, J. A. and Deutsch, D. (1973). "Physiological Psychology" 2nd edn. Dorsey Press, Homewood, Illinois.

Deweer, B., Hennevin, E., and Block, V. (1969). Nouvelles données sur la facilitation réticulaire de la consolidation amnésique. J. Physiol. Povis **60**, 430.

Flexner, L. B. and Flexner, J. B. (1966). Effects of acetoxycycloheximide and of an acetoxycycloheximide-puromycin mixture on cerebral protein synthesis and memory in mice. Proc. Nat. Acad. Sci. USA **55**, 369—374.

Flexner, L. B., Flexner, J. B. and Roberts R. B. (1967). Memory in mice analysed with antibiotics. Science **155**, 1377—1383.

Gaito, J., Davison, J. H. and Mottin, J. (1969). Chemical variation in brain loci during water maze performance. Psychonomic Sci. **14**, 46—48.

Gallistel, C. R. (1973). Self-stimulation: the neurophysiology of reward and motivation. In "The Physiological Basis of Memory" (J. A. Deutsch, ed.), pp. 176—267. Academic Press, London and New York.

Glassman, E. (1969). The biochemistry of learning: An evaluation of the role of RNA and protein. A. Rev. Biochem. **38**, 605—646.

Hackett, J. T. and Marczynski, T. J. (1969). Post-reinforcement electrocortical synchronization and enhancement of cortical photic evoked potentials during instrumentally conditioned appetitive behavior in the cat. Brain Res. **15**, 447—464.

Hebb, D. O. (1949). "The Organization of Behavior". Wiley and Sons, New York.

Hershkowitz, M., Wilson, J. E. and Glassman, E. (1975). Increase in amino acid incorporation during learning. J. Neurochem. **25**, 687—694.

Huang, Y. H. and Routtenberg, A. (1971). Lateral hypothalamic self-stimulation pathways. Physiol. Behav. **7**, 419—32.

Hull, C. L. (1952). "A Behavior System: An introduction to behavior theory concerning the individual organism". Yale University Press, New Haven.

Hydén, H., and Lange, P. W. (1965). A differentiation in RNA response in neurons early and late in learning. Proc. Nat. Acad. Sci. **53**, 946—952.

Hydén, H., and Lange, P. W. (1970). Protein changes in nerve cells related to learning and conditioning. In "The Neurosciences: Second Study Program" (F. O. Schmitt, ed.), pp. 278—288. Rockefeller University Press, New York.

Kety, S. S. (1970). The biogenic amines in the central nervous system: their possible roles in arousal, emotion and learning. In "The Neurosciences: Second Study Program" (F. O. Schmitt, ed.), pp. 324—336. Rockefeller University Press, New York.

Kety, S. S. (1972). Biogenic amines of the central nervous system and their possible involvement in emotion and learning. In "Drugs, Development, and Cerebral Function" (W. L. Smith, ed.), p. 288—304. C. C. Thomas, Springfield, Illinois.

Kimble, G. A. (1961). "Hilgard and Marquis' Conditioning and learning" 2nd edn. Appleton-Century-Crofts, New York.

Landfield, P. W., McGaugh, J. L. and Tusa, R. J. (1972). Theta rhythm: a correlate of post trial memory storage processes in rats. *Science* 175, 87–88.

Mackintosh, N. J. (1974). "The Psychology of Animal Learning" Academic Press, London and New York.

McGaugh, J. L. (1966). Time-dependent processes in memory storage. *Science* 153, 1351–1358.

McGaugh, J. L., and Dawson, R. G. (1971). Modification of memory storage processes. *Behavl Sci.* 16, 45–63.

McGaugh, J. L., and Krivanek, H. (1970). Strychnine effects on discrimination learning in mice. Effects of dose and time of administration. *Physiol Behav.* 5, 1437–1442.

McGaugh, J. L. and Petrinovich, L. (1965). Effects of drugs on learning and memory. *Int. Rev. Neurobiol.* 8, 139–191.

Marczynski, T. J. (1969). Postreinforcement synchronization and the cholinergic system. *Fed. Proc.* 28, 132–134.

Marczynski, T. J. (1971). Cholinergic mechanism determines the occurrence of reward contingent positive variation (RCPV) in cat. *Brain Res.* 28, 71–83.

Marczynski, T. J. and Hackett, J. T. (1969). Post-reinforcement electrocortical synchronization and facilitation of cortical somato-sensory evoked potentials during instrumentally conditioned appetitive behavior in the cat.. *Clin. Neurophysiol* 26, 41–49.

Marczynski, T. J., Rosen, A. J. and Hackett, J. T. (1968). Post-reinforcement electrocortical synchronization and facilitation of cortical auditory evoked potentials in appetitive instrumental conditioning. *Electroenceph. Clin. Neurophysiol.* 24, 227–241.

Morrell, F. (1964) Modification of RNA as a result of neural activity. *In* "Brain Function, Vol. 2. – RNA and Brain Function" (M. A. B. Brazier, ed.), 183–202. University of California Press, Berkeley, California.

Olds, J. and Milner, P. (1954). Positive reinforcement produced by electrical stimulation of septal area and other regions of rat brain. *J. Comp. Physiol. Psychol.* 47, 419–427.

Restle, F. and Greeno, J. (1970). "Introduction to Mathematical Psychology". Addison-Wesley, Reading, Massachusetts.

Rolls, E. T. (1974). The neural basis of brain-stimulation reward. *Prog. Neurobiol.* 3, 71–160.

Rolls, E. T. (1975). "The Brain and Reward". Pergamon, London.

Rose, S. P. R. and Haywood, J. (1977). Experience, learning and brain metabolism. *In* "Biochemical Correlates of Brain Structure and Function" (A. N. Davison, ed.), pp. 249–292. Academic Press, London and New York.

Rowland, V., Bradley, H., School, P. and Deutschman, D. (1967). Cortical steady-potential shifts in conditioning. *Conditioned Reflex* 2, 3–22.

Russell, W. R., and Newcombe, F. (1966). Contribution from clinical neurology. *In* "Aspects of Learning and Memory" (D. Richter, ed.), pp. 15–24. Basic Books, New York.

Schmitt, F. O. (1962). Macromolecular Specificity and Biological Memory. *In* "Macromolecular Specificity and Biological Memory" (F. O. Schmitt, ed.), pp. 1–6. MIT Press, Cambridge, Massachusetts.

Skinner, B. F. (1938). "The Behavior of Organisms: an experimental analysis". Appleton-Century-Crofts, New York.

Squire, L. R. and Barondes, S. H. (1972). Variable decay of memory and its recovery in cycloheximide-treated mice. *Proc. Nat. Acad. Sci., USA* **69**, 1416–1421.

Thorndike, E. (1903). "Educational Psychology". Lemcke and Buechner, New York.

Thorndike, E. L. (1933). A theory of the action of the after-effects of a connection upon it. *Psychol. Rev.* **40**, 434–439.

Ungerstedt, U. (1971). Stereotaxic mapping of the monamine pathways in the rat brain. *Acta Physiol. Scand. suppl.* **367**, 1–48.

Warburton, D. M. (1975). "Brain, Behaviour and Drugs". Wiley and Sons, London.

Warburton, D. M. (1978). Neurochemical Basis of Consciousness. *In* "Chemical Influences on Behaviour" (K. Brown and S. Cooper, eds), pp. 421–462. Academic Press, London and New York.

Warburton, D. M. (1979). *In* "Handbook of Psychopharmacology", (L. L. Iversen, S. D. Iversen and S. H. Snyder, eds), Vol. 8, pp. 385–432. Plenum Press, New York.

8 Vision: Relations between Animal and Human Research

J. B. Davidoff
and G. G. Ratcliff

Abstract Studies of vision in humans and animals may be integrated through the convergence of data derived from different sources. Experimental psychophysics, studies of patients with lesions, animal lesions and histological evidence may often point in the same direction. On the basis of these data we are able to identify brain areas and functional mechanisms involved in a range of visual phenomena. Studies are reviewed which describe the neurophysiological basis of: the noticing and location of stimuli, brightness, colour, feature detection and object recognition. The analogues between human and animal studies must be treated with caution however, since there are many ways in which the two fields of enquiry are separated. Most accounts derived from the animal studies reviewed presume a linear and data-driven system; psychological theories of attention, perception and information processing presuppose an active and selective organism.

I. Sources of Evidence

One can infer some of the properties of the neural mechanisms which subserve human visual perception from purely psychophysical studies of normal intact human subjects. While such psychophysical studies have the merit that they are detailed well controlled investigations of human subjects, the mechanisms suggested by them cannot necessarily be identified with specific brain structures. They have the same logical status as the boxes in cognitive models of word and picture recognition which are not intended to be the representation of specific groups of neurones.

Electrophysiological and anatomical studies of the properties of single neurones and their interconnections are susceptible to different objections. Of necessity they are almost invariably carried out in infra-human species, and while it is reasonable to assume that the human visual system is organized

PHYSIOLOGICAL CORRELATES OF HUMAN
BEHAVIOUR
ISBN 0-12-273901-9

in a basically similar manner it need not be the same in every detail. Further, the knowledge that visually responsive neurones are capable of encoding particular kinds of information does not tell us how that information is used.

The other main source of evidence is the study of the effects of damage to the visual pathway and its projections. If studied through lesions carried out in animals, this evidence is subject to some of the same limitations as single unit studies. Some discoveries made in infra-human species have been shown to apply to man (e.g. the "blindsight" phenomenon discussed below) but others do not seem to have such dual relevance. For example, the visual discrimination learning deficit following infero-temporal damage, which must be one of the most extensively studied phenomena in primate visual perception (see Dean, 1977 for a review), has only a very loose parallel in man; and the phenomenon of hemispheric asymmetry, which has dominated human neuropsychology for several decades, has scarcely any counterpart in the animal literature.

The effects of human brain lesions are obviously relevant to human perception but the data are not easy to interpret. The lesions are typically less well defined than experimental ablations in animals, they are rarely co-extensive with brain areas thought to have a unitary function, and they are not easy to localize. The consequences of a cerebral lesion in man depend on the aetiology of the lesion, the length of time that has elapsed since it occurred, the nature of the associated deficits, the age and possibly the sex of the patient as well as the area and hemisphere damaged.

The fact that all the methods which can be used to discover the physiological basis of visual perception have drawbacks has two implications. First, any conclusions drawn from them must be tentative and second, greater weight should be given to conclusions which are consistent with evidence from several sources. We concentrate our review on a few such cases by looking at psychological functions and relating them to what is known at present of the neural substrate.

II. Noticing and Reacting to the Visual Environment

In mammals most retinal ganglion cells send their axons to the lateral geniculate nucleus of the thalamus which in turn projects to the striate cortex in the occipital lobe. However, the axons of some retinal cells, terminate in the superior colliculi, which form a pair of bulges on the dorsal aspect of the midbrain (see Chapter 3).

Many collicular cells have visual receptive fields and respond best to transient or moving stimuli. Their responses can sometimes be modified by the significance of the stimulus, and the background firing rates of some cells can be inhibited by an eye-movement, giving them the ability to distinguish between actual movement of a stimulus and the displacement of its image across the retina caused by a movement of the eyes. Some cells also discharge before an eye-movement towards a particular part of the field. (For a detailed review see Goldberg and Robinson, 1978). These findings suggest that the colliculi could perform several visual functions including the detection and location of peripheral stimuli, the re-direction of gaze towards these stimuli and the provisions of "efference copy" information to enable the animal to take account of the visual consequences of changing fixation.

Collicular lesions in monkeys have little or no effect on the accuracy of saccadic eye movements (Wurtz and Goldberg, 1972a; Mohler and Wurtz, 1976), but they do reduce the frequency of spontaneous eye movements (particularly to the side contralateral to a unilateral lesion) and the latency of saccades directed to contralateral visual targets is increased (Wurtz and Goldberg, 1972a; Latto, 1978). These results indicate that collicular neurones are not necessary for the specification of the position of the target for an eye-movement or for the execution of the movement itself but they suggest that the colliculi may play some part in the initiation of saccades. Wurtz and Goldberg (1972b) have suggested that their role is to call attention to the stimulus, the extra time taken to shift gaze and the paucity of spontaneous contralateral eye-movements being attributable to a failure to "notice" the stimuli which normally elicit them.

Damage to the human superior colliculus (Heywood and Ratcliff, 1975) and pulvinar (Zihl and Von Cramon, 1979), to which it sends a projection, also cause neglect of the contralateral half of space, which is consistent with the attentional hypothesis. Heywood and Ratcliff's patient also seemed to lack accurate efference copy information about saccadic eye movements contralateral to the lesion. Patients with progressive supra-nuclear palsy, a condition in which the lesions include the colliculi but are not limited to it, perform poorly on tasks requiring complex scanning and visual search (Kimura *et al.*, 1979), as do monkeys with collicular lesions (Latto, 1978). The possibility that these consequences of collicular damage in man are secondary to impairment of the actual motor skill involved in moving the eyes has not been definitely excluded. But, if one takes the electrophysiological, anatomical and lesion data from all species together, it seems reasonable to suggest that the colliculi are involved in directing attention to visual stimuli and co-ordinating shifts of fixation towards them.

The consequences of damage to an area of brain can only tell one that it is *necessary* for a given function. The preservation of some visually-guided behaviour after striate cortex lesions indicates that some non-striate mechanism is nevertheless *sufficient* for some sophisticated visual function. Following Humphrey's (1974) study of residual vision in the monkey after almost total striate ablation, Weiskrantz *et al.* (1974) showed that a patient, who had most of his striate cortex removed during surgical treatment of an angioma, could reach with extraordinary accuracy for a visual stimulus which he could not consciously "see". He could also discriminate horizontal from vertical lines and a cross from a circle when tested by appropriate methods. Weiskrantz has called this residual vision "blindsight" and more recent studies (Weiskrantz, 1980) have shown that some limited visual awareness may return after extensive training.

There is thus good evidence, even in man, to show that non-striate mechanisms are capable of noticing, locating and discriminating visual stimuli. The visual functions which remain after striate lesions need not necessarily be subserved by the superior colliculi, but their anatomy and physiology seem to suit them for the role. The colliculi are probably part of the alternative neural circuit which operates after cortical damage, as the combined effects of collicular and striate ablation are much more devastating than the sum of the effects of the two lesions individually (Mohler and Wurtz, 1976).

Visually responsive neurones have also been found in Brodmann's area 7 (see Fig. 1), which lies in the posterior and superior part of the parietal lobe. The neurones of area 7 have been divided into several classes on the basis of their trigger features, which in many respects are similar to those of collicular

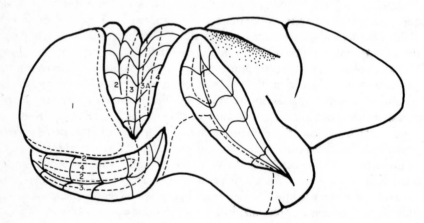

Fig. 1 *Diagram of the right hemisphere of a rhesus monkey showing the position of the visual areas mentioned in the text. The lunate (top), inferior occipital (bottom) and superior temporal sulci have been opened to reveal their depths. Stippling shows the part of area 7 that appears on the lateral surface of the inferior parietal lobule. Area 7 continues down the inferior bank of intraparietal sulcus (from Ratcliff and Cowey, 1979).*

neurones (Mountcastle, 1975; Robinson *et al.*, 1978). Like collicular cells they have large receptive fields and some of them increase their rate of discharge if the visual stimulus in their receptive field is to be the target of an eye-movement. Others exhibit a similar enhancement immediately before the animal (in this case a monkey) extends its arm to grasp the stimulus. This enhancement has been interpreted variously as the physiological correlate of: the "command" to motor systems to fixate or reach for the stimulus (Mountcastle, 1975); the direction of attention to it, which can plausibly be expected to precede such movements (Robinson *et al.*, 1978); and the specification of the position of the target, which is necessary if an accurate movement is to be made (Ratcliff and Cowey, 1979). The last interpretation is based chiefly on lesion studies. Neglect of stimuli in the contralateral half of space is a common result of right parietal lesions in man (Heilman, 1979); however, the lesions are rarely restricted to area 7 and lesions limited to this area in the monkey may be insufficient to cause neglect (Lynch and McLaren, 1979). In both species, damage to posterior parietal cortex severely disrupts the accuracy of visually-guided reaching. When the lesion is bilateral there is a generalized spatial disorientation (Holmes, 1918; Bates and Ettlinger, 1960), and when it is unilateral the misreaching occurs predominantly in the contralateral half field in man (Ratcliff and Davies-Jones, 1972) and with the contralateral arm in the monkey (Hartje and Ettlinger, 1973). The misreaching is not a trivial consequence of sensory or motor impairment and, even in man, the lesions which cause it are clustered quite closely over area 7.

In summary then, there is good evidence that extra-striate mechanisms which include area 7, the superior colliculus and the pulvinar are important in some aspects of visual behaviour, including noticing and locating visual stimuli. Physiological and ablation studies in monkeys (Latto, 1978) and the effects of frontal lobe lesions in man (Luria, 1973) suggest that the frontal eye fields are also included in these functions. However, in view of the multiple interconnections and functional interdependence of these areas of the brain, it may be more appropriate to regard all of them as parts of a single but diverse and widespread system which shares responsibility for vision, than to distinguish "two visual systems" as Schneider (1969) did for the hamster.

III. Lightness Perception

Quite substantial amounts of computation of lightness and darkness occur in the retina and hence at a very early stage of visual processing. The bipolar retinal cells collect input from receptors and provide a suitable mechanism for the detection of edges (sharp discontinuities in the intensity gradient of the luminous flux). This is achieved by collecting light from the receptors and transmitting it to bipolar cells, which have larger receptive areas with on-centres and off-surrounds or off-centres and on-surrounds. These two types of bipolar cell are the beginning of the separate whiteness and blackness channels. These channels remain distinct further into the system; adapting simultaneously to black and white bars of different widths causes the apparent width of subsequently presented black bars to be shifted in apparent width to the width of the black (but not the white) bars in the adapting stimulus. The converse is true when white bars are presented.

Ganglion cells, which receive information from the bipolar cells, also show an antagonistic centre-surround receptive field organization. Marr (1974) has speculated that it is at this level that integration of brightness information takes place from cells with different receptive fields. The fact that a cell will fire to a previously unnoticed target by the inclusion of a stimulus outside its receptive field (McIlwain, 1964) demonstrates this need for a multitude of connections between, as well as within, stages for processing brightness information.

The nature of retinal processing for brightness can explain many illusory brightness phenomena. For example, the Hermann grid (the illusory darkening of the intersections of a white grid placed on a black background; see Fig. 2) is

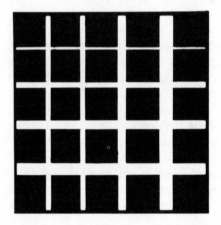

Fig. 2 *Hermann grids with intersections of varying sizes.*

a direct consequence of the receptive field geometry of ganglion cells. At an intersection, a ganglion cell with an on-centre will have the corners of four black squares from the background projecting into the off (inhibitory) surround. As the width of the white lines increases, the illusory darkening decreases because one comes to a point where the receptive field of the cell falls entirely within the white area. This usually happens at fixation (unless the lines are very narrow) because the receptive fields at the fovea are small (Jung, 1973).

Visual processing at the retina enhances contrast and can explain the common brightness contrast effect in which a grey object on a dark ground looks brighter than when it is on a light ground. It also explains the Craik–Cornsweet–O'Brien illusion, in which a sharp gradient of dark to light causes the apparent lightening and darkening of equal grays on either side of the gradient. These illusory effects are achieved by lateral inhibition between neighbouring cells, which causes contour enhancement at the edge of the object, and by an accompanying filling-in inwards from the edge, so that all of the object has the same apparent lightness (Marr, 1974).

There are other contrast effects which are not so easily explained. For example, grey stripes of constant luminous gradient placed alongside each other (see Fig. 3) appear to be bordered by light and dark bands (Mach bands), and contrast effects which usually seem to enhance brightness differences, in some circumstances make a grey ground look lighter by the addition of white lines (Bezold, 1874, cited by Hurvich and Jameson, 1966). We do not have a complete neurophysiological explanation of such illusory contrast effects, but they are presumably a by-product of the improvement in acuity derived from contrast enhancement necessary to compensate for the fuzziness of the retinal image.

It has been suggested that some illusory brightness effects show the existence of higher-order perceptual processes. A uniform grey ring placed half on a black ground and half on a white ground exhibits standard brightness contrasts for each half (see Fig. 4). However, a thin rod placed over the ring at

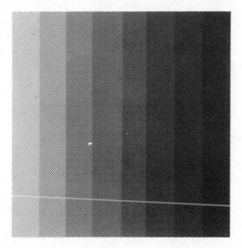

Fig. 3 *Mach bands; from Cornsweet (1970).*

Fig. 4 *Demonstration of simultaneous contrast.*

the boundary between the two backgrounds and slowly moved into the black (or white) ground will draw the perceived grey along with it (Osgood, 1953, p. 235).

Anomalous or illusory contours (see Fig. 5), as demonstrated by Schumann in 1904 (Kanizsa, 1979), have been argued by Gregory (1970) also to show the existence of conceptually based perceptual hypotheses. There are alternative explanations however. Frisby and Clatworthy (1975) give a physiological explanation for the same phenomena and consider them to be side effects of the lightness computation system. Kanizsa (1979) would rather consider the lightness changes to be a result of the formation of contours through Gestalt principles of visual organization, and there is evidence (Kanizsa, 1979, p. 204; Meyer and Phillips, 1980) that contour formation does not necessarily depend on brightness differentials.

IV. Colour Perception

All colours are generated from the responses of only three types of cone, maximally sensitive to red, green and blue; as suggested many years ago by Young (Judd, 1951). The trichromatic theory was thought to be in disagreement with the opponent-process view of Hering, who pointed out that responses to yellow were not as one would have predicted from trichromatic processing. The controversy may be resolved by looking at the output of

Fig. 5 *An anomalous contour of a triangle (after Kanizsa, 1979).*

colour sensitive cells in the lateral geniculate nucleus (LGN). De Valois (1965), recording from the LGN of the macaque monkey, found cells excited by red light and inhibited by green (or vice versa) and similar opponent processes for yellow and blue. These units exhibited almost the same responses to colour as does human colour vision measured psychophysically. De Valois has shown that discrimination of hue and saturation and the apparent variation in hue produced by intensity (Bezold–Brucke phenomenon) can all be predicted from the responses of colour coded units in the macaque monkey.

Colour vision has different properties to the black/white system. The ability to detect colour changes in coloured stripes does not show the same attenuation at low spatial frequencies as the ability to detect brightness contrast. Van der Horst *et al.* (1967) argue that this is due to the fact that no lateral inhibition is found in the colour channels, and hence no Mach bands in equiluminous gradients varying in colour.

Colour vision as a subjective experience is mirrored to a surprising extent in the neurophysiology at stages after the striate cortex, as findings from Zeki (1978) have shown. The fourth visual area in prestriate cortex (V4) contains the most distant colour sensitive cells from the retina. (For a discussion and diagram of the visual areas in prestriate cortex see Cowey, 1979). Compared to colour coded cells in the striate cortex, which themselves have large receptive fields compared to orientation specific cells, these have very large receptive fields and there is no discernible retinotopic organization.

Microelectrode implantation in the monkey has shown (Zeki, 1978) that the action spectrum (wavelength selectivity) of these cells is extremely narrow, varying from 10 to 50 nm. Although we would be able to detect changes of colour caused by such a wavelength change in most parts of the visible spectrum, this nevertheless represents a close neurophysiological approximation to our perception of individual colours. It is very different from the wide bandwidth action spectra of cells earlier in the visual system (Wiesel and Hubel, 1966). The distribution of the peak sensitivities of the cells goes right across the visible spectrum unlike those at the retina, but there does seem to be a clustering at 480 nm (blue), 550 nm (green), and 620 nm (orange-red) and more surprisingly also for the extra-spectral colour of purple. While adjacent cells do not show a consistent pattern with respect to the position of their receptive fields, they do have a common functional component. The peak excitation of the cells successively recorded in one electrode penetration, for example, gradually shifted from short to long wavelengths, with peak inhibition being the complementary colour (Zeki, 1980).

While colour constancy is affected by our memory for colours (Duncker, 1939), colour constancy is also exhibited for the colours of unknown objects. Colours change relatively little when the wavelength energy composition of illumination on objects changes markedly (Land, 1964) and the presence of, say, red in the visual world is determined not only by reflected long wavelength light but also by reflected middle and short wavelength light over a wide area. Zeki (1980) has found a neurophysiological correlate of this phenomenon. A cell with a narrow action spectrum for the red part of a multicoloured display in white light does not output if the display is illuminated by red light alone, nor by middle or short wavelengths alone. This resistance to changes in the relative flux of the component lights corresponds to colour perception since red areas, say, can still look red even when the energies of the incident lights are adjusted so that much more middle than long wavelength light reaches the eye. Although not all cells in V4 behave in this experiential way (some behave simply, i.e. responding when red light is switched on), it would seem that in prestriate cortex we have an area which can act as a colour constancy mechanism and reflects phenomenal colour perception.

Acquired loss of colour vision in man, known as cerebral achromatopsia, follows bilateral damage to the inferior occipital lobes (Meadows, 1974a) and may be the result of damage to the human equivalent of V4. The location of the lesions in achromatopsia suggests that the relevant part of the equivalent of V4 may be located rather lower than it is in the monkey (Damasio *et al.*, 1980). Achromatopsia can occur in patients with normal visual acuity in whom colour information is processed normally at the receptor level and probably reaches the cortex intact (Mollon *et al.*, 1980). The rarity of the disorder is probably due to the rarity of lesions which are sufficiently selective to damage the relevant cortical areas, without causing cortical blindness or other perceptual disorders as a result of damage to neighbouring regions.

V. Line Perception

There is good anatomical and physiological evidence for parallel visual channels (X, Y and W systems) from the ganglion cells onwards (Rowe and Stone, 1977). It has been suggested that the X system which projects to striate cortex subserves discrimination of fine detail. Even though this interpretation has been subjected to some criticism (Lennie, 1980), there is no doubt that the striate cortex with its orientation specific neurones has at least a prima facie connection with line perception.

Microelectrode implantation as pioneered by Hubel and Wiesel (1959) shows that the striate cortex is organized for visual processing into hypercolumns, which contain cells fired by stimulation from a relatively small area of retina. Each hypercolumn extends from the surface of the cortex down through to the white matter, and contains a complete cycle of orientation selective cells and a pair of ocular dominance columns, in which the neurones are maximally sensitive to stimulation from alternate eyes. In monkeys, each hypercolumn is composed of some ¼ million cells, occupies ½−1 mm square on the cortical surface and descends to about 3−4 mm. In humans there is good reason to believe that the hypercolumns are somewhat larger, at around 2 mm. Psychophysical evidence of the inhibition produced by adjacent lines (Wilson, 1978) and sensitivity for spatial frequency (Kelly, 1975), when combined with an estimate (Cowey and Rolls, 1974) of the cortical magnification factor (amount of cortex for a given area of retina), suggests a hypercolumn width of 2 mm, as does the more direct evidence of Dobelle and Mladejovsky (1974). They found that humans implanted with visual prostheses which directly stimulate striate cortex can resolve adjacent electrodes only if they are separated by more than 2−3 mm. Neurophysiological evidence for the existence of hypercolumns comes from the orientation specificity of cells as the microelectrode travels in the cortical surface. Oblique penetrations result in small progressive changes in orientation specificity as the electrode moves from column to column within the hypercolumn, with sudden discontinuities in the steady progression presumably denoting the existence of a new hypercolumn. Chemical uptake of radioactive deoxyglucose by active cells has given us anatomical evidence for hypercolumns (Hubel et al., 1978), as seen from histological sections of the striate cortex of an animal that had been viewing vertical lines just prior to being killed.

There are different types of cell in the hypercolumn which are sensitive to various patterns of light energy. Individual cells respond optimally to edges, slits (light surrounded by dark) or lines (dark surrounded by light) of a particular size and orientation. Adaptation of particular cells should be able to produce a dissociation between orientation effects and width of line effects, which psychophysical procedures have verified. Blakemore and Sutton (1969) found that after inspection of a grating, a finer grating viewed subsequently looked even finer and a coarser one even coarser (Fig. 6). The existence of width specific cells can also be inferred from Blakemore and Campbell (1969), since in that study adaptation was specific to the spatial frequency of the grating. There is a similar orientation specific adaptation which results in an orientation dependent after-effect (Gibson, 1937). Pro-

Fig. 6 An after effect, dependent upon spatial frequency. Inspection of the upper two gratings, by fixation at the bar, should be followed by inspection of the lower two gratings, by fixation at the spot (after Blakemore and Sutton, 1969).

longed inspection of a line rotated clockwise from the vertical by 10° will cause a subsequently viewed vertical line to appear tilted by about 3° in the opposite direction. It has been calculated that the output of cortical cells which have adapted to this clockwise rotation would indeed closely resemble their unadapted output when inspecting a line rotated 3° counter clockwise.

Each discriminable orientation is not represented in the hypercolumn. There are in fact somewhere between 18–20 different orientation columns giving around 10° difference between columns. This explains why the tiltafter-effect decreases markedly if adapting and test gratings differ by more than 10°, but it does not explain why we are able to discriminate between orientations which differ by as little as 2°. There must be a mechanism for pooling the outputs from many simple cells all of which must to some extent fire; however, as yet, no neural correlate of the sharply defined edge at a specific orientation has been found.

Individual cells when adapted show least, in fact zero, adaptation to stimuli at right angles to the inspection figure. This suggests that the right angle is not just a geometric nicety, making it easy to work out area, but that it has a physiological basis. There is not as yet any neurophysiological evidence confirming the special right angle of the horizontal and vertical although human psychophysical data tell us that there should be. Contrast sensitivity and acuity are at their greatest at the meridians of 0° and 90°. Similarly, perceptual organization is at its best at these meridians (Davidoff, 1974). One could speculate that one has vertical and horizontal detection mechanisms which are more finely tuned than those for obliques (Bouma and Andriessen, 1970). Alternatively, there could be more cortex allocated to these orientations. Blakemore and Cooper (1970) provided evidence for this suggestion by showing that kittens raised in vertically striped surroundings did not have horizontally tuned striate neurones and vice versa for kittens raised in an horizontally striped environment. Psychophysical data from non-Caucasian populations have suggested that either or both genetic and experiential factors contribute towards different orientation specificities (Annis and Frost, 1973). The importance of experiential factors is more clearly shown by astigmatism. This refractive error causes blurring along one meridian on the retina and if it is not optically corrected early in life, the patients suffer a permanent reduction in acuity along that meridian (Mitchell *et al.*, 1973). A quite different experiential hypothesis of a more cognitive nature is offered by Gregory (1970), whose explanation of the importance in human vision for the horizontal and vertical is based on the frequency of these meridians in our environment.

Any visual dimension that will produce a simple after-effect can interact with another similar dimension to produce a contingent after-effect. Thus, in the McCollough (1965) effect colour is combined with orientation. After adaptation, differences in orientation produce apparent colours from achromatic stimuli. This effect is orientationally defined in the same way as for simple cortical cells, in that the two gratings have to differ by at least 11° in order to give a contingent after-effect of a tilt producing different colours. Held and Shattuck (1971) found similar orientation tuning for a colour to produce a tilt. Higher order units of one sort or another have been postulated to explain these effects, which would require, for example, both a vertical and a red stimulus to cause firing. Despite the fact that we have many millions of neurones for which to find a function, such specificity has been doubted. Contingent after-effects also behave differently from simple after-effects in that they are very durable. It has been claimed that they last for weeks if the initial adaptation is long enough (Stromeyer and Mansfield, 1970). Mollon (1974) has suggested that doubly tuned cells are formed during adaptation, but there is no neurophysiological evidence for this speculation.

Higher order units have also been put forward to explain the orthogonal after-images of Mackay (1964), in which prolonged exposure to a pattern of concentric circles results in an after-image of radiating lines and vice versa. This effect could arise from the fatigue of cells tuned to detect orientations 90° apart, or as Schwartz (1980) has suggested, the effect is more likely to be due to mapping of orientation within the hypercolumns of the striate cortex. It is suggested that patterns which are 90° rotated will be consistently half of a hypercolumn distance out of phase, giving the complementary image after adaptation.

Explanation of higher-order effects based on combinations of features loses much of its appeal as one realizes that simple cells cannot be feature detectors. A cell which responds optimally to a line at, say, 10° will also respond less well to a line at 20°. However, the responses of such cells are also affected by the brightness of the stimulus. So, how could a cell distinguish between a line, at 10° and a brighter line at 20°? Similarly, cells which fire optimally for slits also fire to some extent for lines. Indeed, John and Schwartz (1978), reviewing the evidence for single cell feature extraction, point out that angle of tilt of body and even auditory stimulation in the appropriate region of visual space all affect the firing rate of these cells. There must be some global process comparing output from many simple cells if the ambiguity is to be resolved. We as yet do not know the neurophysiological correlate of this process, though presumably the hypercolumn is implicated.

VI. Depth Perception

Each hypercolumn of the striate cortex (V1) consists of a pair of ocular dominance columns. At V1 (Fisher and Poggio, 1979) and at V2 (Hubel and

Wiesel, 1970) there is the facility for binocular fusion. In V2 Hubel and Wiesel (1970) show that neurones respond to stimuli falling on non-corresponding points of the two retinae, and therefore that V2 neurones are equipped for coding retinal disparity. Ablation experiments have verified this role for V2 (Cowey, 1979). V2 is known to exist in man but we do not know whether it has a corresponding function (Cowey and Rolls, 1974).

In man it seems that stereoscopic depth perception can be affected by damage to either hemisphere. Different estimates of the frequency of the disorder seem to depend on the different methods which have been used to assess stereopsis (Danta *et al.*, 1978). The responsible lesion is usually in the posterior part of the brain though its precise location varies between cases. Damage to the right hemisphere is more frequently involved, though this may be an artifact of case selection (Danta *et al.*, 1978).

VII. Object Perception

Neurophysiological evidence from microelectrode implantation in the striate cortex of the cat and monkey shows that analysis of visual input, despite the apparent continuity of the visual world in phenomenal perception, is carried out piecemeal. Small parts of the visual field are allocated to particular units of the striate cortex, therefore implying that at a further stage there must be some reintegration. How we manage to obtain structure from the output of the hypercolumns remains unknown. The "features" detected may be further organized by grouping principles not unlike those of the Gestalt psychologists (Marr, 1980), by conjunction through focal attention (Treisman and Gelade, 1980) or alternatively by what might be called context or concept driven hypotheses (Gregory, 1970).

Higher cortical processes do contribute towards form perception and are hard to integrate into the data-driven view of visual perception which constitutes most of this chapter. However, organizational principles have been shown to apply not only to our perception of whole figures when presented only with parts (Leeper, 1935), but also to the after-effects which might be thought to be the sole property of the hypercolumns. Meyer and Phillips (1980) constructed a face-vase ambiguous pattern from a square of horizontal and vertical lines. When subjects who had been exposed to the standard inducing stimulus for the McCollough effect viewed this ambiguous figure, they saw the usual illusory colours when the stimulus was perceived as a face/vase but not when it was perceived as a pattern of rectangles.

A full account of object recognition has proved intractable to computer analysis, one problem being that an object has to be recognized from an infinite number of different views. It would seem unlikely that all such views are represented on a permanent structural basis at the neuronal level, but it could be that there are cells which respond to prototypic versions. Micro-electrode implantation in the monkey has suggested that cells which respond to hand or face-like objects are to be found in the inferotemporal cortex (Gross et al., 1972). There may therefore be some preprogramming, to create higher level neurones responsive to such combinations of features which are important for surivial. How the identification of a particular face maps onto these neurones is still unknown. A single representation for a given face is required if only for acquiring associations, since we would not want to learn the same association for every possible view of the same face.

The rare clinical syndrome of prosopagnosia (inability to recognize familiar faces) arises from bilateral lesions in the inferior occipital–temporal region (Meadows, 1974b), though it may be that the right hemisphere lesion is critical (Whiteley and Warrington, 1977). Visual closure, as measured by the ability to perceive faces in black and white degraded photographs, is certainly more impaired by right than by comparable left hemisphere lesions (Newcombe and Russell, 1969). The more general, though again rare, disorder of visual agnosia arises typically from more diffuse lesions (Rubens, 1979). The lesions which cause visual recognition deficits in man seem to be close to the site of those which cause visual discrimination learning deficits in monkeys (Dean, 1977). With some ingenuity one can discern a similarity between the charac-teristics of the deficit in the two species. However, the kinds of task used are too different to justify a formal comparison, and the location of the lesions – infero-temporal in the monkey and temporo-parietal-occipital in man – do not appear to be identical.

Although there is no convincing evidence for any difference in function between the left and right infero-temporal regions in the monkey, it is not surprising that there should be functional differences between posterior temporal cortex in the two hemispheres of the human brain. The temporo-parietal region is the area in which the most consistent physical asymmetry between the human cerebral hemispheres has been reported (Witelson, 1977). This physical asymmetry is related to cerebral dominance for speech (Ratcliff et al., 1980) and handedness (Hochberg and LeMay, 1975). A physically asymmetric brain has been found in apes as well as man but is not present in monkeys (LeMay, 1976). Speech and handedness are uniquely human characteristics and the temporo-parietal region in the left hemisphere corresponds to Wernicke's area, one of the areas involved in language proces-sing. Given that speech has developed in the left hemisphere, one would expect that parts of the right hemisphere corresponding to the speech areas should have their own special function and this appears to be a capacity for higher perceptual organization.

VIII. Concluding Remarks

As we progress through the complexity of psychological function based on vision, we find less correspondence between man and other species. For visual reception, animal microelectrode implantation and lesion studies give us a picture which resembles human performance, but in man higher-order visual tasks may well have a different neural substrate. For these higher-order tasks we are also less precise as to the neurophysiological correlate. Whereas at the striate (and prestriate) cortex we are concerned with the function of individual cells, all that we can identify as a substrate of higher functions are areas of cortex. In trying to relate a complex psychological process to a cortical site we have to admit ignorance of the nature of the psychological process. Clarification at the behavioural level may help in the formulation of more appropriate experiments concerning neurophysiological correlates.

Acknowledgements

The work done at the Neuropsychology Unit, The Radcliffe Infirmary Oxford, was supported in part by a Medical Research Council Grant G973/144.

Further Reading

Cowey, A. (1979). Cortical maps and visual perception. *Q. J. Exp. Psychol.* **31**, 1–17. A short review of the literature on the visual mechanisms in the primate pre-striate cortex with comments on its implication for visual perception.
Dean, P. (1977). Effects of infero-temporal lesions on the behaviour of monkeys. *Psychol. Bull.* **83**, 41–71. A comprehensive review and critical analysis of the data on infero-temporal lesions in monkeys.
Frisby, J. P. (1980). "Seeing". Oxford University Press, Oxford. A beautifully illustrated, readable book which discusses vision from the point of view of the neurophysiology, psychophysics and computational theory while avoiding technical jargon.
Goldberg, M. E. and Robinson, D. L. (1978). Visual system: superior colliculus. *In* "Handbook of Behavioural Neurobiology, 1: Sensory Integration" (R. B. Masterson, ed.), pp. 119–164. Plenum Press, New York. A comprehensive account of the anatomy, physiology and function of the superior colliculus.
Hubel, D. H. and Wiesel, T. N. (1979). "Brain Mechanisms of Vision in the Brain". W. H. Freeman, San Francisco. A scientific American book. An introduction to the work of these pioneers of visual neurophysiology through microelectrode implantation.
Mountcastle, V. B. (1975). The view from within: pathways to the study of perception. *Johns Hopkins Med. J.* **136**, 109–135.

Robinson, D. L., Goldberg, M. and Stanton, G. G. (1978). Parietal association cortex in the primate: sensory mechanisms and behavioural modifications. *J. Neurophysiol.* **41**, 910–932.
Two accounts of the physiology of area 7 which come to different conclusions about its role in behaviour.
Rubens, A. B. (1979). Agnosia. *In* "Clinical Neuropsychology" (K. M. Heilman and E. Valenstein, eds). Oxford University Press, New York.
A readable review emphasizing the clinical phenomena.
Zeki, S. M. (1980). The representation of colours in the cerebral cortex. *Nature* **284**, 412–418.
A comprehensive account of the author's work on the colour coded areas of the monkey's visual cortex.

References

Annis, R. C. and Frost, B. (1973). Human visual ecology and orientation anisotropies in acuity. *Science* **182**, 729–731.
Bates, J. A. V. and Ettlinger, G. (1960). Posterior bi-parietal ablations in the monkey. *Archs Neurol., Chicago* **3**, 177–192.
Blakemore, C. and Campbell, F. W. (1969). On the existence in the human visual system of neurones selectively sensitive to the orientation and size of retinal images. *J. Physiol., Lond.* **203**, 237–260.
Blakemore, C. and Cooper, G. F. (1970). Development of the brain depends on the visual environment. *Nature* **228**, 477–478.
Blakemore, C. and Sutton, P. (1969). Size adaptation: A new after-effect. *Science* **160**, 245–247.
Bouma, H. and Andriessen, J. J. (1970). Perceived orientation of isolated line segments. *Vision Res.* **8**, 493–507.
Cornsweet, T. N. (1970). "Visual Perception". Academic Press, New York and London.
Cowey, A. (1979). Cortical maps and visual perception. *Q. Jl exp. Psychol.* **31**, 1–17.
Cowey, A. and Rolls, E. T. (1974). Human cortical magnification factor and its relation to visual acuity. *Expl Brain Res.* **21**, 447–454.
Damasio, A., Yamada, T., Damasio, H., Corbett, J. and McKee, J. (1980). Central achromatopsia: Behavioural anatomic and physiologic aspects. *Neurology* **30**, 1064–1071.
Danta, G., Hilton, R. C. and O'Boyle, D. J. (1978). Hemisphere function and binocular depth perception. *Brain* **101**, 569–590.
Davidoff, J. B. (1974). An observation concerning the preferred perception of the visual horizontal and vertical. *Perception* **3**, 47–48.
Dean, P. (1977). Effects of infero-temporal lesions on the behaviour of monkeys. *Psychol. Bull.* **83**, 41–71.
De Valois, R. L. (1965). Analysis and coding of colour vision in the primate visual system. *Cold Spring Harb. Symp.* **30**, 567–579.
Dobelle, W. and Mladejovsky, M. G. (1974). Phosphenes produced by electrical stimulation of human occipital cortex and their application to the development of a prosthesis for the blind. *J. Physiol., Lond.* **243**, 553–576.
Duncker, K. (1939). The influence of past experience upon perceptual properties. *Am. J. Psychol.* **52**, 255–265.

Fisher, B. and Poggio, G. F. (1979). Depth sensitivity of binocular cortical neurones of behaving monkeys. *Proc. R. Soc. ser. B* **204**, 409–414.
Frisby, J. P. and Clatworthy, J. L. C. (1975). Illusory contours: curious cases of simultaneous brightness contrast? *Perception* **4**, 349–357.
Gibson, J. J. (1937). Adaptation with negative after-effect. *Psychol. Rev.* **44**, 222–244.
Goldberg, M. E. and Robinson, D. L. (1978). Visual system: superior colliculus. *In* "Handbook of Behavioral Neurobiology, 1: Sensory Integration" (R. B. Masterson, ed.), pp. 119–164. Plenum Press, New York.
Gregory, R. L. (1970). "The Intelligent Eye". Weidenfeld and Nicolson, London.
Gross, C. G., Rocha-Miranda, C. E. and Bender, D. B. (1972). Visual properties of neurons in inferotemporal cortex of the macaque. *J. Neurophysiol.* **35**, 96–111.
Hartje, W. and Ettlinger, G. (1973). Reaching in light and dark after unilateral posterior parietal ablations in monkey. *Cortex* **9**, 346–354.
Heilman, K. M. (1979). Neglect and related disorders. *In* "Clinical Neuropsychology" (K. M. Heilman and E. Valenstein, eds). Oxford University Press, London.
Held, R. and Shattuck, S. (1971). Color- and edge-sensitive channels in the human visual system: Tuning for orientation. *Science* **174**, 314–316.
Heywood, S. and Ratcliff, G. (1975). Long-term consequences of unilateral colliculectomy in man. *In* "Basic Mechanisms of Ocular Motility and Their Clinical Implications" (G. Lennerstrand and P. Bach-y-Rita, eds). Pergamon, Oxford.
Hochberg, F. H. and LeMay, M. (1975). Arteriographic correlates of handedness. *Neurology* **25**, 218–222.
Holmes, G. (1918). Disturbances of visual orientation. *Br. J. Ophthal.* **2**, 449–468 and 506–516.
Hubel, D. H. and Wiesel, T. N. (1959). The receptive fields of simple neurones in the cat's striate cortex. *J. Physiol., Lond.* **148**, 574–591.
Hubel, D. H. and Wiesel, T. N. (1970). Stereoscopic vision in the macaque monkey. *Nature* **225**, 41–44.
Hubel, D. H., Wiesel, T. N. and Stryker, M. P. (1978) Anatomical demonstration of orientation columns in macaque monkey. *J. Comp. Neurology* **177**, 361–380.
Humphrey, N. K. (1974). Vision in the monkey without striate cortex: a case study. *Perception* **3**, 241–255.
Hurvich, L. M. and Jameson, D. (1966). "The Perception of Brightness and Darkness". Allyn and Bacon, Boston.
John, E. R. and Schwartz, E. L. (1978). The neurophysiology of information processing and cognition. *A. Rev. Psychol.* **29**, 1–29.
Judd, D. B. (1951). Basic correlates of the visual stimulus. *In* "Handbook of Experimental Psychology" (S. S. Stevens, ed.). Wiley and Sons, New York.
Jung, R. (1973). Visual perception and neurophysiology. *In* "Handbook of Sensory Physiology" (R. Jung, ed.). Springer-Verlag, Berlin.
Kanizsa, G. (1979). "Organization in Vision". Praeger, New York.
Kelly, D. H. (1975). Spatial frequency selectivity in the retina. *Vision Res.* **15**, 665–672.
Kimura, D., Barnett, H. J. M. and Burkhart, G. (1979). The psychological test pattern in progressive supranuclear palsy. University of Western Ontario, Dept Psychol. Res. Bull. **477**.
Land, E. H. (1964). The retinex. *Am Scient.* **52**, 247–264.
Latto, R. (1978). The effects of bilateral frontal eye-field, posterior parietal or superior collicular lesions on visual search in the rhesus monkey. *Brain Res.* (Amsterdam) **146**, 35–50.

Leeper, (1935). A study of the neglected portion of the field of learning – the development of sensory organization. *J. Genet. Psychol.* **46**, 41–75.

LeMay, M. (1976). Morphological cerebral asymmetries of modern man, fossil man and nonhuman primate. *Ann. N.Y. Acad. Sci.* **280**, 349–366.

Lennie, P. (1980). Parallel visual pathways: A review. *Vision Res.* **20**, 561–594.

Luria, A. R. (1973). "The Working Brain". Penguin Books, Harmondsworth.

Lynch, J. C. and McLaren, J. W. (1979). Effects of lesions of parieto-occipital association cortex upon performance of oculomotor and attention tasks in monkeys. *Soc. Neurosci. Abstr.* **5**, 794.

Mackay, D. M. (1964). Central adaptation in mechanism of form vision. *Nature* **203**, 993–994.

Marr, D. (1974). The computation of lightness by the primate retina. *Vision Res.* **14**, 1377–1388.

Marr, D. (1980). Visual information processing: the structure and creation of visual representations. *Phil. Trans. R. Soc. Ser. B* **290**, 199–218.

McCollough, C. (1965). Color adaptation of edge-detectors in the human visual system. *Science, N.Y.* **149**, 1115–1116.

McIlwain, J. T. (1964). Receptive fields of optic tract axons and lateral geniculate cells: peripheral extent and barbiturate sensitivity. *J. Neurophysiol.* **27**, 1154–1173.

Meadows, J. C. (1974a). Disturbed perception of colours associated with localised cerebral lesions. *Brain* **97**, 615–632.

Meadows, J. C. (1974b). The anatomical basis for prosopagnosia. *J. Neurol. Neurosurg. Psychiat.* **37**, 489–501.

Meyer, G. E. and Phillips, D. (1980). Faces, vases, subjective contours and the McCollough effect. *Perception* **9**, 603–606.

Mitchell, D. E., Freeman, R. D., Millodot, M. and Haegerstrom, G. (1973). Meridional amblyopia: evidence for modification of the human visual system by early visual experience. *Vision Res.* **13**, 535–558.

Mohler, C. W. and Wurtz, R. H. (1976). Role of striate cortex and superior colliculus in the visual guidance of saccadic eye-movements in the monkey. *J. Neurophysiol.* **40**, 74–94.

Mollon, J. D. (1974). After-effects and the brain. *New Scientist*, 21 Feb. 479–482.

Mollon, J. D., Newcombe, F., Polden, P. G. and Ratcliff, G. (1980). On the presence of three cone mechanisms in a case of total achromatopsia. *In* "Colour Vision Deficiencies V" (G. Verriest, ed.). Hilger, Bristol.

Mountcastle, V. B. (1975). The view from within: pathways to the study of perception. *Johns Hopkins Med. J.* **136**, 109–135.

Newcombe, F. and Russell, W. R. (1969). Dissociated visual perceptual and spatial deficits in focal lesions of the right hemisphere. *J. Neurol. Neurosurg. and Psychiat.* **32**, 73–81.

Osgood, C. E. (1953). "Method and Theory in Experimental Psychology." Oxford University Press, New York.

Ratcliff, G. and Cowey, A. (1979). Disturbances of visual perception following cerebral lesions. *In* "Research in Psychology and Medicine" (D. J. Oborne, M. M. Gruneberg and J. R. Eiser, eds), Vol. 1. Academic Press, London and New York.

Ratcliff, G. and Davies-Jones, G. A. B. (1972). Defective visual localisation in focal brain wounds. *Brain* **95**, 49–60.

Ratcliff, G., Dila, C., Taylor, L. B. and Milner, B. (1980). The morphological asymmetry of the hemispheres and cerebral dominance for speech: a possible relationship. *Brain and Language* **11**, 87–98.

Robinson, D. L., Goldberg, M. and Stanton, G. B. (1978). Parietal association cortex in the primate: sensory mechanisms and behavioural modulations. *J. Neurophysiol.* **41**, 910–932.

Rowe, M. H. and Stone, J. (1977). Naming of neurones. *Brain, Behavior Evoln* **14**, 185–216.

Rubens, A. B. (1979). Agnosia. *In* "Clinical Neuropsychology" (K. M. Heilman and E. Valenstein, eds). Oxford University Press, New York.

Schneider, G. E. (1969). Two visual systems. *Science* **163**, 895–902.

Schwartz, E. L. (1980). Computational anatomy and functional architecture of striate cortex: A spatial mapping approach to perceptual coding. *Vision Res.* **20**, 645–669.

Stromeyer, C. F. and Mansfield, R. J. (1970). Colored after effects produced with moving edges. *Percept. Psychophys.* **7**, 108–114.

Treisman, A. M. and Gelade, G. (1980). A feature-integration theory of attention. *Cognitive Psychol.* **12**, 97–136.

Van der Horst, G. J. C., de Weert, C. M. M. and Bouman, M. A. (1967). Spatiotemporal chromaticity discrimination. *J. Opt. Soc. Am.* **59**, 1482–1488.

Weiskrantz, L. (1980). Varieties of residual experience. *Q. Jl Exp. Psychol.* **32**, 365–386.

Weiskrantz, L., Warrington, E. K., Sanders, M. D. and Marshall, J. (1974). Visual capacity in the hemianopic field following a restricted occipital ablation. *Brain* **97**, 709–728.

Whiteley, A. M. and Warrington, E. K. (1977). Prosopagnosia: a clinical, psychological and anatomical study of three patients. *J. Neurol. Neurosurg. Psychiat.* **40**, 395–403.

Wiesel, T. N. and Hubel, D. H. (1966). Spatial and chromatic interactions in the lateral geniculate body of the rhesus monkey. *J. Neurophysiol.* **29**, 1115–1156.

Wilson, H. R. (1978). Quantitative prediction of line spread function measurements: implications for channel bandwidths. *Vision Res.* **18**, 493–496.

Witelson, S. F. (1977). Anatomic asymmetry in the temporal lobes: its documentation, phylogenesis, and relationship to functional asymmetry. *In* "Evolution and Lateralization of the Brain" (S. J. Dimond and D. A. Blizard, eds) and *Ann. N.Y. Acad. Sci.* **299**.

Wurtz, R. H. and Goldberg, M. E. (1972a). Activity of superior colliculus in behaving monkey. IV Effects of lesions on eye movement. *J. Neurophysiol.* **35**, 587–596.

Wurtz, R. H. and Goldberg, M. E. (1972b). The primate superior colliculus and the shift of visual attention. *Invest. Ophthalmol.* **11**, 441–450.

Zeki, S. M. (1978). Functional specialisation in the visual cortex of the rhesus monkey. *Nature* **274**, 423–428.

Zeki, S. M. (1980). The representation of colours in the cerebral cortex. *Nature* **284**, 412–418.

Zihl, J. and von Cramon, D. (1979). The contribution of the 'second' visual system to directed visual attention in man. *Brain* **102**, 835–856.

9 The Frequency Selectivity of the Auditory System

B. C. J. Moore

Abstract Many aspects of the perception of sound are consistent with the idea that the peripheral auditory system contains a bank of filters which analyse complex sounds into their sinusoidal components. These filters are characterized neurophysiologically by measuring the thresholds of single neurones in the auditory nerve as a function of the frequency of stimulation. The resulting tuning curves bear a striking resemblance to psychophysical tuning curves obtained in masking experiments with humans. It is also possible to demonstrate psychophysical analogues of a second phenomenon which is observed in single neurones: two-tone suppression.

I. The Ear as a Frequency Analyser

The basic stimulus entering the ear consists of fluctuations in air pressure as a function of time. Considered in this form a sound stimulus is completely specified by temporal variations in pressure. However, when a complex sound such as speech or music is presented to the ear, it is transformed in such a way that its neural representation is multi-dimensional. According to Fourier's theory, any complex sound can be analysed into a series of sinusoidal components, a process called frequency analysis. In many ways the ear behaves as if it carries out such an analysis, although it does it in a less than perfect way. The main theme of this chapter will be to compare and contrast physiological and behavioural studies of the frequency analysis carried out by the ear.

One of the simplest waveforms to analyse is the sine-wave, or sinusoidal vibration. An example is given in Fig. 1. This waveform is specified by its frequency, or the number of complete cycles per second (measured in Hz), and its peak amplitude, or maximum pressure deviation from normal atmospheric pressure. Frequency analysis consists of breaking down a sound into sinusoidal components, and so, by definition a sinusoid consists of just one

PHYSIOLOGICAL CORRELATES OF HUMAN
BEHAVIOUR   ISBN 0-12-273901-9

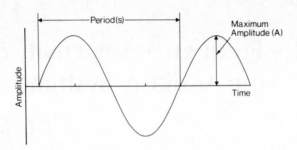

Fig. 1 *The waveform of a sinusoid, also called a simple tone or pure tone. Only 1½ cycles are shown, although the waveform should be pictured as repeating indefinitely. The instantaneous amplitude is given by the expression Asin (2πft), where t is time, f is frequency and A is the maximum amplitude (i.e. the maximum deviation of the sound pressure from the mean). The frequency is the reciprocal of the period.*

component. We shall see later that sinusoids produce relatively simple responses in the auditory system, and thus they are often used as a stimulus to investigate the properties of the system. Subjectively, sinusoids have a very clean or "pure" sound, like that of a tuning fork, and they are often called simple tones or pure tones. When we are presented with a single sinusoid, we hear a single sound with a pitch which is largely determined by the frequency of the sound.

If we are presented with two sinusoids simultaneously, then our perception of this complex sound depends on the frequency separation of the two frequency components. If the components are widely separated in frequency, say 500 Hz and 2000 Hz, then we will hear two separate tones, each with its own pitch and loudness. This illustrates the action of the ear as a frequency analyser; the complex pressure wave has been analysed into the individual sinusoidal components of which it is composed, and the percept is related to these individual components. If, on the other hand, the components are closely spaced in frequency, say 1000 and 1030 Hz, then the two components will not be heard separately; rather we will hear a single sound with a harsh unpleasant quality, quite unlike that of a pure tone. In this case the ear does not have sufficient resolving power to separate the closely spaced components. It is clear then, that the ear does not behave as a perfect frequency analyser; rather its frequency selectivity is limited. One of the main thrusts of auditory research, both physiological and psychological, is to characterize and quantify the limitations of the ear's frequency analysis.

If we wish to carry out a frequency analysis of a complex sound using physical means, one method is to use a bank of band-pass filters. It is convenient to use filters which operate on electrical signals, so we would first need to convert the sound to an electrical form using a microphone. If we use a sinusoidal signal as input to a band-pass filter then over a certain range of frequencies, the pass-band, the signal is passed at full intensity and the output equals the input. However, for frequencies above or below this range the output will drop, or be attenuated. A typical filter characteristic is shown in Fig. 2.

If we apply a complex signal at the input to the filter, then the output will be dominated by those sinusoidal components of the input which fall within the pass-band of the filter. For example, if the filter has a pass-band from 950 Hz to 1050 Hz, and we present an input consisting of the sum of two sinusoids, 1000 Hz and 1500 Hz, the output will consist largely of the component at 1000 Hz. If we had a bank of band-pass filters, each with a pass-band tuned to a slightly different centre frequency, then the 1000 Hz component would produce a strong output in those filters whose pass-bands included 1000 Hz, and the 1500 Hz component would produce a strong output in those filters whose pass-bands included 1500 Hz. Thus our bank of filters would perform a kind of frequency analysis, splitting the complex sound into its sinusoidal components. The ability of the filter bank to resolve closely spaced components (i.e. its frequency selectivity) would be determined by the shapes or characteristics of the filters. Filters with narrow pass-bands and steep slopes outside the pass-band would give a high-resolution analysis, whereas filters with broad pass-bands and shallow slopes would give a low-resolution analysis.

The peripheral auditory system is often likened to a bank of band-pass

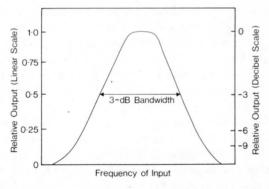

Fig. 2 *A typical filter characteristic. The input to the filter is a sinusoid of constant intensity, but variable frequency. The intensity of the output of the filter is plotted as a function of the input frequency. The bandwidth of the filter (its pass-band) is usually defined as the frequency difference between the two points at which the response has fallen in intensity by a factor of 2, or 3 dB (see text for details).*

filters, with continuously overlapping pass-bands. Many aspects of our perception of complex sounds can be understood in terms of this analogy. This immediately leads to the question of the shapes of the ear's filters; what are their pass-bands and slopes, and how do these vary with centre frequency? In order to answer these questions we need to consider the physical measures which are used to specify filter shapes. We can then go on to compare physiological and psychological estimates of auditory filter shape.

II. The Physical Specification of Filters

A. *Units of Measurement*

The auditory system can deal with a huge range of sound intensities; the most intense sound we can listen to without damaging our ears is about 100 000 000 000 000 times as intense as the faintest sound we can detect. This makes it inconvenient to deal with sound intensities directly. Instead a logarithmic measure is used to express the ratio of two intensities. This unit is the decibel, which is abbreviated to dB. If one sound, the reference sound, has an intensity I_0, and a second sound has an intensity I_1, then their sound levels differ by $10 \log_{10}(I_1/I_0)$ dB. For example, if sound I_1 has an intensity 100 times that of sound I_0, its sound level is 20 dB higher than that of sound I_0. The decibel expresses the relative level of two sounds. If we wish to specify the absolute level of a sound we can do it by referring to an internationally defined reference level, corresponding roughly to the average human absolute threshold for a 1 kHz pure tone. A sound level specified relative to this reference level is known as a sound pressure level, with units dB SPL. It is convenient to remember that each time sound intensity is *multiplied* by a factor of ten, 10 decibels are *added* to the sound level. Thus if the sound intensity is increased by a factor of one million, the sound level is increased by 60 dB. It is also useful to remember that a doubling or halving of intensity corresponds to a change in sound level of about 3 dB (since $10 \log_{10}2$ is roughly equal to 3).

It is sometimes convenient to express frequencies on a logarithmic scale, or in terms of frequency ratios, since this can give a better description of the action of the ear. The most common unit is the octave, which corresponds to a frequency ratio of 2 : 1. In general, for two frequencies f_1 and f_2, the number of octaves separating them is $\log_{10}(f_1/f_2)/\log_{10}2$.

B. *Bandwidth and Slope*

Most physically realizable filters do not have completely flat pass-bands; rather there is a frequency at which the response is maximal, called the centre frequency, and a range of frequencies on either side of that over which the response changes relatively little. Conventionally the width of the pass-band of a filter, its bandwidth, is taken as the difference between the two frequencies at which the response of the filter has fallen by a factor of two in intensity, or 3 dB. This is called the 3-dB bandwidth. A common way of defining the sharpness of tuning of a filter is in terms of the "Q" value, which is defined as the centre frequency divided by the band-width. For example a filter with a 3-dB bandwidth of 250 Hz and a centre frequency of 1 kHz would have a Q of 4. As we shall see, the responses of a single neurone within the auditory nerve can be interpreted as reflecting the output of a filter, but neurophysiologists sometimes find it difficult to measure accurately the characteristics of the pass-band. It is somewhat easier to measure the points 10 dB from the tip, giving the 10-dB bandwidth. The corresponding Q value is known as $Q_{10\text{-dB}}$, and is the ratio of the centre frequency to the bandwidth at the 10-dB down points.

To specify the characteristics of a filter away from the pass-band, we need a measure of how quickly the response falls as a function of frequency (i.e. of the steepness of the slopes). The most common measure has units of decibels per octave (dB/oct). For example, if the response of the filter falls 60 dB, when the input frequency is changed from 1 to 2 kHz, the slope is 60 dB/oct. If a filter response is plotted in dB on a logarithmic frequency scale, the slopes of the filter often approximate straight lines. This means that the slopes of the filter are constant when expressed in dB/oct. However, the slope on the high-frequency side (the HF slope) may be different from that on the low-frequency side (the LF slope).

III. Physiological Measures of Frequency Selectivity

A. *The Basilar Membrane*

The first stage of the frequency analysis which takes place in the auditory system occurs in the inner ear or cochlea. This is a structure which has rigid bony walls, and the shape of a tube coiled like the shell of a snail. This tube is filled with fluid, and it is divided along its length by a membrane called the basilar membrane which vibrates when a sound enters the ear. The physical properties of this membrane, such as its width and stiffness, vary along its length, and because of this each point on the membrane behaves like a filter tuned to a particular frequency. Each different position along the basilar membrane is tuned to a different centre frequency, with the result that different frequencies set up patterns of vibration at different points along its length. The basilar membrane thus acts as a mechanical frequency analyser, performing a frequency-to-place conversion.

A structure called the Organ of Corti lies along the length of the basilar membrane, and contained within the Organ of Corti are the rows of hair cells which are the transducers of the auditory system. The hair cells convert the mechanical movements into electrical activity, which leads to the formation of action potentials in the neurones which make up the auditory nerve. The exact mechanisms by which this takes place are not known.

There is at the moment an active debate about whether the frequency selectivity which is seen on the basilar membrane is sufficient to account for the selectivity seen at other levels of the auditory system. Many workers (e.g. Evans and Wilson, 1973) feel that some other peripheral frequency-selective process must be involved. This hypothetical process has been called the "second filter", the basilar membrane being the first filter. Since this is still an area of controversy, and since there are doubts about the accuracy of some measures of the patterns of vibration on the basilar membrane, we will not pursue this question further. Rather we will concentrate on the frequency selectivity found in single neurones in the auditory nerve. This selectivity does not appear to be markedly enhanced at higher levels of the auditory system, so that measures in primary neurones give a good estimate of the basic frequency resolving power of the auditory system.

B. *Tuning Curves in Primary Auditory Neurones*

Using microelectrodes it is possible to record the activity of single neurones within the auditory nerve. These recordings have shown very clearly that single neurones have frequency selective properties; any single neurone will respond briskly over a certain frequency range, and will respond less briskly, or not at all, to frequencies outside this range. However, if we wish to interpret this pattern of response as indicating that the neurone is driven by the output of a filter, and if we wish to define the characteristics of that filter, then we have to be careful about the response measure that we take. Most primary auditory neurones show some spontaneous activity in the absence of any sound, and most will show saturation of their firing rate for a sufficiently intense sound (see Chapter 4 by Boddy).

Thus the firing rate of a neurone does not provide a linear measure of the effective output of the filter which is driving it. One way to overcome this problem is to measure the filter characteristics for a *fixed output*, in other words for a fixed response from the neurone. Most commonly the response criterion chosen is a small increase in firing rate over the spontaneous rate; this is often called the threshold for the neurone. The intensity of a sinusoidal stimulus necessary to produce this criterion firing rate is measured as a function of its frequency. The resulting function is called a frequency threshold curve (FTC) or tuning curve, and it can be considered as an inverted filter characteristic. An example is given in Fig. 3.

Each curve in the figure is obtained from a different single neurone. Each neurone is most sensitive, or has its lowest threshold at a particular frequency, called the characteristic frequency (CF) or best frequency. Although the tips of the tuning curves (the minima) appear sharply pointed, they are, when studied in sufficient detail, rounded. The sharpness of these filter characteristics, expressed in terms of $Q_{10\,dB}$, varies from about 2 at low CF's up to 6–10 at CF's between 3 and 15 kHz. The low frequency slopes vary from about 30 dB/oct at low frequencies up to 100–200 dB/oct for CF's around 7 kHz, while the high frequency slopes are somewhat steeper at high CF's being around 100–500 dB/oct. Notice also that the FTC's tend to flatten off on the low frequency side, giving what has been called a low-frequency "tail".

It should be pointed out that these results apply to animals (cat, guinea pig and squirrel monkey) whose auditory systems function over a frequency range somewhat higher than that found in man (typically 100 to 45 000 Hz as compared to 20–18 000 Hz). It might well be the case that in man the maximum sharpness of tuning, as measured by $Q_{10\,dB}$, occurs at lower CF's, say around 2–4 kHz. It is also of interest that the sharpness of tuning varies from one neurone to another even when they have the same CF and are

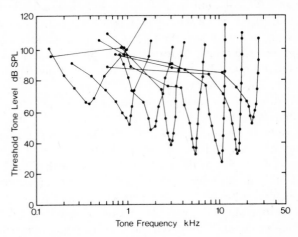

Fig. 3 *Frequency–threshold curves (FTCs) or tuning curves derived from single neurones in the auditory nerve of the guinea pig. Similar results are found in the cat and squirrel monkey. Each curve was derived from a different neurone by measuring the intensity of a sinusoidal stimulus needed to produce a fixed small response from the neurone, as a function of stimulating frequency. The frequency at which the threshold is lowest is called the characteristic frequency (CF). From Evans (1975) by permission of the author.*

measured in the same species. However, the variations within animals are smaller than the variations across animals. It seems to be the case that the filters in some animals are more sharply tuned than those in other animals of the same species. As we shall see, individual differences are also found in the sharpness of tuning revealed in psychophysical studies.

In summary, recordings from single neurones in the auditory nerve support the concept that the peripheral auditory system contains a bank of band-pass filters with overlapping centre frequencies. The filters have well-defined pass-bands, with $Q_{10 \text{ dB}}$ values which depend somewhat on the centre frequency, and the slope on the high-frequency side tends to be somewhat greater than the slope on the low-frequency side. Let us turn now to a psychophysical analogue of the neural tuning curve.

IV. The Psychophysical Tuning Curve

The neurophysiological tuning curve is derived by recording the activity of a single neurone. However, in man any psychophysical judgement that is made about a sound stimulus will almost inevitably be based upon the activity in many neurones. If we wish to devise a psychophysical measure which parallels the neural tuning curve, then the best we can do is to use a stimulus which excites only a very small number of neurones. In that case the decision of the listener must be based on the activity in those neurones. We can achieve this by using as a signal a pure tone with a fixed frequency and a level which is fixed at just above the threshold for detection. Such a tone is often called a probe tone, and it presumably produces neural activity only in those neurones whose CF's are very close to the frequency of the probe.

In order to complete the analogy to the neural tuning curve we can carry out a masking experiment using as a masker a sinusoid with variable frequency and intensity. For each frequency of the masker we determine the level of the masker at which it just masks the probe tone (i.e. at which the probe tone is just made inaudible by the masker). If we assume that the probe will be masked when the masking tone produces a fixed amount of activity in the neurones which would normally signal the presence of the probe, then the curve which we map out in this way will give us a psychophysical analogue of the neural tuning curve. This psychophysical tuning curve (PTC) should reflect the shape of the human peripheral auditory filter with centre frequency at the frequency of the probe tone.

Results from an experiment of this type are shown in Fig. 4. Each curve was obtained with a probe tone of a different frequency, fixed at a level 15 dB above the absolute threshold at that frequency. The curves show a remarkable resemblance to neural tuning curves; they have well-defined tips, the

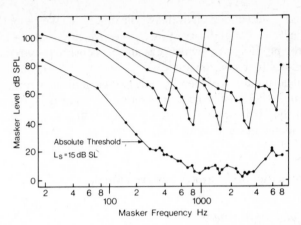

Fig. 4 *Psychophysical tuning curves (PTCs) obtained from human listeners. Each curve was generated using a probe signal of a particular frequency, fixed at 15 dB above the absolute threshold. A sinusoidal masker was presented simultaneously with the probe, and the level of the masker necessary to mask the probe was determined as a function of the masker frequency. The resulting curves are very similar to FTCs obtained from single auditory neurones. From Small (1959) by permission of the author and the Acoustical Society of America.*

slopes are greater on the high-frequency side than on the low-frequency side and the low-frequency side shows a shallow "tail". The curves even change with centre frequency in a similar way to the neural tuning curves. The $Q_{10\,dB}$ values vary from about 4 at 1 kHz to about 6–11 between 2 and 8 kHz (Moore, 1978), with a maximum sharpness around 3–4 kHz. A further point of resemblance is that, just as FTC's can vary in sharpness between animals, so PTC's can be sharper in some individuals than others.

Although the resemblance of FTC's and PTC's is encouraging, we should be cautious in accepting the PTC's as a direct correlate of the FTC's, and concluding on that basis that the peripheral auditory filters in humans are similar in their sharpness to those in animals. The need for caution is indicated by the following differences between FTC's and PTC's.

(i) The FTC is derived from a single neurone, whereas the PTC inevitably involves activity over a group of neurones with slightly different characteristic frequencies. This problem is minimized using very low-level probe tones, but it cannot be completely eliminated. If, for example, the probe is only 3 dB above the nominal "threshold", then on some trials the subject may not detect the probe even when no masker is present. In practice PTC's cannot be determined for probes less than 5 dB above absolute threshold.

(ii) The FTC is determined for primary auditory neurones, but the response of the human observers involves the whole organism. We cannot be certain about the level in the auditory system at which the masking takes place. However, the physiological evidence is at least consistent with the idea that masking can occur at a peripheral level.

(iii) In the determination of the FTC only a single sinusoidal tone is present at any one time, whereas the PTC is determined using two tones presented simultaneously. This last point turns out to be one of some importance, and it will be considered in some detail in the next section.

V. Nonlinearities and Lateral Suppression

A. *The Concept of Linearity*

In our discussion of filters and filter characteristics we have implicitly assumed that the filters are linear. For this to be the case two conditions must be satisfied:

(i) if the input to the filter is changed by a factor k, then the output should also change in magnitude by factor k, but should be otherwise unaltered;

(ii) the output of a filter in response to a number of inputs presented simultaneously should be equal to the sum of the outputs that would be obtained if each input were presented alone.

Provided condition (i) is satisfied, then we can determine a filter characteristic with a sinusoidal input of variable frequency, either by keeping the input magnitude constant and measuring the magnitude of the output or, as in the case of a tuning curve, by determining the magnitude of the input required to maintain a fixed output magnitude. If the second condition applies then, once we have determined the filter characteristic for sinusoidal stimulation, we can apply Fourier's theory to predict the response to any complex stimulus. All we have to do is analyse the complex stimulus into its sinusoidal components, work out what the filter output would be for each component, and then sum the outputs. Notice that in response to a single sinusoidal input, the output of a linear filter will contain only that same component; in general, the output of a linear filter never contains frequency components that were not present in the input signal.

Clearly, if the peripheral auditory system can be considered to contain a bank of linear band-pass filters, then the analysis of tuning characteristics in the way we have described so far can provide a powerful tool for predicting the responses to complex sound stimuli. Several experimenters have tested this idea by measuring the responses of single neurones to complex stimuli such as different types of noise, and comparing their results with the predictions obtained by assuming that the tuning curve represents a linear filter characteristic (e.g. Evans and Wilson, 1973; de Boer and de Jongh, 1978). On the whole, the results fitted the predictions quite well, and this led Evans (1975) to conclude that single neurones in the auditory nerve of the cat "respond to multicomponent stimuli in the manner of linear band-pass filters of the same width and shape as the FTC".

Although, to a first approximation, the FTC's can be considered as linear filter characteristics, there is one important respect in which the behaviour of single neurones in the auditory nerve is distinctly non-linear. This is described in the next section.

B. *Lateral Suppression in the Auditory Nerve*

In a linear filter, the output in response to two simultaneous sinusoids is equal to the sum of the outputs which would be obtained for each sinusoid presented separately. In the determination of the PTC it was assumed that at the masked threshold the masker produced a fixed amount of activity at the output of the filters involved. Thus threshold would correspond to a constant ratio of the output produced by a probe-plus-masker to the output produced by the masker alone. However, in some situations the neural response to a sinusoid of a given frequency can actually be *reduced* by the addition of a second sinusoid with a different frequency to the stimulus. This is known as two-tone suppression, or lateral suppression, and it is clearly a non-linear phenomenon, since the second tone on its own either produces an increase in firing rate, or has no effect.

Figure 5 illustrates the way in which two-tone suppression is normally demonstrated. First the FTC of the neurone is determined. Then the neurone is stimulated with a sinusoid at the CF, at a level 10 dB above threshold (shown by the triangle in the figure). Then a second sinusoid is added to the stimulus and its frequency and intensity are varied. Any tone falling within the hatched area will reduce the response to the tone at CF by 20% or more. Thus, the hatched areas represent suppression regions on either side of the excitatory region defined by the FTC.

This finding complicates the interpretation of the PTC, since the PTC is determined with two tones presented simultaneously. It is possible that in some cases the probe is masked by virtue of the response to the probe being suppressed, while the masker itself does not produce any output in the filters centred around the probe frequency (i.e. the masker does not have an excitatory effect in those neurones with CF's close to the frequency of the probe). If this is true, then the PTC's determined in simultaneous masking should not be interpreted as indicating the shapes of the underlying neural FTC's, but rather as indicating the boundaries of the suppression areas. In the next section we show how this possibility can be investigated psychophysically.

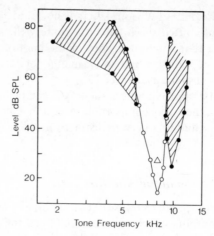

Fig. 5 *Two-tone suppression in a single neurone of the auditory nerve in the cat. The open circles show the FTC of the neurone; a tone falling within the area enclosed by the FTC will produce an excitatory response i.e. an increase in firing rate. The neurone is stimulated with a tone at the CF and about 10 dB above the threshold (shown by the triangle). The solid circles mark the boundaries of areas where a second tone added to the stimulus will reduce the firing rate by 20% or more; these are the suppression areas. From Arthur et al. (1971) by permission of the authors.*

C. *Psychophysical Tuning Curves in Non-Simultaneous Masking*

Recordings from single neurones have shown that suppression begins within a few ms of the onset of the suppressing tone, and ceases within a few ms of its cessation (Arthur *et al.*, 1971). In other words suppression only occurs when the suppressing tone is present simultaneously with the tone being suppressed. Thus, it should be possible to eliminate the influence of two-tone suppression in a psychophysical experiment by presenting the masker and probe non-simultaneously. One way of doing this is to use a forward-masking technique, in which a brief low-level probe tone is presented immediately following a masker of relatively long duration. Typically the probe would have a duration of 10–20 ms, and the masker a duration of 500 ms. Using this method we can determine psychophysical tuning curves (PTC's) exactly as before, by finding the level of a sinusoidal masker required just to mask the probe, as a function of masker frequency. Since the masker is presented prior to the probe, the masking cannot be produced by suppression. It is usually assumed that the masker has its effect by producing fatigue or adaptation in the neurones which would normally respond to the probe. At the masked threshold the masker is assumed to produce a fixed effect in those neurones, and therefore a fixed output from the filters with centre frequencies close to that of the probe. Thus, the PTC's determined in forward masking *will* give a direct indication of the filter characteristic. Furthermore, the differences between the results for simultaneous and forward masking should reflect the influence of lateral suppression (Houtgast, 1972).

Figure 6 shows the results of an experiment in which PTC's were determined for both simultaneous and forward masking. It is clear that the two curves are very different; the PTC obtained in forward masking has a sharper tip and steeper skirts than are found in simultaneous masking. The difference on the high frequency side is particularly marked. Results similar to this have been found by several different workers (Moore, 1978; Vogten, 1978; Houtgast, 1973). The differences between the two curves are consistent with the notion that the threshold of the probe in simultaneous masking may be influenced by lateral suppression.

The $Q_{10\ dB}$ values and slopes for PTC's determined in forward masking are greater than those found in simultaneous masking, and they are also somewhat greater than the values found for FTC's in animals. This could mean that neurones in man have sharper FTC's than those in animals, but it is also possible that some aspect of the psychophysical task gives rise to artificially sharp PTC's. One way in which this might happen was suggested by Moore (1978). When the probe is close in frequency to the masker, the probe will evoke a neural response very similar to that of the masker, so that the observer has difficulty in distinguishing the two. The difficulty will be reduced when the probe and masker differ in frequency, since the patterns of neural activity they evoke will be quite different. Thus the task will be particularly

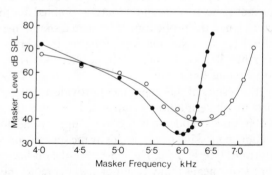

Fig. 6 A comparison of psychophysical tuning curves (PTCs) determined in simultaneous masking (open circles) and forward masking (filled circles). In each case the probe tone was fixed at 6 kHz, and at a level 10 dB above the absolute threshold. Notice that the frequency scale is expanded in this figure in comparison to Fig. 3–5, so that the rounded tips of the PTCs can be clearly seen. From Moore (1978) by permission of the Acoustical Society of America.

difficult for the observer around the tip of the tuning curve, and the PTC will be sharper than the underlying FTC. Given this difficulty of interpretation, it would be premature to conclude that man has sharper peripheral filters than animals. Nevertheless, the differences between PTC's obtained in simultaneous and forward masking have been demonstrated under a sufficiently wide range of conditions for us to conclude that they are real, and that in all probability they reflect at least partially the influence of two-tone suppression.

D. *Two-tone Suppression in Non-Simultaneous Masking*

Houtgast (1972, 1973, 1974), using a variety of techniques, has shown that effects attributable to lateral suppression can be demonstrated in psycho-physical experiments. We will describe the experiment which provides the closest analogue to the two-tone suppression which has been observed in single neurones. In the first part of the experiment the threshold is measured for a brief probe tone at, say, 1 kHz following a sinusoidal masker of the same frequency, i.e. a forward masking technique is used. We assume that the threshold for the probe is determined by the amount of fatigue or adaptation produced by the masker in the neurones with CF's close to the frequency of the probe. If a second sinusoidal component is added to the masker, at say 1·2 kHz, and if that extra component is sufficiently intense, we might expect that the neural response to the 1 kHz component in the masker would be suppressed. Thus the masker will produce less activity in neurones with CF's close to 1 kHz, and there will be less adaptation produced by the masker. This line of reasoning leads us to predict a surprising result: adding the 1·2 kHz component to the masker should actually *reduce* the threshold for the probe signal. This is exactly the result found. Houtgast pointed out that the results are quite different when the probe tone is presented simultaneously with the maskers. In this case the "suppressing" tone at 1·2 kHz suppresses the response both to the 1 kHz component in the masker and to the probe tone, so that no reduction in masking occurs.

In summary, the results of this experiment provide a striking parallel with results obtained in single auditory neurones. It is even the case that the combinations of frequency and intensity of the "suppressing" tone which will produce a reduction in masking resemble closely the suppression areas observed neurophysiologically (see Fig. 5). The existence of non-linearities, such as two-tone suppression, means that we cannot always predict the response to a complex stimulus as the sum of the responses to its sinusoidal components. However, in many cases predictions based on simple linear filtering provide a good first approximation, and the predictions can be modified to take into account lateral suppression, when the stimulus is such that suppression might have a powerful influence.

VI. Summary and General Conclusions

In this Chapter I have concentrated on a limited aspect of the processing of sounds in the auditory system, in order to focus attention on the similarities between physiological and psychophysical measurements. The peripheral auditory system can be considered as containing a bank of band-pass filters with overlapping centre frequencies and limited resolving power. Thus, any complex stimulus entering the ear is subjected to a limited-resolution frequency analysis, being split into the sinusoids of which it is composed. The characteristics of the filters are revealed in frequency-threshold curves (FTC's) in primary auditory neurones, and in psychophysical tuning curves (PTC's) determined using masking experiments. When more than one sinusoidal component is presented simultaneously, non-linear interactions may occur in the form of lateral suppression. This suppression can be observed directly in single neurones, and its influence on the PTC's can be observed by comparing the results obtained in simultaneous masking and forward masking. Forward masking techniques can be used to demonstrate direct psychophysical analogues of the two-tone suppression seen in primary auditory neurones.

As a result of the peripheral analysis described above the distribution of energy in complex sounds as a function of frequency will be represented in the firing rates of different neurones as a function of their characteristic frequencies. However, we should bear in mind that this is not the only way in which stimulus information is coded; the temporal patterns of firing in individual neurones may also be of considerable importance. It has been found that for frequencies up to about 5 kHz these time patterns are closely related to the temporal properties of the stimulating waveform. However, even the time-pattern information is strongly influenced by peripheral filtering. The effective stimulating waveform is not the waveform of the sound stimulus itself, but rather is the waveform resulting from passing the stimulus through the peripheral filtering mechanism (de Boer and de Jongh, 1978). Thus when we stimulate with a complex sound containing a wide range of frequency components, the time-pattern of firing in any single neurone carries information only about frequency components which pass through the peripheral filter driving that neurone; this filter is represented by the FTC of the neurone.

We may think of the peripheral filter bank as a first stage in the analysis and processing of sounds by the auditory system. Inevitably, further analysis and processing takes place at higher levels in the auditory system, but knowledge of the peripheral analysis provides at least a first basis for understanding our ability to hear out the individual sinusoidal components in complex sounds, to detect signals in noise, and to identify the important frequency components in complex sounds such as speech and music.

Acknowledgements

I would like to thank Bernard O'Loughlin, Brian Glasberg and Michael Shailer for their helpful comments on a preliminary version of this chapter.

Further Reading

More detailed and advanced reviews of the physiology and psychology of hearing may be found in the following two books:
Moore, B. C. J. (1982). "Introduction to the Psychology of Hearing" 2nd edn. Academic Press, London and New York.
Green, D. M. (1976). "An Introduction to Hearing". Lawrence Erlbaum Associates, Hillsdale, New Jersey.
The balance of these two books is rather different. Moore's book places greater emphasis on the psychophysical and perceptual aspects of hearing, whereas Green's book provides a more rigorous and detailed coverage of the physics of sound and the anatomy and physiology of hearing.
The following book by Plomp reviews several different aspects of the perception of steady complex tones, and has as its central theme the concept that the ear acts as a frequency analyser. It provides an excellent extension of the basic ideas set out in this chapter.
Plomp, R. (1976). "Aspects of Tone Sensation". Academic Press, London and New York.
In addition, the book by Pickles covers the physiology of the auditory system and includes a chapter comparing physiology with auditory psychophysics.
Pickles, J. O. (1982). "An Introduction to the Physiology of Hearing". Academic Press, London and New York.

References

Arthur, R. M., Pfeiffer, R. R. and Suga, N. (1971). Properties of "two-tone inhibition" in primary auditory neurones. *J. Physiol.* 212, 593–609.
Boer, E. de and Jongh, H. R. de (1978). On cochlear encoding: potentialities and limitations of the reverse-correlation technique. *J. Acoust. Soc. Am.* 63, 115–135.
Evans, E. F. (1975). Cochlear nerve and cochlear nucleus. *In* "Handbook of Sensory Physiology. Vol. V" (W. D. Keidel and W. D. Neff, eds). Springer-Verlag, Berlin.
Evans, E. F. and Wilson, J. P. (1973). Frequency selectivity of the cochlea. *In* "Basic Mechanisms in Hearing" (A. Møller, ed.), pp. 519–551. Academic Press, New York and London.
Houtgast, T. (1972). Psychophysical evidence for lateral inhibition in hearing. *J. Acoust. Soc. Am.* 51, 1885–1894.

Houtgast, T. (1973). Psychophysical experiments on "tuning curves" and "two-tone inhibition". *Acustica* 29, 168–179.

Houtgast, T. (1974). Lateral Suppression in Hearing. Ph.D. Thesis. Academische Pers B.V., Amsterdam.

Moore, B. C. J. (1978). Psychophysical tuning curves measured in simultaneous and forward masking. *J. Acoust. Soc. Am.* 63, 524–532.

Small, A. M. (1959). Pure tone masking. *J. Acoust. Soc. Am.* 31, 1619–1625.

Vogten, L. L. M. (1978). Low-level pure-tone masking: a comparison of "tuning curves" obtained with simultaneous and forward masking. *J. Acoust. Soc. Am.* 63, 1520–1527.

10 Neuropsychology and the Organization of Behaviour

J. G. Beaumont

Abstract This chapter introduces problems encountered in the conceptual basis of neuropsychology. It points to implications of the mind–body problem for neuropsychological theory and research, and questions the validity of many of the kinds of model which are used to describe brain organization for higher cognitive abilities. Difficulties inherent in research strategies in clinical neuropsychology are also outlined. The study of recovery from loss of function, and the investigation of cerebral lateralization, are introduced as important current issues which also illustrate some of the problems faced by neuropsychologists. The current status of neuropsychology is discussed and prospects for future development are assessed.

I. Introduction

While research in the neurosciences has grown at an amazing rate over the past few years, and many significant discoveries have been made, it has to be admitted that with regard to "higher" or "intelligent" abilities we still have little idea of how the brain works. Even less progress has been made towards establishing the relationship between the brain and the mind. Neuro-psychology, or the study of the correlates of behaviour within the structure of the brain, has developed into a specialist field within psychology. Yet it has made this progress only at the expense of ignoring the basic issues raised by searching for mental abilities within the physiological structures of the brain. It does not follow that the search has been futile, or that the knowledge established is without value, but it is important to remember that the basic issues remain unresolved and that a proper understanding of how the brain organizes behaviour is impossible before we can understand how mental processes relate to physiological events.

It is important to remember that neuropsychology rests entirely upon inferences about brain organization derived from the observation of

PHYSIOLOGICAL CORRELATES OF HUMAN
BEHAVIOUR   ISBN 0-12-273901-9

behaviour. There is at present no way in which behaviour can be directly related to brain events, and neuropsychological models are limited by this restriction. Weiskrantz (1973) has discussed the research strategies which neuropsychologists employ, arguing that the brain takes the position of a dependent variable, so limiting the methods to correlational approaches with consequent problems for the interpretation of the findings. It seems better to think of the research designs as ones in which the brain is in fact the independent variable, and behaviour as the dependent variable. In clinical neuropsychology, where the effects on behaviour of damage and disease in the brain are studied, the investigator obviously cannot directly control the location or nature of the pathology. His values of the independent variable are therefore somewhat uncontrolled, but cases are selected and studied to provide particular settings of the independent variable. In experimental neuropsychology, where techniques are used in the laboratory to study the behaviour of normal intact human subjects as a function of their brain state, the experimenter attempts to induce particular states or processes within the brain, in order to study the effects of these states and processes upon the performance of the subjects. Many of the techniques of experimental psychology can therefore be employed to study the organization of behaviour within the brain. Nevertheless the conclusions rest upon relatively remote inferences about the way in which damage might affect "functions" which control behaviour, or about the way in which the experimenter has been able to control the state of the brain by his experimental manipulation.

In human neuropsychology the brain becomes a true dependent variable only rarely, and perhaps only within electrophysiological investigations. The possibilities which are being opened up by this field of research will be mentioned below.

It should be made clear here that human neuropsychology can be roughly divided into three areas: clinical neuropsychology, experimental neuro-psychology and behavioural neurology (Davison, 1974; Buffery, 1977). Clinical neuropsychologists measure deficits in personality, intellect and sensory-motor functions and relate these to specific or diffuse areas of damage or "lesions" within the brain. Their work involves both the study of brain-behaviour relations, and the clinical application of this study to the diagnosis and rehabilitation of the injured brain. Experimental neuro-psychologists work with normal human subjects and conduct research which has much in common with research in general experimental psychology and cognitive psychology.

Behavioural neurology emphasizes conceptual rather than operational definitions of behaviour, and usually involves tests to establish deviations from "normal" functioning. The emphasis is upon the individual case rather than upon group statistics, and the most eminent exponent of this approach has been Luria (1973). However, while these terms provide a useful guide to approaches currently employed, the terms are used very loosely and clear distinctions between the three fields cannot sensibly be made. A useful illustration of how practical issues are addressed by the different approaches, with particular regard to differences between Western and Soviet neuropsychology, is to be found in Luria and Majovsky (1977).

II. The Historical Background

Neuropsychology has a long history, and a particularly rich one in the past hundred years. While there is little space to describe it here, some knowledge of the debates of the last century is important for a proper understanding of the current position of neuropsychology.

The first theoretical approach, founded upon the findings of Broca, Wernicke and others in the second half of the nineteenth century, was known as **localizationist theory**. Derived in spirit if not in substance from the ideas of Gall and the phrenologists, this theory held that a particular part of the brain is responsible for each psychological ability or function. Much research was devoted to identifying the specific regions responsible for each function, and modern versions are to be seen of the maps derived from this line of investigation (Nielsen, 1946; Luria, 1966).

From the beginnings of localizationist theory there were opponents, who argued that specific deficits could be produced by damage to disparate sites in the brain, and that no precise mapping was therefore possible. Flourens, in the 1840s, was responsible for the origins of the alternative **equipotential theory**, which was supported in this century by Kurt Goldstein, Head and Lashley amongst others. Equipotential theory states that while sensory input is localized, perception involves the whole brain, and that the effects of brain lesions depend upon their extent not upon their location. An implication of equipotentiality is that if sufficient cortical material is intact, then it is able to take over functions previously served by the damaged tissue. It should also be possible to derive an index of brain damage, independent of its locus, nature or extent. A recent review of attempts to find such an index is provided by Heaton *et al.* (1978).

The problems with equipotential theory have been that it is possible to demonstrate some kind of a relationship between cortical areas and certain functions, and that it has not been possible to derive an index of the extent of brain damage, independent of the actual location of the damage. These problems are not present in a third general approach, which might be termed **interactionist theory**. Hughlings Jackson is probably responsible for the creation of this approach, with his argument that "higher" abilities are built up by combining a number of more basic skills. To produce speech, the basic skills of hearing, discrimination of speech sounds and control of the speech apparatus are combined with others, to generate the higher skill. The loss of speech may be due to damage to one or more of the areas serving these basic skills, and damage to a particular area may have effects upon a number of higher skills which rely upon that area. Generally accepted findings, that no function or learning process is entirely dependent on any particular area of cortex, and that each part within the brain plays an unequal role in different functions (Chapman and Wolff, 1959; Krech, 1962), support the interactionist position rather than the more extreme localizationist or equipotential theories. The rather looser "regional equipotentiality" (Meyer, 1960) arguing for equipotentiality, but within relatively defined regions, is often also associated with the interactionist position.

The interactionist position is the one most widely adopted or assumed by contemporary neuropsychologists. One of the most elaborate examples of a modern interactionist theory is that of Luria (1964, 1966, 1973), with its interaction between functional systems for each behaviour. Another example is the "associationist" theory of Geschwind (1974), which emphasizes rather the connections between functional regions, and their significance in the learning of complex activities.

Rather fuller introductions to the recent history of neuropsychology are to be found in Brazier (1979), Golden (1978), Hécaen and Albert (1978) and Joynt (1975).

III. Models of Neuropsychological Function

Most neuropsychological models are based upon some organization of functional units. These models, however, almost never make it clear what is to be meant by a "function", nor how the conceptual function might be translated into physiological systems. Even supposing that it were possible to precisely define a function in other than behavioural terms (that is in terms of the behaviour which is to be explained), without tying the model more directly to physiological processes, the model may be only one of a number of alternative models which might be created and equally well "explain" the behaviour. This is a problem known as "complementarity" (Markowitz, 1973).

The difficulty of dealing with the concept of a "function" is illustrated by the work of Luria (1973), who defines a function as a constant task which is served by a variable mechanism leading to a constant result. Luria concludes that neuropsychologists should resist the attempt to seek direct localization of mental processes in the cortex of the brain, and should instead enquire how mental activity is altered by a certain brain lesion and what factors are introduced into mental activity by each brain system. This is an inevitable consequence of constructing models which are in their basic concepts divorced from a consideration of the actual physiological mechanisms involved, and can only lead to, at best, an unsatisfactory description of the way in which the brain is responsible for the conduct of behaviour.

Many of the current models rely upon metaphors (Glassman, 1978). Popular areas from which these metaphors have been derived are engineering, information processing and computer science. The borrowing of models from these areas has not been unprofitable, but it has restricted the kind of investigation which has been pursued, and not all the metaphors which have been employed have been appropriate ones. Gregory's (1961) metaphor of the television receiver, and his argument that an understanding of the operation of a television set is unlikely to follow from observing the effects upon the performance of the set of removing components one by one, has been much quoted, and many of his points are no doubt valid. Although not proposed as a model of brain organization, but as an objection to models then current, it has been discussed as an approach to understanding cerebral function, and it is important to question whether the metaphor is in fact an appropriate one. Similarly, to think about the brain as if it were a computer may well be valuable in generating ideas about how one might go about investigating the operations of such a "machine", but if the brain does not work like a computer, and it is highly probable that it does not, the value of this model is likely to be limited, and the inferences drawn from it possibly erroneous.

A final example will be given. In a current influential theory (Kinsbourne, 1976), cerebral function is conceived as being built up from the "simplest building blocks", which have some locus within the brain, which are then built up into a "hierarchy". Kinsbourne employs the metaphor of a telephone exchange, for which a "map" of cerebral space is to be generated. Apart from the problem of seeing how a telephone exchange is an appropriate model for a hierarchical system, and asking whether a "map" is the best way to describe a telephone exchange, many questions remain unanswered. For example, how one might know that the simplest level of building block has been described, how the connections are to be made, how the system might be governed, and so on. This is not to point to the difficulties with any one current model, but to underline the general weakness with current ways of thinking about and describing models of the organization of behaviour within the brain.

There are other problems. The concepts of inhibition and facilitation, which are valuable and appropriate for the neurophysiologist working with systems of individual cells at another level of analysis, are used loosely and unhelpfully in neuropsychology. If a "centre" which serves a function becomes inoperative, then facilitation should be the result if the previous effect were one of inhibition. This however relies upon the assumption, not necessarily well founded, that lesions cause centres to become inoperative, and that previous inhibition or facilitation will be reversed. This also conflicts with a model of "information" being "transmitted", in which damage to the centre results in no information being received from that centre subsequently. Mix the two kinds of explanation, as is commonly done, add the possibility that a lesion might affect a function, a process or a cognitive strategy, and the result is that almost any effect of a lesion can be explained, but in a variety of ways and with very little validity attached to any one.

There are additional methodological problems attached to the inferences which may be drawn from the effects of various "treatments", and these have been excellently discussed by Weiskrantz (1968a, b). The problems include the multi-determinacy of behavioural tasks and the imperfect sensitivity of tests designed to assess performance on these tasks. If some variable affects performance, to generate a 'U' shaped function, then the direction of change in performance following changes in the value of this variable will depend upon the initial value of the variable. There may even be no quantitative change in performance, even though there has been a change in the value of the associated variable. A spectrum of effects is likely to follow from a single treatment, and while one treatment may affect a single task, a second treatment may affect this task as well as a second task. Multiple treatments will almost certainly interact in a complex way in affecting a specific task, and there will in addition be the effect of unknown background treatments.

Finally, there is the difficulty that even the most successful neuro-psychological models lack validity in physiological terms. Many current models, among them that of Luria, rely upon a hierarchical model of sensory systems passing information to secondary areas where perceptual processes occur. From there the information goes to higher, tertiary, "association" areas, where the highest intellectual functions are performed. Many of these models are stated as if they reflect the physiological organization of the cerebral cortex. It is, however, clear that the physiological basis for such a model is inaccurate, and that cortical areas cannot be regarded as organized and interconnected in this way (Masterton and Berkley, 1974; Creutzfeldt, 1979). All neocortical areas receive their main excitatory input from a subcortical thalamic projection nucleus. Neuropsychological models must take account of such arrangements, or remain divorced from any valid roots in the physiological processes of the brain.

IV. Models from Cognitive Psychology

If we are to explain how the brain organizes behaviour, we need not only a model which is valid in terms of the physiological operation of the brain, but a model of behaviour at the purely psychological level to which to relate the brain events. Unfortunately for neuropsychology, models and explanations in cognitive psychology which have been heavily used in the study of brain-behaviour relationships suffer from many of the problems of neuropsychological theories. In order to have a good neuropsychological understanding of memory, for example, it is important that the operation of the processes of memory can be accurately described at the cognitive psychological level. This is not to say that the psychological description must come first. Memory is in fact a good illustration of a field in which there has been a fruitful interchange between psychological experimentation and theory, and data and theories derived from the study of patients with brain lesions. However, while neuropsychological evidence may usefully contribute to psychological theories, it is difficult to think that there might be a valid neuropsychological description of some ability without it being related to a sound psychological understanding of that ability. This psychological understanding must also account for individual differences and how these are expressed in psychological and neuropsychological variables (Newcombe and Ratcliff, 1979).

Examples of the way in which contemporary cognitive models have been utilized in neuropsychology are to be found in the work of Kinsbourne (1971, 1976), Bryden (1978) and Moscovitch (1979) among many others. The cognitive models however suffer from many conceptual weaknesses and ambiguities (Neisser, 1976; Lachman *et al.*, 1979), so bringing additional problems into neuropsychological explanations, particularly when applied rather uncritically. An example is the way in which principles of serial or parallel processing are employed to explain differences between the specializations of the two cerebral hemispheres (Carmon, 1975; Levy, 1978; Moscovitch, 1979). At least in cognitive psychology there is some recognition of the necessity to establish criteria by which such processes can be identified (Townsend, 1971; Das *et al.*, 1979). In neuropsychology the terms are used loosely, not as operationally defined descriptions but as rather vague conceptual principles, which neither add to the explanation being generated nor stimulate useful testable hypotheses for further investigation.

Neuropsychology is unlikely to be better than the cognitive psychology from which it is partly derived, and it is important that when cognitive models are employed, they are employed with accuracy and with a recognition for the role which they are playing.

V. Research Strategies in Clinical Neuropsychology

The clinical neuropsychologist is naturally forced to rely upon the research material which comes along as a result of injury and disease. The best research strategy which can be employed in this situation is to collect groups of cases with lesions in particular areas, or cases exhibiting a particular deficit, and to study the relationship between psychological abilities and lesion sites or disease processes within and between these groups. Aside from the purely practical problems, and the obvious point that accidental, or even surgical, lesions are no respectors of the anatomical boundaries investigators use in their analyses, there are some more fundamental problems in this approach.

It is convenient to think of lesions as classifiable on a number of dimensions: whether the lesion is focal or diffuse, if localized then the hemisphere and lobes to which it is restricted, whether acute or chronic, static or progressive, the mass of the lesion, and the type of pathology from which the lesion results. Reitan (Reitan and Davison, 1974) employs factors of this kind quite explicitly. A research design would ideally select groups of patients with particular lesions (assuming that lesions could always be so accurately diagnosed), which would be classified along dimensions of this kind, and then contrast these groups holding all but one or perhaps two of the factors constant.

This is the design used implicitly in clinical neuropsychological research. It must however remain an unsatisfactory approach because of the nature of cerebral lesions. For instance lesions of a particular type, certain kinds of tumour for example, do not occur randomly over the surface of the brain. Certain types of tumour tend to occur more frequently in certain areas. Modern missile wounds, in which high velocity projectiles commonly pass straight through the head, do not occur randomly in surviving patients. This is not only because the injuries tend to occur when the individual is either facing towards or fleeing from the source of the missile, but because it is more likely than an object entering through the frontal or occipital lobes can pass straight through the brain without damaging subcortical areas essential to survival, than if the entry is through the temporal lobes of the brain. Even in comparing the effects of surgical lesions for the removal of tumours in either the right or left hemisphere, the research design is complicated by the fact that patients tend to arrive for surgery with larger tumours in the right hemisphere. This is because right hemisphere pathology interferes less with verbally related skills, is therefore less immediately obvious to the patient and his relatives, and medical advice is sought rather later when the tumour has grown to a larger size.

The result of these, and many other similar inherent confounding complications, means that in the hypothetical research strategy many cells must remain empty, or at best contain highly atypical cases from which valid conclusions cannot be drawn. The problem is of course equally acute in multivariate research designs, and no adequate solution has been found to this methodological problem.

One refinement of the research strategy should, however, be noted and that is the use of **double dissociation** in the analysis of lesion effects (Teuber, 1955; Weiskrantz, 1968b; Luria, 1973). This principle states that it is insufficient to associate a particular functional deficit with a particular cerebral region. At least in terms of the logic of the analysis, it is necessary to consider two locations and two functions. If lesions of area A affect function X more than function Y, and lesions of area B affect function Y more than function X, then double dissociation has been demonstrated. This is an undoubted contribution to the conceptual analysis of lesion effects. It does however rely upon a model of relatively strict and stable localization, and may also be quite difficult to apply in a complex situation in clinical neuropsychology with varied and interacting behavioural deficits resulting from a complex pattern of cerebral lesions.

An additional problem with the double dissociation strategy, as well as with less elegant research designs, is that the investigator may be trying to establish that a particular ability is *not* affected by particular lesions. This is the problem of trying to affirm the null hypothesis and is beset with various methodological and statistical difficulties. The investigator can never really be sure that no effect is present, and that he has not failed to employ sufficiently sensitive tests or use an adequate research design (Teuber, 1975a; Laurence and Stein, 1978). The general sensitivity of standard psychometric procedures when applied in neuropsychology has also been rightly questioned and remains a problem for many studies of the effects of brain injury (Dawson, 1973; Isaacson, 1975).

VI. Recovery from the Effects of Lesions

Leaving aside conceptual and methodological problems, an important current issue is the extent and the nature of the recovery of the initial deficits which follow brain injury (LeVere, 1975; Laurence and Stein, 1978; Kertesz, 1979). Apart from the issue of actual neural regeneration, which is extremely limited yet may have some important functional consequences, the mechanisms in operation may be both structural and functional.

The structural mechanisms may include redundancy, reactivation and changes in the accessibility of structural components. Redundancy is of course implied by equipotential conceptualizations of the brain, the idea that a function may be served by one of a number of structures, so that structural reorganization is possible without the need for relearning. It has been suggested (Chow, 1967) that this effect may operate less in primates than in lower animals. Reactivation of non-functional areas is also a possibility, depending in part on the type of pathology (LeVere and Morlock, 1973,

1974), although it is difficult to demonstrate whether this actually occurs. Lastly, changes in the accessibility of structural components may be caused by changes in the balance of inhibitory and excitatory effects of one structure upon another (Sprague, 1966), or by the renewal of access to memory engrams important in the control of cerebral systems (Meyer, 1972).

Functional mechanisms essentially involve functional substitution, either by reorganization or by the emergence of new functional systems (Meyer, 1973). With complex cognitive tasks, it is clear that the same cognitive task may be performed by employing different basic functional units, and utilizing one of a variety of cognitive strategies. The same end result may be achieved in a variety of ways, and new learning may play a role in functional recovery. The complexity of many cognitive tasks, the different strategies which have been identified, and the long-term course of recovery often over several years, all support the importance of functional mechanisms in recovery and restitution.

Diaschisis, the idea that recent lesions have effects at a distance in the brain, with widespread consequences which diminish with the passage of time, has been much discussed recently, and accounts are to be found in Gazzaniga (1975), Laurence and Stein (1978) and Brown (1979).

Laboratory studies with animals are relevant to the issue of recovery and have been well reviewed by Dru *et al.* (1976). Relevant also is the general issue of plasticity, the idea that the brain becomes less capable of re-adaptation with developmental progress. A good introductory review to this issue is to be found in Bach-y-Rita (1975). Lastly, those interested in long term recovery should consult the accounts of long term follow-up of war injuries described by Newcombe (1969), Newcombe and Ratcliff (1979) and by Teuber (1975a).

VII. Cerebral Lateralization

Lateralization and specialization of the cerebral hemispheres has been the major topic of investigation in experimental neuropsychology in recent years. A number of texts which review this area are available (Dimond and Beaumont, 1974; Milner, 1975; Kinsbourne, 1978; Beaumont, 1982). The idea that there are functional differences between the hemispheres, and that these may be based on fundamentally different cognitive mechanisms, while often accepted as a basic principle of neuropsychological organization, is however derived from some very problematic evidence. For example from commissurotomy ("split brain") patients, and experiments with normal subjects which are characterized by methodological problems and rather distant inferences to neuropsychological organization. Clearly the data do link with clinical findings (although there are clear exceptions, see for instance LeDoux *et al.*, 1980), and may well illustrate something fundamental about the way in which the brain is organized. Nevertheless, the data are often treated rather uncritically, and theories are erected with cavalier disregard for inconsistencies within the data, and for the basis of the concepts employed within the theories. Of the problems discussed above with models in neuropsychology, almost all are to be clearly seen within theories in this area. The failure to take effective account of subject variables (Marshall, 1973) and the confusion between process and modality oriented mechanisms (Teuber, 1975b; Whitaker and Ojemann, 1977), without regard to any proposed physiological basis for the theories formulated, have contributed to the unsatisfactory state of current accounts of hemisphere lateralization, and have even hindered progress in this area.

The issue of cerebral lateralization is important, if only because technical advances have enabled experimental neuropsychological investigation of this area. It is an exciting and still developing field, but students of this topic would be wise to inspect very carefully both the foundations of the explanatory ideas in the actual data, and the nature of the models of brain-behaviour relationships from which the theories are derived.

VIII. Comparative Neuropsychology

While this book is concerned with human physiological psychology, it is important to note the contribution of the neuropsychological study of lower animals to that of man. Indeed until recently an experimental neuropsychologist would most likely have been engaged upon lesion experiments with rats, cats or monkeys, and much important work is still conducted in this area.

There has been in the past an unfortunate division between human neuropsychologists, interested primarily in the cortex of the brain and higher functions and (until the last decade) dealing mostly with clinical material, and animal neuropsychologists working with more basic functions and examining subcortical structures. The result was a divorce between considerations of the cortex and subcortical systems. Only very recently has there been a move to consider cortical lesions as extending subcortically, as they almost invariably do (Teuber, 1975a; Brown, 1979), and attempts to integrate studies from the two approaches into a unified account of neuropsychology (Dimond, 1980).

Nevertheless, problems remain in comparing the effects of experimental lesions in animals with the effects of clinical lesions in man. It is clear that even fairly cautious and specific generalizations from monkey to man may well be invalid (Drewe *et al.*, 1970; Weiskrantz, 1977). This is because, despite the strong similarity between the monkey and the human brains, there are fundamental differences between the cortex of the two, particularly in the association areas. These differences are sometimes masked by apparently similar but misleading nomenclature. Behaviour which carries the same descriptive label may in detail be quite different between the two species. There are differences in the localization of even quite similar functions. There are also important and fundamental differences between the primary modes of communication in monkey and man which must have a fundamental effect upon the cognitive, and thus the neuropsychological, organization of their respective cortices. The wider issues raised by comparative neuropsychology are well discussed in Blakemore *et al.* (1972) and Warren and Kolb (1978).

IX. Current Status of Neuropsychology

Neuropsychology has made progress over the past two decades in a variety of directions, but this has only been by accepting a questionable implicit model of the relationship between the behaviour and the way in which psychological functions might be organized. The progress has only been possible because the philosophical foundations and the conceptual models and theories have not been carefully considered. This cannot be a healthy situation, and it is likely that a return will have to be made to these basic issues before any dramatic progress can be made.

  The implicit model of relative localization of basic functional units, based upon regional equipotentiality, with some kind of organizational structure, possibly hierarchical, which may be modified by psychological variables, is readily detected in recent reviews of the effects of cerebral lesions upon behaviour (Dimond, 1980; Hécaen and Albert, 1978; Heilman and Valenstein, 1979; Kinsbourne, 1971, 1976; Lezak, 1976; Milner and Teuber, 1968; Teuber, 1975a; Walsh, 1978). The model accommodates a wide range of philosophical positions on the mind–body problem by remaining vague about the precise ways in which the cognitive organization of the brain is controlled and modified by psychological factors, and the ways in which functions are exercised by anatomical structures in the brain.

  There are, however, signs that the implicit model is being questioned, for example with respect to the role of the frontal lobes (Jouandet and Gazzaniga, 1979), as well as more widely within clinical neuropsychology (Pincus and Tucker, 1978). There is renewed interest in the philosophical issues relevant to neuropsychology (see, for example, Bunge, 1980; CIBA, 1979) and the form and operation of models of neuropsychological function (Finger, 1978). It is difficult to assess as yet the impact that this may have upon routine research in neuropsychology and the application of neuropsychology in clinical settings. Possibly the rather belated growth of interest in recovery and rehabilitation, which particularly demands that a workable model be available of how functions operate and just what happens when functions are recovered, will act as a stimulus to consideration of the basic issues.

One exciting possibility, currently in the early stages of development, is the use of electrophysiological investigation in neuropsychology. The recording of cerebral event related potentials and new analysis techniques in EEG research, such as frequency analysis and coherence analysis now within the capabilities of even modest laboratories, offer the possibility of studying brain events as the dependent variable, while the experimenter manipulates independent psychological variables. It is now possible to record just what relatively specific areas of the cortex are doing, within short time periods, and to relate these to psychological events under the control of the experimenter. Therefore it is feasible to observe, in "real time", brain events and behaviour in a highly specific way, using complex high level behaviours, and therefore for the first time to have a bridge between mental events and psychological events amenable to experimental investigation, and with a resolution never before available.

A recent report (Merton and Morton, 1980) that electrical stimulation of the cortex is possible in normal intact subjects, without discomfort or harmful effects, opens other exciting avenues of experimental investigation.

Neuropsychology also awaits a better understanding of the principles of high level operation of the brain. While we may assume some kind of very complicated neural network, which might be modelled as if it were an electronic machine (by extrapolation from the understanding of networks of neural cells at lower levels of analysis, successfully generated by neurophysiologists), it is clear that this may not be the best way of conceiving how the brain works. An alternative in thinking of the processes in terms of waves and the interference patterns between waves generated over the surface of the cortex has been proposed (Szentagothai and Arbib, 1974; Szentagothai, 1975). But it may well be that we must await a very radical new insight into the operation of the brain before more satisfactory functional models can be created. Recent stimulating discussions of some of the possibilities, by Hubel *et al.*, Nauta and Feirtag, and Crick, appeared in a special issue of Scientific American (September, 1979).

Another issue, which has received less attention than it deserves, is that of prediction and control, and the moral and ethical problems raised by a successful science of neuropsychology. As yet these have only been discussed with reference to psychosurgery (Smith and Kling, 1976; Smith and Kiloh, 1977), but the questions raised by successful prediction and the possibility of control are relevant to much wider areas in the neurosciences, and should be faced in as calm, rational and well informed a way as possible.

Finally, there is always the intriguing possibility that valid neuropsychological explanation may be inherently impossible. Because our descriptions of the brain are conveyed within language and other artifacts of the brain itself, it has at least to be considered that a full understanding of the brain is impossible, that the brain may not be used to think about the brain. I do not believe that this is the case, and an incomplete understanding is still worth striving for, but it is a salutory thought that no neuropsychologist can ever entirely afford to forget.

X. Summary

Neuropsychology faces particular problems in that it attempts to generate descriptions of the relationship between the brain and behaviour in the absence of any agreed position on the philosophical issue of the mind–body problem. Brain states and behavioural events are related without any consideration of how mental activity is linked to physiological processes. Another facet of this problem is that the brain-behaviour relationships proposed are only based on relatively indirect inferences, and not on clearly demonstrated associations.

Models have been employed rather uncritically and sometimes misleadingly. It is still unclear what kind of model we should adopt to characterize cerebral processes, and how this model can be related to current models in cognitive psychology. Neuropsychology has advanced by essentially ignoring this problem.

There are particular methodological difficulties associated with research in clinical neuropsychology, because of the nature of the brain injuries and disease which are incidentally available for study.

The investigation of recovery of behavioural deficits, and of cerebral lateralization, provides two examples where the conceptual difficulties are clearly to be seen, and yet where some progress is currently being made in empirical research and theoretical discussion. The degree to which this progress may be challenged, and the extent to which further progress may be made, given the underlying conceptual weaknesses, should be carefully considered.

The problems of having a valid and useful way to conceive of how the brain works, as well as of having a good model of how cognitive processes are organized psychologically, underlie many of the difficulties of contemporary neuropsychology, and significant developments in these areas are probably a prerequisite of successful neuropsychology.

Further Reading

Current Neuropsychological Findings

Beaumont, J. G. (1983). "Introduction to Neuropsychology". Grant McIntyre, London.
A comprehensive introductory text covering both clinical neuropsychology and human experimental neuropsychology.
Dimond, S. J. (1980). "Neuropsychology". Butterworths, London.
An excellent stimulating overview drawing together a broad variety of neuro-psychological data.
Kinsbourne, M. (1976). The neuropsychological analysis of cognitive deficit. *In* "Biological Foundations of Psychiatry" (R. G. Grenell and S. Gabay, eds), Vol. 1, pp. 527–589. Raven Press, New York.
A review which emphasizes the application of models drawn from cognitive psychology.
Walsh, K. W. (1978). 'Neuropsychology: A Clinical Approach". Churchill Livingstone, Edinburgh.
A sound introduction to clinical neuropsychology for students.

Models of Cerebral Function and Methodological Issues

Glassman, R. B. (1978). The logic of the lesion experiment and its role in the neural sciences. *In* "Recovery from Brain Damage" (S. Finger, ed.), pp. 4–31. Plenum Press, New York.
A discussion of conceptual issues, rather wider than the title implies.
Scientific American, September, 1979. Special issue entitled "The Brain". See papers by Hubel, Nauta and Feirtag, and Crick in particular.
Stimulating, if occasionally speculative discussion of a variety of issues. Also reprinted by W. H. Freeman, Oxford (1979).
Weiskrantz, L. (1968). "Analysis of Behavioural Change" especially Chapters 14 and 15. Harper and Row, New York.
A central text on the methodological issues.

Philosophical Issues

Bunge, M. (1980). "The Mind–Body Problem". Pergamon, Oxford.
An excellent critical review of current theoretical positions, and the statement of an important new approach.
CIBA Foundation (1979). "Brain and Mind" Symposium 69 (new series). Excerpta Medica, Amsterdam.
Proceedings of a symposium, but a good and lively introduction to both theories and issues.

Recovery and Restitution

Laurence, S. and Stein, D. G. (1978). Recovery after brain damage and the concept of localisation of function. *In* "Recovery from Brain Damage". (S. Finger, ed.), pp. 369–407. Plenum Press, New York.
A discussion both of recovery and its implications for neuropsychological models.

LeVere, T. E. (1975). Neural stability, sparing and behavioural recovery following brain damage. *Psychol. Rev.* **82**, 344–358.
A valuable discussion of ideas about recovery and restitution.

References

Bach-y-Rita, P. (1975). Plasticity of the nervous system. *In* "Cerebral Localization" (K. J. Zülch, O. Creutzfeldt and G. C. Galbraith, eds), pp. 313–327. Springer-Verlag, Berlin.
Beaumont, J. G. (ed.) (1982). "Divided Visual Field Studies of Cerebral Organisation". Academic Press, London and New York.
Blakemore, C., Iversen, S. D. and Zangwill, O. L. (1972). Brain functions. *A. Rev. Psychol.* **23**, 413–456.
Brazier, M. A. B. (1979). Challenges from the philosophers to the neuroscientists. *In* "Brain and Mind" Ciba Foundation Symposium 69 (new series), pp. 5–30. Excerpta Medica, Amsterdam.
Brown, J. W. (1979). Language representation in the brain. *In* "Neurobiology of Social Communication in Primates" (H. D. Steklis and M. J. Raleigh, eds), pp. 133–195. Academic Press, New York and London.
Bryden, M. P. (1978). Strategy effects in the assessment of hemispheric asymmetry. *In* "Strategies of Information Processing" (G. Underwood, ed.), pp. 117–149. Academic Press, London and New York.
Buffery, A. W. H. (1977). Clinical neuropsychology: a review and preview. *In* "Contributions to Medical Psychology" (S. Rachman, ed.) Vol. I, pp. 115–136. Pergamon, Oxford.
Bunge, M. (1980). "The Mind–Body Problem". Pergamon, Oxford.
Carmon, A. (1975). The two human hemispheres acting as separate parallel and sequential processors. *In* "Signal Analysis and Pattern Recognition in Biomedical Engineering" (G. F. Inbar, ed.), pp. 219–236. Halstead Press, New York.
Chapman, L. F. and Wolff, H. (1959). The cerebral hemispheres and the highest integrative functions of man. *Arch. Neurol.* **1**, 357–424.
Chow, K. L. (1967). Effects of ablation. *In* "The Neurosciences, First Study Program" (G. C. Quarton, M. Melnechuk and F. O. Schmitt, eds), pp. 705–713. Rockefeller University Press, New York.
CIBA (1979). "Brain and Mind" Ciba Foundation Symposium 69 (new series). Excerpta Medica, Amsterdam.
Creutzfeldt, O. D. (1979). Neurophysiological mechanisms and consciousness. *In* "Brain and Mind" Ciba Foundation Symposium 69 (new series), pp. 217–233. Excerpta Medica, Amsterdam.
Das, J. P., Kirby, J. R. and Jarman, R. F. (1979). "Simultaneous and Successive Cognitive Processes". Academic Press, New York and London.
Davison, L. A. (1974). Introduction. *In* "Clinical Neuropsychology: Current Status and Applications" (R. M. Reitan and L. A. Davison, eds) pp. 1–18. V. H. Winston and Sons, Washington, D.C.
Dawson, R. G. (1973). Recovery of function: implications for theories of brain function: *Behav. Biol.* **8**, 439–460.
Dimond, S. J. (1980). "Neuropsychology". Butterworths, London.
Dimond, S. J. and Beaumont, J. G. (eds) (1974). "Hemisphere Function in the Human Brain". Elek Science, London.

Drewe, E. A., Ettlinger, G., Milner, A. D. and Passingham, R. E. (1970). A comparative review of the results of neuropsychological research on man and monkey. *Cortex* 6, 129–163.

Dru, D., Walker, J. B. and Walker, J. P. (1976). CNS recovery of function: serial lesion effects. *In* "Advances in Psychobiology" (A. H. Riesen and R. F. Thompson, eds), Vol. III, pp. 197–218. Wiley-Interscience, New York.

Finger, S. (ed.) (1978). "Recovery from Brain Damage". Plenum Press, New York.

Gazzaniga, M. S. (1975). The concept of diaschisis. *In* "Cerebral Localization" (K. J. Zülch, O. Creutzfeldt and G. C. Galbraith, eds), pp. 328–331. Springer-Verlag, Berlin.

Geschwind, N. (1974). The anatomical basis of hemispheric differentiation. *In* "Hemisphere Function in the Human Brain" (S. J. Dimond and J. G. Beaumont, eds). Elek Science, London.

Glassman, R. B. (1978). The logic of the lesion experiment and its role in the neural sciences. *In* "Recovery from Brain Damage" (S. Finger, ed.), pp. 4–31. Plenum Press, New York.

Golden, C. J. (1978). "Diagnosis and Rehabilitation in Clinical Neuropsychology". C. C. Thomas, Springfield, Illinois.

Gregory, R. L. (1961). The brain as an engineering problem. *In* "Current Problems in Animal Behaviour" (W. H. Thorpe and O. L. Zangwill, eds), pp. 307–330. Cambridge University Press, Cambridge.

Heaton, R. K., Baade, L. E. and Johnson, K. L. (1978). Neuropsychological test results associated with psychiatric disorders in adults. *Psychol. Bull.* 85, 141–162.

Hécaen, H. and Albert, M. L. (1978). "Human Neuropsychology". Wiley-Interscience, New York.

Heilman, K. M. and Valenstein, E. (eds) (1979). "Clinical Neuropsychology". Oxford University Press, New York.

Isaacson, R. L. (1975). The myth of recovery from early brain damage. *In* "Aberrant Development in Infancy" (N. R. Ellis, ed.), Lawrence Erlbaum, Potomac, Maryland.

Jouandet, M. and Gazzaniga, M. S. (1979). The frontal lobes. *In* "Handbook of Behavioural Neurobiology: – Vol. 2 Neuropsychology" (M. S. Gazzaniga, ed.), pp. 25–59. Plenum Press, New York.

Joynt, R. J. (1975). Neuroanatomy underlying the language function. *In* "Reading, Perception and Language" (D. D. Duane and M. B. Rawson, eds), pp. 39–54. York Press, Baltimore, Maryland.

Kertesz, A. (1979). Recovery and treatment. *In* "Clinical Neuropsychology" (K. M. Heilman and E. Valenstein, eds), pp. 503–534. Oxford University Press, New York.

Kinsbourne, M. (1971). Cognitive deficit: experimental analysis. *In* "Psychobiology" (J. L. McGaugh, ed.), pp. 285–348. Academic Press, New York and London.

Kinsbourne, M. (1976). The neuropsychological analysis of cognitive deficit. *In* "Biological Foundations of Psychiatry" (R. G. Grenell and S. Gabay, eds), Vol. I, pp. 527–589. Raven Press, New York.

Kinsbourne, M. (ed.) (1978). "Asymmetrical Function of the Brain". Cambridge University Press, Cambridge.

Krech, D. (1962). Cortical localization of function. *In* "Psychology in the Making" (L. Postman, ed.), pp. 31–72. Knopf, New York.

Lachman, R., Lachman, J. L. and Butterfield, E. C. (1979). "Cognitive Psychology and Information Processing". Laurence Erlbaum, Hillsdale, New Jersey.

Laurence, S. and Stein, D. G. (1978). Recovery after brain damage and the concept of localization of function. *In* "Recovery from Brain Damage". (S. Finger, ed.), pp. 369–407. Plenum Press, New York.

LeDoux, J. E., Smylie, C. S., Ruff, R. and Gazzaniga, M. S. (1980). Left hemisphere visual processes in a case of right hemisphere symptomatology. *Arch. Neurol.* 37, 157–159.

LeVere, T. E. (1975). Neural stability, sparing and behavioural recovery following brain damage. *Psychol. Rev.* 82, 344–358.

LeVere, T. E. and Morlock, G. W. (1973). The nature of visual recovery following posterior neodecortication in the hooded rat. *J. Comp. Physiol. Psychol.* 83, 62–67.

LeVere, T. E. and Morlock, G. W. (1974). The influence of pre-operative learning on the recovery of a successive brightness discrimination following posterior neodecortication in the hooded rat. *Bull. Psychonomic Soc.* 4, 507–509.

Levy, J. (1978). Lateral differences in the human brain in cognition and behavioural control. *In* "Cerebral Correlates of Conscious Experience" (P. A. Buser and A. Rougeul–Buser, eds), pp. 285–298. Elsevier North Holland, Amsterdam.

Lezak, M. D. (1976). "Neuropsychological Assessment". Oxford University Press, New York.

Luria, A. R. (1964). Neuropsychology in the local diagnosis of brain injury. *Cortex* 1, 3–18.

Luria, A. R. (1966). "Higher Cortical Functions in Man". Basic Books, New York.

Luria, A. R. (1973). "The Working Brain". Penguin, Harmondsworth.

Luria, A. R. and Majovsky, L. V. (1977). Basic approaches used in American and Soviet clinical neuropsychology. *Am. Psychol.* 32, 959–968.

Markowitz, D. (1973). Generalized complementarity re-entered. *J. Theor. Biol.* 40, 399–402.

Marshall, J. C. (1973). Some problems and paradoxes associated with recent accounts of hemispheric specialization. *Neuropsychologia* 11, 463–470.

Masterton, R. B. and Berkley, M. A. (1974). Brain function: changing ideas on the role of sensory, motor and association cortex in behaviour. *A. Rev. Psychol.* 25, 277–312.

Merton, P. A. and Morton, H. B. (1980). Stimulation of the cerebral cortex in the intact human subject. *Nature* 285, 227.

Meyer, D. R. (1972). Access to engrams. *Am. Psychol.* 27, 124–133.

Meyer, P. M. (1973). Recovery from neo-cortical damage. *In* "Cortical Functioning in Behaviour" (G. French, ed.), pp. 115–138. Scott, Foresman, Glenview, Illinois.

Meyer, V. (1960). Psychological effects of brain damage. *In* "Handbook of Abnormal Psychology" (H. J. Eysenck, ed.), pp. 529–565. Pitman, London.

Milner, B., ed. (1975). "Hemispheric Specialization and Interaction". MIT, Cambridge, Massachussetts.

Milner, B. and Teuber, H-L. (1968). Alterations of perception and memory in man: reflections on methods. *In* "Analysis of Behavioural Change" (L. Weiskrantz, ed.), pp. 268–375. Harper and Row, New York.

Moscovitch, M. S. (1979). Information processing and the cerebral hemispheres. *In* "Handbook of Behavioural Neurobiology: – Vol. 2 Neuropsychology" (M. S. Gazzaniga, ed.), pp. 379–446. Plenum Press, New York.

Neisser, U. (1976). "Cognition and Reality". W. H. Freeman, San Francisco.

Newcombe, F. (1969). "Missile Wounds of the Brain". Oxford University Press, Oxford.

Newcombe, F. and Ratcliff, G. (1979). Long term psychological consequences of cerebral lesions. *In* "Handbook of Behavioural Neurobiology: – Vol. 2

Neuropsychology" (M. S. Gazzaniga, ed.), pp. 495–540. Plenum Press, New York.

Nielsen, J. M. (1946). "Agnosia, Apraxia, Aphasia". Hoeber, New York.

Pincus, J. H. and Tucker, G. J. (1978). "Behavioural Neurology" 2nd edn. Oxford University Press, New York.

Reitan, R. M. and Davison, L. A. (1974). "Clinical Neuropsychology: Current Status and Applications". V. H. Winston and Sons, Washington, D.C.

Smith, J. S. and Kiloh, L. G. (1977). "Psychosurgery and Society". Pergamon, Oxford.

Smith, W. L. and Kling, A. (eds) (1976). "Issues in Brain/Behaviour Control". Spectrum, New York.

Sprague, J. M. (1966). Visual, acoustic and somesthetic deficits in the cat after cortical and midbrain lesions. In "The Thalamus" (D. P. Purpura, and M. Yahr, eds), pp. 391–417. Columbia University Press, New York.

Szentagothai, J. (1975). The module concept in cerebral cortex architecture. *Brain Res.* **95**, 475–496.

Szentagothai, J. and Arbib, M. A. (1974). Conceptual models of neural organization. *Neurosci. Res. Prog. Bull.* **12**, 305–510.

Teuber, H-L. (1955). Physiological psychology. *A. Rev. Psychol.* **6**, 267–296.

Teuber, H-L. (1975a). Recovery of function after brain injury in man. In "Outcome of Severe Damage to the CNS" Ciba Foundation Symposium 34 (new series), pp. 159–190. Elsevier, Amsterdam.

Teuber, H-L. (1975b). Why two brains? In "Hemispheric Specialization and Interaction" (B. Milner, ed.), pp. 71–74. MIT, Cambridge, Massachussetts.

Townsend, J. T. (1971). A note on the identifiability of parallel and serial processes. *Percep. Psychophys.* **10**, 161–163.

Walsh, K. W. (1978). "Neuropsychology. A Clinical Approach". Churchill-Livingstone, Edinburgh.

Warren, J. M. and Kolb, B. (1978). Generalizations in neuropsychology. In "Recovery from Brain Damage". (S. Finger, ed.), pp. 36–48. Plenum Press, New York.

Weiskrantz, L. (1968a). Treatments, inference and brain function. In "Analysis of Behavioural Change". (L. Weiskrantz, ed.), pp. 400–414. Harper and Row, New York.

Weiskrantz, L. (1968b). Some traps and pontifications. In "Analysis of Behavioural Change". (L. Weiskrantz, ed.), pp. 415–429. Harper and Row, New York.

Weiskrantz, L. (1973). Problems and progress in physiological psychology. *Br. J. Psychol.* **64**, 511–520.

Weiskrantz, L. (1977). Trying to bridge some neuropsychological gaps between monkey and man. *Br. J. Psychol.* **68**, 431–446.

Whitaker, H. A. and Ojemann, G. A. (1977). Lateralization of higher cortical functioning: a critique. *Ann. N.Y. Acad. Sci.* **299**, 459–473.

11 Psychophysiological Measurement: Methodological Constraints

S. W. Porges, P. A. Ackles and S. R. Truax

Abstract To understand the why, what and how of psychophysiological measurement, the decision-making processes associated with each of these questions must be described. General paradigms, such as those focusing on stimulus–response relationships or individual differences, establish different rationales for why physiological variables are measured. The research question pursued determines, in part, the approaches, strategies, and assumptions adopted. For example, questions concerning the relationship between psychological and physiological variables differ in the degree of focus on either the neural or psychological substrates of the physiological response as well as the type of psychological–physiological connection involved. The selection of physiological variables to monitor, the what of psychophysiological measurement, is influenced by tradition, research question, and technology. How physiological variables are monitored includes a consideration of variable definition, measurement, and quantification strategies.

I. Introduction

Psychophysiological research is concerned with the relationships between physiological activity and psychological processes. This chapter will be concerned with the decision-making processes that the investigator encounters in attempting to infer psychological process from physiological activity. We will focus on three questions: (i) *why* are physiological measures monitored; (ii) *what* are the dimensions of physiological activity monitored; and (iii) *how* are the physiological variables monitored? The chapter will elucidate specific assumptions made by the investigator as each question is addressed.

PHYSIOLOGICAL CORRELATES OF HUMAN
BEHAVIOUR   ISBN 0-12-273901-9

II. Why Measure Physiological Variables?

A. Paradigms

The selection of a research paradigm limits the choice of research questions, determines the theoretical constructs, and leads to particular methodologies. Until recently, psychology has been dominated by the search for stimulus–response (S-R) laws. Similarly, S-R paradigms have been adopted by psychophysiologists in attempts to identify relationships between externally manipulated stimuli and specific physiological response patterns. Many of the chapters in this volume provide examples of these psychological–physiological parallels. In fact, it was the early emphasis on psychological and physiological parallels that led to this experimental discipline being named "psycho-physiology."

Stimulus–response paradigms are not simply defined as investigations of parallels between a physical stimulus or input and a physiological response or output. Rather, S-R paradigms vary in complexity. For example, stimulus manipulations may involve either physical (e.g., sound intensity) or psychological (e.g., importance or relevance) dimensions. When physical characteristics are manipulated and physiological responses monitored, the paradigm is a simple S-R model. If the characteristics of the physical stimuli influence a psychological process (e.g., orienting, habituation or classical conditioning) or the context of a stimulus presentation conveys information (e.g., threat), then the physiological response may be used to infer information about psychological processes. The S-R paradigm is then elaborated into a S-I-R paradigm, in which the "I" represents some intervening psychological process (Donchin, 1979; Donchin and Israel, 1980). A third type of S-R paradigm is the S-O-R model, where the "O" represents the structure and function of the organism.

The search for general S-R laws may involve any of these paradigms. Each paradigm advances different assumptions about the *control* a stimulus imposes on a response and the sensitivity of the response to convey information concerning either psychological process and/or physiological organization.

All S-R paradigms may have inferential limitations. It is possible that obtained effects result from one or more unmeasured or uncontrolled variables, such as motivation or deficits in sensory reception or motor performance. Thus inferences drawn from response topographies concerning psychological processes or atypical physiological organization depend frequently on the assumption that other potential influences are random.

Individual difference paradigms may be contrasted with the above S-R paradigms. Individual difference approaches seek to establish relationships between individual variations in physiological activity and behavioural systems, through correlational rather than manipulative means. It is often assumed that the distinctive behaviour of organisms may be reflected by covariations between behaviour and physiological activity. In the central and autonomic nervous systems, correlations are sought between measures of spontaneous physiological activity and behaviour or behavioural states. This type of paradigm may be characterized as an organism-response (O-R) model. Its major limitation centres on the inability to determine cause and effect relationships. Although research within this paradigm dates back to the late 1800's and early 1900's (see Porges and Coles, 1976; Stern *et al.*, 1980), more recent investigations of the individual differences in behaviour have focused on the assessment of the physiological characteristics of atypical groups such as sociopaths, the developmentally disabled, or the unusually creative. The study of the phases of sleep exemplifies an area where behavioural states have been elaborately investigated with psychophysiological techniques. Psychophysiological techniques have been particularly valuable in broadening our understanding of sleep states because they can be applied to intact, normally functioning human subjects.

The study of individual differences may be viewed as contradictory to the search for general S-R laws. For example, how could a general law, relating stimulus manipulations to response dimensions, be described if the response characteristics differed among the subjects? One way this apparent conflict may be resolved is to adopt a research strategy which includes the search for general S-R laws along with the assessment of individual differences in spontaneous physiological activity. Individual differences in the nervous system reflected by psychophysiological measures may influence the characteristics of both spontaneous activity and the responses to stimulus manipulations. For example, brain-damaged organisms often exhibit atypical response patterns both spontaneously and to stimulus manipulations. Thus one could measure the changes in "state" of the organism, as well as S-R relationships. Hence, the S-O-R strategy, which combines O-R and S-R strategies, allows the partition of sources of response variation into stimulus and organism determined components.

In summary, the interrelationships between physiological activity and psychological processes may be investigated along two general dimensions: (i) assessing the relationship between stimulus manipulations and response elicitation to describe "general laws" of processing; (ii) assessing the relationship between individual differences and state variations in spontaneous physiological activity and behaviour (e.g., temperament, behavioural style, sleep states). It is not necessary to place these paradigms in conflict. Psychophysiological techniques lend themselves to reconciling these approaches, by the nature of both the methods used and the variables measured. Psychophysiological techniques permit continuous data collection for analysis of both spontaneous and elicited activity.

B. General Psychophysiological Research Questions, Approaches and Assumptions

In this section several psychophysiological research questions and approaches will be discussed within the context of assumptions made regarding the information conveyed by physiological variables. Underlying these questions is the general assumption that the measurement of physiological activity will provide meaningful information about psychological processes. However, different questions and assumptions lead to research strategies which differ in the degree they explicitly attempt to link measures of physiological activity to underlying neural or psychological substrates.

Question 1: What are the relationships between one psychological process and another psychological process when one is indexed by a physiological variable?

Research addressing this question uses physiological measures (e.g., evoked-cardiac responses) associated with one psychological process (habituation of orienting) to investigate other psychological processes (e.g., recognition and/or discrimination of phonemes). Questions concerning the reliability and validity of the physiological indices or the specific neural mechanisms underlying these indices are typically *not* investigated. Two related research approaches have emerged which focus on this question. Both are based on the research described below under Question 2 and view physiological activity as "covert" behaviour.

In the first approach, it is assumed that *physiological measures are simply another dimension of the organism's responsivity to the environment* (Assumption 1) and are not a reflection of specific psychological process. Many of the specific research questions within this approach have been concerned with various aspects of stimulus–response relationships. For example, evoked heart-rate responses have been used to assess the full-term and preterm human infant's sensory thresholds to tactile stimulation (see Rose *et al.*, 1976).

In the second approach to this question, two far reaching assumptions are made concerning the nature of the physiological activities measured. First, it is assumed that *specific physiological measures are isomorphic (correlated) with specific psychological process* (Assumption 2). Thus, specific changes in physiological activity (e.g., level, direction, amplitude, latency) are presumed to be reliable and valid indices of certain psychological processes (e.g., orienting, habituation, arousal, affect). If this assumption is accepted a priori, then it follows that the physiological measure should be a sensitive index of a psychological process.

However, Assumption 2 frequently invites the further assumption that *a physiological measure is in fact a "component" of a specific psychological process* (Assumption 3). The implication of this assumption is that the psychological process does not occur without the component physiological response. For example, if increased heart rates are assumed to be a component of a heightened state of arousal, then an individual would be in a heightened state of arousal if, and only if, there was an increase in heart rate. Assumption 2, however, only implies that the physiological measure is a correlate of the psychological process. Therefore, it is possible for an individual to be in a heightened state of arousal without exhibiting an increase in heart rate.

Although few investigators have adopted Assumption 3 and Assumption 2 both assumptions have played a major role in labelling physiological response patterns as manifestations of psychological processes. Consistent with these assumptions, psychological constructs have been defined in terms of the occurrence of certain psychological response patterns. The literature contains references to terms such as "cardiac orienting" when a heart-rate deceleration was observed; "defensive reflex" when a heart-rate acceleration was observed; and "expectancy" when a specific cortical potential pattern was observed prior to stimulus onset or change. Moreover, many developmental psychophysiologists have accepted these assumptions and employed these research approaches because the infant has a limited verbal and motoric behavioural repertoire. The literature contains numerous examples of the use of physiological dependent variables in studies of infant sensory-perceptual capacities (e.g., Chang and Trehub, 1977), classical conditioning (see Fitzgerald and Brackbill, 1976), habituation (see Clifton and Nelson, 1976), and social-emotional development (Campos, 1976; Sroufe and Waters, 1977).

Question 2: What are the psychological substrates of specific physiological measures?

Question 2 is perhaps the major focus of psychophysiological research. This research is more explicitly concerned with the basic problem of *identifying* the relationships between psychological and physiological variables. The assumptions of the previously described approaches under Question 1 serve as working hypotheses for research attempting to answer Question 2.

Although questions concerning the reliability and validity of physiological measures are emphasized, questions concerning the neural substrates of these physiological measures frequently are not investigated.

Within the context of Question 2, several research strategies have been employed to provide estimates of the reliability and validity of the physiological indices of psychological processes. One strategy focuses on the extent to which physiological measures are consistently predictable from experimental manipulations of psychologically relevant variables. The reliability of the measure is supported, if the physiological measure is consistently elicited under theoretically equivalent experimental conditions. If the same measure is reliably predicted for the experimental conditions subsumed under a specific psychological construct (e.g., orienting) but not elicited under conditions subsumed under another construct (e.g., defensive reactions), then some degree of validity is established for the physiological measure. (It should be noted that questions of reliability and validity are not all or none, but a matter of degree.)

A second strategy involves the use of correlations between physiological events and performance measures thought to be mediated by the same psychological process. If two measures, one physiological and one performance, are thought to reflect the same process, then the two variables should be correlated. For example, under certain experimental conditions heart rate deceleration may covary with reaction time, suggesting that heart rate deceleration may index attention. Reaction time performance is the criterion variable against which the validity of the physiological measure is evaluated. This correlational strategy may also be used in reverse. The *lack* of correlation between physiological measures or between physiological and performance measures has been used as evidence that these measures subserve different psychological processes.

Although these strategies have met with some success in psychophysiology, there are many instances of negative findings. For example, the magnitude of anticipatory heart-rate decelerations in warned reaction-time studies are not always correlated with reaction-time performance either between- or within-subjects (Jennings et al., 1970; Coles et al., 1975; Walter and Porges, 1976; Duncan-Johnson and Coles, 1974; Van der Molen and Orlebeke, 1980). One major problem is the identification of performance variables. Performance variables may not be manifestations of a single psychological process or their occurrence may lag behind the psychological process (e.g., choice behaviours in stimulus discrimination tasks). Moreover, there may not be an overt performance variable which corresponds to a particular psychological process. Thus, it is not always the case that the validity of a physiological measure can be estimated by correlating it with an overt behaviour (see, e.g., Donchin et al., 1978; Donchin et al., 1981).

Question 3: Do *physiological measures reflect the occurrence of general psychological states?*

Research on this question focuses on the problem of identifying physiological indices of general psychological states and is based on the assumption that *physiological activity represents a general state which parallels a variety of psychological processes* (Assumption 4). It does not assume that physiological activity is a sensitive index of *specific* psychological events. This view does not necessitate an isomorphic relationship between physiological activity and specific psychological events. Rather, certain physiological measures are viewed as reflecting a *general process* which facilitates a global state, enabling more specific processes to occur.

Research on this question assumes that general psychological states subsumed under constructs such as arousal, stress and emotion may be measured along specific physiological dimensions. However, it also assumes that a variety of psychological processes may occur within each of these states. Much of the early psychophysiological research, especially on the concepts of emotion and arousal originated from the latter assumption. More recently cognitive psychophysiologists have pursued this question in studies on such concepts as subject involvement, effort and mental load.

Question 4: Are individual differences in spontaneous physiological activity related to behaviour?

Research investigating this question attempts to identify measures of spontaneous or basal physiological activity which reflect individual differences in the general integrity or status of the central nervous system. It is assumed that *physiological activity reflects individual differences in the nervous sytstem organization which predispose and limit behaviour* (Assumption 5). Thus, if these measures reflect individual differences in the nervous system, they should be sensitive to, or predictive of, performance and other behavioural variables. Assumption 5, unlike Assumptions 1–3, does not require a simultaneity of physiological activity and specific psychological process.

Much of the research on this question involves the development of measures of spontaneous physiological activity for use as diagnostic instruments (Ahn *et al.*, 1980; Eysenck, 1967; John *et al.*, 1980; Johnson, 1980; Porges, 1980). Research has attempted to identify individual differences in physiological activity which are related to *trait* constructs or diagnostic categories such as personality type, hyperactivity, schizophrenia and senility.

Historically, psychologists have recognized that the concept of individual differences is important to the understanding of human behaviour. Unfortunately, since individual differences cannot be manipulated, the construct is difficult to incorporate into experimental paradigms. Although most psychologists are aware of individual differences, individual differences are usually ignored in the scientist's quest for *general laws*. In physiological psychology, for instance, powerful manipulations, such as lesions, tend to mask individual differences. However, psychophysiological research tends to focus on human and animal subjects with intact nervous systems. These *intact* subjects often exhibit a large range of individual differences (behavioural and physiological) which may interact with desired stimulus–response relationships.

Question 5: What neural mechanisms are involved in the physiological response systems of interest to psychophysiologists?

This final research question emphasizes a more explicit reductionist strategy. Although human subjects may be studied in special situations to answer this question, obvious experimental constraints on measurement and manipulation often necessitate the use of animal preparations. Increasingly, invasive techniques commonly employed by physiological psychologists and neurophysiologists (e.g., pharmacological manipulations, single cell recording and stimulation, lesioning, etc.) have been adopted in an attempt to gain a more comprehensive knowledge of central nervous system activity and the mechanisms governing its transduction into peripheral activity (e.g., Lacey and Lacey, 1978; Obrist, 1976; Porges *et al.*, 1982; Schneiderman *et al.*, 1974). Underlying much of the research on this question is the assumption that *the neural mechanisms which transform psychological events into physiological processes are manifested in peripheral physiological activity* (Assumption 6).

This assumption may also imply a continuity between individual differences in the central nervous system which are related to behaviour and peripheral physiological activity (see Porges, 1980; Porges and Smith, 1980). Hence, accurate description of central control mechanisms may be derived from peripheral physiological activity. This assumption has led to research attempting to validate the relationship between peripheral patterns and central mediation through invasive techniques. It also calls for a refinement in measurement strategy, since an important goal in psychophysiological measurement is to partition the variance of the peripheral response system into components that are associated with central control. With heart rate, this assumption has led to research attempting to derive measures of neural control (e.g., vagal) of the heart from the complex pattern of heart rate (see Porges *et al.*, 1982).

C. *Summary*

The general psychophysiological question evaluating the relationship between physiological and psychological phenomena has produced several lines of research. Each has posed different research questions based upon different assumptions. The approaches differ along a continuum which varies in the extent to which they focus on isolating the neural or psychological substrates of the physiological measures. At one end of this continuum, the psychophysiological research questions have not been concerned with the issues of reliability and validity of the measure, but rather, the focus is on the relationship between one psychological process and another psychological process when one is measured by physiological responses. At another level of this research continuum, the reliability and validity of physiological measures are the focus of the research questions being asked. At still another level, the emphasis is on a more explicitly reductionist approach to describe central and peripheral mechanisms of the physiological systems commonly measured by psychophysiologists.

It should be obvious from the discussion above that the research conducted is based upon an experimenter's belief that a research question has an answer. Often research has been based upon assumptions which have not been evaluated. A researcher may accept certain assumptions a priori and conduct research on that basis, or experiments may be conducted to evaluate the validity of those assumptions. It seems clear that one researcher's assumptions are very often another's research questions.

III. What Physiological Variables are Monitored?

The factors governing the specific physiological measurement dimensions selected include: existing traditions, specific research questions, and available technology. Exemplifying the effects of tradition, certain measures have become associated with cognitive processes (directional heart rate responses or event-related cortical potentials) while other measures have been associated with states of arousal (levels of heart rate or skin conductance). Still other physiological parameters have been associated with states of sustained attention and mental effort (pupillary activity, suppression of respiration, and heart rate variability). A brief review of the historical roots of psychophysiological measurement may help identify traditional influences leading to the selection of specific physiological measures.

A. *Historical Trends in Measurement*

Concepts relating physiological states to psychological processes are historically old (see Mesulam and Perry, 1972; Neumann and Blanton, 1970).
However, psychophysiology has only recently become an experimental discipline of contemporary science. Modern psychophysiology focuses on the
description and quantification of subtle physiological variations. The antecedents of contemporary psychophysiology are found in a variety of scientific
disciplines.

Careful observers of behaviour (e.g., Darwin, 1872) have known that
humans and other animals are sensitive to subtle overt physiological cues
such as the "blush" of the face or the "tear" in the eye. Researchers who study
personality and social psychology often describe physiological components
of emotion without direct physiological measurement. In an intake interview,
a physician may observe subtle signs of physiological activity as an aid in
diagnosis. Crude quantitative indices of physiological activity have been
made of body temperature, vasomotor activity (redness of the skin), pulse
rate and breathing rate. These measures focus on the dimension of changes in
level or rate rather than changes in pattern.

Once electricity was harnessed, the galvanometer was used to study the
bio-electric nature of living systems. (The galvanometer measures slight
variations in electrical activity.) Consequently, bio-electrical change became
an important focus of research. In the 1800's, for example, researchers
attempted to measure the bio-electric characteristics of behavioural and
medical disorders. For the interested reader, early papers in this area may be
found in Porges and Coles (1976).

Following the advent of the galvanometer, methods were devised to record
patterns of electrical activity. One early instrument was the smoked
kymograph, a rotating drum covered with smoked paper in contact with the
stylus of the galvanometer. As the drum rotated, the stylus etched the changing electrical activity. Later, the polygraph became the principal measurement tool in psychophysiology. The polygraph is a series of galvanometers
with styli. Each galvanometer is associated with a transducer, amplifier and
filter which can transform, amplify and condition the biological process into
electrical impulses which drive the stylus for a permanent record. A
polygraph may contain high impedance input circuits which allow the
recording of very small shifts in voltage at low current levels without affecting
normal bioelectric characteristics. Moreover, the polygraph is capable of
transducing biological processes not inherently bioelectric. Recently there
has been a dramatic increase in the use of modern high speed computer
technology in interface with the polygraph for immediate (on-line) or

delayed (off-line) storage, transformation and analysis of the physiological activity.

To summarize, the history of psychophysiological measurement began with observation of physiological changes and activity (e.g., tears, pupil dilation, sweating); proceeded to crude quantification of physiological activity (e.g., counting pulses or breaths); and then developed more precise measurement of subtle "bio-electric" characteristics with the use of the galvanometer and permanent recordings. Contemporary measurement evolved with the development of complex transduction, amplification and filtering equipment for the modern polygraph and the interface with computer facilities.

One can trace the history of the measurement of heart rate responses as an example of the effects of tradition and technology on the use of psycho-physiological variables (for a review of heart rate response measures see Woodcock, 1971). Initially, heart rate was assessed by counting pulses. Observers noted that the heart rate accelerated during apparent anxiety. Thus, heart rate level evolved as a standard index of arousal or activation. In the early part of this century, research focused on emotion; heart rate level was used as an index of this construct. Stimuli external to the subject were presented and heart rate level was assessed. The heart rate response was interpreted as an emotional response since theories related visceral activity to the psychological concept of emotion.

Research interest shifted from emotion to theories of cognition. Physiological responses which had been used as indices of emotion were applied to assess cognitive processes (e.g., attention). The assumptions relating the physiological process to a psychological construct also shifted. During the late 1950's and early 1960's the method of quantifying the heart rate response drastically changed. No longer were mean pulse counts per time unit an adequate measure. Heart rate responses were viewed as sensitive reflections of higher level cortical events associated with specific cognitive activity. To demonstrate this parallel, the heart rate response was investigated as a temporal pattern rather than a discrete event. The pattern, and not the mean level, conveyed the information regarding the cognitive processing of the experimental manipulation. Second-by-second or beat-by-beat measurements became common and the directionality of the pattern became critical. The cardiotachometer which measured the time between successive heart beats fostered this change in methodology. For recent discussions on the use of measures of heart rate variability and time series models for evaluating evoked heart rate responses and patterns of basal cardiac activity, the reader is referred to Siddle and Turpin (1980) and Porges *et al.* (1980).

More recently the cardiac cycle (the time between successive heart beats) has been partitioned to study the sensitivity of components of the EKG and cardiac cycle to external stimuli. This became feasible with the development of computer technology which can sense, on-line, the onset of a given heart beat and insert the stimulus at various points in the cardiac cycle. Thus, the measurement of the heart rate response has evolved from counting pulses per unit time, through describing the directional characteristics of the pattern, to investigating the individual cardiac cycle. These measures define a class of evoked heart rate responses. They share the assumption that the cardiac system responds to stimulation with a change in rate, although they define this change on a variety of dimensions.

B. *Psychophysiology without Electrodes*

A limited number of techniques exist to assess the internal processes (e.g., emotion and cognition) which mediate overt behaviour. In psychophysiological research, the emphasis is on the monitoring of physiological activity. However, careful observation of behaviour and elicitation of the subject's own report may provide important convergent information.

1. Self report

As indicated above, many psychophysiologists are concerned with the validity of their measures. They question whether the measurements are sensitive to the appropriate process or dimension. One important source of validation is the self report. Sometimes self report provides reliable and valid measures of behaviour and internal states; at other times, the self report may be of limited validity. Often, individuals may not be fully aware of the true cause or consequences of their behaviour, or they may be reluctant to provide full disclosure because they fear their response may present them unfavourably. Self report should be considered as a potential index when the subject: (i) is likely to have accurate knowledge of the desired information; and (ii) has no self-interest in its presentation. These two rules seem obvious and simple but they are often neglected. Self reports may contribute information important in successful psychophysiological research. First, self reports may be used as criterion variables to evaluate the predictive value of physiological activity; or second, self reports may provide all the information needed for researchers interested solely in the internal process and not specific physiological–psychological relationships.

Self report data may be obtained in a variety of ways. The classic psychometric approach entails the presentation of written verbal stimuli to elicit responses. The verbal stimuli are usually questions or statements, selected on the basis of factor analysis or other methods, which obtain presumably reliable information regarding a specific psychological dimension. The response characteristics of a questionnaire are controlled by the design of the testing instrument. It may provide categorical alternatives (e.g., true/false) or dimensions with several alternatives between extremes (e.g., strongly disagree to strongly agree). The Taylor manifest anxiety scale (Taylor, 1953) is an example of a psychometric device for measuring anxiety. Open-ended self reports have the advantage of obtaining information free of the instrument constructor's biases, but are rarely used because they are difficult to quantify.

2. *Other behavioural measures*

Under conditions when self report is of questionable validity, a good approach is to look for other measures, which are at least subject to different sources of invalidity. Even when self reports are used, other behavioural or physiological variables may serve as significant convergent indices of internal states. However, as with all forms of measurement, the data may be modified unacceptably by the device employed. Considerable caution is required when the data are derived from behavioural observations. Observers may introduce systematic bias through faulty interpretation.

There are many behavioural variables which have been used as indices of internal state, in addition to self reports. Peripheral changes in the body appear to be important cues of emotion. One class of cues associated with autonomic change (in addition to bio-electric measurement) is the overt changes which can be observed without special equipment and associated with specific physiological systems. Pupilometry is an area of research which infers sympathetic and parasympathetic changes from the overt behaviour of the iris of the eye (Rubin, 1962). Changes in peripheral blood flow (blushing or blanching of the skin) may serve as a similar, although less sensitive, observable index of autonomic response. Facial expressions (Izard, 1971) have distinct characteristics in different emotional states. Also, activity level may be defined to represent arousal or emotional agitation.

The distinction between a behavioural and a physiological response is not always clearcut. In general, overt behaviour such as breathing, pupillary dilation and limb tremor are considered physiological variables if they are monitored by equipment which provides a continuous record of changes and requires the attachment of sensors to the subject. An example is a polygraph with transducers to record breathing and limb tremor.

IV. How are Physiological Variables Measured?

How physiological variables are translated into empirical measurements depends first on what responses are to be measured. The characteristics of the variable dictates the measurement strategy. The experimenter must operationally define the response parameters to be studied (the "what" aspect) prior to data collection. This determines how the data are collected, the monitoring and recording equipment necessary, and the characteristics of the data set to be analysed.

Factors in signal transduction, amplification and conditioning as well as quantification strategies contribute to the final method of monitoring employed. The *how* may be partitioned into two strategies: (i) measurement (recording the physiological process); and (ii) quantification and analysis (defining the response). The analysis strategy focuses on the partitioning of the variance of the physiological process into identifiable components associated with experimental manipulations (i.e., treatments), individual differences and repeated observations.

A. *Measurement Strategy*

For practical purposes, biological variables may be partitioned into two broad categories: discrete events and continuously changing levels. Events can be discretely measured while levels represent a continuous process whose amplitude is generally sampled across time. The heart rate system provides an example in each of these domains. Counted pulses are obviously discrete measurable events. However, the actual electrical pattern generated by the contracting heart, the EKG, is a continuous process which has a voltage pattern associated with various biological processes. The measurement strategy includes methods of transducing the physiological process into a permanent record. This strategy necessitates a series of processes described below.

1. *Signal transduction*

The method of transduction is dependent upon the physiological system being monitored and the a priori definition of the response. Numerous topographical characteristics may be quantified from any physiological system. There are no compelling theoretical or empirical reasons for assuming that all response dimensions of a given physiological system will behave similarly.

The process of signal transduction begins with the identification of a specific physiological system. The signal in its natural context may be a bio-electric process (e.g., EKG, EEG, EMG, SC, etc.) or it may be physical activity such as movement (e.g., limb tremor), or an overt biological activity (e.g., fluctuations in pupillary diameter). After the system is identified and the dimensions of the response agreed upon, specific sensors are applied to the subject to monitor this activity. The sensor must be capable of transducing the biological event into electrical energy, quantitatively related to the physiological parameter studied, so that instruments such as the polygraph or computer can record the activity permanently. If the system produces a bio-electric potential, suitable electrodes are all that is needed. Responses such as skin potential, EEG and EKG are examples. If the physiological system produces a mechanical event such as blood pressure, then a suitable mechano-electrical transducer is required. If the system is characterized by fluctuating temperatures, then a thermo-electrical transducer is needed. Thus, the sensor-transducer unit in psychophysiological research permits the system being studied to be represented by electrical activity.

2. *Signal amplification and conditioning*

After the biological activity is transduced, a useful signal waveform is extracted from the incoming electrical information. In many cases, components of the polygraph, often called "couplers" or specialized "preamplifiers", perform the initial signal conditioning process. The signal conditioner may filter the signal to obtain information in the desired frequency band, or it may produce a signal whose amplitude is proportional to some parameter of the incoming signal.

Often the voltage from the organism or the transducer is very small. Virtually all recording devices have a *preamplifier* to amplify the magnitude of the input signal from the electrodes or the transducer. Once the signal is amplified to a specific level the polygraph has a *driver amplifier* which increases the voltage output sufficiently to operate the galvanometers, which change the electrical signal into the mechanical force necessary to move the polygraph's pen over the chart paper. (Preamplification is necessary because the driver amplifiers generally require a relatively high input voltage signal.) A chart drive passes the paper under the pen and a permanent visible record of the input signal is produced. Computers are rapidly replacing polygraphs for record storage.

B. *Quantification Strategy*

In order to effectively conduct psychophysiological research, the investigator should have an a priori definition of the response parameters being investigated. In this section we will discuss some of these response parameters and how they lead to specific types of analyses and hypotheses.

In most physiological research, background spontaneous activity is considered unimportant. Meaningful responses can be easily identified as a discrete change in the ongoing activity of a behavioural system. However, when investigating physiological processes, it becomes obvious that most physiological systems function continuously. Although we can easily identify the occurrence of many overt behavioural responses, the physiological responses are much more difficult to define and isolate. In the process of quantifying physiological activity, the background information may be removed by *difference* scores or *change* measures. More sophisticated trend removal may be accomplished with the application of complex time-series techniques. Basically, one must assume that virtually every physiological system is continuous even though the manifestation of the system may occur at discrete times (e.g., heart beats).

Physiological systems have a variety of quantifiable parameters. Does frequency, level, amplitude, slope, magnitude of change or mere occurrence of an event signify the appropriate parameter of the system that will be sensitive to the psychological manipulation? When more than one physiological system is being monitored the complexity is multiplied. Is it the temporal coupling, the phase, the common periodicities or the correlation between events, that appropriately characterizes the relationships between and among a series of physiological systems (see Porges *et al.*, 1980)? The research questions selected and the assumptions adopted force the investigator into specific quantification strategies. Some questions relate to the nature of the underlying physiological process and necessitate quantification strategies which are designed to partition the variance of the process into specific neural and non-neural influences. Other questions may merely necessitate a consistent change in some response system.

Two studies with hyperactive children provide examples of different quantification strategies. In the first study, discrete changes in heart rate and heart rate variability during a warned reaction-time task were quantified (Porges *et al.*, 1975). In the second study, the focus was on spontaneous patterns of heart rate activity (Porges *et al.*, 1981).

The Porges *et al.* (1975) study examined the widely hypothesized attention deficit linked to hyperactivity, as well as the effects of methylphenidate (Ritalin) on heart rate and reaction time measures of sustained attention in a within-subjects design. Significant differences were found between the placebo and Ritalin conditions in the heart rate and reaction time measures. The reaction times were longer in the placebo than in the Ritalin condition, and the tonic heart rate and heart rate variability responses measured in the latter portion of the foreperiod, shifted from increases during placebo administration to decreases during Ritalin treatment. Thus, in the placebo condition, the direction of change in the heart rate and heart rate variability responses was consistent with the hypothesized sustained-attention deficit, associated with the hyperactivity syndrome. During the Ritalin treatment, the performance and direction of the tonic heart rate and heart rate variability responses shifted to that typically found in normal samples.

Let us now consider the physiological mechanisms which may underlie these heart rate responses. Since the heart rate decreases observed in the latter portion of the foreperiod of the warned reaction time tasks can be blocked with atropine, it appears that these responses are mediated by the efferent inhibitory influences of the vagus nerve to the heart (see Obrist *et al.*, 1970). The data cited from the Porges *et al.* (1975) study would then suggest that hyperactive children may have less vagal influence on the heart during the placebo condition than during the Ritalin condition. Thus, one may ask the question whether diminished vagal influences on the heart result in characteristic heart rate response topographies (i.e., direction and magnitude of change) which, in turn, reflect deficits in sustained attention. Also, one may ask the question whether diminished vagal influences on the heart are a characteristic of the untreated hyperactive children.

Questions concerning the neural control of the heart could not and were not tested directly in the Porges *et al* (1975) study. In order to provide a more direct test of this hypothesis, a non-invasive quantification technique of vagal influences on the heart was needed. Porges *et al.* (1981) applied such a quantification strategy with hyperactive children to test the question of whether Ritalin enhanced vagal influences on the heart in spontaneous cardiac activity.

The quantification strategy used by Porges *et al.* (1981) sought to capitalize on a phenomenon known as respiratory sinus arrhythmia (RSA). RSA refers to the apparent covariation of rhythmic changes in heart rate with those of respiration (i.e., during inspiration heart rate tends to increase and during expiration decrease). These changes in heart rate are thought to result from the phasic modulation in the brainstem of the efferent-inhibitory vagal influences (vagal tone) to the heart mediated by respiration. Thus, quantification of RSA should provide a non-invasive estimate of these vagal influences (Porges *et al.*, 1982).

Porges *et al.* (1981) used spectral and cross-spectral techniques to quantify RSA. Spectral analysis is a time-series technique which decomposes the fluctuations of heart rate and respiration into a series of sinusoidal functions which describe the variance of the frequency components of heart rate and respiration. From these analyses, two measures of RSA were derived. The first, called $\hat{V}$, assessed the amplitude of RSA to provide an estimate of vagal tone. This estimate of vagal tone ($\hat{V}$) was derived by summing the variances attributed to each frequency of the heart rate rhythms within the frequency band characteristic of respiration. The second measure, weighted coherence (C_w), was derived from the cross-spectral analysis of the heart rate and respiration and reflects the degree of temporal coupling between respiration and heart rate. C_w quantifies the percent of rhythmic co-variation between heart rate and respiration within the primary respiratory frequency band (see Porges *et al.*, 1980). Thus the amplitude of RSA, or vagal tone, may be independent of C_w.

C_w was found to be significantly greater during the low dose of Ritalin than during either the predrug or placebo conditions. $\hat{V}$ was also found to vary significantly across the drug conditions. The highest levels of $\hat{V}$ occurred during the predrug condition and the lowest occurred during the high-dose of Ritalin condition. The results suggest that the absolute amount of vagal tone, as measured by $\hat{V}$, may not be diminished in the untreated hyperactive child and that the Ritalin treatment does not result in increases in vagal tone. This would also suggest that the changes for the placebo and Ritalin conditions in the direction of the heart rate responses in the Porges *et al.* (1975) study were not the result of increases in vagal tone. However, the results for the C_w variable suggest that C_w may be related to the heart rate response patterns associated with attention. A study was conducted to evaluate the relationship between C_w and the heart rate pattern during a reaction-time task (Porges and Coles, 1982). When adult subjects were partitioned into high- and low-C_w groups, only the high-C_w subjects responded with a statistically significant heart rate response pattern characterized by an acceleration to the warning signal and a deceleration in anticipation of the imperative signal.

To summarize, the measurement strategy is a complex aggregate of processes associated with selection, transduction, recording, sampling and analysing physiological processes. The physiological process is transduced into electrical activity, the electrical activity is monitored by recording equipment which shapes and conditions the signal by filtering and amplifying. The quantification of the electrical activity is dependent upon an a priori defined measure which dictates the dimensions of quantification.

C. *Conclusions*

Quantification of physiological processes in psychophysiological research is a complex problem. We have reviewed some of the basic issues that must be considered. Unlike many other scientific disciplines, which are defined by paradigm or measurement strategy, psychophysiology contains a variety of approaches. Therefore, defining oneself as a psychophysiologist who studies cardiovascular variables, for instance, does not in itself convey information regarding the specific dependent variables measured, experimental design employed and assumptions accepted regarding physiological–psychological relationships. It is the variety of approaches and questions that can be pursued that makes psychophysiology such an inviting domain for adventurous researchers.

Acknowledgements

Preparation of this manuscript was supported, in part, by a National Institute of Mental Health Research Scientist Development Award (K02-MH-0054) to the first author and a postdoctoral traineeship (MH-15128) to the second author.

Further Reading

Martin, I. and Venables P. H. (eds), (1980). "Techniques in Psychophysiology". Wiley and Sons, New York.
This text contains a collection of chapters which focus on various aspects of methodological issues surrounding the most common, but not all, psychophysiological measures (e.g., electrodermal, cardio vascular, spontaneous EEG, event-related brain potentials, and peripheral vascular activity). Many of the chapters discuss the physiological mechanisms underlying various psychophysiological variables as well as data collection and processing. Also included are separate chapters devoted to biochemical methods, setting up a psychophysiology laboratory, measurement problems, and computers in psychophysiology.
Porges, S. W. and Coles, M. G. H. (eds), (1976). "Psychophysiology". Dowden, Hutchinson and Ross, Stroudsburg, Pennsylvania.
"Psychophysiology" provides a collection of papers which have had theoretical impact on the development of psychophysiology as a scientific discipline. The volume covers a broad range of psychophysiological concepts and includes the earliest published papers on cortical potentials and electrodermal activity as well as the more contemporary papers on arousal, attention, and autonomic conditioning. These landmark papers are organized into four parts: methodology; arousal theory; orienting reflex; attention, emotion and autonomic conditioning.
Stern, R. M., Ray, W. J. and Davis, C. M. (1980). "Psychophysiological Recording". Oxford University Press, New York.
This is an introductory textbook which provides the beginning student with a very readable, self-contained overview of psychophysiology which does not assume prior knowledge of the field. The book is subdivided into three parts. The first contains six chapters with the first chapter providing a brief historical introduction to psychophysiology. Subsequent chapters in Part I deal with background materials such as physiology, electronics and recording equipment, basic concepts, and safety and ethics. Part II surveys the basic areas of psychophysiology according to the response system measured. Part III concludes the text with a discussion of research and applications of psychophysiological recordings.
The following four committee reports are suggested readings for beginning students in psychophysiology. The first report provides a proposed standard nomenclature for psychophysiological measures. The last three provide brief and relatively nontechnical discussions of methodological issues surrounding the collection, quantification, and analysis of evoked-brain, electrodermal, and cardiac responses in humans.
Brown, C. C. (ed.), (1967). A proposed standard nomenclature for psychophysiologic measures. *Psychophysiology* 4, 260–264.

Donchin, E., Callaway, E., Cooper, R., Desmedt, J. E., Goff, W. R., Hillyard, S. A. and Sutton, S. (1977). Publication criteria for studies of evoked potentials (EP) in man. *In* "Attention, voluntary contraction and event-related cerebral potentials: Progress in Clinical Neurophysiology, Vol. 1" (J. E. Desmedt, ed.), pp. 1–11. Karger, Basal.

Fowles, D., Christie, M. J., Edelberg, R., Grings, W. W., Lykken, D. T. and Venables (1981). P. H. Publication recommendations for electrodermal measurements. *Psychophysiology* 18, 232–239.

Jennings, J. R., Berg, W. K., Hutcheson, J. S., Obrist, P., Porges, S. and Turpin, G. (1981). Publication guidelines for heart-rate studies in man. *Psychophysiology* 18, 226–231.

References

Ahn, H., Prichep, L., John, E. R., Baird, H., Trepetin, M. and Kaye, H. (1980). Developmental equations reflect brain dysfunction. *Science* 210, 1259–1262.

Campos, J. J. (1976). Heart rate: A sensitive tool for the study of emotional development in the infant. *In* "Developmental Psychology: The significance of infancy" (L. P. Lipsitt, ed.). Lawrence Erlbaum, Hillsdale, New Jersey.

Chang, H. W. and Trehub, S. E. (1977). Infant's perception of temporal grouping in auditory patterns. *Child Dev.* 48, 1666–1670.

Clifton, R. K. and Nelson, M. N. (1976). Developmental study of habituation in infants: The importance of paradigm, response system, and state. *In* "Habituation: perspectives from child development, animal behavior, and neurophysiology". (T. J. Tighe and R. N. Leaton, eds.). Lawrence Erlbaum, Hillsdale, New Jersey.

Coles, M. G. H., Porges, S. W. and Duncan-Johnson, C. C. (1975). Sex differences in performance and associated cardiac activity during a reaction time task. *Physiol. Psychol.* 3, 141–143.

Darwin, C. (1872). "The expression of emotions in man and animals". Appleton, London. Reprinted (1965) by University of Chicago Press, Chicago.

Donchin, E. (1979). Event-related brain potentials: A tool in the study of human information processing. *In* "Evoked brain potentials and behavior". (H. Begleiter, ed.). Plenum Press, New York.

Donchin, E. and Israel, J. B. (1980). Event-related potentials and psychological theory. *In* "Motivation, motor, and sensory processes of the brain: Electrical potentials, behavior, and clinical use: Progress in brain research" (H. H. Kornhuber and L. Deecke, eds). Elsevier/North Holland, Amsterdam.

Donchin, E., McCarthy, G., Kutas, M. and Ritter, W. (1981). Event-related potentials in the study of consciousness. *In* "Consciousness and self regulation" (R. Davidson, G. Schwartz and D. Shapiro, eds), Vol. 3. Plenum Press, New York.

Donchin, E., Ritter, W. and McCallum, W. C. (1978). Cognitive psychophysiology: The endogenous components of the ERP. *In* "Brain event-related potentials in Man" (E. Callaway, P. Tueting and S. Koslow, eds). Academic Press, New York and London.

Duncan-Johnson, C. C. and Coles, M. G. H. (1974). Heart rate and disjunctive reaction time: The effects of discrimination requirements. *J. Exp. Psychol.* 103, 1160–1168.

Eysenck, H. J. (1967). "The Biological Basis of Personality". C. C. Thomas, Springfield, Illinois.

Fitzgerald, H. E. and Brackbill, Y. (1976). Classical conditioning in infancy: Development and constraints. *Psychol. Bull.* **83**, 353–376.

Izard, C. E. (1971). "The face of emotion". Appleton-Century-Crofts, New York.

Jennings, J. R., Averill, J. R., Opton, E. M. and Lazarus, R. S. (1970). Some parameters of heart rate change: Perceptual versus motor task requirements, noxiousness, and uncertainty. *Psychophysiology* **7**, 194–212.

John, E. R., Ahn, H., Prichep, L., Trepetin, M., Brown, D. and Kaye, H. (1980). Developmental equations for the electroencephalogram. *Science* **210**, 1255–1258.

Johnson, L. C. (1980). Measurement, quantification, and analysis of cortical activity. *In* "Techniques in psychophysiology" (I. Martin and P. H. Venables, eds). Wiley and Sons, New York.

Lacey, B. C. and Lacey, J. I. (1978). Two-way communication between the heart and the brain: Significance of time within the cardiac cycle. *Am. Psychol.* **33**, 99–113.

Mesulam, M. and Perry, J. (1972). The diagnosis of love-sickness: Experimental psychophysiology without the polygraph. *Psychophysiology* **9**, 546–551.

Neumann, E. and Blanton, R. (1970). The early history of electrodermal research. *Psychophysiology* **6**, 453–475.

Obrist, P. A. (1976). The cardiovascular–behavioral interaction – as it appears today. *Psychophysiology* **13**, 95–107.

Obrist, P. A., Webb, R. A., Sutterer, J. R. and Howard, J. L. (1970). Cardiac deceleration and reaction time: An evaluation of two hypotheses. *Psychophysiology* **6**, 695–706.

Porges, S. W. (1980). Individual differences in attention: A possible physiological substrate. *In* "Advances in special education" (B. K. Keogh, ed.), Vol. 2. JAI Press, Greenwich, Connecticut.

Porges, S. W. and Coles, M. G. H. (eds). (1976). "Psychophysiology". Dowden, Hutchinson and Ross, Stroudsberg, Pennsylvania.

Porges, S. W. and Coles, M. G. H. (1982). Individual differences in respiratory-heart period coupling and heart period responses during two attention demanding tasks. *Physiol. Psychol.* **10**, 215–220.

Porges, S. W., Bohrer, R. E., Cheung, M. N., Drasgow, F., McCabe, P. M. and Keren, G. (1980). New time-series statistic for detecting rhythmic co-occurrence in the frequency domain: The weighted coherence and its application to psychophysiological research. *Psychol. Bull.* **88**, 580–587.

Porges, S. W., Bohrer, R. E., Keren, G., Cheung, M. N., Franks, G. J. and Drasgow, F. (1981). The influence of methylphenidate on spontaneous autonomic activity and behavior in children diagnosed as hyperactive. *Psychophysiology* **18**, 42–48.

Porges, S. W., McCabe, P. M. and Yongue, B. G. (1982). Respiratory heart-rate interactions: A psychophysiological measure with implications for pathophysiology and behavior. *In* "Focus on Cardiovascular Psychophysiology" (J. T. Cacioppo and R. E. Petty, eds). Guildford Press, New York.

Porges, S. W. and Smith, K. M. (1980). Defining hyperactivity: Psychophysiological and behavioral strategies. *In* "Hyperactive children: The social ecology of identification and treatment" (C. K. Whalen and B. Henker, eds). Academic Press, New York and London.

Porges, S. W., Walter, G. F., Korb, R. J., and Sprague, R. L. (1975). The influence of methylphenidate on heart rate and behavioral measures of attention in hyperactive children. *Child Dev.* **46**, 727–733.

Rose, S. A., Schmidt, K. and Bridger, W. H. (1976). Cardiac and behavioral responsivity to tactile stimulation in premature and full-term infants. *Dev. Psychol.* **12**, 311–320.

Rubin, L. S. (1962). Patterns of adrenergic–cholinergic imbalance in the functional psychoses. *Psychol. Rev.* **69**, 501–519.

Schneiderman, N., Francis, J., Sampson, L. D. and Schwaber, J. S. (1974). CNS integration of learned cardiovascular behavior. *In* "Limbic and autonomic nervous system research" (L. V. DiCara, ed.). Plenum Press, New York.

Siddle, D. A. T. and Turpin, G. (1980). Measurement and quantification, and analysis of cardiac activity. *In* "Techniques in Psychophysiology" (I. Martin and P. H. Venables, eds). Wiley and Sons, New York.

Sroufe, L. A. and Waters, E. (1977). Heart rate as a convergent measure in clinical and developmental research. *Merrill-Palmer Quarterly* **23**, 3–27.

Stern, R. M., Ray, W. J. and Davis, C. M. (1980). "Psychophysiological recording". Oxford University Press, New York.

Taylor, J. A. (1953). A personality scale of manifest anxiety. *J. Abnorm. Soc. Psychol.* **48**, 285–290.

Van der Molen, M. W. and Orlebeke, J. F. (1980). Phasic heart-rate change and the U-shaped relationship between choice reaction time and auditory signal intensity. *Psychophysiology* **17**, 471–481.

Walter, G. F. and Porges, S. W. (1976). Heart rate and respiratory responses as a function of task difficulty: The use of discriminant analysis in the selection of psychologically sensitive physiological responses. *Psychophysiology* **13**, 563–571.

Woodcock, J. M. (1971). Terminology and methodology related to the use of heart-rate responsitivity in infancy research. *J. Exp. Child Psychol.* **11**, 76–92.

12 Polygraphic Interrogation: the Applied Psychophysiologist

D. T. Lykken

Abstract Some of the earliest developments in psychophysiology were for the purpose of the detection of deception (Munsterberg, 1908). Indeed, the polygraph itself, that central fixture in any psychophysiologist's laboratory, was invented by a policeman for purposes of lie detection (Larson, 1923). The administration of lie detector tests has become a big business, especially in the United States. The growing use of lie test results as evidence in court or for purposes of hiring (or firing) employees, however, is attended by considerable controversy. Yet few psychophysiologists know enough about this original application of their science to make a useful contribution to the debate. Fewer than 1% of all practising polygraph examiners are psychophysiologists; their backgrounds typically are in police work or military intelligence and their training consists of a 6 week course and an apprenticeship. This chapter examines the assumptions of the most highly regarded method of lie detection, the control-question polygraph test, and the surprisingly slim evidence available concerning its validity. A quite different method of polygraphic interrogation, the guilty knowledge test, also is considered. It is the thesis of this chapter that psychophysiologists *should* know about polygraphic interrogation; it is an interesting topic, our roots lie there, important social and ethical questions are implicated, and the history of lie detection illustrates what happens when the psychological component of psychophysiology is neglected.

I. Introduction

Psychophysiologists work with those accessible physiological phenomena that reflect covert mental states and processes. The classic example of a covert psychological state is the state of mind of a guilty suspect in a criminal investigation. "Lie detector" is the popular name for the device, a three or four channel polygraph, used to record the physiological responses of persons under interrogation. The man who coined that name asserted in 1938 that, ". . . secret knowledge can be read like print by the lie detector." (Marston, 1938). Forty-one years later, after a lifetime in the profession, an eminent

PHYSIOLOGICAL CORRELATES OF HUMAN
BEHAVIOUR
ISBN 0-12-273901-9

polygrapher extolled "... the polygraph, that complex, delicate, and totally impartial device that almost always enabled me to clear the innocent and make certain of the guilty" (Gugas, 1979). In the standard modern textbook of polygraphic interrogation, Reid and Inbau (1977) contend that, in the tens of thousands of lie detector tests conducted by them and their associates, fewer than 1% have yielded erroneous conclusions. Dr. David Raskin, one of the few psychologists in the polygraphy business, recently asserted that the "control question" polygraph test is 96% accurate, "even on hardened criminals behind bars." (Dunleavy, 1976). Thus it would seem that polygraphic interrogation may be the pre-eminent achievement not only of psychophysiology but of all applied psychology. Like the sabretooth tiger, perjury soon may be extinct; the Age of Truth is nigh.

II. The Specific Lie Response

Most of us, alas, have some experience of lying and can recall the emotional disquiet that accompanies the intention to deceive. It is easy therefore to believe that a modern polygraph, monitoring a variety of involuntary or partly voluntary physiological processes, might be able to detect that covert emotional response and hence the lie. But to achieve 99 or 96 or even 90% accuracy with such an instrument, it is necessary to assume that there is a **specific lie response,** a reaction or pattern of involuntary reactions that nearly all people emit when they are lying but which they seldom or never exhibit when they are telling the truth. W. H. Marston, who could be said to have invented the lie detector some 60 years ago, explains: "It is necessary to test for some emotion which will not be present unless a person is lying ... some *one* bit of behaviour which would *always* mean a person was lying. Early in the twentieth century this long-sought symptom of deception was discovered." (Marston, 1938). Marston's specific lie response was an increase in systolic blood pressure that he thought accompanies only a deceptive answer. Unhappily, however, this "discovery" was an illusion. Falsely accused persons answering truthfully with innocent emotion also are likely to show increases in systolic blood pressure; the systolic pressure of some liars decreases.

There is a lesson in this example. Marston was not an ignorant man; his doctorate was in psychology, obtained at Harvard under Hugo Munsterberg. There is no evidence that Marston was himself a liar. Determining the actual relationship of psychophysiological changes to the underlying psychological events, then as now, is a difficult business full of pitfalls, and these pitfalls gape their widest for the enthusiastic investigator dazzled by high hopes and expectations. Modern instrumentation merely compounds this problem by providing a plethora of dependent variables that weave complex patterns into which the creative and expectant eye can read important, but unreplicable, "truths". Marston estimated blood pressures by ausculation; it was the whisper of a simple stethoscope that he mistakenly interpreted. The modern polygraph, in which the pens move "as subtly as Raskolnicov's soul" (Younger, 1966), provides greater opportunity for the "experimenter expectancy effect" (Rosenthal, 1966) to manifest itself. Marston ended his career as the author of the comic-strip called "Wonder Woman." Some of his intellectual descendents are still writing psychophysiology.

Is there a specific lie response? Careful laboratory studies have been able to demonstrate a difference between the average patterns of autonomic response of subjects who are angry and those who are frightened (Ax, 1953; Schachter, 1957), but these were group differences and there is considerable variability from person to person. Some frightened subjects will show "angry" patterns; some angry subjects would be classified by the polygraph as frightened; the patterns of other subjects are idiosyncratic. There is no reason to suppose that the intention to deceive should itself produce any particular autonomic reaction at all; it is the emotional accompaniment of this intention that one expects to be revealed on the polygraph recordings. The liar should feel guilty and, perhaps, afraid; will *all* liars always feel guilty when they lie? This seems doubtful. Of those liars who do experience the pangs of guilt, will the autonomic effects of this emotion be the same for each liar and always different from the effects of the emotions of fear or outrage that these same persons would experience when, in a different situation, they are innocently accused? This seems doubtful, too. Many people report that, when truthfully denying a false accusation, they still feel guilty. Is there a machine that can distinguish the false guilt of chagrined innocence from the true guilt of the liar? No such device has been invented.

Some modern polygraphers seem to believe that there are several different specific lie responses. Reid and Inbau (1977), for example, speak of "typical deception responses" and give as examples shallow breathing, heavy breathing, a speeding up of respiration or, equally "typical", a slowing down. Raskin (Raskin and Hare, 1978) has referred to a certain change in abdominal respiration and to a tendency for the liar to show cardiac deceleration following his deceptive answer. The truth is, however, that no qualitatively distinctive physiological response has ever been shown to be pathognomic of deception.

There has been considerable recent interest in **voice stress analysis** for purposes of lie detection. Just as it seems plausible to use the polygraph to look for "tremors in the blood" (Lykken, 1980) and other covert symptoms that might betray deception, so also it seems credible that tremors in the voice might serve the same purpose. Most of us have heard our own voices, strained by some suppressed emotion, sounding unnatural in our ears. One type of voice stress analyser looks for changes in the frequency spectrum when the subject utters the suspected lie. Another device, the "Psychological Stress Evaluator" (PSE), looks for a decrease in low-frequency (e.g., 10 Hz) warble in the voice. This frequency modulation is allegedly produced by micro-tremor of the muscles of the vocal apparatus, a tremor that is said to fade under stress. Although hundreds of these devices have been sold, there is no consistent evidence that they in fact can measure emotional "stress" ("strain" would be a better term). In one study for example (Lynch and Henry, 1979), subjects were required to speak into a microphone a list of neutral words and also a list of taboo words of a sexual or scatological nature. Using the PSE, the investigators tried to discriminate the presumably stressed voices speaking taboo words from the same voices speaking innocuous words but they were unsuccessful. Several studies of the PSE applied to lie detection have yielded consistently negative results (Barland, 1978; Horvath, 1978, 1979; Kubis, 1973; Nachshon, 1979): one could do as well by flipping a coin.

III. The Control-Question Approach

Although there may be no specific lie response, one can at least tell from the polygraph that the subject responded more strongly to Question B than he did to Question A. If Question A could somehow be designed to have the same impact on the subject that Question B would have if he is innocent and truthful, then a larger response to B than to A might be interpreted to indicate that he is not in fact innocent and truthful. This approach to inferring deception or guilt from a different autonomic response to "relevant" and "control" questions is the basis of most modern polygraphic interrogation.

A. *The Truth Control Test (TCT)*

John Jones is suspected of shooting and killing a bank guard in the course of a robbery. He is told that he is also suspected of a similar robbery-murder that occurred a year previously and is questioned at length about the earlier crime. In fact, however, this prior crime is fictional; Jones is being psychologically prepared to believe that he is in equal jeopardy with respect to two separate incidents. In the subsequent polygraph test, Question B is as follows: "On June 6th, a month ago, did you shoot the guard at the University Bank?" (referring to the real incident). Question A is: "On August 24th, 11 months ago, did you shoot the guard at the Fifth Northwestern Bank?" (referring to the fictional incident.) If the deception has been effective *and if Jones is innocent of the actual crime,* then these two questions should be equivalent stimuli; the polygraphic response elicited by Question A should predict the response that Jones will give to Question B. If Jones is guilty of the actual crime, then the two questions will not be equivalent. To be accused of a crime one did not commit (Question A) may be a threat but it should not be so great a threat as to be accused of a crime of which one is guilty (Question B). Moreover, Question A can be answered spontaneously and truthfully while a guilty suspect must answer Question B with a lie, while at the same time attempting to appear sincere and natural. It seems reasonable to expect that the *"relevant"* question, Question B, will elicit a stronger psychophysiological response from a guilty, deceptive respondent than will the *"control"* question, Question A.

As used in scientific parlance, a "control" manipulation involves using all of the same conditions and independent variables present in the experimental manipulation except for that single factor the effect of which one is attempting to assess. In lie detection, this critical factor is the need for deception. We know that the suspect will deny his guilt; we want to know whether this denial will require him to lie. But we also know that being asked an accusatory question will be an evocative stimulus for anyone whether guilty or innocent. Even if his denial is truthful, Question B should produce in Jones an emotional arousal that will include an autonomic reaction visible in the polygraph tracings. The strength of this reaction will depend on a number of factors: how serious the accusation is, how much jeopardy Jones feels himself to be in, how much confidence he has that his innocence will be revealed by the test he is now taking, how emotionally reactive Jones happens to be. All these factors are idiosyncratic; if Jones and Smith are both innocent suspects in the same affair, we would not expect them both to show exactly the same polygraphic reaction to the relevant question. Jones may have more faith in the test than Smith does and therefore feel less threatened; Smith may have the more labile autonomic nervous system and therefore show a stronger reaction than Jones does to almost any stimulus. Since we cannot predict how Jones will react to the relevant question if he is innocent, we cannot predict how he should respond if he is guilty and must answer deceptively. But, if we can make him believe that he is equally suspected of an equally serious crime, one that we know he did not commit because it never happened, then the "truth control" question about Crime A presents him with the same stimulus conditions that the relevant question about Crime B does, if he is innocent. His response to Question A should predict how Jones will respond to Question B if his answer to Question B is truthful, as is his answer to Question A.

This reasoning seems plausible; how certain is it? More than most psychological tests, a polygraphic lie test may have important social and human consequences. If we conclude that Jones is innocent and he is released from custody then, if we are wrong, we have been responsible for turning a

246 D. T. Lykken

murderer loose to prey upon the community. If we conclude erroneously that Jones is guilty then he may be prosecuted, even convicted, for a crime he did not commit. One source of uncertainty is the possibility that Jones, although guilty, might manage by covert self-stimulation to augment his polygraphic reaction to the control question, causing it to be as strong as his response to the relevant question, so that he "passes" the lie test. We shall discuss the problem of countermeasures in a later section. What if Jones' reaction to the relevant question is only slightly stronger than his control response? All human behaviour is variable; since we would not expect a subject to respond in exactly the same way even to repetitions of the same question, small differences between Jones' relevant and control responses should not be over-interpreted. A solution to this problem might be to use several relevant and control questions and to require that the relevant responses be consistently stronger than the control responses.

How certain can we be that Jones will in fact give stronger reactions to the relevant question if he is guilty? "Did you kill Mr. Brown?" should be a stronger stimulus than "Did you kill Mr. Green?" if Jones really did kill Brown but never laid eyes on Green, our fictional decedent. But will this always be true, for every Jones? A particular defendant with especially good emotional control might have rehearsed the interrogation about the Brown killing many times in his mind, knowing that his vulnerability lies there. This might have the effect of a self-administered desensitization treatment, so that the relevant stimulus will have less of an impact than it would have produced without all this preparation. Although a few guilty suspects might escape detection for such reasons (false-negative errors), the Truth Control method of polygraph testing might have the advantage of a low rate of false-positive errors, if one could successfully deceive the suspect about the fictional crime and if one could be comfortable about the ethics of such deception.

B. The Lie-Control Test (LCT)

In the standard method of polygraphic interrogation, the answers to the control questions are not known to be truthful but, on the contrary, are assumed to be deceptive. The TCT was discussed first because it most clearly illustrates the basic concept of a control question lie test, but the TCT is seldom if ever used in practice.

The question format for a typical lie control test is illustrated in Table I. The subject in this case had been accused of raping a woman, whom he met in the bar of a hotel where they were both staying. The defendant admitted going with the complainant to her room and having intercourse with her, but he insisted that the act had been consensual. For a variety of reasons, the prosecutor doubted the woman's story and he therefore offered to drop the charges against the defendant, Sam K., if he could pass a polygraph test. However, Sam had to stipulate that, should he fail the test, the results could be used as evidence against him in court. The three control questions shown in Table I had some thematic connection to the issue in question but were not directly related to the specific charge. They were chosen by the polygraph examiner because (i) he felt they would be disturbing to the suspect in this context, and (ii) he assumed that "No" answers to these questions would probably be lies or, at least, that the suspect would be ". . . very concerned about them" (Podlesny and Raskin, 1977). The theory of the lie control test

Table I Example of a typical lie-control test

Question	Answer	Question Type
Is today Tuesday?	Yes	Irrelevant
Are you concerned that I might ask you a question that we have not reviewed?	No	Outside Issue
Regarding the incident with Mary V., do you intend to tell me the truth about that?	Yes	Sacrific Relevant
On the night of May 15th, did you force your way into Mary V's motel room?	No	Relevant
Have you ever committed an abnormal sex act?	No	Control
On the night of May 15th, did you threaten to choke Mary V.?	No	Relevant
Prior to last year, have you ever forced a woman to have sex with you?	No	Control
Is your name Sam?	Yes	Irrelevant
Prior to last year, did you ever lie to someone in authority to get out of trouble?	No	Control
On the night of May 15th, did you rape Mary V.?	No	Relevant

holds that a guilty suspect, who must answer the relevant questions deceptively, will be more disturbed by the stimulus package consisting of a relevant question and his deceptive reply than he will by the control questions (even if he answers them also deceptively.) The theory also holds that an innocent suspect will feel less threatened by the relevant questions, which he can answer truthfully, than he will by the control questions. Therefore, if the suspect consistently shows a stronger polygraphic reaction to the relevant than to the control questions, then he is classified as Deceptive. Only if he consistently responds more strongly to the control than to the relevant questions is he classified as Truthful.

1. The validity of the lie-control test

Laboratory studies using volunteer subjects and mock crimes cannot reliably estimate the validity of the LCT in actual criminal investigation. The truthful subject, for example, should be far more disturbed by the relevant questions in real life than in a laboratory, although truthful in both situations, and therefore field studies will show more false-positive errors than laboratory research would predict. In some field studies the polygrapher who administered the tests is allowed to make the diagnosis of Truthful or Deceptive. This is an unfortunate practice because the original examiner is privy to many sources of extra-polygraphic information, and it is impossible to determine to what extent (if any) his judgements depended upon the autonomic measurements. In the US Army study by Bersh (1969), for example, the examiners based their diagnosis to an unknown extent on the same case facts and other materials that were furnished to the judges, who provided the criterion determination of guilt or innocence. Therefore, as Bersh himself admits, his findings probably over-estimate the accuracy of the polygraph test itself. Six studies have been reported in which the polygraph records have been scored "blindly", by someone other than the original examiner. Four of these must be discarded because the records to be scored were selected to conform with LCT theory, and thus were not representative of the general run of LCT results. This leaves us with just two studies that are useful for estimating the field validity of the current standard polygraphic lie test. When the first of these appeared in print, the LCT had been in use for 30 years (Reid, 1947), while the myth of the lie detector had been abroad for 60 (Marston, 1917).

Horvath (1977) asked 10 professional polygraphers to score the polygraph records from tests given to 56 criminal suspects. Half of these 56 had subsequently confessed and thus were known to have lied on the test; half were subsequently cleared by the confession of another person. Horvath's polygraphers scored 63% of the tests as Deceptive; 77% of the guilty suspects were correctly classified but 49% of the innocent suspects were erroneously called "deceptive" also. Barland and Raskin (1976) reported findings on 109 criminal suspects tested by Barland with the polygraph records scored blindly by Raskin. Excluding cases where guilt or innocence could not be established or where Raskin scored the charts as Inconclusive, 78% of these suspects were criterion-guilty. Since Raskin scored 88% of the charts as Deceptive, it is perhaps not surprising that most (98%) of the guilty suspects were classified Deceptive. However, more than half (55%) of the innocent suspects were also classified as Deceptive. The two studies agree reasonably well. The LCT tends to classify most subjects as Deceptive; therefore, most guilty persons are correctly classified. But the price of this accomplishment is to misclassify about half of the innocent respondents. The LCT is strongly biased against the innocent.

This bias of the LCT is a natural consequence of the fact that the "control" questions used are not control stimuli at all. In the TCT discussed earlier, the control questions should be indistinguishable from the relevant questions to the innocent suspect; they all seem to accuse him of equally serious crimes that he did not commit. The only reason for a suspect to respond more strongly to the relevant questions would be if he was actually involved in the real crime; then the two accusations would carry a different weight and his answers to the relevant questions would have to be deceptive. In the LCT, only the relevant questions seem to place the respondent in serious jeopardy, whether he is innocent or guilty. In either case, the "control" questions will at once be seen as different from the relevant questions and, indeed, it is expected that all subjects will respond differently to the two stimuli. One might suppose that everyone would respond more strongly to the relevant questions, that all respondents, truthful or deceptive, should fail the LCT. In fact, truthful suspects often respond more to the "control" questions, a surprising result that deserves further investigation. Perhaps these individuals are so persuaded that the lie detector will demonstrate their innocence that the relevant questions do not disturb them. But, as the Horvath, and Barland and Raskin studies demonstrate, about half of all truthful respondents *do* fail the LCT.

C. Counter-measures

John Reid, inventor of the LCT, reported in 1945 that it is possible to simulate polygraph responses in a manner that is imperceptible to the operator. This can be done by pressing one's arm against the chair arm, abducting the toes, biting the tongue, or tightening the gluteal muscles. If these manoeuvers are carried out when the "control" questions are asked, responses to these questions would be selectively augmented and even a guilty respondent should be more likely to pass the test. How might one test this hypothesis experimentally? Laboratory studies would not be convincing. One would have to somehow contact persons scheduled to be given polygraph tests in actual criminal investigations. These suspects would have to be willing to admit their guilt privately to the experimentor in return for advice on how to "beat" the impending lie test. The ordinary scientist might despair of being able to make such arrangements.

In 1978 a man named Floyd Fay was arrested in Toledo, Ohio, on a charge of murder. The victim, a liquor store manager, had been shot by a masked man in the course of a robbery. Before he died, the victim described his assailant as a big man, like his friend "Buzz" Fay but said, "it wasn't Buzz." Later, drugged and at the point of death, urged by the police to make a positive identification, he said that he thought it was Fay after all. After Fay had been arrested and his affairs investigated thoroughly, nothing could be found to link him to this robbery. His previous record was without blemish. At this point the prosecutor offered Fay a deal: "If you agree to take a polygraph test and pass it, Floyd, we will drop the charges. But you must agree that, should you fail the test, we can use that fact in evidence against you." Fay agreed, failed the polygraph test, failed a second one, went to trial and was convicted of aggravated murder and sentenced to life in prison. More than two years later the actual killers were apprehended and confessed; Floyd Fay was totally exonerated and released.

In the prison where Fay had been incarcerated, inmates charged with violations of prison regulations were required to submit to polygraph testing. Fay had been studying about the polygraph in the prison library and had found an article of mine describing how the LCT might be beaten by covert self-stimulation. He decided to conduct his own experiment. He would contact inmates scheduled for polygraph testing. Those who admitted their guilt privately to Fay were shown my article. Some of them were instructed to bite their tongues covertly after each control question. Later, Fay's experimental subjects were instructed to secrete a nail in their sock and to press down on the sharp edge of the head of that nail during each control question. By the time Fay was released from prison he had thus counseled 27 guilty inmates; 23 of the 27 had been succesful in beating the lie test. When these results become widely known, the only people who fail the lie-control polygraph test may one day be those truthful suspects who, because they are innocent, do not try to beat the test.

IV. The Guilty Knowledge Test

Some years ago, a certain deputy sheriff was accused by a prisoner in the county jail of having smuggled a gun to that prisoner for a large sum of money. The inmate volunteered to take a polygraph test, was administered the standard LCT, and passed it easily. The deputy was also given a LCT and failed it. Subsequent events showed beyond doubt that both tests were wrong. The prisoner had lied: someone else had smuggled the gun and the deputy was innocent.

I would have handled this investigation differently. After attaching the bewildered deputy to the polygraph, I would have asked the following: "One of the prisoners has made a serious charge against you. If you have committed this offence, you will know which of these men was involved. Just repeat each name after me. Which prisoner is concerned in this charge against you? Is it – (i) Johnson? (ii) Ekblad? (iii) Wilson? (iv) Gevenda? (v) Franzen?" This multiple-choice question has 5 alternatives which should all appear equally plausible to the innocent deputy. He may respond autonomically to each one but there should be only a 20% chance that his largest response will be to the "correct" alternative, (iv). If he is guilty, on the other hand, the deputy will know at once that Gevenda is the prisoner to whom he gave the gun, and it is likely that he will respond more strongly to that name than to the others. Next I might ask him: "You are charged with smuggling contraband to this prisoner. What is it that you are supposed to have smuggled in. Is it – (i) Some pills? (ii) Some whiskey? (iii) A weapon? (iv) Some Marihuana? (v) A file?" If the deputy is innocent and without guilty knowledge, then his chances of responding most strongly to the relevant alternative on both these items are about $0 \cdot 2 \times 0 \cdot 2 = 0 \cdot 04$. With 10 such items, an innocent subject would have about 2 chances in 1000 of "hitting" on as many as 6 items and only 1 chance in 10 million of giving his strongest response to the relevant alternative on all 10 items. In contrast to the LCT, this **guilty knowledge test** (GKT) employs genuine control stimuli; the incorrect alternatives provide a valid estimate of how an innocent subject ought to respond to the correct alternative since a suspect who is without guilty knowledge will not be able to distinguish the one from the other.

Laboratory studies using volunteer subjects and mock crimes have produced promising results with the GKT; 100% accuracy with innocent subjects and from 80 to 95% correct detection of guilty subjects (Lykken, 1959; Davidson, 1969; Podlesny and Raskin, 1978; Giesen and Rollison, 1980), even with only 5 or 6 good items. The GKT depends upon the orienting response, the tendency for people to respond differentially to stimuli recognized as significant in some way, rather than on responses of fear or guilt and the dubious assumption that only the liar will be fearful of the relevant question. Therefore, one might hope that the GKT should perform in real life as well as it does in the laboratory. But this hope remains to be tested in practical trials.

It seems doubtful that lying will ever be detectable with very high accuracy from autonomic measurements. The unavoidable weakness of any lie test is that both deceptive and truthful suspects can immediately identify the relevant questions, and both have reason to be autonomically aroused by these questions. The guilty knowledge technique, on the other hand, seems to have real potential as an aid in criminal investigation. How this potential will be realized will depend on future collaboration between psychophysiologists and resourceful policepersons.

V. Summary

There is no consistent symptom of deception, that most people display when they are lying but not when they are truthful. For this reason, most polygraphers base their inference of deception on whether the subject's response to the relevant questions is larger than his response to "control" questions. A true control question would provide an estimate of how this subject should respond to the relevant question if his answer is truthful but such controls would require extravagant deception and would be both unethical and unworkable in real life. The "control" questions actually employed in lie detection are merely comparison stimuli, meant to be less evocative than the relevant question when the subject is deceptive but more evocative when he is truthful. Without knowing how strongly this suspect will respond to the relevant question when he is lying or when he is truthful, the examiner must design "control" questions that will elicit responses midway between these two unknown values. It seems implausible to expect polygraphers to consistently accomplish such a delicate titration, even after six weeks in polygraph school. Research confirms what common sense predicts; when lie tests are scored strictly from the polygraph charts, their validity ranges from 63 to 72% (where 50% equals chance expectancy) and about 50% of truthful respondents are erroneously classified as deceptive.

A fundamentally different procedure is designed to detect, not lying, but guilty knowledge. The guilty knowledge test assumes that a suspect who recognizes the correct answers to a series of multiple-choice questions about a crime should show different autonomic reactions to the correct than to the incorrect alternatives – and that an innocent suspect, without guilty knowledge, will be unable to react differentially in this way. The GKT might prove useful in the investigation of certain crimes. Lie detection, in contrast, seems useful mainly as a method of inducing the gullible to confess.

Further Reading

Munsterberg, H. (1908). "On the Witness Stand: Essays on Psychology and Crime". Doubleday, Page and Co., New York.
An early and influential discussion of the use of psychological techniques in criminal investigation. Munsterberg thought that guilt detection, but not lie detection, might be feasible. Yet his student, Marston, was a progenitor of the modern lie detector industry.
Marston, W. M. (1938). "The Lie Detector Test". Richard R. Smith, New York.
A self-aggrandizing review of his own colourful career by the man who first claimed to be able, almost infallibly, to detect lying from autonomic changes.

Gugas, C. (1979). "The Silent Witness: A Polygraphist's Casebook". Prentice-Hall, Englewood Cliffs, New Jersey.
A companion piece to Marston's "The Lie Detector Test". It seems apparent from these anecdotes that the author, like many of his fraternity, is principally an interrogator who uses the polygraph as a stressor rather than as a test. Under this bloodless third degree, his subjects confess or otherwise betray themselves.
Reid, J. E. and Inbau, F. E. (1977). "Truth and Deception: The Polygraph ("Lie-detector") Technique" 2nd edn. Williams and Wilkins, Baltimore, Maryland.
The principal textbook of polygraphy today. Inbau is a professor of law. The late John Reid, also an attorney, operated a large polygraph testing service and also the Reid College for the Detection of Deception in Chicago.
Lykken, D. T. (1980). "A Tremor in the Blood: Uses and Abuses of the Lie Detector". McGraw-Hill, New York.
This book attempts an objective appraisal of the modern Diogenes and the tools of his trade. The various forms of lie test, the questionnaire tests of "honesty", and the guilty knowledge method, are analyzed, their assumptions made explicit, and their present or potential applications are appraised.

References

Ax, A. F. (1953). The physiological differentiation between fear and anger in humans. *Psychosom. Med.* 15, 433–442.
Barland, G. (1978). Use of voice changes in the detection of deception. *Polygraph* 7, 129–140.
Barland, G. and Raskin, D. (1976). "Validity and reliability of polygraph examinations of criminal suspects" US Department of Justice Report No. 76–1, March, 1976, Contract 75-NI-99-0001. University of Utah, Department of Psychology, Salt Lake City.
Bersh, P. (1969). A validation of polygraph examiner judgements. *J. Appl. Psychol.* 53, 399–403.
Davidson, P. (1969). Validity of the guilty knowledge technique: The effects of motivation. *J. Appl. Psychol.* 53, 399–403.
Dunleavy, S. (1976). Patty wasn't guilty. *The Star,* December 14, pp. 24–25.
Giesen, M. and Rollison, M. (1980). Guilty knowledge versus innocent associations: Effects of trait anxiety and stimulus context on skin conductance. *J. Res. Personality* 14, 1–11.
Gugas, C. (1979). "The Silent Witness". Prentice-Hall, Englewood Cliffs, New Jersey.
Horvath, F. (1977). The effect of selected variables on interpretation of polygraph records. *J. Appl. Psychol.* 62, 127–136.
Horvath, F. (1978). An experimental comparison of the Psychological Stress Evaluator and the galvanic skin response in detection of deception. *J. Appl. Psychol.* 63, 338–344.
Horvath, F. (1979). Effect of different motivational instructions on detection of deception with the Psychological Stress Evaluator and the galvanic skin response. *J. Appl. Psychol.* 64, 323–330.
Kubis, J. F. (1973). "Comparison of voice analysis and polygraph as lie detection procedures". Report of contract DAAD05-72-C-0217 August, 1973, prepared for the US Army Land Warfare Laboratory. US Army Land Warfare Laboratory, Aberdeen Proving Ground, Maryland.

Larson, John, A. (1923). The cardio-pneumo-psychogram in deception. *J. Exp. Psychol.* **6**, 420–454.

Lykken, D. T. (1959). The GSR in the detection of guilt. *J. Appl. Psychol.* **43**, 385–388.

Lykken, D. T. (1980). "A tremor in the blood: Uses and abuses of the lie detector." McGraw-Hill, New York.

Lynch, B. and Henry, D. (1979). A validity study of the Psychological Stress Evaluator. *Can. J. Behav. Sci.* **11**, 89–94.

Marston, W. M. (1917). Systolic blood pressure changes in deception. *J. Exp. Psychol.* **2**, 117–163.

Marston, W. M. (1938). "The lie detector test". Richard R. Smith, New York.

Munsterberg, H. (1908). "On the witness stand: Essays on psychology and crime". Doubleday, Page and Co., New York.

Nachshon, I. (1979). "The Psychological Stress Evaluator: Validity study". Final report, Grant No. 953-0265-001, Israeli Police Department of Criminology, Bar Ilan University, Ramat Gal, Israel.

Podlesny, J. and Raskin, D. (1977). Physiological measures and the detection of deception. *Psychol. Bull.* **84**, 782–799.

Podlesny, J. and Raskin, D. (1978). Effectiveness of techniques and physiological measures in the detection of deception. *Psychophysiol.* **15**, 344–359.

Raskin, D. and Hare, R. (1978). Psychopathy and detection of deception in a prison population. *Psychophysiol.* **15**, 126–136.

Reid, J. (1947). A revised questioning technique in lie detection tests. *J. Criminal Law Criminol.* **37**, 542–547.

Reid, J. E. and Inbau, F. E. (1977). "Truth and deception: The polygraph ("lie-detector") technique" 2nd edn. Williams and Wilkins, Baltimore, Maryland.

Rosenthal, R. (1966). "Experimenter effects in behavioral research". Appleton-Century-Crofts, New York.

Schachter, J. (1957). Pain, fear, and anger in hypertensives and normotensives. *Psychosom. Med.* **19**, 17–29.

Younger, I. (1966). Review of "Truth and Deception" by J. E. Reid and F. E. Inbau. *Saturday Rev.* December 31, 20–21.

13 The Psychological and Physiological Response to Stress

T. Cox, S. Cox
and M. Thirlaway

Abstract This chapter discusses what is meant by the term "stress", and in doing so presents a model which outlines the nature of the psychological and physiological responses to stress.

The authors discuss the different coping strategies that may accompany the experience of stress, and examine the importance of information and control for coping. They then consider the involvement of the adrenal glands (cortex and medulla) in the physiological response to stress. The chapter outlines some of the relationships between the psychological and physiological responses, and traces out their implications for health. Throughout the discussion questions are posed concerning the design and execution of experiments in this area of research, and often in particular reference to the collection of data. Suggestions for further research and for further reading are made.

I. The Nature of Stress

Man is a living system entirely dependent on maintaining a satisfactory relationship with his total environment. His life depends on his ability to maintain an optimum body temperature, on his intake of food, of fluids and of air, on the elimination of waste products, and on achieving a balance between activity and rest. Given his ability to fulfil these critical requirements, Man can *survive*. Beyond this, however, the *quality of human life* is dependent on the ability to resist disease, and to adapt to the physical and psychological demands of the environment. Failure to adapt can result in impaired physical and psychological well-being, in disease, and ultimately in death. These demands, their experience, and effects represent *stress*.

When the concept of "stress" was first proposed by Selye (1950), it was as a description of the common (non-specific) physiological effects of a large

PHYSIOLOGICAL CORRELATES OF HUMAN
BEHAVIOUR   ISBN 0-12-273901-9

number of different noxious, or at least aversive, agents. Such an "economy" of description is appealing in the analysis of human behaviour. However, the treatment of the concept, by Selye, and others, as a *response* within a relatively restricted stimulus–response paradigm is inadequate. It is so both in terms of the available data, and against current psychological and psychophysiological models of Man. These lay emphasis on the dynamic nature of the person's interaction with his environment, and on the mediating role of individual psychological processes.

Several interactional models of stress have been proposed, reflecting the person's interaction with and adaptation to his environment (Lazarus, 1976; Cox, 1978; Cox and Mackay, 1981). It has been suggested that the person routinely assesses his relationship with his environment: this process has been termed "primary cognitive appraisal". Initially, the present authors described appraisal in terms of the "matching" or "balancing" of four basic elements of the person–environment "transaction": (i) the external demands made on the person; (ii) his ability to cope with them (his personal resources); (iii) his needs (internal demands); (iv) the degree to which his situation supplied their fulfilment. However, it has become obvious that *social support, and constraints on behaviour* are important aspects of the appraisal process. The model has, therefore, been developed to include consideration of social support, of external constraints on coping and of the internal constraints imposed by personal values and belief systems. An "imbalance" in the elements of this primary appraisal is associated with the experience of negative emotion and with psychological and physiological change. Certain responses to stress have been termed "coping" and are instrumental in altering the source of the mismatch or imbalance, or in reducing the discomfort associated with it. However, in some circumstances, they may contribute to impaired well-being and disease.

The body of this chapter considers some of the psychological and endocrine responses associated with the experience of stress.

II. The Psychological Response to Stress

There has been a great deal of research on the psychological response to stress, although much of it has not attracted that particular title. Research with "animals" has tended to concentrate on the behavioural correlates of emotional states, like anxiety, fear or anger, or on the response to danger, conflict or punishment. Until recently, interest in Man's response to stress has been largely confined to clinical, industrial and military studies. Two criteria of concern exist, often side by side. The first related to Man's ability to perform effectively, either at specific tasks or in terms of his social skills. The second concerns his well-being or health, both physical and mental. While obviously related in many situations, these two criteria can be independent, and this independence can be a problem: changes and strategies which are good for the individual's health may or may not be the best for maintaining his performance on a task, or in a social situation. Some of the strategies adopted in response to stressful situations are discussed below.

A. *Coping*

A key concept in discussing the psychological response to stress is that of "coping", and this owes much to the work of Lazarus (1976). A person experiencing stress will remain in trouble unless and until he does something to remove the source of the problem, or reduce the distress experienced. He must deal with at least some of the different elements contributing to the stress-producing mismatch in the appraisal of the problem. What a person does to master the situation is most commonly called *coping*.

Coping may involve both cognitive and behavioural strategies. It is best considered as a form of problem solving, where the risk is to the person's well-being, and manageable solutions are not always clear, possible, or totally effective. It involves either an adjustment *to* the situation, or an adjustment *of* the situation.

Lazarus suggests that there are two main types of coping strategy: direct action and palliation. Direct action refers to behavioural attempts by the person to alter some aspect of the physical or social environment, or their own capacity – to remove the source of their problem. Palliation is directed at reducing, or eliminating the distress associated with the experience of stress. Taking palliative action often means to seek comfort, and often without altering the source of the discomfort.

1. *Direct action*

This can take several forms: preparation against harm, aggression (fight), avoidance and escape (flight), and possibly inaction (freezing).

Preparation against harm can be a form or component of avoidance behaviour in which the person seeks information and takes action in anticipation of danger. If this preparation is successful then the signs of danger will recede, and the person's anxiety will be reduced. The problem situation or the threat it embodies may be avoided or reduced, the person's resources may be strengthened, or failure to cope allowed for. If preparation is unsuccessful then the danger or problem will become manifest.

Fight and flight are descriptions of behavioural strategies adopted by many different species in response to dangerous or emergency situations. Early research on these behaviours was carried out by the American physiologist Walter Cannon (1932). He described an active pattern of response in cats to acute stress in terms of aggressive or escape behaviour. He believed that preparing for and facilitating these behaviours was the function of the sympathetic – adrenal medullary system (see p. 266).

Another behavioural response often observed in animals exposed to danger is *freezing*. Gray (1971) described freezing as "silent, tense immobility". There is some debate as to whether freezing is an active response. It is passive only in that the animal shows no locomotor activity, but it is active in that the immobility observed is tense, involving considerable skeletal muscle activity and energy expenditure.

The literature on the response to aversive stimulation (and punishment) presents a similar view of the possible types of response pattern. Miller and Weiss (1969), for example, have described two contrasting response patterns. One, the suppression of behaviour, involves freezing, muteness, piloerection, defaecation and possibly feigned death. The other, the activation of behaviour, involves increased startle responses, vocalizations, and running and leaping. To these two may be added the third pattern, aggression.

Gray (1971) has attempted to show how these different patterns of response relate to one another. Freezing, he has suggested, tends to occur during the anticipation of danger. Escape and aggression occur, by contrast, as a response to the presence of danger. It is adaptive, he has argued, for an animal to respond to pain inflicted by a predator, by struggling or running away. However, the adaptive response to impending danger may be to remain still, and thus escape attention. Such a scheme holds true for many species, for example for the hare, the pheasant and the partridge, but not for all. It is obvious that there is a natural variation in the dominant pattern of response from species to species. Some show a tendency towards behavioural activation, others a tendency towards behavioural suppression. Furthermore the response demonstrated in any situation will also reflect the physical (and psychological) constraints imposed by that situation. It has been shown, for example, that an approaching cat will elicit escape behaviour in a rat which is not confined and freezing in one which is.

Although these considerations are drawn from animal studies, they would seem to map onto what is known about Man's behavioural response to stressful situations.

2. Palliation

Palliation is a matter of moderating the distress caused by the experience of stress. This may be achieved in several ways. Lazarus (1976) distinguishes between symptom-directed modes and intra-psychic modes. The former include the use of alcohol, tranquillisers and sedatives, relaxation and other body centred techniques. Intra-psychic palliation, on the other hand, has been discussed in terms of cognitive defence mechanisms. In psychodynamic theories the term "defence mechanism" has been used to refer to an unconscious psychological manoeuvre by which means the person may deceive himself about the presence of danger. It is the threat of danger that is reduced and not the actual danger. Cognitive defence may thus be maladaptive. Several specific mechanisms have been named, and are described elsewhere (Freud, 1946; Lazarus, 1976; Cox, 1978): identification, displacement, repression, denial, reaction formation, projection and intellectualization. It has been suggested that cognitive defence occurs in situations where behavioural coping is not possible or where there are high levels of fear.

B. *Information, Control and Predictability*

There is much experimental data relating to the control and the predictability of aversive events and the experience of stress. That evidence suggests that lack of control over events is a source of stress, and that increasing a person's control over his situation can reduce his experience of stress and his physiological response to it. The literature is, however, confusing in that predictability sometimes appears to decrease, and sometimes to increase that experience.

Miller (1980) has reviewed the available evidence and proposed a "blunting" hypothesis, which specifies the situations in which predictability can reduce stress and those in which it cannot. Her hypothesis also describes individual differences in coping strategies and in the preference for predictability. Miller first distinguishes between events which are "controllable", when one is able to do something about them, and those which are "predictable", when one knows something about them. Her hypothesis concerns "uncontrollable" and thus potentially stressful events, which may or may not be "predictable". She then develops her hypothesis around the concept of "safety signals" (Seligman, 1968). When such a signal reliably predicts danger (predictability), the absence of a signal predicts safety. By contrast when no signal reliably predicts danger (unpredictability), equally no signal predicts safety: and the person or animal can never relax. Thus if given a choice they should prefer the condition of predictability. They then know when danger is threatened, but can otherwise relax.

To provide an adequate account of human behaviour, this theory has to be further developed to distinguish between the physical and psychological presence of danger signals. The two can be independent. Four situations are therefore possible.

(i) The person is aware of the physical presence of danger signals: they are attending to danger cues, possibly expressing realistic anxiety.

(ii) The person is unaware of the physical presence of the danger signals. This can occur for a variety of reasons, including the operation of a "coping" strategy, for example through distraction, or through the use of defence mechanisms (see p. 274). This can cause the unrealistic inhibition of anxiety.

(iii) The person is aware of danger, but in the absence of danger signals. They brood, worry, ruminate and rehearse, expressing unrealistic anxiety.

(iv) Finally, the person is not aware of danger, and there are no danger cues physically present. They are attending to "safety" cues, realistically inhibiting anxiety.

There appear to be two types of individual in relation to this hypothesis: those that attempt to defend themselves against danger cues (blunters), and those that continually seek information and scan for danger cues (monitors). Blunters, according to Miller (1980), often achieve their goal through distraction. The appropriateness of these two strategies will obviously vary from situation to situation.

III. Physiological Response to Stress

The psychological reactions to the experience of stress are accompanied by other changes involving body state. These physiological responses appear to be dominated by activity in the autonomic nervous system and in various endocrine systems. Overall, the changes which occur appear to be integrated, and in some situations, to have an obvious relationship with the behavioural response. For example, enhanced activity in the sympathetic–adrenal medullary system in emergencies prepares the animal for a prolonged and strengthened behavioural response (Cannon, 1932).

A. Selye

The early work of Selye (1950) was instrumental both in establishing the concept of stress, and in providing insights into its physiology. Selye adopted a "response-based" definition, treating stress as the non-selective and non-specific physiological response to noxious stimuli. From his observations on patients, and his experimental research using "animals", he outlined the important role that the central and autonomic nervous systems and the endocrine agents played in that non-specific response. Perhaps, his major concern was for adrenal activity, in particular that of the adrenal cortex. He suggested that the response to stress occurred in three phases, which described a *general adaptation syndrome* (GAS). The first phase, the alarm reaction, he suggested was dominated by increased sympathetic–adrenal medullary activity. This represented the immediate response to the onset of "stress". The alarm stage, however, gave way to the second phase, that of resistance, dominated by increased anterior pituitary–adrenal cortical activity. This stage was maintained with the continuing presence of "stress", facilitating coping and short-term survival, but at a cost. The cost is analogous to that attracted by running a car with the choke permanently out. The increased "wear and tear" on the body accumulates, along with the "drain" on available resources. If stress persists and is sufficiently severe, the third phase of exhaustion and collapse is reached. Adrenal cortical function begins to fail, adrenal medullary activity temporarily increases, but death can occur.

Selye's research and ideas provided a major impetus to research on stress, but have also attracted (recent) criticism. This has concerned at least three aspects of his work. The first criticism is his treatment of stress within a response–based paradigm. The three major paradigms used in the study of stress have been discussed by the authors (Cox, 1978; Cox and Mackay, 1981), and the conceptual and practical inadequacies of stimulus-and-response based models highlighted. Second, his concept of non-specificity has been challenged, and it has been shown that different stressors may produce specific patterns of reaction. The general nonspecific pattern of neuro–endocrine response to stressors is not as easy to demonstrate as Selye suggests. The third criticism is that the GAS does not accurately describe the response to stress, and that there is no clear separation of adrenal medullary, and cortical activity as suggested. In most stressful situations both can occur, although with different latencies and durations of effect. What appears to occur is more simply, an increase in patterns of catabolic activity during the experience of stress, with a suppression of anabolic activity, which is reversed with its removal or offset (Mason, 1968).

B. *Stress and Health*

When the overall pattern of psychophysiological response is inappropriate, too severe or too prolonged, damage to the body may occur. There are several different pathways by which the response to stress can impair health:

(i) The way in which the person copes may increase their exposure to health damaging agents, e.g. through smoking or drinking.
(ii) The physiological response may promote or initiate changes which

contribute to actual health damage, e.g. high noradrenaline levels may promote the eventual deposition of fat in the coronary arteries.

(iii) The physiological response may suppress the body's natural defences, allowing the spread of infection, or the failure to contain malignant cell growth.

(iv) The psychological response may distort the person's perception of himself or others, isolating him and disrupting normal life.

More information concerning the possible impairment of health is included in the following sections of this chapter which deal with particular aspects of the physiology of stress.

Largely following on from the work of Selye and Cannon, research into the physiological response to stress has tended to concentrate on the sympathetic–adrenal medullary system and the pituitary–adrenal cortical system. It is not possible to present a comprehensive review of all aspects of the physiology of stress here, and the rest of this chapter therefore concentrates on those two neuro-endocrine systems.

C. The Adrenal Glands

The adrenal glands are situated at the superior pole of each kidney, although there are extra-adrenal sites in the body at which both cortical and medullary tissue can be found.

There are two endocrine organs in the adrenal gland: the outer cortex which secretes steroids and the inner medulla which secretes the catecholamines. The two areas appear functionally separate. Secretion of the catecholamines from the medulla is controlled by activity in the sympathetic nervous system. By contrast, secretion of the steroids by the cortex is controlled by the level of adrenocorticotrophic hormone (ACTH) and other chemicals in the blood.

D. Adrenal Medulla

The chromaffin cells of the medulla elaborate adrenaline and noradrenaline, also referred to collectively as catecholamines. Histochemical evidence shows the presence of two separate types of cell: adrenaline-secreting and noradrenaline-secreting. The ratio of adrenaline to noradrenaline secreted varies between species: in Man about ten times more adrenaline than noradrenaline is released from the medulla. Despite this, measured levels of adrenaline in both plasma and urine are lower than those of noradrenaline, due to the additional secretion of the latter by the sympathetic nerve endings.

The chromaffin cells of the medulla are intimately connected with preganglionic (cholinergic) fibres of the sympathetic nervous system (splanchnic nerve). The secretory activity of the cells is controlled through these pathways.

1. *The functions of the catecholamines*

The physiological effects of the catecholamines are ubiquitous, but generally involve cardio-circulatory and metabolic effects similar to those occurring at the beginning of exercise. The main effects of adrenaline are the mobilization of glucose as a source of energy, and an increase in heart rate and cardiac output. Noradrenaline is by contrast a more potent vasoconstrictor, and is important in the maintenance of blood pressure through changes in peripheral resistance. Increased blood pressure may serve in turn to *reduce* heart rate. Both hormones accelerate the rate and increase the depth of respiration, and both affect smooth muscle.

2. *The measurement of catecholamine levels*

Advances in analytical techniques have made studies involving catecholamines more reliable. The traditional bioassays of catecholamine content have now been formally replaced by fluorimetric techniques; the most recent research has used high pressure liquid chromatography.

Provided the conditions under which urine is sampled are carefully controlled, the excretion of catecholamines, especially that of adrenaline can be reliably measured, and has been shown to be related to physical and psychosocial aspects of the person's interaction with their environment.

Large inter-individual differences exist in the levels of both the catecholamines. However in a study of urinary catecholamine excretion over a twelve month period, Johannson and Post (1974) showed a marked consistency in intra-individual levels. In the same study neither variations over the year nor differences between men and women in the excretion of adrenaline and noradrenaline were statistically significant.

Plasma catecholamine levels have also been studied but the more invasive nature of blood sampling makes it a less favoured measure in human experimental studies. In a study on the validity of plasma catecholamine estimations (Carruthers *et al.*, 1970), venepuncture itself was found to significantly raise blood catecholamine levels.

3. *Factors controlling catecholamine levels*

Many different types of *physical* stimuli have been shown to increase the activity of the medulla. Furthermore, the proportion of catecholamines secreted by the medulla can vary with the nature of the stimulus e.g. asphyxia and hypoxia increase the ratio of noradrenaline to adrenaline. There is less agreement, however, over the general and selective effects of *psychological* stimuli.

In *laboratory studies* on the effects of various psychosocial stressors (Frankenhaeuser, 1975), the output of adrenaline and noradrenaline is increased not only in response to threatening stimuli, but also in situations involving mental work under noise or time pressure, and in situations where subjects lack control of events. For example, Frankenhaeuser and Rissler (1970) have shown how increasing the degree of control exercised by the individual over his environment can be an effective means of counteracting the adrenaline response to unpredictable and aversive events. It has also been shown that enhanced sympathetic–adrenal medullary activity occurs in subjects exposed to a wide variety of *real life* situations, for example: before boxing matches, during acrobatics, or supersonic or space flight, while car driving or taking University examinations, on having medical or dental examinations, and on admission to hospital (see Cox, 1978).

The effects of different types of job and work environment have been studied, both in *real and simulated workplaces*. For example, recent studies in the Swedish Sawmill industry have highlighted *machine-paced* jobs as "high risk", in which the worker has no control over pace and in which body posture and mobility are constrained. Workers engaged in these "jobs" show greatly elevated catecholamine levels at work. Furthermore, these elevated levels do not readily return to baseline levels after work (Johansson *et al.*, 1978). Somewhat similarly, the authors have shown, using simulated work, that repetitive work is associated both with higher levels of urinary adrenaline than non-repetitive work, and with a disruption of the normal diurnal rhythm (Cox *et al.*, 1982).

4. Interpretation of catecholamine data

The research referred to above represents but a fraction of the studies which exist. With most of these studies several important questions need answering before the available data can sensibly be interpreted. These questions apply equally well to the role of other hormones in the response to stress; including the corticosteroids (see later).

First, it is necessary to know whether there are normal diurnal rhythms for the catecholamines, and to what extent they can be disrupted. Second, if disruption can occur, whether and in what way this is detrimental to performance or general well-being. This naturally leads into the question of the relationship between hormone levels, performance and general well-being. Fourth, it is necessary to know to what extent the hormones react individually or respond in a unitary fashion to psychological stimuli. Furthermore, it is interesting to know to what extent catecholamine release is moderated by individual psychological factors, such as personality differences, and by other parameters, such as sex differences, posture and age.

5. Diurnal rhythms and catecholamine secretion

A diurnal rhythm in catecholamine output exists, and is most obviously displayed by adrenaline secretion: the lowest levels occur during the night and the highest between midday and late afternoon. However, results from experimental work indicate that fluctuations in catecholamine levels of diurnal origin are considerably smaller than those engendered by typical daytime activity patterns.

Akerstedt and Froberg (1978) have related diurnal patterns to levels of arousal and have looked at people whose rhythms have been altered, e.g. night shift workers. The evidence suggests that an adaptation of catecholamine rhythms occurs during long term exposure to permanent night shift, but that exposure to rotating shifts "flattens" the normal pattern of variation, producing very low levels of both adrenaline and noradrenaline which take a long time to recover.

6. Catecholamines and performance

The role of catecholamines in the performance of different types of task has been exhaustively researched. Work carried out by O'Hanlon and Horvarth (1973) has shown that plasma concentrations of adrenaline are positively related to the capability for performing "mental" work, characterized by low energy expenditure and sustained level of attention. Similarly, Frankenhaeuser and her co-workers have shown that, amongst healthy individuals, those who have high tonic levels of catecholamine excretion perform better that those with low tonic levels, both in terms of speed and accuracy (Frankenhaeuser, 1971). In a recent study on parachute trainees, Ursin (1978) has examined the underlying structure of the physiological response to stress. He has reported the existence of a "catecholamine factor", which he showed to be positively related to performance.

However, despite these and similar studies, it would be wrong to assume that high levels of the catecholamines are always necessary for good performance. Research by Frankenhaeuser has shown that high catecholamine excretion may be detrimental to performance in complex tasks requiring selective attention. This may be explained in terms of an association between catecholamine levels and drive; high drive interfering with the choice between competing responses. Frankenhaeuser's research has also established that those people whose catecholamine levels readily return to baseline (rapid decreasers) are psychologically better adjusted, and perform more efficiently in achievement situations than those whose levels return slowly to baseline (slow decreasers).

7. Catecholamines and health

Chronic alterations in catecholamine levels have been said to increase the amount of "wear and tear" on the body and significantly contribute to the aetiology and poor prognosis of several diseases (Selye, 1950). Often mentioned in this context are gastric ulcers and coronary heart disease. The mechanisms by which the latter may occur have attracted much attention.

Carruthers (1980), for example, has suggested that coronary heart disease has a multi-factorial aetiology, in which the emotions of aggression, anger and frustration play a significant role. The experience and expression of these feelings are often associated with significant increases in catecholamine levels, and in particular with increases in noradrenaline levels. The overall change in catecholamine activity tends, in turn, to be associated with increased levels of free fatty acids, triglycerides and glucose. The triglycerides have been directly implicated in the precipitation of coronary heart disease.

8. Catecholamine response: unitary or differential?

There is some debate in the literature as to whether the adrenaline and noradrenaline secreting cells of the medulla respond to psychosocial stimuli in the same way and to the same degree, or whether they respond differentially. The evidence is beginning to support the notion of a differential response.

Davies and Tune (1970), using a serial discrimination task, have established that although adrenaline secretion initially increases, as a result of psychophysiological mobilization, and then declines in a manner related to performance, levels of noradrenaline are unaffected.

Several other studies in the literature have demonstrated differential catecholamine responses, but related more to individual differences than to external stimulation. Goodall (1951) for example, in his studies on "animals", showed greater concentrations of noradrenaline in aggressive than in non-aggressive individuals. Funkenstein's (1956) theory developed in a similar vein. He postulated that the response to psychological stress in persons who direct anger inwardly is characterized by adrenaline secretion and those who respond more outwardly secrete mainly noradrenaline. However, many of these studies have been hampered by the type of methodology referred to in the final section of this chapter (see p. 275).

More recent research has centred on comparisons between type "A" and type "B" individuals (Friedman and Rosenman, 1959). One of the characteristics of type A behaviour is "increased hostility and aggression", and at least three studies in this area report that type A's display elevated noradrenaline levels in response to stressful situations, whereas type B's fail to show this responsiveness (Friedman *et al.*, 1975). However, studies carried out by Lundberg and Forsman (1979) showed no consistent differences in catecholamine response between the two types. This may highlight the problems associated with using students as subjects in this area of research. The latter study used students, while the former studies did not.

There is a need in all studies to control variables such as physical activity and posture, morphology and sex. A lack of such control tends to cause inconsistencies in results gained from different studies.

9. *Catecholamine activity and other variables*

Posture It has been shown in studies on healthy individuals that plasma catecholamine levels can be dramatically affected by posture; for example the levels obtained in recumbancy are approximately half those obtained in a corresponding head-up tilted position.

Sex differences Although it has been generally assumed that, provided catecholamine excretion is expressed in terms of body weight, no sex differences can be demonstrated (Karki, 1956), recent studies have provided important qualifications to this assumption. Work carried out by Frankenhaeuser and her colleagues (see Cox, 1978) has shown that men are more physiologically responsive than women, and show greater increases in adrenaline levels in demanding situations. However, in a study of female employees in an insurance company, unusually high levels of catecholamines were found in a large proportion of the work force, in response to a period of prolonged overtime (Rissler, 1977). High levels of catecholamines have also been measured in women working at simulated repetitive tasks (Cox, *et al.*, 1982).

10. *Comments*

In conclusion, therefore, provided the conditions under which urine is sampled are carefully standardized, catecholamine excretion rates constitute fairly sensitive indices of how people relate to the demands and emotional impact of the environment. It is important to note, however, that some of the physiological actions of the catecholamines do not occur in the absence of the adrenal cortical hormones, the latter being necessary to maintain the responsiveness of the tissues.

E. *The Adrenal Cortex*

The adrenal cortex is composed of three discrete cellular regions; zona reticularis, zona fasciculata and zona glomerulosa. These regions produce three different groups of steroid hormones: mineralocorticoids, androgens and glucocorticoids. The **mineralocorticoids** function primarily in the regulation of the electrolyte–water balance, largely by promoting sodium reabsorption in the kidney tubule. Aldosterone is the main salt-retaining hormone of the adrenal cortex. Synthesized in the zona glomerulosa, its production is subject to a diurnal variation. The exact function of the **adrenal androgens** is not yet clear. However they appear to have some role in the development of secondary sexual characteristics. The **glucocorticoids**, largely produced in the zona fasciculata, form the bulk of adrenal cortical secretion. They are essential for the maintenance of life. In humans, 85% of glucocorticoid secretion is as **cortisol**, the remainder being predominantly corticosterone. The activity of the glucocorticoids is regulated by the level of adrenocorticotropic hormone (ACTH) in the blood. This is secreted by the anterior lobe of the pituitary gland and its production is in turn controlled by the secretion of corticotropic factor (CRF) from the median eminence of the hypothalamus. There is general agreement that a negative feedback mechanism operates to control the levels of glucocorticoids in the blood: levels of CRF are reduced in response to increases in plasma cortisol.

Although all three groups of steroids operate in response to stress, the emphasis of the main body of research has been on the glucocorticoids.

1. Glucocorticoid function

Increased levels of cortisol (and corticosterone) have a major effect on carbohydrate metabolism. They cause an increase in the formation of glucose from tissue protein (gluconeogenesis), an increased deposition of glycogen in the liver, and depression of fat synthesis from carbohydrate. They also enhance the release of free fatty acids from adipose tissue and facilitate the absorption of insoluble fats through the stomach lining. During stress, elevated levels of the glucocorticoids, effect a redistribution and suppression of circulating white blood cells; reducing activity in the thymus and blocking the migration of neutrophils to inflammatory sites. Other reactions to stress include minor increases in blood pressure. In this respect increased levels of circulating glucocorticoids enhance and maintain the vascular reactivity to the catecholamines.

In summary the overall effect is *catabolic*, releasing energy to enable the body to cope with stress.

2. Measurement of adrenal cortical activity

Adrenocortical activity has been measured in various ways: through plasma levels of cortisol and ACTH and through levels of 17-hydroxycorticosteroids (metabolites of cortisol and corticosteroid) excreted in urine. Very little cortisol or corticosterone is excreted in the urine. Studies on plasma have tended to neglect the assessment of *free* cortisol. Approximately 95% of cortisol secreted into the systemic circulation is immediately *bound* to various plasma proteins, but it is the free cortisol which exerts a functionally active effect and levels may change drastically, while total plasma cortisol levels exhibit only small changes. Methods for the assay of corticosteroids have become extremely sophisticated in the past decade. Techniques include gas chromatography, colorimetric and fluorescence techniques and, perhaps most reliable of all, radioimmunoassay. In practical terms the most useful measure of adrenocortical activity for the psychologist has been urinary excretion of 17-hydroxycorticosteroids (17-OHCS).

3. *Biochronology and sex differences*

In man the adrenal cortex functions throughout life, but is most active during the foetal stage, although it continues to respond adequately into old age.

A **circadian rhythm** has been demonstrated in plasma cortisol levels: they peak early in the waking hours and decline across the day, rising again in the early hours of the evening (Guignard *et al.*, 1979). This rhythm is sensitive to disrupted sleep cycles, and permanent night shift workers can show a reversal of the rhythm.

Although corticosteroid secretion appears to be relatively stable over the course of the **menstrual cycle**, adrenocortical reactivity to psychological stress has been shown to be significantly greater in women during the pre-menstrual phase compared to mid-cycle (Marinari *et al.*, 1976). This effect seems only to occur in non-pill taking women; women taking oral contraceptives, although exhibiting elevated baseline levels of cortisol, do not exhibit the same differences between phases.

There appears to be a correlation between body weight and excretion of 17-OHCS, obese individuals excrete comparatively high levels.

4. *Corticosteroid activity and the stress response*

Although speculative suggestions of a link between emotions and the adrenal cortex were advanced as early as 1922 (Uno, 1922), the foundations of work concerned with the adrenocortical response to stress were developed from the work of Selye (1950). The "resistance" and "exhaustion" stages of his general adaptation syndrome were characterized by increased activity and ultimate atrophy of the pituitary-adrenocortical mechanism. In the light of later work it is necessary to recognise that changes in adrenocortical activity also occur during the "alarm" reaction and that other endocrine systems are involved in the resistance stage.

Experimental work largely with animals has confirmed the general observation that adrenal cortical activity increases under conditions of experimentally induced stress, (e.g. immobilization, electric shock, noise). Similar
effects on adrenal cortical activity have been observed in more natural
stressful situations e.g. overcrowding or the establishment of dominance
hierarchies.

Examples of *real-life situations* where increases in plasma and urinary
17-OHCS have been demonstrated in man are numerous: flying activities,
pre-operative states, University examinations, parachute jumping, novel or
hostile environments and combat activity. Psychiatric patients, particularly
acutely disturbed or depressed patients show marked elevations in excretion
of 17-OHCS.

An important point to note, is that corticosteroid activity can also be
suppressed. Reduced levels of plasma 17-OHCS have for example been
demonstrated in states of hypnotic trance.

5. Coping and corticosteroid activity

While the evidence for a significant adrenal cortical response to a wide variety
of stimuli is clear, factors such as cognitive defences, coping strategies and
early experience may well affect that response.

Wolffe, in a prospective study on the parents of leukemic children, demonstrated that the most meaningful differences in urinary 17-OHCS were those
between individuals and not those related to changes from normal values.
Consistently lower levels of 17-OHCS were excreted by subjects who had
adopted successful methods of coping with their childrens' fatal illness
(Wolffe, *et al.*, 1964). Although the evidence is largely correlational, it seems
that while denial is a successful psychological defence and maintains low
corticosteroid activity, personality traits such as repression and denial seem
to be associated with high levels of corticosteroids (Fox, 1978).

Studies on rhesus monkeys have confirmed the importance of being able to
cope with stressful situations. Mild increases in corticosterone levels in rhesus
monkeys who had learned an avoidance response to electric shock contrast
dramatically with elevated levels in those monkeys who had learned the
response, but were presented with unavoidable shocks (Mason, 1968). Withdrawal of the coping response was more effective in elevating corticosteroid
levels than shock itself.

Levine and his co-workers have somewhat similarly demonstrated that
corticosteroid levels in monkeys exposed to high noise or shock, but with
some means of control over the stimulus, are equivalent to those levels found
in control animals. However, they are significantly lower than levels found in
animals experiencing the same stimuli but with no effective control.

Lack or loss of control thus appear to be important factors in determining the magnitude of the adrenal cortical response. Similarly *feedback* providing information about the success of a control response (coping) also seems to be important (Weinberg and Levine, 1980).

6. Corticosteroids and disease

The role of the adrenal cortical response in the aetiology of disease is again receiving much interest. In his early studies, Selye (1950) induced a variety of pathological changes in laboratory rats: hypertension, arthritis, atherosclerosis and gastrointestinal ulcers. He attributed these states to a maladaptive function of the adrenal steroids; the suppression of the inflammatory reaction, permitting the spread of infection and inhibiting healing. Later authors have emphasized the catabolic nature of the adrenal response (Mason, 1968) and implicated this in the aetiology of degenerative disease.

One particular interest in recent years has centered on the specific relationship between corticosteroid activity and cancer. Several studies with animals have demonstrated a link between increased corticosteroid activity and increased susceptibility to infection, reduced lymphocyte activity and cancer. The effect of the glucocorticoids on the suppression of immune activity has been documented (Faucci, 1979) and there is increasing evidence to suggest a link between stress induced modulation of the immune system and the promotion of human cancer (for review see Cox and Mackay, 1982). Studies indicating a link between personality traits, such as anxiety and repression, and stressful life events, and susceptibility to cancer have also been extensively reviewed by Fox (1978). Personality traits of repression, obsessiveness and denial are correlated with a high incidence of cancer as are life stresses such as bereavement. Lack of emotional support during crises and inappropriate coping styles have been variously associated with increased adrenal cortical activity.

IV. The Integrated Study of Human Stress

It must now be obvious that the most satisfactory studies on stress are those which consider the psychological and physiological aspects together. The value of these different measures is that they complement each other and extra information is provided by the relationship between them. An individual reporting high arousal and showing high catecholamine levels is in a different state (say fear) to a person reporting low arousal and showing high catecholamine levels (say boredom).

Future studies should be characterized by their adequate methodology.

Beyond this, a more specific examination of the relationship between particular demands and patterns of response should be attempted. The demands of interest must be those generated by the development of theory, for example, those related to information, predictability and control, or those which reflect real world problem situations, such as the demands inherent in the visual display unit (VDU) operators' job. A fruitful cross validation of ideas and findings may be afforded by the parallel development of pure and applied research in this area. This chapter ends with examples of studies which have adopted this integrated approach. In doing so, it highlights the problems inherent in this area of research.

The authors have established a workshop for the study of the demands inherent in repetitive work and their effects on the worker. A machine paced button sorting system has been devised, which involves three separate but related tasks: loading, sorting and minding (see Mackay and Cox, 1979). The repetition inherent in both the loading and sorting tasks is often associated with understimulation and severe constraints on behaviour; this inevitably leads to feelings of boredom. The boredom manifests itself as a decrease in self-reported arousal, decreases in mean heart-rate and increases in heart rate variability. Interestingly, catecholamine excretion may show either an increase or a decrease depending on the experimental conditions. It is the authors' hypothesis that these apparent differences in response reflect the consequences of boredom. A decrease in catecholamine excretion occurs when a decrease in arousal is acceptable and not detrimental to the person, while increases occur in situations when arousal has to be increased in order to cope with the situation. The latter is usually accompanied by high levels of self-reported stress, and may be a compensatory reaction.

The problems encountered in this type of research are primarily those of identifying and controlling extraneous variables, both of a physiological and a psychological nature. In previous sections several of these variables have been discussed, for example, time of day effects and age and sex differences. In addition to these, the following factors must be considered in the design and execution of experiments: the establishment of base-lines, without which the interpretation of data is difficult; degree of subjects' familiarization with the situation; their food and fluid intake before and during the experiment and their alcohol and caffeine intake; their smoking behaviour; and their behaviour before starting the experiment. All these factors can affect subjects' responses, particularly those related to neuroendocrine systems. However, although strict control of caffeine intake and smoking should be adhered to wherever possible, in some subjects non-smoking and non-coffee drinking situations can themselves be inherently stressful.

Having taken these and other factors into consideration there usually remains the question of what is an adequate control condition for the experience of stress, say at work. Should stressful work be compared with non-stressful work, or should the person be studied at work and out-of-work? Base-line measures could be taken in the subjects' own home environment at similar times of the day. In most cases this is not always feasible.

The authors' subjects were recruited in groups of three to work in the simulated workshop. No work was carried out on the first day and subjects were able to familiarize themselves with their fellow workers, the experimenter and the surroundings. On the following three days subjects sat in the same work environment engaged in the three tasks under study; two repetitive tasks, "loading" and "sorting", and a non-repetitive "minding" task. Minding was seen as an "at work" control. Each person performed every task, but on different days. Order of presentation of task was controlled. The "minders" were required to watch over automatic collection of the sorted buttons, replacing the few that fell from the collection chute, and notifying the supervisor of any faults which occurred. Although an adequate experimental control for the repetitive jobs, minding has important equivalents in industry. Indeed the proportion of deskilled minding jobs may increase with the technological changes which are currently occurring.

Within the experimental workshop at Nottingham it has been possible to control many of the important extraneous variables. The work schedule and sampling procedures were identical on all three days and a standard dietary regime was designed which provided low carbohydrate, low protein food and caffeine-free drink for all subjects, in controlled quantities at specified times. Wherever possible subjects were asked to refrain from smoking unless this caused undue distress. However in this type of research all controls can be rendered ineffectual by inadequate collection and handling of samples. In urinary catecholamine determinations, accurate measurement of time between voiding, sample volume and, most important of all, immediate stabilization of samples are all essential for good experimental practice.

The results gained through the authors' research have highlighted the demands inherent in repetitive work and their effects on workers' mood, performance and physiological state. Exposure to repetitive and monotonous work produces feelings of boredom, and a loss of arousal and alertness. This may have serious implications for performance (and safety), and appears to be associated with increased tension and feelings of stress. The loss of arousal is accompanied by a decrease in mean heart rate and an increase in heart rate variability. Urinary adrenaline excretion appears to increase. Performance often becomes poorer and more variable as the worker attempts to compensate for becoming drowsy by gross body movements (fidgetting, moving around), by socializing (talking to other workers), or by a variety of other strategies, including leaving the task for "a walk" or "a cigarette". These changes are conditioned by the nature of the task being carried out, by the degree of machine pacing, by the form of payment, by the time of day, and by the social cohesiveness of the work group.

Research of a similar nature has been carried out by Frankenhaueser and her colleagues. In one particular study, male and female students, previously classified as Type A or Type B, were studied in different situations (Lundberg and Forsman, 1979). Three conditions were used: understimulating and overstimulating tasks and a "no" task control. The urinary excretion of catecholamines and of cortisol, and self reported mood were measured. The results showed that both task conditions increased hormone levels. However, during the understimulating condition cortisol predominated, whereas during the overstimulating condition adrenaline excretion increased markedly especially for male subjects. The self report measures also distinguished between the two task conditions. Feelings in both tasks were characterized by effort, tenseness and irritation. However, those in the under-stimulating task were also related to boredom.

Acknowledgements

The authors acknowledge the support of the Medical Research Council, and the United States Army Research Institute. The views expressed here are their own and do not reflect those of either supporting body. The authors would also like to acknowledge the help of Ann Cooke in preparing the manuscript.

Further Reading

Cox, T. (1978). "Stress". Macmillan, London.
This is a broadly based and well integrated book which provides more discussion of the nature of stress and its psychological and physiological aspects. At the same time it provides a background and a development of the information presented in this chapter.
Gray, J. (1971). "The Psychology of Fear and Stress". Weidenfeld and Nicholson, London.
This relatively short text provides an interesting supplement to the ideas introduced in "Stress" by T. Cox.
Ganong, W. F. (1977). "Review of Medical Physiology". Blackwell, Edinburgh.
This is a very usable standard textbook of medical physiology, which provides useful background information on the neuro-endocrine systems discussed in this chapter.
Levine, S. and Ursin, H. (1980). "Coping and Health". Plenum Press, New York.
This is an edited volume of papers largely dealing with the behavioural aspects of stress, but also introducing some physiological considerations. It is useful for the interested student to read for a more *advanced* insight into stress research.

References

The references marked with an asterisk (*) are primary references or papers of immediate interest. The references not so marked are included to support important points in the chapter, and as "leads" for advanced study.

Akerstedt, T., and Froberg, J. E. (1978). Inter-individual consistency of catecholamine excretion in relation to circadian rhythms. *J. Psychosomatic Res.* 22, 433–438.
*Cannon, W. B. (1932). "The Wisdom of the Body". Norton, New York.
*Carruthers, M. (1980). Hazardous occupations and the heart. *In* "Current Concerns in Occupational Stress" (C. L. Cooper and R. Payne, eds). Wiley and Sons, Chichester.
Carruthers, M., Taggart, P., Conway, N., Bates, D. and Somerville, W. (1970). Validity of plasma catecholamine estimations. *Lancet* ii, July, 62–67.
Cox, T. (1978). "Stress". Macmillan, London.
*Cox, T. and Mackay, C. J. (1981). A transactional approach to occupational stress. *In* "Stress, Work Design and Productivity" (N. Corlett and P. Richardson, eds). Wiley and Sons, Chichester.
Cox, T. and Mackay, C. (1982). Psychosocial factors and psychophysiological mechanisms in the aetiology and development of cancers. *Soc. Sci. Med.* 16, 381–396.
Cox, S., Cox, T., Thirlaway, M. and Mackay, C. (1982). Effects of simulated repetitive work on urinary catecholamine excretion. *Ergonomics* 25, 1129–1141.
Davies, D. R. and Tune, G. S. (1970). "Human Vigilance Performance". Staples Press, London.
Faucci, A. S. (1979). Mechanisms of the immuno-suppressive and anti-inflammatory effects of the glucocorticoids. *J. Immunopharmacol.* 1, 1–25.
*Fox, B. H. (1978). Premorbid psychological factors as related to cancer incidence. *J. Behav. Med.* 1, 45–133.
Frankenhaeuser, M. (1971). Behaviour and circulating catecholamines. *Brain Res.* 31, 241–262.
*Frankenhaeuser, M. (1975). Experimental approaches to the study of catecholamines and emotions. *In* "Emotions: their parameters and measurement" (L. Levi, ed.). Raven Press, New York.
Frankenhaeuser, M. and Rissler, A. (1970). Effects of punishment of catecholamine release and efficiency of performance. *Psychopharmacology* 17, 378–390.
Freud, A. (1946). "The Ego and Mechanisms of Defense". International University Press, New York.
Friedman, M. and Rosenman, R. H. (1959). Association of specific overt behaviour pattern with blood and cardiovascular findings. *J. Am. Med. Ass.* 169, 1286–1296.
Friedman, M., Byers, S. O., Diamant, J. and Rosenman, R. H. (1975). Plasma catecholamine response of coronary prone subjects (type A) to a specific challenge. *Metabolism* 24, 205–210.
Funkenstein, D. M. (1956). Nor-epinephrine and epinephrine-like substances in relation to human behaviour. *J. Ment. Disorders* 124, 58–68.
Goodall, McC. (1951). Studies of adrenaline and noradrenaiine in mammalian heart and suprarenals. *Acta Physiol. Scand.* 24, suppl. 85.
*Gray, J. (1971). "The Psychology of Fear and Stress". Weidenfeld and Nicholson, London.

Guignard, M. M., Pesquies, P. C., Serrurier B. D. and Reinberg, A. (1979). Circadian rhythms in cortisol, dehydroepiandrosterone, A-4-androstenedione, testosterone and dihydrotestosterone of healthy young human males. *Chronobiologia* 6, 104.

Johansson, G. and Post, B. (1974). Catecholamine output of males and females over a one year period. *Acta Physiol. Scand.* 92, 557–565.

Johansson, G., Aronsson, G. and Lindstrom, B. O. (1978). Social, psychological and neuroendocrine stress reactions in highly mechanised work. *Ergonomics* 21, 583–588.

Karki, N. T. (1956). The urinary excretion of noradrenaline and adrenaline in different age groups, its diurnal variation, and the effect of muscular work on it. *Acta Physiol. Scand.* 39, suppl. 132.

*Lazarus, R. S. (1976). "Adjustment". McGraw-Hill, New York.

Lundberg, U. and Forsman, L. (1979). Adrenal-medullary and adrenal-cortical responses to understimulation and overstimulation: comparison between type A and type B persons. *Biol. Psychol.* 9, 79–89.

Mackay, C. J. and Cox, T. (1979). "Response to Stress: occupational aspects". International Publishing Corporation, London.

Marinari, K. T., Leshner, A. I. and Doyle, M. P. (1976). Menstrual cycle status and adrenocortical reactivity to psychological stress. *Psychoneuroendocr.* 1, 213–218.

*Mason, J. W. (1968). A review of psychoendocrine research on the pituitary-adrenal cortical system. *Psychosomatic Med.* 30, 576–607.

Miller, N. E. and Weiss, J. M. (1969). Effects of the somatic or visceral response to punishment. *In* "Punishment and Aversive Behaviour" (B. A. Campbell and R. M. Church, eds). Appleton-Century-Crofts, New York.

Miller, S. M. (1980). When is a little information a dangerous thing? Coping with stressful events by monitoring versus blunting. *In* "Coping and Health" (S. Levine and H. Ursin, eds). Plenum Press, New York.

O'Hanlon, J. F. and Horvarth, S. M. (1973). Interrelationships among performance circulating concentrations of adrenaline, noradrenaline, glucose and the free fatty acids in men performing a monitoring task. *Psychophysiology* 10, 251–259.

Rissler, A. (1977). Stress reactions at work and after work during a period of quantitative overload. *Ergonomics,* 20, 577–580.

Seligman, M. E. P. (1968). Chronic fear produced by unpredictable electric shock. *J. Comp. Physiol. Psychol.* 66, 402–411.

Selye, H. (1950). "Stress". Acta Incorporated, Montreal.

Uno, T. (1922). Effect of general excitement and of fighting on some ductless glands of male albino rats. *Am. J. Physiol.* 61, 203.

Ursin, H. (1978). Activation, coping and psychosomatics. *In* "Psychobiology of Stress: a study of coping men" (H. Ursin, E. Baade, and S. Levine, eds). Academic Press, New York and London.

Weinberg, J. and Levine, S. (1980). Psychobiology of Coping in Animals: the effects of predictability *In* "Coping and Health" (S. Levine and H. Ursin, eds). Plenum Press, New York.

Wolffe, C. T., Friedman, S. B., Hofer, M. A. and Mason, J. W. (1964). Relationship between the psychological defences and mean urinary 17-hydroxycorticosteroid excretion rates. *Psychosomatic Med.* 26, 576–591.

14 Mechanisms for Habitual Substance Use: Food, Alcohol and Cigarettes

D. M. Warburton
and K. Wesnes

Abstract In this chapter we consider the mechanisms which underlie the habitual consumption of commonly used substances, taking food, alcohol and tobacco as examples. We illustrate how well the opponent-process theory can be used to describe the psychological processes which underlie habitual substance use and also how similar these processes appear to be. We then describe the neural mechanisms which underlie these psychological processes. For food and alcohol the reward mechanisms which maintain substance use are similar and fit well with the opponent-process theory. For smoking, however, the neural mechanisms are different and we propose that the factors which maintain smoking are different from those which maintain the use of most other common substances. To support this proposal we discuss the neurochemical and the electrophysiological effects of nicotine, the effects of smoking withdrawal, smoking under stress, and the personality of smokers.

I. Introduction

Every year the average European and North American eats about a million calories, drinks ten litres of absolute alcohol and smokes three and a half thousand cigarettes. Most people find that the use of these substances improves the quality of their lives and that they suffer no ill effects. However, excessive use of food, alcohol and tobacco are three of the major *identifiable* causes of illness and premature death. They have been implicated in the causation of cardiovascular, hepatic, neoplastic and pulmonary diseases and so an understanding of their excessive use has important implications for preventive medicine.

PHYSIOLOGICAL CORRELATES OF HUMAN
BEHAVIOUR   ISBN 0-12-273901-9

The question arises whether the cost to public health is the only factor that is common to the excessive use of the substances or whether a common process underlies over-indulgence. Apart from the fact that all three are oral consummatory activities, there does not appear to be much in common with munching a solid, gulping a liquid and puffing a smoke. However, it is true that most over-users are aware of the health risks and wish to control use, but are unable to stop over-indulgence even with professional help. Thus it is sensible to ask whether there are common psychological processes which can explain these behaviours and whether the same physiological mechanisms underlie these processes. It should be emphasized that similarity of the psychological process does not necessarily mean that the physiological mechanism is the same (A bridge can be blown up by an explosion, but many different mechanisms could produce the explosion). Before considering these two separate questions it is useful to distinguish between use, misuse and abuse.

II. Habitual Substance Use, Misuse, and Abuse

Even the most distinguished professionals in the fields of law and medicine confuse use, misuse and abuse. The United States President's Advisory Commission on Narcotic and Drug Abuse defined drug abuse as "either drug taking in amounts to endanger his own health or the health of others, or when drugs are obtained illicitly, or when drugs are taken on the person's own initiative without the authorization of a doctor". (Smart, 1974). This definition is obviously ridiculous because it equates abuse with any sort of use, and would include aspirin taking, laxative use and a sleeping tablet given by a friend. It does not distinguish harmful drug use from harmless, and states that any drug use without a doctor's stamp of approval is "abuse"! It seems to us that substance use, including drug use, can only be evaluated with respect to purpose of use, the situation of use, the manner of use and the consequence of use, as Balter (1974) suggested.

Habitual substance *use* can thus be defined as responsible intake of a substance for an innocuous or a constructive purpose, in moderate amounts and in the appropriate context in terms of place and culture. Thus food taken regularly at meal times by a hungry person, in amounts sufficient to make up the energy deficit, would fit this definition. A cigarette smoked to relieve stress in places where smoking was not restricted and in quantities that did not impair health would constitute correct use of the substance. A glass of wine or marijuana smoked for relaxation in the early evening at a party would constitute normal substance use.

Habitual substance *misuse* occurs when the substance is used wrongly in terms of either purpose, or situation, or manner, or consequences. Most of us at one time or another violate these conditions and misuse substances. We continue to eat after satiation, eat between meals, eat the wrong foods and exceed the correct calorie intake for that day. Cigarettes that are smoked automatically and alcohol or marijuana taken just before driving would constitute habitual substance misuse.

Habitual substance *abuse* is the emotive term and, as we have pointed out already, it is a term that is most misused and abused in the literature. The dictionary definition of abuse implies that it is use which results in harm. Thus the definition of habitual substance abuse focuses on consequences of use in terms of psychological and physiological effects. Among these consequences are impairment of personal and social functioning, personal development, personality disturbance including psychoses, organic damage and even death. Indirectly, abuse refers to the manner of use by the person, and is related to the pattern of use and the doses that are taken. It must be emphasized that the problem is in the person's interaction with the drug and not a fault in the drug itself, although some drugs are more likely to be abused than others.

The person–drug interaction that leads to abuse may be termed the *abuse potential* of a drug (Balter, 1974), and it depends on three aspects of substance use.

(i) The substance must have adverse consequences when taken excessively. However, this is a necessary but not a sufficient condition, because most substances are dangerous if taken in large enough quantities and/or over a long enough time. Thus, not all substances have abuse potential, for example, strychnine. The magnitude of this factor can be estimated from the probability of occurrence of adverse consequences in the user population.

(ii) The substance must have some degree of intrinsic attractiveness, that is it must be in some way psychologically or socio-culturally rewarding for the user. This is a sufficient condition for a substance having abuse potential. This factor can be estimated from the incidence of use.

(iii) The substance can have dependence liability, that is it has intrinsic properties which can lead to excessive use, either due to intrinsic attractiveness or to avoid the psychological and physical discomfort that results from abstinence. This risk of dependence can be estimated from the ratio of dependent users to the total number of users (see Balter, 1974). In this Chapter we will be considering in detail the common aspects of factors (ii) and (iii). They determine substance use and the tendency to habitual misuse and abuse in terms of a psychological theory, providing a unified approach to habitual substance use – the opponent-process theory of acquired motivation (Solomon and Corbit, 1974).

III. Opponent-process Model for Habitual Substance Use

The opponent-process model of Solomon and Corbit (1974) was proposed as a useful model to explain acquired motivation in such disparate areas as imprinting, masochism and thermoregulation. The authors also claim that it can be used to increase our understanding of all types of habitual substance use and abuse, including that of food. In the next sections we will outline the model, consider the possible physiological bases for the processes and examine how well the model can explain alcohol use, food use and cigarette use.

The main features of the model are two processes and two conditioned states that are associated with the processes. Process *a* is the initial affective mechanism that is activated by substance intake and the person experiences pleasure (State *A*). Thus all habitually-used substances must be capable of eliciting some pleasure initially, otherwise they will not be sampled again. Thus State *A* rewards behaviours that are associated with getting and using the substance. During the early phases of substance intake, previously neutral stimuli can become classically conditioned to State *A* and become elicitors of State *A* and act as positive secondary reinforcers of substance use behaviours.

Process *b* is an opponent "slave" process that is a consequence of a negative feedback loop from State *A*. It is a slave process because it can only be produced indirectly by eliciting State *A*. If substance use is repeated then Process *b* will be strengthened so that if substance use is stopped State *B* is produced. State *B* is an unpleasant state of withdrawal which becomes so aversive and persistent that the user will attempt to eliminate it. As Process *b* is the opponent of Process *a*, the quickest and most effective way to eliminate State *B* is to use the substance in order to produce State *A*. Thus abstinence produces craving and the degree of craving will be a function of the amount of substance use and the consequent strength of Process *b*. Behaviours which result in the acquisition and use of the substance will be doubly rewarded, because they both produce State *A* (positive reinforcement) *and* simultaneously terminate State *B* (negative reinforcement). Process *b* will be strengthened further as a result and as the amount of pleasure depends on the difference $(a - b)$, then the amount of the substance that is taken, must be increased in order for the difference to be greater than zero. Process *b* will continue as long as Process *a* is evoked, but it will weaken gradually over time when substance use stops because it is a slave process and cannot continue without evocation of Process *a*.

In a similar fashion to State *A*, neutral stimuli that are associated with the eliciting of State *B* become conditioned to it and become elicitors of State *B*, the aversive withdrawal symptoms and craving for the substance. Initially substance use is escape behaviour that terminates State *B*. However, as the aversively conditioned stimuli become stronger, substance use will become anticipatory and the chronic substance user will be exhibiting more avoidance behaviour than escape i.e. he will take the substance often enough so that he only experiences State *B* occasionally. Unfortunately, repeated use of a drug with escalating doses is liable to be harmful i.e. "use" becomes "abuse".

In summary, there is behavioural evidence that there are two related processes in the brain which maintain behaviour. Activation of one process initially produces pleasure, but repeated activation results in a strengthening of an opponent process which decreases the pleasure, and, at the same time, the absence of activation results in aversive effects. It follows from this model that any intense pleasure should lead to repetition of the behaviour that leads to its production, especially if stopping the behaviour results in aversive consequences. In combination, the pleasure and the aversive effects of cessation will result in powerful mechanisms for maintaining behaviour. Basically, all pleasures have the seeds of their own abuse.

IV. Neurochemical Substrate for Reward

One of the most important findings for the theory of reward mechanisms was the discovery that animals would respond in order to receive electrical stimulation of the brain. When rats were placed in an operant chamber in which a lever press delivered electrical stimulation to the brain, the probability of the lever pressing response increased very rapidly and they continued to press for hours with no signs of satiation (Olds and Milner, 1954). Some parts of the brain were "neutral", in the sense that stimulation in those regions did not change the probability of responding, which demonstrated that the results were not merely an artifact of stimulating the brain.

A. *Anatomy of Reward*

Olds and Olds (1963) mapped the places in the brain where electrical stimulation appeared to be reinforcing and found that the medial forebrain bundle in the hypothalamus was the most sensitive site, with the highest response rates for the lowest levels of current. This bundle of fibres runs through the hypothalamus from the hindbrain to the forebrain. It is a neurochemically heterogeneous bundle of neurones, which have differing origins in the brain stem and separate terminals. Electrical stimulation in the medial forebrain bundle will activate all of these pathways and the behavioural effects will be the resultant of changes in many structures. One model for self stimulation

(Deutsch and Deutsch, 1966) suggested that there are two pathways involved in self-stimulation, but that only one of the pathways is involved with reward, while the other is a motivational pathway. The motivational pathway carries excitation from the motivational cells sensitive to imbalances in homeostatic systems, and hormones to the cells that mediate action i.e., a drive system. The reward pathway acts as a "gate" for the drive pathway, so that the excitation will pass from the motivational cells to the motor cells to activate behaviour.

Huang and Routtenberg (1971) used very fine electrodes and low current to try to stimulate specific fibre tracts in the medial forebrain bundle. They found that quite different response rates were obtained from various regions of the medial forebrain bundle; stimulation of the ventral fibres produced lower response rates than the more dorsal and lateral pathways. Deutsch argued that a higher response rate would be obtained from the "drive" pathway than the reward, so that we can tentatively suggest that the reward pathways were running at a ventral level in the medial forebrain bundle. The important distinction between the drive and reward pathways is in terms of their origins in the hindbrain and terminals in the forebrain. Huang and Routtenberg implicated the brachium conjunctivum in "slow rate" self-stimulation, and the origins of these fibres are the dorsal nuclei of the brainstem around the locus coeruleus. Electrodes were implanted in this region, and the rats were tested for self-stimulation responding (Crow, 1972), and slow rate self-stimulation responding was obtained from electrode sites close to the locus coeruleus.

B. *Biochemistry of Reward*

In conventional self-stimulation, each lever press delivers trains of current fixed intensity to the posterior hypothalamus, but a technique of threshold titration has proved useful in determining the biochemical substrate of reward. In this procedure each press produces a train of current, but also reduces the intensity by a small step. A second lever is available which will reset the current at its original intensity, so the animal can reset the current when it reaches a non-rewarding level, i.e. subthreshold. The thresholds have been found to be stable over many months of testing. A number of drugs have been tested for their effects on the threshold for self-stimulation, and Stein (1962) found that amphetamine lowered the threshold.

It is a well established fact that amphetamine increases the amounts of functional catecholamines, noradrenaline and dopamine, in the brain by increasing release from the neurone, and by preventing inactivation of the transmitters by reuptake. This evidence suggests that amphetamine is reducing the reward threshold by enhancing activity in the catecholamine neurones ascending in the median forebrain bundle, and leads to the hypothesis that either a noradrenaline or dopamine pathway mediates reward. Both Olds (1962) and Stein (1964) have suggested that it is noradrenaline.

In order to test this possibility and to rule out dopamine, Wise and Stein (1969) administered disulphiram, which inhibits the synthesis of noradrenaline and dopamine, to rats with electrodes in the median forebrain bundle. Self-stimulation responding was suppressed, but was restored by an intraventricular injection of L-noradrenaline, the isomer of the transmitter that occurs naturally in the body, but not by D-noradrenaline or dopamine. This result implies that L-noradrenaline is the transmitter which mediates reward. However, as a direct test of this hypothesis, Stein and Wise (1969) implanted electrodes in the median forebrain bundle, a push-pull cannula in the lateral hypothalamus, and injections of radioactive noradrenaline were made. After three hours, background levels of radioactivity were recorded in the perfusate of unstimulated animals, but stimulation of rats, who would press for self-stimulation, produced large increases in radioactivity. Electrodes which did not produce high self-stimulation rates did not produce increase in radioactivity. Chemical analysis disclosed that most of the radioactivity was due to noradrenaline metabolites which would be produced by enzymatic inactivation of released noradrenaline. This study gives strong support for the idea that noradrenaline is the transmitter that is involved in the function of the brain reward system.

C. *Neurochemistry of Reward*

An important concept in theories of the neurochemistry of behaviour is that the place where the biochemical change happens is just as important as the change itself (Warburton, 1981). Modern theorists no longer think of centres exerting exclusive control over a particular function, but formulate hypotheses in terms of neurochemical networks, systems of pathways. Consequently we have to abandon the notion of a "reward centre" in the hypothalamus and instead look for a noradrenaline system that passes along the medial forebrain bundle.

Fluorescence staining techniques for brain sections have enabled precise extensive mapping of the neuronal pathways containing dopamine, noradrenaline and serotonin. In the reticular formation, two groups of noradrenaline neurones ascend in the medial forebrain bundle and terminate in the hypothalamus, neocortex and parts of the limbic forebrain, including the septal area and hippocampal formation. Ungerstedt (1971) demonstrated that there is a dorsal noradrenaline pathway, which has its cell bodies in the locus coeruleus and passes along the brachium conjunctivum. At the level of the nucleus mamillaris it turns ventrolaterally to meet the ascending dopamine fibres, and the fibres ascend together in the medial forebrain bundle, but have separate projections. The dorsal noradrenaline pathway innervates many areas of the brain, including the cerebral cortex, and the hippocampus. If lesions were made in the brachium conjunctivum at sites that support self-stimulation, fluorescence histochemistry showed that there was an accumulation of noradrenaline in the dorsal pathway from the locus coeruleus (Clavier and Routtenberg, 1974). These results suggest that reward is a consequence of activity in the dorsal noradrenaline pathway to the hippocampus and neocortex.

Further support for the involvement of the dorsal noradrenaline pathway from the locus coeruleus to the cortex was obtained from another study by Crow and his colleagues (Anzelark, Walter, Arbuthnott, Crow and Eccleston, 1975). Rats with electrodes implanted in the locus coeruleus were allowed to press for stimulation for an hour and a control group of rats were stimulated through electrodes which did not support reward. Both groups were sacrificed and a metabolite of noradrenaline was extracted from the cortex, and it was found that there was a marked rise in the level of the metabolite from the cortex of the rewarded rats, but not the cortex of the control animals. If the ascending dorsal noradrenaline pathway from the locus coeruleus in the brain stem is the reward system, then Process *a* of the opponent-process model is activation of this pathway.

V. Alcohol Use

Alcohol is the most commonly used drug in the world and its use is only restricted in Muslim countries. As well as its widespread use, alcohol is the most widely misused and abused drug. The level of abuse in a particular culture seems to be directly proportional to the level of use. In this section we will analyse alcohol use and abuse in terms of the opponent-process model.

A. *Alcohol and the Opponent-process Model*

Most people's first experience of alcohol is pleasurable, and it is usually taken in some sweetened diluted form. The pleasure is more intense if it is taken quickly so that a sizeable dose reaches the brain quickly. The initial "impact" pleasure is followed by a feeling of relaxation that persists for some hours (State *A*). As the alcohol wears off the person experiences mild depression and perhaps some anxiety (the beginnings of partial State *B*). However, when alcohol is taken repeatedly, the same quantity produces less intense pleasure (State *A*) than before, and the dose must be increased in order to produce the same impact and coasting effects. The drinker starts to take the first two or three drinks rapidly to increase the dose reaching the brain. In terms of the opponent-process model, this tolerance effect is the result of the strengthening of an opponent process b and a decrease in the difference $(a - b)$. Continued use of alcohol with escalating doses increases the tolerance effect (Process b) and withdrawal results in abstinence symptoms of depression, restlessness and anxiety (partial State B). The drinker can eliminate these effects by taking more alcohol, until eventually alcohol is required for effective functioning even in routine activities, so that the alcoholic drinks repeatedly and is intoxicated for days (continual cravings). Abstinence at this stage results in severe symptoms of hallucinations, disorientation, severe anxiety, restlessness and tremor (Severe State B). These symptoms are eliminated by alcohol. For the alcoholic the sum $(a - b)$ has become small and so alcohol use is employed to avoid or escape the aversive State B that occurs when the blood alcohol level falls. Thus the drug serves a different function from the initial use which was to produce pleasurable State A, and instead serves to terminate or postpone the unpleasant State B. The alcoholic shows impaired interpersonal relations and social and economic functioning and sometimes disturbed mental functioning. Eventually repeated, excessive use produces liver and brain damage and so use has become abuse.

If the alcoholic abstains completely, the abstinence symptoms decrease gradually because, according to the model, Process b that produces the aversive symptoms (State B) is fading since Process a is no longer being elicited. It might be thought that after these extremely unpleasant withdrawal symptoms the alcoholic would never drink again, but the relapse rate is high. Relapse seems to be due to a desire for the pleasure of State A. After a period of abstinence the difference $(a - b)$ will be increased and the rewarding effects will be large. In addition, conditioned stimuli will still elicit State B and the craving for alcohol.

B. *Alcohol and Brain Reward Systems*

Alcohol produces pleasurable effects in man, and animal studies also show that alcohol has rewarding properties; Deneau (1972) demonstrated that most monkeys would self-administer alcohol and maintain themselves in a state of extreme "intoxication" by repeatedly pressing the injection lever. We have hypothesized that the rewarding effect of the other dependence-producing drugs results from increased activity in the ascending noradrenergic neurones from the locus coeruleus in the brain. There is some evidence that alcohol does increase the release of noradrenaline in the brain stem, but more importantly Duritz and Truitt (1966) have demonstrated that acetaldehyde, the first product of the metabolism of alcohol, releases and depletes brain stem noradrenaline. Thus the pleasurable sensations produced by alcohol are correlated with increased activity in the noradrenaline pathway that is produced by acetaldehyde. This evidence is consistent with the hypothesis that the pleasurable State *A* effects of alcohol result from the release of noradrenaline in the reward pathways which we identified with Process *a* earlier.

These neurochemical studies account for the acute effects of alcohol, but do not explain tolerance or physical dependence, and the opponent Process *b* and State *B*. Increased metabolism by the liver enzymes seems to play only a small part in alcohol tolerance, and so we are left with changes in the central nervous system to explain the opponent process. It seems likely that the partial State *B* can be explained in terms of depletion of noradrenaline, but there do not seem to be any plausible hypotheses for the role of the central nervous system amines in the development of tolerance and physical dependence, that develops after years of boozing.

VI. Eating

"Food is the most commonly eaten substance in the world" (Anon, personal communication) and it is the most widely misused and abused chemical. As the ratio of pleasure to penalty is so small for eating, one would expect that obesity should only be the result of metabolic problems, and yet most obesity results from overeating. The opponent-process model gives a convincing explanation of why this should be so.

A. *Food and the Opponent-process Model*

At first it appears strange that a process as normal as eating should be compared with cigarette smoking or alcohol use, but the opponent-process model has been applied to eating by Solomon (1977). He identified hunger and satiety as the interacting processes which maintain body-weight within fairly narrow limits in the long term. In terms of the model, hunger is the Process *a*, and satiety is the "slave" Process *b* which is elicited by Process *a* and serves to reduce the hedonic quality of that state. Both processes are influenced by many variables, including blood sugar level, body temperature, body fat deposits and stomach loading.

However, in the short-term eating is also controlled by other variables such as the taste, odour and textural qualities of foods. Solomon proposed that the control of eating based on the sensory properties of food is mediated by two other processes that result in taste-pleasure and taste-craving. Taste-craving results from the slave process (Process *b*) to taste-pleasure (Process *a*) and is an aversive motivator which has a fairly rapid decay. Altogether there are four processes controlling eating beahaviour at any given moment, producing satiety and taste-pleasure as positive reinforcers, and hunger and taste-craving as negative reinforcers. During eating, hunger gradually fades causing satiety to gradually increase, but the two taste processes will be constantly interacting with hunger and satiety.

This model can be easily applied to many typical eating experiences and has great intuitive appeal. The first bite of a meal is primarily motivated by hunger, but if food is tasted and eaten its taste fades quickly and then taste-craving the opponent-process will be elicited. Because both taste-craving and hunger are aversive, they will summate and the total motivation for eating will be greater than it was before the first taste, assuming of course that the post-ingestinal effects have not yet significantly activated the satiety system. This would explain the frequently made observation: "I didn't know how hungry I was until I started eating", and the saying of Rabelais "L'appetit vient en mangeant". As more food is ingested, satiety will oppose hunger and eating will decrease unless something is done to increase taste-craving. Solomon described this as the "dessert effect", because by altering the taste of the food to a different quality the taste-craving will become more intense, and at its peak the pleasurable results from this process will exceed the aversive effects and therefore eating will continue.

If a break (say of three minutes) is introduced towards the end of a meal, hunger and satiety will be of similar strength and only taste-craving, occurring as the result of the prior taste pleasure, will be maintaining eating. The break allows the peak of taste-craving to occur and then fade to zero and thus prevent the resumption of eating. Certainly this prediction is consistent with the common saying that leaving the table while still feeling a little hungry is a sensible procedure for those wishing to lose weight with the minimum of will-power.

From these examples it is clear that the opponent-process theory can be easily applied to eating. In the next section we will consider the neural mechanisms which may underly these processes.

B. *Eating and Brain Reward Systems*

A group of scientists at Oxford University have carried out much of the crucial research in identifying the systems which are involved in the interaction of taste and eating (Rolls, 1981). These workers have identified a population of neurones in the lateral hypothalamus and substantia innominata (an area lateral to the lateral hypothalamus) of primates, the activity of which is associated with the taste of food. These neurones are specific in the sense that they only respond to solutions of particular taste and the intensity of the response of these neurones decreases as eating proceeds. Could these neurones form the substrate of the taste-pleasant and taste-aversive processes described in the preceding section?

As eating proceeds we would predict that the activity of taste-pleasure neurones would decrease and that the decrease in firing of these neurones would stop and reverse if, despite the onset of satiation, the food was changed, which is consistent with the findings of Rolls and his colleagues. We would not expect taste-pleasure neurones to be directly involved in changes in hunger, and this is supported by the finding of Rolls that the baseline firing rate of the taste-sensitive neurones is not affected by the transition from hunger to satiation.

It is important that in the studies described above, the behaviour of the primates often corresponded to the effects of feeding to satiety. Thus the animal would reject the food on which he had been fed to satiety, but accepted other foods upon which he had not been fed. In addition, Rolls has studied the eating behaviour of human subjects in conditions comparable to those of the primates. He found that subjects who were given a second course consumed much less if it was of the same food than if it was of a different food. It was also observed that the reported pleasantness of the taste of food which had been eaten to satiety decreased more than for foods which had not been eaten.

It is now pertinent to consider the role of hypothalamic neurones in positive reinforcement produced by eating. As discussed earlier, self-stimulation studies suggested that activity in noradrenergic self-stimulation pathways is pleasurable. It is therefore significant that all of the hypothalamic food neurones discovered by Rolls were activated by electrical stimulation of a number of self-stimulation sites in other regions, and animals would work to obtain stimulation of these neurones in the lateral hypothalamus. The noradrenergic pathways from the locus coeruleus pass close to the taste-sensitive neurones in the hypothalamus, and so it is reasonable to hypothesise that these taste neurones are interconnected with the noradrenaline reward system (Crow, 1972).

Major pieces of evidence on this issue have been collected by Rolls and his colleagues. Rolls recorded from single cells in the lateral hypothalamus in the squirrel monkey during self-stimulation. Some cells responded after a short latency to reinforcing stimulation. These were tested further with food. It was found that some of these units responded when food was in the mouth of a hungry animal, but not when isotonic saline was introduced or when air was blown from a syringe onto the tongue. Some food neurones were activated not only when the hungry monkey tasted food, but even when it saw or smelled food. Thus, these hypothalamic brain stimulation cells were activated selectively by both food and by conditioned stimuli associated with food, the sight and smell of food. This evidence suggests that the brain pathways that mediate reward are interconnected with food neurones.

VII. Smoking

Cigarette smoking is a remarkable phenomenon, and certainly the inhalation of the smoke of burning leaves would be considered a most bizarre practice, were it not for the fact that tens of millions of people in the world today spend a large proportion of their waking lives doing exactly that. Yet, despite the widespread extent of the habit and the almost universal condemnation of the effects of smoking on health, very little is known about the mechanisms which underly the development and the maintenance of the smoking habit. This situation is well illustrated by an editorial in the British Medical Journal which considered the evidence for the involvement of nicotine in smoking and was forced to conclude that ". . . what makes people smoke is still largely a mystery" (Editorial, Br. Med. J., 1977).

A. *Smoking and Opponent-processes*

Solomon and Corbit (1973) argued that they could describe cigarette smoking within the empirical framework of the opponent-process theory of motivation. In the early stages of the development of the smoking habit, the positive affect produced by smoking (State *A*) and other (unstated) social reinforcers are the crucial determinants in the maintenance of the habit. However, the initially weak slave response (State *B*), produced by the termination of State *A*, gradually becomes stronger with the repeated activation of State *A*. A point is eventually reached at which the strength of the aversive state is sufficient to motivate the smoker to smoke, not because of the positive affect it produces but in order to terminate the unpleasant withdrawal effects (State *B*). Thus, according to Solomon and Corbit, the well-addicted smoker is exhibiting avoidance behaviour by smoking so frequently that he rarely lets State *B* occur. However, although they suggest that the same mechanisms operate in smoking as in other forms of drug dependence, we can find little evidence for this assertion.

B. *Smoking, Nicotine and Brain Reward Systems*

In this section we will discuss the possible mechanisms for occurrence of the smoking habit, and compare them with the mechanisms underlying habitual use of other substances. Most researchers assume that nicotine is the pharmacological reinforcer in smoking behaviour, and the evidence for its role is impressive, although there is still insufficient evidence to put this beyond reasonable doubt. Certainly it would be a most remarkable coincidence that hundreds of millions of tobacco smokers in the world today restricted their smoking habits to one particular type of leaf, and this leaf was the *only* one which contained nicotine. A twenty a day, ten puff per cigarette, smoker receives over 70 000 "shots" of nicotine per year. It has been estimated that with inhalation this highly toxic drug reaches the brain in seven seconds, over twice as fast as heroin when mainlined into the arm.

However, there are a large number of concomitant non-pharmacological experiences which accompany these 70 000 doses of drug to the brain, such as the taste and inhalation of the smoke, together with the oral and tactile manipulation of the cigarette. Thus it is not surprising that the pattern of smoking behaviour develops some sort of independence over a lifetime of smoking. In addition, the psychological effects of nicotine are much more subtle than alcohol, and are hard to pin down. In this section we will present evidence that although the psychological effects of nicotine are crucial to the maintenance of the smoking habit in the vast majority of smokers, the mechanisms by which the drug achieves these effects are quite different from those of other habitual substances.

Most other habitually used substances are positively reinforcing because they have psychological effects which are described as pleasurable. If nicotine is producing such effects by acting upon the brain reward mechanisms then there are a number of predictions which can be made (Warburton and Wesnes, 1979).

The first is that smoking should produce feelings of pleasure. However, in contrast to the intense feelings of pleasure which follow the administration of amphetamine or heroin, there are no sensations produced by nicotine or smoking which can be described as highly enjoyable in this way (Johnson, 1942). Furthermore, very few smokers claim to smoke for pleasurable effects and these only do so in terms of the enhancement of other rewarding experiences, for example the pleasurable relaxation of smoking after a meal.

The second prediction is that nicotine would act on the noradrenergic pathways, described earlier, which are believed to control reward. However, although there is some evidence that nicotine affects brain noradrenaline, this effect is secondary to the action of the drug on cholinergic neurones in the midbrain (Fuxe *et al.*, 1977). Furthermore, an elegant series of studies has clearly demonstrated that the ability of rats to determine whether or not they have been injected with nicotine is solely determined by the cholinergic effects of nicotine and not the adrenergic effects (Rosencrans, 1977).

The third prediction is that nicotine would increase self-stimulation responding in animal studies. However, the drug has little effect upon self-stimulation, and it seems that "smoking doses" of the drug have a depressant effect upon this sort of responding (Domino, 1973).

The fourth prediction is that it should be possible to set up an animal model of nicotine self-administration which closely resembles human self-administration. However, while there is a huge literature concerned with the self-administration of heroin, amphetamine, cocaine and the barbiturates, there are very few papers on nicotine self-administration. When animals do self-administer the drug, the amount varies considerably from day to day (Deneau and Inoki, 1967). Some monkeys have been shown to puff cigarette smoke after prolonged training, but when the researchers stopped the tobacco smoke and switched to hot air, no immediate change was observed in the number of puffs the animals took from the tube which had previously delivered the smoke. Although the puffing response of some animals did extinguish over a few days, many did not alter their puffing rates even over a fourteen day period (Jarvik, 1967). Thus while nicotine may have some rewarding properties for some animals, it is extremely weak in relation to other substances and the pattern of use does not closely resemble human smoking.

Finally, if nicotine is acting on the same neural mechanisms as other habitually-used substances, we would expect that human smoking would be decreased by other habitually-used drugs, but amphetamine, heroin and alcohol actually increase cigarette smoking.

Thus as none of the predictions from the brain reward system hypothesis are supported by experimental evidence, we must conclude that the mechanism by which nicotine produces reward is not the same as that activated by alcohol, food and other habitually-used substances.

An alternative possibility is that nicotine acts as a negative reinforcer, and certainly both animal and human studies provide much support for this action. Russell *et al.* (1974) found that many smokers claimed to smoke when they were anxious or angry, and there is much laboratory evidence that not only does smoking reduce feelings of anxiety and aggression, but that it also reduces objective measures of tension. In a recent study we found that fifty out of fifty one student smokers smoked more cigarettes in an examination period than in a non-examination period, and they reported that they inhaled the smoke more deeply during the examination period (Warburton *et al.*, 1983). Similar findings have been reported with executives during stressful work periods and drivers performing simulated driving tasks. Thus there would appear to be fairly good evidence that smoking is capable of producing negative reinforcement, but it seems that the mechanisms are not the same as those for tranquillizers (Warburton and Wesnes, 1979).

There are three main pieces of evidence for this statement. The first is that the direct neurochemical effects of nicotine are to increase the activity in cholinergic pathways, while anxiolytics typically decrease the activity in cholinergic and serotonergic pathways, and increase the activity in noradrenergic pathways. The second is that nicotine's action upon the electrical activity of the brain closely resembles that produced by arousing stimuli, whereas other tranquillizers produce changes which are indicative of a relaxed state with lowered mental alertness. Finally, tranquillizers should reduce smoking if they were acting upon common brain mechanisms, but there has been no evidence of such an effect. Thus, there is behavioural evidence that nicotine acts as a negative reinforcer, but the mechanism of action is not the same as that of tranquillizers.

How then does nicotine provide reinforcement? We propose that nicotine increases mental efficiency and, by enabling greater mastery of the environment, is rewarding. Nicotine does this by increasing the activity in the ascending reticular cholinergic pathways, which travel from the ventral tegmental area to all parts of the cortex (Warburton and Wesnes, 1979). This increased activity results in a pattern of electrical activity at the cortex which is characteristic of heightened alertness and efficient information processing. Thus smoking should improve human concentration, and our research during the last eight years bears this out. In one task we have found that performance after smoking is actually improved. This finding has now been replicated in six separate studies, and the improvement takes the form of both an increase in the speed and accuracy of performance over the rested baseline level, and sometimes a decrease in the already small number of errors. Nicotine was the crucial ingredient of cigarettes because nicotine tablets produce the same effect in both smokers and non-smokers. In a second series of studies we have demonstrated that nicotine and scopolamine (a cholinergic blocking agent) act in a mutually antagonistic fashion, showing that it is the drug's cholinergic properties which are producing the effects of smoking on attention. This research together with some previous work from other laboratories clearly demonstrates that smoking facilitates performance by improving alertness. Further, using the Stroop test, we have been able to show that nicotine improves performance by reducing distraction (Wesnes and Warburton, 1978). These data provide strong evidence for the claims of many smokers that cigarettes help them think and concentrate. We have administered the Russell Smoking Motives Questionnaire (Russell *et al.*, 1974) to our experimental subjects and 86% of them gave this answer as one of their reasons for smoking, which compares well with 86% for Russell's clinic population and 59% for his hospital workers group.

As we have pointed out the evidence that smoking provides negative reinforcement is fairly strong, but there is little evidence that nicotine is acting in the same way as a tranquillizer. We believe that the increased mental efficiency is also the basis for the negative reinforcing effects, although the way that it helps may differ between individuals or in the same individual in different situations. One of the characteristics of improved alertness and concentration is the ability to attend to particular stimuli while ignoring others. The improved concentration would help to relieve anticipatory stress which precedes various challenges, such as public speaking, meeting strangers, and important conferences, by increasing the confidence of the smoker that he will be able to perform competently in the situation. In addition, the decreased distractability will be anxiety reducing by enabling the individual to ignore stressful distracting thoughts and stimuli, while coping with the task in hand. This explanation resolves the much discussed paradox of nicotine, a "stimulating" drug, having a "tranquillizing" action.

It is now time to return to the application of the opponent-process model to smoking. The positive and negative reinforcing effects of nicotine can be described in terms of State A, but what are the effects of the drug which constitute State B? For most habitually used substances State B is a result of body mechanisms becoming dependent upon the particular substance for normal functioning. Let us now consider the evidence that bodily mechanisms become dependent upon nicotine by looking at the effects of smoking cessation. One of the most prominent researchers in this area has recently reviewed the findings and has concluded that: "The tobacco with-drawal syndrome is characterized objectively by changes in the EEG and cardiovascular function, by decrements in psychomotor performance, and by weight gain. Subjective symptoms of irritability, anxiety, inability to concen-trate, and disturbances in arousal are characteristic of tobacco users in withdrawal . . ." (Shiffman, 1979, p. 178). Thus the subjective reports tally well with the objective measures in showing abstinence symptoms. However, the crucial question is whether these symptoms represent true dependence responses produced by the withdrawal of a chronically-administered drug.

A major problem with drawing this conclusion is that smokers and non-smokers differ in their personality prior to some of them taking up the habit (Cherry and Kiernan, 1978), and we cannot validly compare the state of ex-smokers with that of non-smokers. Secondly, because smoking cessation studies are only carried out after the smoker has stopped a habit that he has indulged in for many years, there is no way of determining what the smoker was like before he took up the habit. It is interesting that the cessation effects correspond to the differences in the behavioural attributes of the personality differences between smokers and non-smokers. Thus smokers are typically more extraverted than non-smokers and it has been found that the degree of extraversion is related inversely to the ability to concentrate and the level of EEG arousal. In addition, smokers are more neurotic than non-smokers and neuroticism is directly related to anxiety and irritability. Thus without nicotine it is not too surprising that such effects are observed, particularly as nicotine reduces anxiety and improves EEG arousal and concentration. Thus we would suggest that the effects of smoking cessation are not withdrawal effects in the classical sense, but simply a return to the pre-smoking state.

However, it is then necessary to explain why a drug which is often chronically administered over decades, does not produce dependence. Note that we are using dependence here in the classical sense of a dependence of the body on the drug for normal functioning. It may well be the case that the smoker becomes dependent upon the beneficial effects of the drug, but this is a different matter. One reason for this may lie in the remarkable similarity between the molecular structure of nicotine and that of acetylcholine. Obviously the brain cannot develop a tolerance for its own transmitters, and so it does not become insensitive to nicotine either. This might also explain the remarkable stability of the smoking habit once it has been established. Smokers show remarkably little change in the number of cigarettes they smoke each day over a lifetime of smoking, which is quite inconsistent with the idea that they are becoming increasingly dependent on nicotine. It is also inconsistent with the idea that they become more tolerant to the effects of the drug. Thus, although in the very early stages of the habit smokers develop a tolerance to some of the more unpleasant effects of nicotine such as nausea, there is no evidence that smokers gradually become tolerant to the other effects of smoking.

VIII. Conclusion

In view of the evidence considered in this chapter, it seems that although the opponent-process model can be used to describe eating, drinking and smoking and is useful for various types of habitual substance use, the underlying mechanisms are not necessarily the same. In particular, nicotine maintains the smoking habit by quite different mechanisms from the mechanisms by which other substances maintain self-administration. People use nicotine because it improves the efficiency of coping with situations. Firstly, it can help the person think and concentrate and be more successful (positive reinforcement). Secondly, experience of this enhanced efficiency will reduce an individual's anticipatory stress about their behavioural competence, and thirdly by enabling the individual to ignore stressful, distressing and distracting thoughts it will be anxiety reducing (both effects being negatively reinforcing). The effects of smoking cessation are well documented, but because of the absence of evidence of nicotine tolerance we believe that the most suitable explanation is that these symptoms are a return to the pre-drug state, as opposed to the chronic dependence symptoms observed with the withdrawal of other habitually-used substances. Thus, nicotine acts in a completely different way from other habitually used substances and ignorance of this fact has contributed to the limited success of most smoking cessation strategies.

Acknowledgement

The research from our laboratory was supported by Carreras-Rothmans Ltd., the Medical Research Council and the Tobacco Research Council.

Further Reading

Royal College of Psychiatrists (1979). "Alcohol and Alcoholism". Tavistock, London.
A good general account of the effects of alcohol on the brain and the consequences of repeated use.
Eysenck, H. J. (1981). "The Causes and Effects of Smoking". Maurice Temple Smith, London.
A rigorous analysis of the smoking motives, including genetic data.
Monro, J. F. (1979). "The Treatment of Obesity". M.T.P. Press, London.
An outline of the major factors in obesity and the implications for treatment of the condition.

References

Anzelark, G. M., Walter, D. S., Arbuthnott, G. W., Crow, T. J. and Eccleston, D. (1975). The relationship between noradrenaline turnover in cerebral cortex and electrical self-stimulation through electrodes in the region of locus coeruleus. *J. Neurochem.* 24, 677.
Balter, M. B. (1974). Drug abuse: a conceptual analysis and overview of the current situation. *In* "Drug Use: Epidemiological and Sociological Approaches" (E. Josephson and E. E. Carroll, eds), pp. 3–21. Wiley and Sons, New York.
Cherry, N. and Kiernan, K. (1978). A longitudinal study of smoking and personality. *In* "Smoking Behaviour: Physiological and Psychological Influences" (R. E. Thornton, ed.), pp. 12–18. Churchill Livingstone, Edinburgh, London and New York.
Clavier, R. M. and Routtenberg, A. (1974). Ascending monoamine-containing fiber pathways related to intracranial self-stimulation; histochemical fluorescence study. *Brain Res.* 72, 25.
Crow, T. J. (1972). Catecholamine-containing neurones and electrical self-stimulation, Part 1 (a review of some data), *Psychol. Med.* 2, 414.
Deneau, G. A. (1972). The measurement of addiction potential by self-injection experiment in monkeys. *In* "Drug Abuse" (W. Keup, ed.), pp. 73–79. C. C. Thomas, Springfield, Illinois.
Deneau, G. A. and Inoki, R. (1967). Nicotine self-administration in monkeys. *Ann. N.Y. Acad. Sci.* 142, 277–279.
Deutsch, J. A. and Deutsch, D. (1966). "Physiological Psychology." Dorsey Press, Homewood, Illinois.

Domino, E. F. (1973). Neuropsychopharmacology of nicotine and tobacco smoking. *In* "Smoking Behavior: Motives and Incentives" (W. L. Dunn, Jr., ed.), pp. 5–31. V. H. Winston and Sons, Washington, D.C.

Duritz, G. and Truitt, E. E., Jr. (1966). Importance of acetaldehyde in the action of ethanol on brain norepinepherine and 5-hydroxytryptamine. *Biochem. Pharmacol.* **15**, 711–715.

Editorial (1977). Do people smoke for nicotine? *Brit. Med. J.*, 1041–1042.

Fuxe, K., Agnati, L., Eneroth, P., Gustafsson, J.-Å., Hokfelt, J., Löfstrom, A., Skett, B., and Skett, P. (1977). The effect of nicotine on central catecholamine neurons and genadotrophia secretion. *Med. Biol.* **55**, 148–157.

Huang, Y. H. and Routtenberg, A. (1971). Lateral hypothalamic self-stimulation pathways in *Rattus norvegicus*. *Physiol. Behav.* **7**, 419.

Jarvik, M. E. (1967). Tobacco smoking in monkeys. *Ann. N.Y. Acad. Sci.* **142**, 280–297.

Johnson, L. M. (1942). Tobacco smoking and nicotine. *Lancet* **2**, 742.

Olds, J. (1962). Hypothalamic substrates of reward. *Physiol. Rev.* **42**, 554–604.

Olds, J. and Milner, P. M. (1954). Positive reinforcement produced by electrical stimulation of septal area and other regions of rat brain. *J. Comp. Physiol. Psychol.* **47**, 419.

Olds, J. and Olds, M. E. (1963). Approach-avoidance analysis of rat diencephalon. *J. Comp. Neurol.* **120**, 259.

Rolls, E. T. (1981). Central nervous mechanisms related to feeding and appetite. *Br. Med. Bull.* **37**, 131–134.

Rosencrans, J. A. (1977). Nicotine as a Discriminative Stimulus to Behavior: its characterization and relevance to smoking behavior. *In* "Cigarette Smoking as a Dependence Process" (N. A. Krasnegor, ed.), pp. 58–69. NIDA Research Monograph 23.

Russell, M. A. H., Peto, J. and Patel, U.A. (1974). The classification of smoking by factorial structure of motives. *J. Roy. Stat. Soc.* A **137**, 313–333.

Shiffman, S. M. (1979). The tobacco withdrawal syndrome. *In* "Cigarette Smoking as a Dependence Process (N. A. Krasnegor, ed.). NIDA Research Monograph **23**, Rockville, Maryland.

Smart, R. G. (1974). Addiction, dependency, abuse, or use: which are we studying with epidemiology? *In* "Drug Use: Epidemiological and Sociological Approaches" (E. Josephson and E. E. Carroll, eds), pp. 23–42. Wiley and Sons, New York.

Solomon, R. L. (1977). *In* "Learning Mechanisms in Food Selection" (L. M. Barker, M. R. Best and M. Domjau, eds). University Press.

Solomon, R. L. and Corbit, J. D. (1973). An opponent-process theory of motivation: II Cigarette addiction. *J. Abnorm. Psychol.* **81**, 158–171.

Solomon, R. L. and Corbit, J. D. (1974). An opponent-process theory of motivation: I Temporal dynamics of affect. *Psychol. Rev.* **81**, 119–145.

Stein, L. (1962). Effects and interactions of imipramine, chlorpromazine, reserpine and amphetamine on self-stimulation. Possible neurophysiological basis of depression. *In* "Recent Advances in Biological Psychiatry" (J. Wortis, ed.), pp. 288–308. Plenum Press, New York.

Stein, L. (1964). Self-stimulation of the brain and the central stimulant action of amphetamines. *Fed. Proc.* **23**, 836–849.

Stein, L. and Wise, C. D. (1969). Release of norepinephrine from hypothalamus and amygdala by rewarding medial forebrain bundle stimulation and amphetamine. *J. Comp. Physiol. Psychol.* **67**, 189–198.

Ungerstedt, U. (1971). Stereotaxic mapping of the monamine pathways in the rat brain. *Acta. Physiol. Scand. suppl.* 367, 1–48.

Warburton, D. M. (1981). Neurochemical bases of behaviour. *Br. Med. Bull.* 37, 121–125.

Warburton, D. M. and Wesnes, K. A. (1979). The role of electrocortical arousal in the smoking habit. *In* "Electrophysiological effects of nicotine" (A. Remond and C. Izard, eds), pp. 183–200. Elsevier, Amsterdam.

Warburton, D. M., Wesnes, K. A. and Revell, A. D. (1983). Personality factors in self-medication by smoking, to be published. *In* "Response Variability to Psychotropic Drugs" (W. Janke, ed.). Pergamon, London.

Wesnes, K. A. and Warburton, D. M. (1978). The effects of cigarette smoking and nicotine tablets upon human attention. *In* "Smoking Behaviour: Physiological and Psychological Influences" (R. E. Thornton, ed.), pp. 131–147. Churchill Livingstone, Edinburgh, London and New York.

Wise, C. D. and Stein, L. (1969). Facilitation of brain self-stimulation by central administration of norepinephrine. *Science* 163, 299.

15 Sexual Arousal in the Human: Love, Chemistry or Conditioning?

Marvin Zuckerman

Abstract Although scientists may never be able to define the complex emotion of "love" they have been making considerable progress on the subject of sex. Methods of measuring sexual physiological arousal, by measuring genital changes, have opened the field of research to intensive study. The results show that sexual arousal is a complex phenomenon influenced by stimuli, cognition, biochemical factors and personality characteristics. Although based on unconditioned reflexive responses, sexual arousal is regulated by everything that affects the brain; conditioned stimuli may elicit arousal and voluntary or involuntary inhibitory factors may override the effects of the stimulation.

The sex hormones and central biogenic amines may affect the degree of arousability at a given time, but the range of stimuli that elicit arousal seems to be determined by past conditioning. Sex is not "just chemistry" or "just conditioning"; it is a function of both.

I. Introduction

"Birds do it, bees do it, even educated fleas do it, lets do it, lets fall in love." "Falling in love" is Cole Porter's sly euphemism for sexual activity, and the line from his song points up the phylogenetic universality of reproductive sex. But sexual behaviour is far from a universal instinctual pattern in humans, primates or other species.

Sexual behaviour in non-human species may, or may not, occur depending on a variety of biological and environmental conditions. Monkeys raised in socially isolated conditions may never do it (although they may attempt to). In some species only a minority of the more dominant and aggressive males do it, while the others are excluded from the activity. We all know that many humans never do it or do it only sporadically and think about it a lot. The transformation of sexual arousal into sexual activity is dependent upon other acquired and innate traits of the organism.

PHYSIOLOGICAL CORRELATES OF HUMAN
BEHAVIOUR
ISBN 0-12-273901-9

Is sex a drive in which arousal of the inclination to do it is dependent on sensitization of neural structures by hormones produced by the gonads (sex glands)? In the musical comedy "Guys and Dolls", Sky Masterson and his girl sing a charming duet in which they debate the nature of their mutual attraction. "Its love" she sings while the cynical gambler replies "No, its just chemistry." But many persons whose chemistry is quite normal do not do it and feel no inclination to do it. Recent studies of sexual dysfunction have revealed that in addition to those who want to do it but cannot, there are a great number of persons who feel insufficient desire to do it even though they can. On the other hand there are many who are inclined to and do do it at reasonable intervals despite extremely low levels of the hormones which are supposed to be the requisite for the drive.

Is sex a learned drive and sexual behaviour a conditioned response? Freud and others have argued that while sexual arousal is unlearned, the forms that sexual behaviour assumes and the objects of sexual activity are learned in a complex interaction between civilization and "eros". According to Freud sexual motives may underlie much behaviour that is not obviously sexual, including the "disinterested" scientific study of sex or any other field of human knowledge.

Whatever the motive for sex research a great quantity of it has been done, particularly in the last 30 years. Until the 1960's most of the research on the physiological aspects of sexual arousal was confined to non-human species. Most information, and considerable amounts of misinformation, came from second-hand reports of behaviour or cognition from cultural anthropologists, psychoanalysts, and compendiums of sexual deviation such as the classics of Havelock Ellis and Kraft-Ebbing. While such data contributed some interesting speculations, the inadequate sampling of the populations, the theoretical biases of the observers, and the inevitable distortions by the subjects of study, restricted the scientific value of the work. As Freud himself noted, the men (of his time) "wear a thick overcoat, a pack of lies, to conceal it [their sexuality] as though it were always bad weather in the world of sex."

It was not until the monumental survey studies by Kinsey and his colleagues in the 1950's that any large scale survey of sexual practices and experience in the general population was forthcoming. But even this study was not based on adequate sampling techniques and, despite some ingenious methods of obtaining interview data, suffered from the essential limitations of all self report data.

Another important landmark in sexual research was the publication of the work by Masters and Johnson in 1966. These studies were based on the physiological recording of sexual response in the human. They were preceded by studies on peripheral autonomic responses, but most of that work dealt with only the first stage of sexual arousal, did not follow the reactions during genital stimulation and orgasm, and did not study the genital reactions. The physiological experiments of Masters and Johnson were not controlled, and little of the data have been presented in a quantified or comparative form, that would enable other investigators to verify the findings in their own populations. They defined 4 stages of sexual arousal: (i) excitement; (ii) plateau, or the high level of arousal usually preceding orgasm; (iii) orgasm; (iv) resolution, or the subsiding of sexual arousal. The physiological reactions, including genital changes, accompanying each of these stages are well described.

The great value of the work of Masters and Johnson was the breaking down of the taboo on direct study of human sexual physiology and behaviour in the laboratory. New methodologies were evolved to study genital responses and with these advances in methodology a great number of hypotheses about sex began to be put to the test of experimental study.

An often repeated expression is that scientific knowledge raises more questions that it answers. In 1971, I reviewed the area of the physiology of human sexual arousal and pointed out many of these new questions (Zuckerman, 1971). In the decade since that review, studies of sexuality have increased with an exponential function. The request to write this chapter inspired me to take another look at this literature to see how many of these questions have been answered. I will try to present the general findings in a manner that is readable for the student who has persevered through the previous chapters of this book. The reader should be warned that I am oversimplifying complex findings for the sake of exposition.

This chapter will be divided into two parts: (i) measurement of sexual arousal; (ii) determinants of sexual arousal and arousability. The writer assumes that a number of basic concepts such as psychophysiological measurement (skin conductance, heart rate, etc.), classical and instrumental conditioning, and others have been mastered from the preceding chapters.

II. Physiological Measurement

Why don't we just ask people if we want to know if they are sexually aroused, or how much they are aroused? One reason is the imperfect correlation between self-report and genital arousal, an issue that will be dealt with later. Most people are not like Mae West who, in a film, asked her partner who was dancing close to her: "Do you really love me or is that just a pencil in your pocket?"

There is no reason to expect a perfect or even a very high correlation between subjective sexual arousal and the physiological state of the genitals. When subjects are asked to rate their sexual arousal on a scale of 1 to 5 from "not at all aroused" to " extremely aroused" the terms defining the scale are likely to have highly individualized meanings for subjects. One person may interpret arousal strictly in terms of felt genital sensations, while another may rely on other body sensations or purely affective feelings related to the stimuli.

A. *Autonomic Activity: non-genital*

Sexual arousal is a specific pattern of activity of the autonomic nervous system. Once the sexual arousal mechanism is activated, by either psychological (visual, auditory or fantasy) or tactual stimuli, an autonomic pattern is seen which consists of diversion of blood flow toward the genital structures and vasocongestion of these tissues. This initial vasocongestion in the genital and secondary (breasts, nipples) sexual areas during the excitement phase is largely mediated by the parasympathetic branch of the autonomic system, but some non-specific sympathetic system arousal, such as a rise in body temperature, sweating, and increase in heart rate or heart rate variability, may also occur. Recordings of these indicators show that large increases are typically seen during genital stimulation, with peaks during orgasm and drops after orgasm if stimulation ceases. A question asked early in the research was whether these measures of sympathetic system arousal were sensitive to excitement produced by psychological stimuli. A second question was whether the arousal measured by autonomic indicators was specific to sexual arousal, or could be produced by other kinds of emotional arousal such as fear or shame.

1. *Skin conductance*

The skin conductance response (SCR) is uniphasic and measures transient changes in arousal produced by a discrete stimulus. It cannot tell us what kind of arousal it reflects; whether the stimulus has produced sexual arousal, fear, anger, disgust, or some combination of these, or some other feeling. When we examine a continuous sequence of stimuli, as in a motion picture, changes in the general level of skin conductance (SC) over larger periods of time may be examined or the number of spontaneously occurring skin conductance responses (No. SCRs) may be evaluated. These findings show that the arousal produced by sexual stimuli, relative to blander stimuli, is generally reflected by greater changes in palmar skin conductance, but they do not tell us whether the response is indicative of sexual arousal or more unpleasant feelings.

When responses to sexual stimuli and stimuli which elicit unpleasant subjective reactions (e.g., Nazi atrocity films) are compared, generally no significant differences are found; both types of stimuli produce electrodermal arousal. When responses of males or females, or heterosexuals and homosexuals, to nudes of the opposite and same sex are compared, the differences in SCR elicited by the stimuli are not impressive, despite differences in subjective responses. When genital reactions are measured, the differences in response to the preferred and nonpreferred sex are much clearer. The SCR and genital response measures are usually not found to be correlated. The results suggest that electrodermal measures reflect general arousal, but do not differentiate between sexual arousal and other kinds of arousal.

2. Heart rate

Masters and Johnson and others, who have recorded heart rate changes from the sexual excitement phase to orgasm and resolution, have found that the heart rate is variable during foreplay but increases sharply when genital stimulation or coitus begins. Heart rate briefly peaks at very high levels during orgasm in both sexes (110 to 180+ beats per minute – bpm), and subsides after orgasm unless stimulation of the female is continued. In which case, heart rate may again increase up to additional orgasms.

The case is less clear for stimulation produced by slides, movies, auditory, or textually presented erotic stimuli. In the majority of experiments heart rate is not significantly higher in response to sexual rather than to neutral stimuli. Even when greater increases or decreases in heart rate are found they are not of great magnitude (typically 5 to 10 bpm), compared to the great increases recorded during masturbation, coitus and orgasm.

Several studies have found that heart rate *decreases* in immediate response to static erotic stimuli and one found this in subjects low in sex guilt. The findings of heart rate decrease in the immediate response to erotic stimuli may reflect a positive interest in these stimuli, while acceleratory reactions may indicate a negative, defensive attitude to the stimuli. A few findings of negative correlations between heart rate change and genital arousal would also support this hypothesis.

3. Pupillary response

Pupillary dilation is controlled by the sympathetic branch, and constriction by the parasympathetic branch, of the autonomic nervous system. Studies by Hess and his colleagues (1965) on pupillary responses to sexual stimuli suggested that dilation of the pupil indicates positive affective arousal while contraction indicates negative arousal in response to such stimuli. These conclusions were based on studies contrasting responses of small numbers of men and women and heterosexual and homosexual males to pictures of nude males and females. Subsequent research using more adequate samples did not support these conclusions. Pupillary dilation is a sign of arousal that may be produced by any kind of novel, intense, or interesting stimuli, but pupillary contraction is primarily a protective reflex response to bright light. Studies have shown a differential response to sexual and neutral stimuli but not generally to male and female sexual stimuli. Furthermore, there are no consistent findings of correlation between pupillary dilation and self-reports of sexual arousal or genital response. The results suggest that the pupillary dilation response is a non-specific measure of arousal.

4. Temperature

Skin temperature changes are undoubtedly part of the advanced stages of sexual arousal. The term "hot" is the most frequently used one to describe the subjective sensation of high sexual arousal. Whether such generalized temperature changes accompany initial excitement is another matter. Most studies have failed to find differential skin-temperature changes to erotic and neutral stimuli. Some studies have reported *decreases* in skin temperature, particularly in the groin region, as blood flow is diverted to the genital areas. Studies using thermographic measurement have confirmed the observation that the abdomen and groin areas cool as blood is diverted to the genitals during plateau and orgasmic phases. Skin temperatures in non-genital areas do not seem to be sensitive indices of sexual arousal.

5. Muscle tension

Masters and Johnson have reported that general muscle tension increases as orgasm is approached. Orgasm itself is usually characterized by the discharge of muscle tensions in involuntary muscle spasms. But such muscle tension is a sign of high levels of sympathetic system arousal that would probably be incompatible with the parasympathetic arousal which predominates during the excitement phase and might prevent arousal. Studies that used forehead electromyogram measures (EMG) have found no relationship to sexual arousal produced by erotic stimuli. However, forehead tension is an unreliable index of tensions in other muscle groups and measures of muscle tension in many other areas should be studied.

6. Pulse amplitude

Measurement of changes in finger pulse amplitude have been employed as a measure of arousal. Most studies have not found a differential arousal of finger pulse amplitude to erotic and non-erotic stimuli. This would not seem to be a useful measure of sexual arousal. As we will see, pulse amplitude in the vagina has been shown to be a very good measure of sexual arousal.

7. Blood pressure

Masters and Johnson reported that blood pressure elevations in the excitement phase increase "in direct parallel to rising tension." Other studies have confirmed their findings of high peaks of systolic blood pressure during orgasm. Blood pressure is one measure that often shows a graded response to psychological stimuli of different intensities (e.g., erotic movies as opposed to slides). Studies using blood pressure as a dependent variable have found differential response to erotic and neutral stimuli, or a graded response from stimuli of less intensity to those of greater intensity. However, like other peripheral autonomic measures, blood pressure does not differentiate between responses to erotic and suspenseful or depressing films.

8. *Respiratory rate*

The hyperventilation (heavy breathing) response was said by Masters and Johnson to be more characteristic in the late plateau phase (approaching orgasm) of sexual arousal. Studies using respiration rate, have not found a differential response to erotic and non-erotic stimuli. While respiratory rate may reflect the arousal produced by intercourse, it is at a rate compatible with the mild exercise of that activity. The measure is not a sensitive index of the initial excitement produced by psychological stimuli.

9. *Summary*

Of all the non-genital autonomic measures examined, only the electrodermal (skin-conductance) and blood pressure measures show any sensitivity to the sexual arousal produced by psychological stimuli. During the plateau and orgasm stages of coitus mobilization of the entire autonomic system is more apparent and changes can be seen on almost any kind of measure of autonomic arousal. The two measures that are more sensitive to the more subtle arousal of the excitement phase do not differentiate between sexual and dysphoric arousal. Only direct genital measures can be used for this discrimination and these will be discussed next.

B. *Genital Measures*

1. *Penile*

Penile erection may be reflexly stimulated by tactile stimulation of the penis or "psychogenically' from impulses passing down the spinal cord from the brain. Severance of the spinal cord above the sacral level prevents psychogenic arousal of penile erection but does not interfere with the reflexive tactile pathway. Feedback sensations from the body create sexual feelings. Such feelings may be impaired by spinal cord lesions of the ascending sensory pathways. The extent of the impairment of "feeling" depends on how far down the lesion is in the spinal cord; the further down, the more areas of the body are still contributing to the sensory feedback. However, as long as the sacral section of the cord (containing the reflexive centres for erection) is intact, penile erection can occur, even in the absence of "feelings" of sexual arousal.

Penile erection is accomplished through dilation of the penile arteries, diverting larger quantities of blood into the arterioles in the spongy tissue which runs through the penis. This response is believed to be under parasympathetic innervation. Erection may be lost when sympathetic arousal causes constriction of the penile arteries (as when anxiety causes impotence). However, the high sympathetic arousal in the plateau and orgasmic phases does not interfere with, and even enhances, penile tumescence. Sympathetic and parasympathetic arousal seem to be antagnostic in the initial arousal phase but synergestic in the plateau and orgasmic phases.

There are two major approaches to the measurement of penile erection: measures of penile circumference and measures of penile volume. In circumference measures a ring or loop is placed around the penis, which changes in circumference with variations in the diameter of the penis at the point where the loop is attached. The volumetric devices are sealed plethysmographic chambers which enclose the penis and record changes in volume through a water or air medium. The air-filled plethysmographs have been used more widely than the water-filled devices.

The literature on both circumference and volume devices has shown that they are reasonably sensitive to sexual arousal produced by erotic stimuli and further discriminate between responses to preferred and non-preferred sexual objects of heterosexuals and homosexuals. They are the only physiological measures that can reliably discriminate sexual arousal from other types of emotional arousal in the male.

2. Vaginal

Just as penile erection is due to a vasocongestion in the tissues of the penis, female sexual arousal is expressed in the vasocongestion of the vagina, clitoris and labia. The blood flow to the vagina, and ensuing vasocongestion, produces the vaginal lubrication, a kind of "sweating" reaction, which facilitates penile penetration.

The first attempts to measure female sexual arousal in a quantifiable fashion consisted of devices to measure temperature changes or changes in the acidity (pH) of the vaginal secretions. This attempt was followed by a more successful effort to measure blood flow in the vaginal wall using thermistors attached to a diaphragm ring, or a photoelectric cell which measured light transmission through the vaginal capillary bed. But the device which has become most widely used in the last several years is the vaginal plethysmograph developed by Sintchak and Geer (1975).

The device consists of a clear acrylic plastic probe about the size of a menstrual tampon. The probe contains a light source (lamp) and a photocell.

The light illuminates the vaginal tissue and is reflected back to the photocell surface which is in direct contact with the vaginal wall. Changes in blood flow make the capillaries more or less opaque and thereby change the amount of reflected light. These changes are recorded on two channels: one system used at low sensitivity (DC) measuring blood volume changes, and a second channel (AC coupled) which registers pulse volume (pressure pulse). Pressure pulse is said to measure the distensibility of the vascular bed in response to changes in blood pressure resulting from the heart forcing blood into the arterial system" (Geer *et al.*, 1974, p. 561).

There are several problems with this type of measurement. Unlike the male measurement of penile circumference, that can be calibrated for direct measurement of a physical property of the organ (centimeters-size), the blood volume and pulse pressure have no calibration scale and changes are measured in centimeter change on the recording paper. Relative within-subject comparisons can be made during one session if there is no change in position of the probe. Comparisons of subjects on change scores can be made, but to the extent that changes are influenced by differences in initial levels (law of initial limits). Variations between individuals may introduce error or impreciseness in these comparisons. The light source may emit enough heat to change the local blood flow. The device has been modified by using an infrared light-emitting diode which generates less heat, but this device is more subject to movement artifact (Heiman, 1977).

Despite these problems in measurement, the vaginal plethysmograph has shown a sensitivity to a range of sexual arousal from excitement produced by psychological stimuli to the more intense arousal produced by masturbation and orgasm. Like the male penile measurements, it discriminates between responses to erotic and non-erotic stimuli. Heiman feels that the vaginal pulse pressure is more sensitive to arousal-producing stimuli and better correlated with subjective arousal than the blood-volume change measure.

3. Labial temperature

Henson *et al.* (1977) have reported a method for assessing female sexual arousal that may provide a measure with a known physical scale: temperature. The device consists of a thermistor attached with a clip to the minor-labia at a comfortable tension. While skin temperature measures have not proven to be sensitive to erotic stimuli (see previous section), Henson *et al.* have found increases of labial temperature in women exposed to an erotic film that were larger than those in response to a non-erotic film. Henson and Rubin (1978) found high correlations between the labial temperature measures and vaginal blood volume using the Sintchak and Geer probe, but subjective arousal correlated more highly with labial temperature ($r = 0.84$) than with vaginal blood volume ($r = 0.40$).

4. Anal

Although the anus is not, properly speaking, a genital organ, Masters and Johnson observed that anal contractions during orgasm were synchronized with vaginal contractions in the female and penile contractions in the male. Bohlen and Held (1979) developed an anal probe to measure these contractions. Their device registers increased, irregular activity during the excitement produced by masturbation and a series of high amplitude regular contractions during orgasm. Little research has been done using this device as a measure of arousal in response to psychological stimuli.

C. Biochemical Measures

The role of sex hormones in the control of human sexual behaviour is an issue that will be addressed in the second major section of this chapter. In this section I will look at the response of these hormones, as well as other biochemicals, to sexual stimulation.

1. Sex hormones

There have been only a few studies of the effects of sexual stimulation and coitus or masturbation on levels of gonadotropic and gonadal hormones. One investigator (Fox; see Fox et al., 1972) obtained blood samples of a single male subject before and during coitus and within 5 minutes after ejaculation. He also studied levels in 7 subjects before and immediately after masturbation. Testosterone levels in samples of blood collected shortly before orgasm were almost always higher than the control values, taken before coitus or masturbation, suggesting some elevation of testosterone by sexual arousal. Levels of testosterone were also higher than control values in samples collected within 5 minutes after orgasm. There was no difference in levels collected just before and just after orgasm in the one subject in coitus, or the 8 subjects in masturbation. While one cannot generalize too far from these limited samples, the results suggest that sexual arousal may elevate testosterone but that orgasm and ejaculation have no immediate effects in testosterone levels. Other investigators have found increases in testosterone and luteinizing hormone (LH) in male subjects, who have been watching sexually arousing films; these increases were not seen after the subjects watched neutral films.

2. Non-specific arousal measures from blood

Other kinds of biochemicals including the peripheral catecholamines (adrenaline and noradrenaline) and free fatty acid (FFA) have also shown some increase in response to erotic films. Although these measures increased more in response to erotic films than to neutral or merely romantic "love" films, the levels during erotic arousal did not exceed those reached after viewing films producing unpleasant arousal such as anxiety or depression.

3. Acid phosphotase (AP)

Acid phosphotase may be found in urine or blood. In men, urinary AP may be produced by secretions from the prostate gland discharged into the urinal tract during sexual excitement or at other times. Studies have shown elevated urinary AP levels in heterosexual men, but not in women, after viewing heterosexual erotic films. Homosexual males did not respond to the same films. Barclay and Little (1972) found that the AP secretion increased in response to a sexual videotape, in contrast to the lack of increase in response to videotapes eliciting anger, anxiety, or laughter. Another study found that sex guilt decreased AP secretion.

4. Summary

There is some limited evidence that increased levels of sex hormones (testosterone and LH) are produced during sexual arousal. Acid phosphotase (AP) in the urine of males also seems to increase as a function of sexual arousal. Non-specific arousal of the sympathetic nervous system may also be produced by erotic stimulation as reflected in blood levels of adrenaline, noradrenaline and free-fatty acids. However, like the peripheral autonomic measures, skin conductance and blood pressure, these changes in adrenaline, noradrenaline and free fatty acids are not specific to sexual arousal, but are seen in dysphoric arousal as well.

III. Relationships between Subjective Arousal and Physiological Arousal

There are many reasons why reports of subjective arousal might not correlate with measured physiological arousal during sexual stimulation. The verbal report may be distorted by defensiveness or secondary reactions to the sexual arousal. A lack of sensitivity to the physical changes during the sexual arousal may attenuate the relationship. The subjects may have a personal meaning for "sexual arousal" that is broader than simple physical response. Subjective sexual arousal is often measured by a simple self-rating scale of questionable reliability and validity.

Despite these problems, male genital arousal generally correlates between + 0·5 and + 0·6 with subjective ratings of sexual arousal. The only exceptions to this moderately high range of correlation is found in subjects who have reason to deny their arousal, for instance rapists who report less arousal to rape scenes than their penile tumescence indicates.

The correlation between vaginal plethysmograph recordings and self-reported arousal in females, is typically lower than that for males, with correlations of $+ 0.4$ to $+ 0.5$ in some samples, and lower and insignificant correlations in a few studies. Heiman (1977) found that no male ever reported a lack of arousal during large erections, but that 42% of females claimed to experience no sexual arousal in periods where blood volume measures were maximal. Females showed higher relationships between the vaginal pulse amplitude measure and subjective arousal, coming close to the high relationship found for men on this kind of measure.

There is no question that the cues of physical sexual arousal are more salient for men than they are for women. This anatomical reality may have more profound effects on the nature of sexuality in men and women than is generally realized. For instance the higher proportion of males than females masturbating shortly after puberty may be a function of the more conspicuous penile reactions to internal and external stimulation. Some of the therapies for "pre-orgasmic" women incorporate sensitivity to cues of sexual arousal in themselves. Such cues may be discriminated better by sexually experienced women.

IV. Determinants of Sexual Arousal

A. *Stimuli*

Visual and auditory stimuli seem to be the primary source of initial sex excitation in humans, in contrast to the more powerful role of the olfactory sense in other mammals. There is some evidence, however, that the same volatile acids that have sex-attractant properties for males in infra-human primates are produced by human women (Michael *et al.*, 1975). Such olfactory stimuli have not been used in experiments on humans though, so I will focus on the visual and auditory stimuli that have been popular.

1. Sexual relevance

In the previous section the criterion of differential response to sexually relevant and non-relevant stimuli has been used to evaluate the adequacy of different response measures of sexual arousal. Generally, the genital physiological measures plus some biochemical ones, such as acid phosphotase (AP) and perhaps the sex hormones such as LH and testosterone, did reveal differential response to sexual and non-sexual stimuli. In recent years, research has investigated the specific aspects of sexual stimuli that produce arousal.

A hypothesis by Kinsey is that women respond in general less to visual sexual stimuli and less to more explicitly sexual stimuli than to stimuli that produce romantic fantasies. Studies of self-reports of reactions to erotic stimuli support this hypothesis, but studies of genital reactions show that as many women as men respond to such stimuli. The magnitudes of male and female genital responses cannot be compared since they are based on different kinds of measurement. But it is interesting that womens' vaginas respond to explicit "non-redeeming" erotic stimuli as much as they do to erotic stimuli with more romantic elements (Heiman, 1977). Furthermore, purely romantic stimuli (audiotapes) do not elicit as much genital arousal *in either sex* as more blatantly erotic stimuli. Films of group sex usually elicit self reports of "disgust" in females, but one study showed that such portrayals elicited the greatest amount of vaginal arousal in women, in contrast to more conventional erotic scenes.

One caveat to the conclusion that women are as physiologically aroused as men to explicit sexual stimuli is the fact that a greater proportion of men than women actually volunteer for such experiments. Participating women may constitute a highly select sample of the female population, with only the least inhibited women volunteering.

Both sexes show more genital response to sexual scenes presented in movies than in slides, or in self-generated fantasy. Males respond more to film scenes of women who are nude, or in the act of undressing, than to clothed women. They also respond more to sexually suggestive non-verbal behaviour, such as swinging hips and smiles, than to non-erotic behaviour. Heterosexual males responding to static pictures of females show more penile response to the pubic area than to breasts, more to breasts than to legs, and more to female legs than to landscape scenes. Homosexual males show a similar hierarchy of response to pictures of other males: (i) pubic; (ii) face, rear; (iii) legs and chest. Other studies of homosexuals, and homosexual and heterosexual paedophiles, show specific arousal directly related to pictures of their favoured object choices, or films showing homosexual rather than films showing heterosexual activity. Bisexuals show the same pattern of response as homosexuals: greater penile response to sexual activities between males, than between males and females.

2. Disinhibition

The prospect of seeing erotic stimuli tends to arouse anxiety and guilt in some persons and these reactions may interfere with sexual arousal. In one study of males, penile volume responses to erotic stimuli tended to increase over trials while skin conductance responses decreased. Another study showed a decrease in heart rate with repeated trials. Studies have shown a greater vaginal response of women to erotic films presented in the second session than to the same films presented in the first session. There is even some evidence that if an erotic stimulus is preceded by a non-erotic stimulus the arousal is greater than that produced if the erotic stimulus is presented first. All of these results suggest that disinhibition by an initial experience with another erotic stimulus, or even a neutral stimulus, may reduce anxiety in the situation and thereby increase response to the subsequent erotic stimulus.

3. Habituation

Beyond the disinhibition effect, continued exposure to erotic stimuli may decrease their novelty value and thereby dampen sexual arousal. A study (Michael and Zumpfe, 1978) was done of sexual behaviour in male rhesus monkeys who were paired regularly over a period of three and a half years with females made continuously receptive by daily injections of oestrodiol (a condition analogous to the human one where female receptivity is not restricted by the menstrual cycle). Despite the fact that each male was paired with four different female partners they soon tired of their "harem" and drastically reduced their sexual behaviour. The introduction of a new group of four females resulted in an abrupt increase in potency. The replacement of the new females by the old ones resulted in an immediate return to the habituated, low levels of sexual activity seen previously.

A similar phenomenon is seen in human response to pornography. A group of male subjects exposed to a pornographic "cafeteria" for 5 days a week for three weeks showed a large initial rise in acid phosphotase (AP) on the first day, and a sharp decline on the second day and thereafter. Time spent looking at the erotic stimuli also declined, although more gradually than AP. This group showed a decline in penile response to new erotic films presented after the three week period, in contrast to a control group not sated on pornography. There was a recovery of penile response to an erotic film in the experimental group after a 3 week "rest" period.

4. Conditioning

Stimuli may acquire their capacity for producing sexual arousal through classical conditioning if they are somehow associated with an unconditioned stimulus which reflexly elicits arousal. In higher order conditioning, a stimulus which has been strongly conditioned can be used to condition a new stimulus. The sight of the nude form of the opposite sex, for instance, might be associated with another stimulus which in turn would be conditioned to elicit sexual arousal. It is also possible that some stimuli, such as the nude form, are "biologically prepared" to be easily conditioned while others would be more difficult to condition.

A number of case studies and some better controlled group studies have used tactual stimulation of the genitals, or masturbation, as an unconditioned stimulus, and slides of nude sex objects or recorded voices as conditioned stimuli. These studies have been done in the context of treating heterosexual dysfunction or changing object preferences of homosexuals, paedophiles, or fetishists. The studies that have employed physiological measures have generally shown changes in sexual arousal as a function of the conditioning, although the therapeutic gains are often lost where they are in opposition to long established conditioning patterns. However, the studies are of interest in suggesting how sexual arousal patterns might be established through conditioning.

Personality differences in conditionability have been found. Extraverts conditioned more readily to a stimulus associated with sexual arousal than introverts, and neurotics more readily acquired an inhibitory response conditioned to dearousal than stable persons (Kantorwitz, 1978).

Instrumental aversive conditioning has been extensively used in the treatment of homosexuals and others who want to change their object arousal patterns. The usual method is to present nude pictures of the current objects (nude males for male homosexuals) followed by electric shock. Pictures of nudes of the opposite sex are then presented without shock (relief from shock). Generally, changes in penile tumescence patterns are established, with increased erection in response to heterosexual as opposed to homosexual objects. The same effects have been accomplished through "covert sensitization", that is by following verbally stimulated fantasies of homosexual arousal with unpleasant images of nausea, vomiting, or embarrassment. While the immediate conditioning effects of such treatments are easy to demonstrate, their long term effectiveness depends on many factors not under the control of the therapist. What has been counter-conditioned can easily be reconditioned, or new patterns of arousal may be aversively counter-conditioned by subsequent life experiences, for example a humiliating failure of performance in a heterosexual encounter. But apart from their therapeutic effectiveness, the treatments suggest the role of punishment in producing inhibitions of sexual arousal.

Instrumental reward conditioning may also affect sexual arousal. One method is to reward increments or decrements in penile tumescence with a signal of reward. Such signals may be used to increase or decrease erection. Biofeedback has been used in a similar fashion. The subject is simply told to keep on (or off) a light or tone and the stimulus is hooked up with the recording of penile tumescence so that increases (or decreases) of specific magnitudes turn the stimulus on (or off). A usual type of control is a yoked feedback group in which the feed-back stimuli are not contingent on the subject's own penile responses. These instrumental methods have also demonstrated control of sexual arousal by consequent reinforcements. How do subjects control their own erections? Probably through relaxation and erotic fantasies to stimulate erection, and distraction or other cognitive devices to inhibit erection. One study showed that subjects with high levels of tension, reflected in high and irregular cardiac and respiratory responses, could only produce jerky and insubstantial erections in contrast to the smoothly increasing erections produced by more relaxed subjects. High sympathetic system arousal of the type produced by "fear of performance" is antagonistic to the parasympathetic arousal necessary for initial erection. What these studies of positive reinforcement suggest is that the sensations produced by sexual arousal may be employed as positive reinforcers in a relaxed, non-threatening atmosphere. This is precisely what happens in the "sensate focusing" technique of Masters and Johnson where couples are encouraged to provide tactual stimulation but refrain from attempts at intercourse. The arousal produced is reinforcing to patients who had thought their sexuality was "dead".

B. Cognitive Factors

Although sex is not "all in the head", the head (cognition) plays a major role in sexual arousal as well as in sexual behaviour. Since male sexual arousal is a conspicuous response, most males learn during adolescence to inhibit the erection response under socially inappropriate conditions. Laboratory studies have demonstrated that instructions to inhibit penile tumescence while watching an erotic film are usually sufficient to reduce erections by at least 50%, although one study showed that feedback information of the erectile response was necessary to effect inhibition (presumably the internal feedback from the penis itself is not as sensitive as the mechanical feedback devices). The inhibition is not accomplished by avoiding looking at the erotic stimulus since the subjects have to monitor the film to report a signal. Even forcing the subjects to describe the film, thus preventing covert shift of attention, did not interfere with inhibition of response.

While voluntary inhibition of erection is relatively easy, the production of erection is not so readily accomplished. Laws and Rubin (1969) found that instructions to produce an erection in the absence of an external stimulus did have some results, but the erections were relatively small, short-lived and variable. Other studies have shown some effects when male and female subjects have been asked to fantasize a sexual scene, but the effects are rarely as strong as those produced by external erotic stimuli. However, the combination of instructions and biofeedback of genital changes has produced more substantial arousal in both sexes.

The voluntary inhibition of sexual arousal is an important issue for psychologists using the penile tumescence response to diagnose paedophilia. While only 5% of those who admit to this sexual deviance fail to show the expected pattern of arousal to slides depicting nude children, almost a third of "non-admitters" succeed in inhibiting arousal. New methods consisting of "priming" the subjects with an adult erotic slide, presented before the deviant one have been more successful. Inhibition of penile erection is more rapid in the normal heterosexual than in the paedophile.

Expectancies are not always a reliable guide to sexual arousal. Although most persons are familiar with the dampening effects of high doses of alcohol on sexual arousal, they also expect mild to moderate doses to enhance sexual arousal. The effect of alcohol on both males and females is actually a depression of genital arousal in direct proportion to the dosage. Because of the expectation that alcohol releases sexual arousal, subjects who were told that they were getting alcohol but actually given a placebo drug, showed increased arousal in response to less socially acceptable kinds of sexual stimuli, such as heterosexual rape, or homosexual films. Apparently the suggestion that they were getting alcohol relaxed social inhibitions against responding to these films. This may provide the key to the common misconception that moderate doses of alcohol enhance sexual arousal. Alcohol may enhance sexual arousal to the extent that arousal is inhibited by other social factors. But the belief that one is ingesting alcohol is at least as important as the disinhibiting effects of the alcohol itself. This may also explain some of the aphrodisiacal powers claimed for other drugs such as marijuana.

Subjects given false heart rate feedback could be manipulated into rating certain nudes (those producing an "increase" in heart rate) as more attractive than others (those producing a "decrease" in heart rate). Actually a real decrease in heart rate would be more indicative of a positive sexual interest, but most subjects are not very conversant with psychophysiology.

The effectiveness of voluntary inhibition or enhancement of sexual arousal may be in some part dependent on personality factors. In the bogus heart rate experiment subjects who scored high on a sexual-guilt scale were most affected by the bogus heart rate information. In another study sex-guilt did not correlate with penile tumescence, but it correlated negatively with subjectively assessed arousal.

1. Summary

The research has confirmed the powerful role that cognitive factors may play in sexual arousal, at least in the subjective level. Subjects can actually inhibit or enhance their physical arousal, although facilitation is more readily accomplished with the aid of biofeedback. Subjects' beliefs about the effects of alcohol or the meaning of heart rate increases may affect arousal, even when their beliefs are inaccurate. The beliefs (i) that alcohol enhances sexual arousal and (ii) that ingestion of alcohol may enhance arousal to stimuli, where normally both the stimulus and the drug would inhibit or dampen arousal. Personality factors also influence sexual arousal through their effects on conditioning and cognitive states.

C. Anxiety and Guilt Arousal

The influence of personality traits such as extraversion, neuroticism and sex-guilt on conditioning and cognitive factors has been mentioned. One study showed that subjects high in neuroticism showed more non-specific electrodermal responses (GSR's), often a sign of anxiety arousal, during the presentation of erotic stimuli than did less neurotic subjects. Another study showed that low sex-guilt females responded to erotic stimuli with cardiac deceleration, while those with high sex-guilt showed a tendency toward heart rate acceleration. Still another study demonstrated that male subjects who were high in sex guilt secreted less acid phosphotase during exposure to erotic stimuli than low guilt subjects. Presumably anxiety or guilt prone subjects are in an anxious or guilty state during or even prior to exposure to erotic stimuli. But do anxiety and guilt necessarily dampen sexual arousal?

One study showed that moderate levels of anxiety, produced by a video-tape, actually enhanced sexual arousal in women produced by an erotic videotape. Presumably higher levels produced by subjectively threatening situations would inhibit sexual arousal. Up to some optimal level, non-sexual arousal may potentiate sexual arousal. This could apply to arousal by emotions such as anger or joy as well as anxiety. Beyond this optimal level, the arousal of other emotions may be accompanied by high levels of sympathetic system arousal, that are reciprocally inhibiting to para-sympathetic sexual arousal. Cognitive factors are important here too. Subjects with rapid heart rates produced by exercise, who did not perceive their residual arousal as the after-effects of the exercise, rated their subjective arousal in response to an erotic film higher than subjects who attributed their arousal to the exercise. If the residual anxiety from arousal by a prior stimulus is perceived as part of the arousal produced by the erotic stimulus, the sexual arousal may be felt as more intense.

D. Sleep

Spontaneous erections occur in males during sleep and a corresponding phenomenon may occur in vaginal pulse pressure in women, although the latter phenomenon is less firmly established. Most of the erections in males occur during the REM phase of sleep, associated with dreaming in humans (see Chapter 6). The REM (rapid-eye-movement) period is sometimes called "paradoxical sleep", because the EEG and autonomic response indicators show an arousal pattern in contrast to the low levels of cortical and autonomic activity seen in other phases of sleep. Penile erection in males is almost as reliable as rapid-eye-movements as an indicator of paradoxical sleep. The erection is not always, or even usually, accompanied by erotic dreams. Apparently the phenomenon is due to a general autonomic outflow during the activation of REM sleep which, in the absence of inhibition from higher centres, activates the reflexive centres for erection in the sacral part of the spinal cord (see Chapter 6).

Because of the involuntary reflexive nature of nocturnal penile tumescence (NPT) it has been suggested that it might be used in the differential diagnosis of organic and psychogenic impotence. The former may be produced by a variety of diseases, drugs, and hormone insufficiencies, while the latter is generally a function of some kind of "fear of performance." If there is some impairment of the arousal mechanism itself then there could be a dampening or elimination of NPT in addition to the problems found in waking, stimulated erections. But there is no immediate reason to expect inhibition of NPT in psychogenic impotence.

E. *Hormones*

1. *Prenatal hormones*

Sex hormones may affect sexual development, arousal, or behaviour at any point in the life cycle from conception to death. Abnormal prenatal hormone influences on the developing foetus may result in the development of external genitalia that are not congruent with the genetically programmed sex of the individual. If such children are assigned to the sex-role on the basis of their superficial sex appearance they usually fit into that role and develop "heterosexual" interests congruent with the role. But longitudinal studies of these individuals, who were correctly assigned at birth (and surgical corrections made), reveal differences between them and most persons of their sex, which show that prenatal hormones influence more than sexual object choices.

Two conditions may produce an excess of androgens in the developing foetus. In the 1950's mothers with a history of miscarriages were treated with progestinic drugs, producing a pseudo-hermaphroditism. The other, called the adrenogenital syndrome, is transmitted as a recessive genetic trait with a hyperactive adrenal gland in the foetus producing too much androgen.

Girls exposed to an excess of androgens (male hormone) because of these conditions show less interest in dolls and more propensity to engage in the "rough-and-tumble" play more typical of boys. This "tomboyism" is generally accepted by parents and society and the girls generally develop the usual heterosexual interests when they reach puberty. Study of a group of

Russian girls with a late-treated (12–40 years of age) virilizing adrenogenital syndrome showed that all had heterosexual and none had homosexual interests, but most had strong sex drives and a high frequency of sexual dreams and masturbation. The result is understandable in view of evidence that androgen is the major influence in female as well as male sex drive. Androgen sensitizes the clitoris as well as the penis. Three-quarters of these women had enlarged clitorises and erections of the clitoris during sexual arousal (not an invariant phenomenon in normal female arousal).

Turner's syndrome (gonadal dysgenesis) and testicular feminization (androgen insensitivity) may produce boys who fail to develop a penis or scrotal sac and have the external appearance of girls. But the penis may develop enough to result in correct sex assignment. In one study of such boys at 16 years of age some residual effects of the feminizing influence were seen. Observers rated their behavioural mannerisms as more feminine than those of controls, they had fewer stereotypical masculine interests, were less assertive and aggressive and had less heterosexual experience. Another group of 6 year old boys exposed to oestrogens in utero were rated by their teachers as less aggressive, assertive and athletically coordinated than their classmates.

While prenatal exposure to androgens in girls or oestrogens in boys does not necessarily lead to homosexual object choices, it seems to affect the developing temperament along masculine or feminine lines. Such exposure may also affect sexual arousability and intensity of the later developing sex drive, with androgen heightening it in girls and oestrogen dampening it in boys.

2. Post-natal hormones and heterosexual behaviour

Sexual arousal and intercourse in the adult male are possible without the sensitizing influence of testosterone, but the observations of hypogonadal men who come for treatment show a diminishing desire, and erections are more difficult to obtain and sustain. Ejaculate is diminished or eliminated. Money (1961) demonstrated that the substitution of a placebo injection for the testosterone that hypogonadal patients were receiving, resulted in a recurrence of their impotence. However, studies of men whose hypogonadism was discovered in the course of examinations for sterility have *not* revealed markedly impaired sexual performance despite drastically reduced levels of testosterone. Apparently there is some self-selection in the low-testosterone men who came for treatment of their sexual problems. The results on the second type, whose low testosterone is discovered in another context, show that in some men very low testosterone levels are not incompatible with a satisfactory sex life. However, studies of men with low levels of testosterone, even prior to adolescence, report lower frequencies of intercourse than normal men. Testosterone levels at or before puberty may be quite important in establishing sexual patterns that may persist in spite of lowered testosterone levels in later years.

Within the normal range of sexual behaviour, levels of testosterone in males do not correlate with frequency of intercourse, masturbation, orgasms, sexual interests or sexual thoughts (Brown *et al.*, 1978). However, Daitzman and Zuckerman (1980) found that testosterone correlated positively with *cumulative* sexual experience of the subjects. Both of these studies used unmarried male college students. Frequency measures in this type of population may have more to do with current opportunities than sex drive.

Married men, or others with a constantly available partner, provide a better test of the effect of testosterone on frequency of sexual activity. Persky (1978) studied a small group of young married men and their wives over a three month period. He found no relationship between testosterone levels in either sex and the frequency of initiating sexual intercourse, but the receptivity of *either partner* to the initiation of the other correlated positively with the husband's testosterone level. The wives' own testosterone levels correlated with their reports of sexual gratification.

Only one study has examined the relation between testosterone levels and responses to erotic stimuli in the laboratory (Rubin *et al.*, 1979). The study used only 6 subjects, tested in 6 experimental sessions. Within subject correlations between testosterone and penile response revealed high positive correlations for 2 subjects, non-significant correlations for 3 subjects, and a significant negative correlation for the final subject. This study bears repeating with a larger number of subjects.

While oestrogen (the primary hormone produced by the ovaries) serves a function in vascularization of the vaginal tissue and the lubrication of the vagina during stimulation, androgens seem to mediate sexual arousability and orgasmic capacity in females as well as in males. In females the larger proportion of androgens is produced by the adrenal cortex, so that loss of function in the ovaries through surgical removal or natural menopause does not have any necessary physiological effect on sexual desire (although lack of oestrogen may produce some problems in lubrication). However, most women whose adrenal glands are removed show a marked reduction in sexual desire, activity and responsiveness, showing the primary role of androgens in these characteristics. A recent study suggests that testosterone, combined with even infrequent counselling, may help sexually unresponsive women. Women receiving testosterone reported greater increases in sexual arousal and satisfaction and frequency of orgasm than those receiving a tranquilliser (diazepam).

Studies of the role of androgens in male sexual dysfunction have yielded inconsistent evidence of a hormonal basis for impotence, and treatment with testosterone does not generally ameliorate the disorder without treatment of the psychological factors. But more recent studies have shown that men classified as organically impotent, on the basis of clinical criteria, are subsequently found to have lower testosterone levels than those classified as having "psychogenic" impotence. Medical opinion has been that impotence is purely "psychogenic" in 90–95% of the cases. A recent study (Spark et al., 1980) has challenged this estimate. These investigators found that 35% of 105 consecutive patients with complaints of impotence had demonstrable disorders of the hypothalamic-pituitary gonadal axis. All but one of these patients had low testosterone levels and some also had deviant gonadotropic hormone levels. Potency was restored in 18 of 19 patients with low gonadotropic and gonadal hormones by injections of testosterone. This study underlines the importance of the differential diagnosis of organic and "psychogenic" impotence, and the necessity for a complete hormonal screening of patients, particularly those where the psychogenic factors are not obvious.

3. Hormonal cycles

Although the human female's sexual arousability is not limited to the ovulatory period of the menstrual cycle, as in other animals, nature has provided some inducements for activity in this period. It has been known for many years that oestrogen peaks just before the ovulating period, but recent evidence has also shown a peak in testosterone, the hormone most relevant to arousability in both sexes, at or just after ovulation. Obviously, women's understanding of the menstrual cycle and its role in conception will have an influence on their sexual behaviour and possibly their arousability. Studies have shown little relationship between sexual arousability or behaviour and the menstrual cycle. If anything, intercourse tends to occur more frequently just after the menstrual period and arousability is highest during menstruation (an interesting fact in view of the widespread taboos on coitus during that period).

Do males also have "cycles" for sex hormones? Such cycles have been found in other species of animals. Doering et al. (1975) present evidence for 8 to 30 day cycles in 60% of a group of human males where testosterone blood levels were sampled every 2 days for 2 months. One wonders if males' cycles would fall into synchrony with the menstrual cycles of their mates.

4. Homosexuality

All of the hormonal studies of homosexuality have been done on male homosexuals. In 10 studies comparing the testosterone levels of homosexual and heterosexual males, 3 studies found heterosexuals had higher levels, 2 found homosexuals had higher levels, and 5 found no significant differences. Two studies found that homosexuals had higher levels of one of the oestrogens, but one study found no difference in oestradiol. Several of these studies compared subjects' ratings on Kinsey's heterosexual–homosexual scale, based on the lifetime sexual history, with testosterone levels. There was no relationship between degrees of homosexuality or heterosexuality and testosterone. Exclusive homosexuals had the same levels as bisexuals. The data, with the methods used thus far, suggest that hormone levels in adult life have little to do with homosexuality. This is not surprising in view of the fact that most homosexuals realize their sexual object preferences fairly early, often before puberty. If hormones are involved at all in homosexuality it must be the earlier levels of hormones, or even pre-natal hormone influences, that affect the sexual disposition. Most of the work has focused on androgens. There is some evidence that oestrogens may be involved in male homosexuality.

5. *Ageing*

Gonadal hormonal output declines with age as a consequence of changes in the glands. There is some debate about the decline in testosterone in males, some maintaining that little decline is seen until relatively late, if at all, and others reporting a constant decline from the twenties onwards. The data in older groups depend on whether unselected samples are used or only physically healthy men are studied; the former show more decline than the latter. A parallel age decline is seen in sexual activity and interest; usually activity goes before interest. It is easy to reach the conclusion that the hormone decline is responsible for the decline in sexual interest and activity. But we know the effect a new sexual partner can have on activity and interest of either sex at any age. Perhaps habituation has more to do with the age decline than hormones. The disinhibiting effect of new sexual partners for male rhesus monkeys (Michael and Zumpfe, 1978), discussed previously, showed that their new "harems" raised their testosterone levels from the levels they had fallen to during their habituation to the old sexual partners. The results suggest that a fall in testosterone might be a function of, rather than a cause of, the reduction in sexual activity.

F. *Drugs*

1. *Alcohol*

The porter in Shakespeare's Macbeth, commenting on the effect of alcohol on male sexuality, says: ". . . it provokes the desire but it takes away the performance . . . it sets him on and it takes him off . . . makes him stand to, and not stand to." Shakespeare's observations are accurate concerning the effects of high blood levels of alcohol on sexual behaviour. Alcohol reduces psychological inhibition ("provokes the desire") but high doses may cause temporary impotence ("not stand to"). The cognitive factors in alcohol were described in a previous section. Some of the loss of inhibition can occur even when the drinker only believes he has ingested alcohol. But alcohol actually reduces penile erection and vaginal vasocongestion in direct proportion to dose level, regardless of what the drinker believes. At very high blood levels alcohol narcotizes the brain, making it insensitive to the sensations from the body, slowing reflexes, and generally depressing sympathetic system arousal. But at intermediate levels, where the reduction in genital response is not enough to cause impairment of erectile capacity, alcohol prolongs time to orgasm and ejaculation. This can provide some benefit to premature ejaculators but would be a detriment to males or females with orgasmic dysfunctions. In spite of the physiological effects of alcohol, a majority of drinkers report experiencing greater sexual enjoyment after drinking. This is a testimony to the role of guilt, inhibition and fear in reducing sexual enjoyment, rather than any intrinsic aphrodisiacal powers of alcohol.

Chronic alcoholism may produce chronic impotence or orgasmic dys-function, because it stimulates the activity of an enzyme in the liver that catabolizes testosterone, produces atrophy of the testes and inhibits testicular testosterone synthesis. These changes are not irreversible if liver and testes damage is not permanent. If the alcoholic stops drinking, testosterone will rise and potency may be restored.

2. Other drugs

Segraves (1977) has reviewed this field. Certain anti-psychotic drugs and some of the anti-depressant drugs inhibit ejaculation in males. Chronic heroin use may have the same effect. Female orgasmic capacity is probably also affected, but few studies have been done of females taking these drugs. The ejaculation inhibition probably occurs because of the blocking effects of the drugs on the sympathetic nervous system, as well as bioamines in the central nervous system which mediate neural circuits involved in sexual response.

Some of these drugs, particularly the antidepressant ones, have been reported to interfere with erection in males. This may be due to their primary blocking of parasympathetic function.

It should be emphasized that only a minority of patients using these drugs are affected, and few studies have been done in a double-blind fashion. Severely depressed patients normally report a loss of sexual desire and this may be confused with the effects of the drugs used to treat depression if proper placebo and double-blind controls are not used. The best procedure would be to use these controls in studies of sexually active persons without psychiatric disorders. Stringent ethical standards would make such research nearly impossible today, even with willing volunteers.

3. Aphrodisiacs

For centuries men and women have experimented with substances reported to produce sexual arousal. Most of these, like alcohol, work strictly through cognitive mediation or suggestion. Some, such as cantharides ("Spanish-fly", actually a powder from a beetle), irritate the genito-urinary tract. The inflammation produces dilation of blood vessels in the genitals, the effects of which can produce erection in the male and some kind of sensations in the female. Generally these drugs are dangerous and not effective sexual stimulants.

Stimulants, such as amphetamine and cocaine, are also widely thought to have aphrodisiacal properties, but 90% of their effect is probably suggestion and the remainder may be due to the heightened sympathetic system arousal that slows sexual arousal and increases the felt intensity of orgasm when it does occur. However, there is another possibility: both of these drugs release dopamine from neurones in the limbic system that may be involved in sexual function.

4. Biogenic amines

Recent experimental evidence suggests that sexual behaviour in male rats is enhanced by drugs which increase levels of dopamine in the brain. Clinical reports have suggested some stimulation of sexual behaviour in patients with Parkinsonism treated with L-dopa, a precursor of dopamine. However, these effects only occur in a minority of the patients and could be a function of the alleviation of their dopamine-deficit illness and restoration of general health.

Other studies on rats show that drugs that decrease brain serotonin levels increase sexual behaviour, and drugs that increase brain serotonin inhibit copulatory behaviour. The monamine oxidase inhibitors, used in the treatment of depression in humans, have the effect of *increasing* the levels of brain serotonin, which might account for their reported inhibitory effect on erection in the male. However, these drugs also increase the levels of the other monoamines in the brain, including dopamine. The results of drugs affecting the monoamines in the brain are quite interesting, and the rat studies suggest that there is some involvement of these central amines in sexual behaviour. In my other chapter in this title, on "Sensation Seeking" (Vol. 3, Ch. 7), I suggest that two of these monoamines, noradrenaline and dopamine, are involved in this personality trait, and that an important expression of the trait is in sexual arousability and experience. As yet these are speculative hypotheses. The only chemical known to be directly linked to sexual arousability so far is the one produced in the gonads and adrenal cortex: testosterone.

Further Reading

Kinsey, A. C., Pomeroy, W. B. and Martin, C. E. (1948). "Sexual behavior in the human male". Saunders, Philadelphia.
Kinsey, A. C., Pomeroy, W. B., Martin, C. E. and Gethard, P. H. (1953). "Sexual behavior in the human female". Saunders, Philadelphia.
These two volumes represent the first systematic study of human sexual behaviour. Although most of the data consists of statistics on the sexual habits and experiences of a large sample of Americans, a number of sections are devoted to the biological aspects of sex. Part III of the female volume (Ch. 14–18) deals with the anatomy and physiology of sexual response and orgasm and neural hormonal and conditioning factors in sexual response.
Masters, W. and Johnson, V. (1966). "Human sexual response" Little, Brown and Co., Boston.
This book describes the results of the research of the authors on the physiology of the sexual response. It represents the first direct laboratory study of changes in the genitals and other body areas during sexual arousal and orgasm. The four stages of sexual excitement, plateau, orgasm and resolution are described in males and females.
Rosen, R. C. and Keefe, F. J. (1978). The measurement of human penile tumescence. *Psychophysiology* 15, 366–376.
This article reviews the techniques that were developed to measure penile tumescence, listing the advantages and disadvantages of each technique.
Heiman, J. R. (1978). Issues in the use of psychophysiology to assess female sexual dysfunction. *J. Sex Marital Therapy* 2, 197–204.
The paper reviews some methods developed to measure changes in the vagina during sexual arousal and some of the issues in research with these methods such as: (i) whether the laboratory studies reflect changes occurring in a natural environment; (ii) the sources of individual differences in response; (iii) the influences of the menstrual cycle on arousal; (iv) the reason for a lack of high correlation between genital response and self-rated arousal.
Heiman, J. R. (1977). A psychophysiological explanation of sexual arousal patterns in females and males. *Psychophysiology* 14, 266–274.
This controlled experimental study explores some of the sources of variation in arousal including the type of stimulus material and how it is presented, sexual experience of subjects, and desensitization and habituation. A number of different types of psychophysiological indicators are used including genital pulse amplitude and blood volume, heart-rate and finger pulse amplitude. Scaled subjective reports are also used and correlated with genital measures.
Zuckerman, M. (1971). Physiological measures of sexual arousal in the human. *Psychol. Bull.* 75, 297–329.
This article reviews genital and non-genital psychophysiological and biochemical studies of human sexual arousal. The article was written at the end of the first decade of experimental study of human sexual response. It pointed out the many methodological problems in the research and suggested areas for study in the years ahead.
Schiavi, R. C. and White, D. (1976). Androgens and male sexual function: A review of human studies. *J. Sex Marital Therapy* 2, 214–228.
This article reviews the role of androgens in normal male sexual response, in erectile disorders, and in homosexuality.
Segraves, R. T. (1977). Pharmacological agents causing sexual dysfunction. *J. Sex Marital Therapy* 3, 157–176.

This article reviews the effects of various drugs on sexual arousal and ejaculation in the male. The authors speculate on the brain pharmacology that might mediate the effects of the drugs.

Whalen, R. E. (1976). Brain mechanisms controlling sexual behavior. *In* "Human sexuality in four perspectives" (F. A. Beach, ed.). Johns Hopkins University Press, Baltimore.

This chapter presents an up-to-date conceptualization of the way that sexual behaviour is organized and directed from the brain. The conceptualization is a systems approach which describes the interaction of neural subsystems and hormonal systems with feedback-regulation that controls sexual behaviour.

Beach, F. A. (1976). Hormonal control of sex-related behavior. *In* "Human sexuality in four perspectives" (F. A. Beach, ed.). Johns Hopkins University Press, Baltimore.

This chapter by the editor is an updating of his views on the role of hormones in human sexual behaviour. Those who cite his earlier work (Ford and Beach, 1951) as evidence of the irrelevance of hormones in human sexual behaviour should read the current views of Beach on this subject.

References

Barclay, A. M. and Little, D. M. (1972). Urinary acid phosphotase secretion under different arousal conditions. *Psychophysiology* 9, 69–77.

Bohlen, J. G. and Held, J. P. (1979). An anal probe for monitoring vascular and muscular events during sexual response. *Psychophysiology* 16, 318–323.

Brown, E., Brown, G. M., Kofman, O. and Quarrington, B. (1978). Sexual function and affect in Parkinsonian men treated with L-DOPA. *Am. J. Psychiat.* 135, 1552–1555.

Daitzman, R. and Zuckerman, M. (1980). Disinhibitory sensation seeking, personality and gonadal hormones. *Personality and Individual Differences* 1, 103–110.

Doering, C. H., Kraemer, H. C., Brodie, K. H. and Hamburg, D. A. (1975). A cycle of plasma testosterone in the human male. *J. Clin. Endocr. Metab.* 40, 492–500.

Fox, C. A., Ismail, A. A. A., Love, D. N., Kirkham, K. E. and Loraine, J. A. (1972). Studies on the relationship between plasma testosterone levels and human sexual activity. *J. Endocr.* 52, 51–58.

Geer, J. H., Morokoff, P. and Greenwood, P. (1974). Sexual arousal in women: The development of a measurement device for vaginal blood volume. *Arch. Sexual Behav.* 3, 559–564.

Heiman, J. R. (1977). A psychophysiological exploration of sexual arousal patterns in females and males, *Psychophysiology* 14, 266–274.

Henson, D. E. and Rubin, H. B. (1978). A comparison of two objective measures of sexual arousal of women. *Behav. Res. Therapy* 16, 143–151.

Henson, D. E., Rubin, H. B., Henson, C. and Williams, J. R. (1977). Temperature change of the labia minora as an objective measure of female eroticism. *J. Behav. Therapy Exp. Psychiat.* 8, 401–410.

Hess, E. H., Seltzer, A. L. and Shlien, J. M. (1965). Pupil response of hetero- and homosexual males to pictures of men and women: A pilot study. *J. Abnorm. Psychol.* 70, 165–168.

Kantorwitz, D. A. (1978). Personality and conditioning of tumescence and detumescence. *Behav. Res. Therapy* 16, 117–128.

Kinsey, A. C., Pomeroy, W. B., Martin, C. E. and Gebhard, P. H. (1953). "Sexual behavior in the human female". Saunders, Philadelphia.

Laws, D. R. and Rubin, H. B. (1969). Instructional control of an autonomic sexual response. *J. Appl. Behav. Analysis* **2**, 93–99.

Masters, W. and Johnson, V. (1966). "Human sexual response". Little, Brown and Co., Boston.

Michael, R. P. and Zumpfe, D. (1978). Potency in male rhesus monkeys: Effects of continuously receptive females. *Science* **200**, 451–453.

Michael, R. P., Bonsale, R. W. and Kutner, M. (1975). Volatile fatty acids, "copulins," in human vaginal secretions. *Psychoneuroendocrinology* **1**, 153–163.

Money, J. (1961). Sex hormones and other variables in human eroticism. *In* "Sex and internal secretions, VIII" (W. C. Young, ed.). Williams and Wilkins, Baltimore.

Persky, H. (1978). Plasma testosterone level and sexual behaviour of couples. *Arch. Sexual Behav.* **7**, 157–173.

Rubin, H. B., Henson, D. E., Falvo, R. E. and High, R. W. (1979). The relationship between men's endogenous levels of testosterone and their penile responses to erotic stimuli. *Behav. Res. Therapy* **17**, 305–312.

Segraves, R. T. (1977). Pharmacological agents causing sexual dysfunction. *J. Sex and Marital Therapy* **3**, 157–176.

Sintchak, G. and Geer, J. H. (1975). A vaginal plethysmograph system. *Psychophysiology* **12**, 113–115.

Sparks, R. F., White, R. A. and Connolly, M. S. (1980). Impotence is not always psychogenic. *J. Am. Med. Assoc.* **243**, 750–755.

Zuckerman, M. (1971). Physiological measures of sexual arousal in the human. *Psychol. Bull.* **75**, 297–329.

Glossary

Most of the technical terms in this volume are explained in detail within the text or in the context of anatomical and physiological diagrams. Many readers will be unfamiliar with biochemical terminology and most of the items in the Glossary are devoted to biochemical aspects of the nervous system.

Acetylcholine (ACh) The transmitter of cholinergic neurones, it is found in the central nervous system, at neuromuscular junctions, in parasympathetic and the pre-ganglionic sympathetic neurones.

Acidity The capacity of a compound to yield hydrogen ions when dissolved in water, giving a pH lower than 7.

ACTH *See* adrenocorticotrophic hormone.

Adenosine diphosphate (ADP) *See* adenosine triphosphate.

Adenosine triphosphate (ATP) A triple phosphorylated organic compound that functions as the "energy currency" for cells. One of the phosphate groupings is readily transferred to other substances by enzyme action (leaving ADP, which is rephosphorylated to ATP), making available a considerable amount of energy for use by the cell.

Adrenal gland (a) medulla, inner core innervated by sympathetic nervous system, which stimulates release of adrenaline and noradrenaline into circulatory system. (b) cortex, outer part secreting steroid hormones, glucocorticoids, mineralo-corticoids and sex hormones, the release of which is controlled by ACTH.

Adrenaline Hormone secreted by the adrenal medulla, certain of its actions resemble those of sympathetic system.

Adrenocorticotrophic hormone (ACTH) Polypeptide secreted by anterior lobe of pituitary, it controls secretory activity of adrenal cortex, in particular stimulating secretion of glucocorticoids. Its own release is controlled by secretion of a factor by the hypothalamus.

Affective disorder A form of psychopathology affecting emotional state; including anxiety, depression and manic-depressive illness.

Alkalinity The capacity of a base or alkali substance to increase hydroxyl ion concentration when dissolved in water, giving a pH higher than 7.

Amino acid Organic compound containing both a basic amino $(-NH_2)$ and an acidic carboxyl $(-COOH)$ group. Fundamental unit of proteins.

Amphetamine A stimulant drug, which blocks the re-uptake of both noradrenaline and dopamine, potentiating their affects, but also eventually resulting in their depletion from the neurones.

Amygdala Part of the limbic system and believed to have importance in the control of emotional expression.

Anabolism See metabolism.

Atherosclerosis A form of arteriosclerosis in which fatty deposits build up within an artery, so reducing the cross-sectional area.

Atropine A drug which blocks the effect of acetylcholine at synapses with muscarinic receptors. Acts as a false transmitter.

Autonomic nervous system The nerves that innervate smooth muscle, viscera, glands, heart and sweat glands in the skin. Classically separated into the sympathetic and parasympathetic nervous systems.

Carbohydrates Compounds of general formula $C_x(H_2O)_y$, e.g. sugar, starch, cellulose.

Catabolism See metabolism

Catecholamine A general term for compounds containing the catechal nucleus, which is a benzene ring with two adjacent hydroxyl groups and one amine group. The most important are: noradrenaline, adrenaline and dopamine.

Catechol-o-methyltransferase An enzyme which breaks down extracellular noradrenaline and dopamine.

Cholesterol Technically, an unsaturated secondary alcohol, but better known as a waxy fatlike substance widespread throughout the body, playing important roles in cell membranes and atherosclerotic thickening of the arterial wall.

Cholinergic A neurone or synapse having acetycholine as the transmitter substance.

Cholinesterase Enzyme which catalyses hydrolysis of acetyl-choline, thus inactivating it, after its release as a transmitter.

Cocaine A drug that limits the action of the transmitter substance noradrenaline at the receptor sites.

Cystathionine A complex sulpher containing amino acid thought to act as an inhibitory neurotransmitter.

D-sleep Stands for desynchronized or dream sleep. It is the portion of sleep during which dreams and rapid eye movements (REMs) occur. Also called REM sleep and paradoxical sleep.

Delta waves Slow synchronous waves recorded from the cortex which cycle at a rate of about 1–3 Hz. They are characteristic of NREM sleep.

Deoxyribonucleic acid (DNA) A nucleic acid found in the cell nucleus, the sequence of its component units constituting the genetic code which forms the basis of heredity.

Dopamine A catecholamine which is a neurotransmitter found in high concentrations in the basal ganglia and in the substantia nigra and ventral hypothalamus.

Electrodermal resistance The resistance of the skin to current passed through it. High resistance usually is associated with relaxation, low resistance with autonomic arousal. Related to the galvanic skin response.

Electron A negatively charged primary subatomic particle.

Emergent stage 1 A stage of sleep during which the EEG activity is low voltage and desynchronized, and during which rapid eye movements occur. Now called REM sleep or D-sleep, this state of sleep received the name emergent stage 1 for historical reasons.

Endorphin Neuromodulatory peptide, derived from a 91 amino acid peptide, β-lipotropin, itself a fragment of ACTH. A "natural opiate", i.e. morphine is thought to have its affects by mimicking the actions of endorphin and related compounds.

Enkephalin As for endorphin, of which it is a fragment.

Enzyme A protein that acts as a biological catalyst.

Fatty acids Acid of a chain of from sixteen to eighteen carbon atoms. See lipids.

Gamma-aminobutyric acid (GABA) A substance found in the brain and spinal cord thought to be an inhibitory neurotransmitter.

Glutamic acid An amino acid believed to act as a neurotransmitter in the central nervous system.

Growth hormone releasing factor A biochemical which stimulates the release of growth hormone from the anterior pituitary. Its effects on the anterior pituitary are antagonized by growth hormone inhibitory factor, also called somatostatin.

Hormones Chemical messengers, produced in one part of an organism, and usually released from endocrine glands into the circulatory system, to exert their effect elsewhere. They affect the rates and ongoing activity of cells, their influence usually being more widespread and longer lasting than that of nervous transmission.

Human growth hormone Hormone produced by the human anterior pituitary; it promotes growth of whole body. Among other functions, it facilitates the production of protein via the mediation of compounds produced in the liver.

4-Hydroxy-3-methoxyphenylethylene glycol (MOPEG) A breakdown metabolite of noradrenaline.

5-Hydroxytryptamine *See* serotonin

Hypothalmus A cluster of important nerve cells, located below the thalamus, playing an essential role in autonomic and endocrine function.

Insomnia Literally means no sleep, but actually a misnomer. It should be dyssomnia – disruption of sleep. Refers to a family of disorders characterized by subjective complaints of insufficient sleep.

Isomers Compounds comprising the same number and type of atoms, but arranged differently and so having different properties. Isomerism may be structural, geometric or optical.

K-complexes Electrophysiological signals recorded from scalp electrodes, consisting of a spike and followed, at times, by spindles. Occur during stage 2 of sleep. Believed to be evoked potentials.

Lactic acid Organic acid formed as an end-product of glucose breakdown (glycolysis) which is essential for utilization of energy of food. Also formed in metabolism of micro-organisms.

Limbic system A circle of complex brain structures, consisting of about 53 regions and 35 associated tracts, lying below the cerebral cortex. Appears to integrate endocrine, autonomic and central systems into a smooth functioning whole.

Lipids Any of a variety of compounds insoluble in water but soluble in ethers and alcohols; includes fats, oils, waxes, phospholipids and steroids.

Lipoproteins Combination of lipids (e.g. cholesterol) and protein found within cells and in the blood.

Lysergic acid diethylaminde (LSD-25) An hallucinogenic drug that is thought to act on serotoninergic receptors.

Macromolecule Compound with a MW in the order of thousands or millions of units, e.g. proteins, nucleic acids, polysacchorides.

Melatonin A compound synthesized in the pineal gland and thought to have a role in bodily rythyms.

Metabolism The sum of the chemical reactions within a cell (or whole organism), including anabolism (synthesis or build up) and catabolism (break down).

3-Methoxy-4-hydroxyphenylglycol (MHPG) A breakdown metabolite of noradrenaline.

Monoamine oxidase An enzyme that breaks down noradrenaline and dopamine.

Morphine Powerful analgesic drug, having both stimulant and depressant affects, derived from an alkaloid of plant origin.

Muscarinic receptors One of two types of cholinergic receptor. Stimulated by muscarine and acetylcholine. *See also* nicotinic receptors.

Myelin Fused membranes of Schwann cells or glial cells forming a high resistance sheath around an axon.

Neuromodulator/neuroregulator A chemical modifying a nerve cell rather than acting directly as a neurotransmitter. Has a longer time course of action compared to a neurotransmitter.

Neurotransmitters A chemical synthesized within a neurone and liberated by the presynaptic terminals in response to an action potential. It causes an effect on the postsynaptic cell membrane, usually an increase in permeability to one or more ions. The effect may be inhibitory or excitatory.

Nicotinic receptors One of two types of cholinergic receptor. Stimulated by nicotine and acetylcholine. *See also* muscarinic receptors.

Noradrenaline A transmitter substance found in the brain and the post-ganglionic neurones of the sympathetic system.

NREM sleep Non-REM sleep, a synonym for S-sleep. *See* S-sleep.

Nucleic acid Any of several organic acids that are polymers of nucleotides and function in the transmission of hereditary traits, in cellular activities.

Paradoxical sleep A synonym for D-sleep. Called paradoxical sleep because of the paradox of scalp EEG recordings similar to those of alert waking, and other physiological signs consistent with deep sleep.

Pepsinogen The inactive precurser of the digestive juice proteolytic enzyme, pepsin.

Pheochromocytoma A disease in which the patient suffers from a benign tumour of the adrenal medulla, resulting in excessive amounts of adrenaline and noradrenaline being released into the body.

Phospholipids A major component of cell membranes, composed of glycerol or sphingosine, fatty acids, a phosphate group and a nitrogenous group.

Physostigmine A drug which inhibits the enzyme cholinesterase, resulting in a build-up of acetylcholine, thus potentiating the transmitter's effects.

Polysaccharide *See* carbohydrates.

Polypeptide chain *See* proteins.

Protein An abundant, diverse class of high MW organic compounds, which are the primary constituents of living things. They are composed of long polypeptide chains, formed from amino acids joined together by peptide bonds. Proteins may be fibrous or globular.

Proton A positively charged primary subatomic particle.

Rapid eye movements Rapid conjugate movements of the eyes which occur during D-sleep and which are believed to accompany dreaming.

Receptive field Denotes the area of the periphery which influences the firing of a neurone. For cells in the visual pathway it refers to an area on the retina, the illumination of which affects the activity of a neurone.

REM rebound The tendency for REM sleep, or D-sleep, to occur at significantly greater density when a person finally is permitted to sleep after having been deprived of D-sleep.

REM sleep A synonym for D-sleep, so-called because of the characteristic rapid eye movements which occur during this state.

REMs *See* rapid eye movements.

Reverberatory synaptic circuits Concept relating to memory, i.e. proposed as the physiological mechanism for short term memory.

Ribonucleic acid (RNA) Linear polymer of ribonucleotides, there being three main types in cells, messenger, ribosomal and transfer. They translate the genetic code of nuclear DNA into actual proteins.

S-sleep One of two stages of sleep. Is frequently subdivided into four sequential stages. Also called NREM or non-REM sleep.

Scotophobin Polypeptide coded for the specific learning of light avoidance.

Sensory gating A process by which sensory information is excluded from high level processing in the nervous system. The reticular formation is believed to be involved. Has the adaptive value of permitting selective attention.

Serotonin A brain neurotransmitter found in high concentration in the raphe nuclei of the brain stem and the hypothalamus.

Sleep deprivation One of several tools for the sleep researcher. Involves either depriving a person completely of sleep for specified periods of time, or selectively depriving the individual either of S-sleep or D-sleep.

Sleep spindles A characteristic cortical sign of stage 2 sleep, so-called because of their spindle shape. Occur also during barbiturate anaesthesia. Function or significance unknown.

Sleep stage One of four arbitrary subdivisions of S-sleep, the subdivisions based upon the presence or absence of characteristic rhythms. *See* K-complexes, sleep spindles, delta waves.

Sleep state Refers to S and D sleep, which are believed each to be a state unto itself in the same way as waking is considered to be a state unto itself.

Slow wave sleep (SWS) A synonym for stage 4, and sometimes stage 3, of S-sleep. So-called because of the characteristic slow delta waves which occur during this period.

Synaptic facilitation Concept relating to memory, i.e. proposed as the physiological mechanism for long term memory.

Taurine A derivative of the amino acid cysteine. It is thought to act as an inhibitory neurotransmitter.

Thought disorder A type of psychopathology characterized by abnormal, at times bizarre, thinking. Includes schizophrenia.

Triglyceride A fat synthesized from glycerol and three different fatty acids and stored in adipose tissue.

Trypsin An enzyme which catalyses the hydrolysis of proteins to peptones and peptides, cleaving at specific peptide links. It has a MW of 34 000, but only one active site, with optimal activity in alkaline solution.

Ventromedial hypothalamus A nucleus in the ventral portion of the hypothalamus, believed to be important in feeding behaviour and in the control of growth hormone secretion.

Author Index

The numbers in italics refer to the reference lists at the end of each chapter.

Subject Index

Conditioning and sexual arousal, 300,
    312–314
Consciousness, 15, 16, 22, 25, 67, 68, 74,
    75, 106, 112, 114
Consolidation, 144, 145, 149, 150
Control, 211, 212, 259, 260, 270, 271
    corticosteroid activity, and, 270, 271
Control-question polygraphy, 244–249
Coping
    corticosteroid activity, and, 270, 271
    direct action, 257, 258
    palliation, 258, 259
Corpus callosum, 38, 41–44
    "split-brain" patients, 208
Correlation, 8, 9, 17, 18
Cortex, *see* Cerebral cortex
Cortical desynchronization, 148, 149,
    291, 292, 294
Corticosteroids, 262, 267–270, 274
    coping and, 270, 271
    disease and, 271
    measurement, 268, 269
    stress and, 268–270, 274
Corticotrophic releasing factor, 268
CRF, 268

dB *see* Decibel
Decibel, 184
Defensive reflex, 223
Delta waves, 108, 109, 113, 133–135
    see also Slow wave sleep, S-sleep
Deoxyribonucleic acid, 86, 87
    memory and, 95, 153–155
Dependence,
    alcohol, 284–286
    defined, 279
Depression, 98, 127
Depth perception, 172, 173
Desynchronized EEG
    attention and, 149
    sleep and, 106, 108, 113, 115–120,
        122, 125
Diaschisis, 208
    see also Brain damage, Recovery
Diencephalon, 38, 39, 41
Direct action coping, 257, 258
Disinhibition of sexual arousal, 311, 312
Diurnal rhythms *see* Biological rhythms
DNA, *see* Deoxyribonucleic acid

Dopamine, 93, 94, 102
    growth hormone, sleep and, 134, 138
    self-stimulation and, 147, 284, 285
    sexual arousal and, 323
Double dissociation, 207
Dreaming, 105, 112–114, 137
    memory consolidation and, 137
    see also D-sleep
Drive, 146, 147, 282
Drugs, 34
    habitual use of, 277–286, 289–295
    sexual arousal and, 321–323
    see also Amphetamine, Protein
        synthesis inhibitors
D-sleep, 108–114, 120, 122, 127, 128,
    135–138
    dreaming, 105, 112–114, 137
    function of, 135–138
    memory consolidation and, 136, 137
    patterns of, 108–114
    physiological correlates of, 112–114,
        122, 125, 127, 128
    repair and maintenance of
        noradrenaline systems, 136, 137
    see also Sleep, Slow wave sleep

Eating, *see* Food intake
EEG, *see* Electroencephalogram
Electrochemical techniques, 99
Electroconvulsive shock, 150
Electrodermal resistance, *see* Skin
    conductance
Electroencephalogram, 60, 61, 148, 149,
    211
    see also Sleep
Electromyographic activity
    sexual arousal and, 304
    sleep and, 107, 112–114, 122, 128
Electrophysiology, 200, 211
Emergent stage 1, *see* D-sleep
EMG, *see* Electromyographic activity
Emotion
    lie detection and, 242–246
    sleep and, 105, 119, 120, 126, 137
    see also Limbic system
Encoding of sensory input, 8–10, 12
    50–52
    pulse, 50
    place, 50–52

Personality
  sexual arousal and, 313, 316
  sleep and, 136
Phrenology, 201
Pineal gland, 92
Pituitary gland, 38, 40, 72, 94
Place coding, 50, 52
Plasticity
  brain, 201, 207, 208
  neural, 58, 143–145
Polygraph, 228
Polygraphic interrogation, 241–254
  control-question approach, 244–249
  counter-measures in, 249, 250
  guilty knowledge test, 250–252
  lie-control test, 246–29
  specific lie response, 242–246
  truth-control test, 244–246
Pons, 148, 150, 282
  sleep and, 106
  see also Brainstem
Pornography and sexual arousal, 312
Post-reinforcement synchronization,
  148, 149
Potentials
  evoked, 61–64, 67, 148, 149
  postsynaptic, 33, 34, 35, 144, 145
Predictability, 259, 260
Protein, 82, 83, 100
  amino acid transmitters, 92
  neuroregulatory peptides, 92, 93
  synthesis, 82
    growth hormone, sleep and, 134,
      136, 137
    inhibitors, 152, 153
    memory and, 95, 96, 136, 137, 145,
      151–154
Psychophysical tuning curve, 188–194
Psychophysiology, 219–236
Psychosurgery, 211
PTC, *see* Psychophysical tuning curve
Pulse amplitude and sexual arousal, 304
Pulse coding, 50, 195
Pupillary response and sexual arousal,
  303, 304
Puromycin, *see* Protein synthesis
  inhibitors

Raphe nucleus, 120–127
  see also S-sleep

Rapid eye movements, 108, 109, 111,
  113, 114
  see also D-sleep
Rapists, *see* Sexual deviation
Reaction time, 106, 224
Reactivation, 207, 208
  see also Brain damage, Recovery
Receptive fields, visual, 160, 161, 164,
  165
Receptor–transmitter interaction, 33,
  34, 145
Recognition, 13
  visual, 173, 174
Recovery, 201, 207, 208, 211
  see also Brain damage
Recurrent collateral inhibition, 56, 57
Redundancy, 207
  see also Brain damage, Recovery
Regeneration, neural, 207
  see also Recovery
Rehabilitation, *see* Brain damage,
  Recovery
Reinforcement, 69, 145–149, 153,
  280–284
  alcohol and, 285
  contingent positive variation, 148
  food and, 146–149, 286–289
  noradrenaline and, 147, 148,
    282–284
  secondary, 147, 288, 289
REM rebound, 135
REM sleep, 110, 114, *see* D-sleep
REMs, *see*, Rapid eye movements
Research strategies, 200, 202–207
Respiratory rate, 243
  sexual arousal and 305
  sleep and, 112–114
Retention, 150, 152, 153
Reticular activating system (RAS), 38,
  66, 67, 106, 107, 115–120, 150,
  282–284
Reticular formation, *see* Reticular
  activating system
Retrieval, 145, 152, 153
Retrograde amnesia, 149, 150, 152, 153
Reward systems, *see* Reinforcement
Rhinencephalon, 42
  see also Limbic system
Rhythms, *see* Biological

Spectral analysis, 237, 238
Speech, 174, 202
Spinal cord, 36, 37
Spindles, *see* Sleep
Split brain, *see* Commissurotomy
S-sleep, 108–114, 120–122, 127, 128,
    132–135, 137, 138
  functions of, 132–135
  stages and patterns of, 108–113
  see also D-sleep, Slow wave sleep,
      Sleep
Strategies (cognitive), 208
Stress, 257–278
  cancer and, 271
  integrated study of, 271–274
  physiological response to, 260–271
  psychological response to, 256–260
  nature of, 255, 256
  sleep and, 136
Striate cortex, *see* Occipital lobe, Visual
    system
Strychnine, 150
Subcortex, 209
Substitution, 208
  see also Recovery
Suppression, 191–194
Suprachiasmatic nucleus
  sleep and, 127, 128
  see also Biological rhythms
SWS, *see* Slow wave sleep
Synapse, the, 23–27, 32–36, 88, 89
  electrophysiology
    EPSP, 32, 33
    IPSP, 34, 35
    inhibition, 34, 35
    spatial and temporal summation, 35,
      52
  structure, 23–27
  synaptic facilitation, 94, 145
  synaptic integration, 52, 144
  synaptic transmission, 32–36, 89, 90,
    146–147
  transmitter–receptor interaction, 33,
    34, 145
  see also Neurotransmitters
  vesicles, 32, 33, 147
  see also Axonal transmission, Neurone
Sympathetic activity, *see* Autonomic
    nervous system

Synchronized EEG
  reinforcement and, 149
  sleep and, 112, 115, 116, 118–124

Taste, 286–288
Tegmental area, 38, 149, 150
Temperature, body,
  sexual arousal and, 304, 306, 307
  sleep and, 112, 113
Temporal lobe, 44, 45, 206
Testicular feminization, 318
Testosterone
  sexual arousal and, 308, 318–321
  sex-typed interests and, 317, 318
Thalamus, 38–43, 126, 204
  diffuse thalamic projection system, 41,
    68
    see also Recticular activating system
  non-specific thalamic nuclei, 67, 116,
    118
Thought disorders, sleep and, 106, 126,
    127
Time-pattern of neural firing, *see* Pulse
    coding
Tolerance, 281, 285, 294
Tractus Solitarius, nucleus of the, 118,
    119
Trace memory theory, 150
Transactional model of stress, 255, 256
Transmission of information, 8–10, 12
  see also Axonal, Synaptic
Transmitter–receptor interaction, 33,
    34, 145
Transmitters, *see* Neurotransmitters
Truth-control test, 244–246
Tuning curves, *see* Frequency threshold
    curves, Psychophysical tuning
    curves
Turner's syndrome, 318
Two-tone suppression, *see* Suppression

Vaginal response to sexual arousal, 306,
    307, 310, 319
Vagus nerve,
  sleep and, 119, 239
  vagal tone (V̂), 235, 236
Ventral tegmental area, 38, 150